I0815899

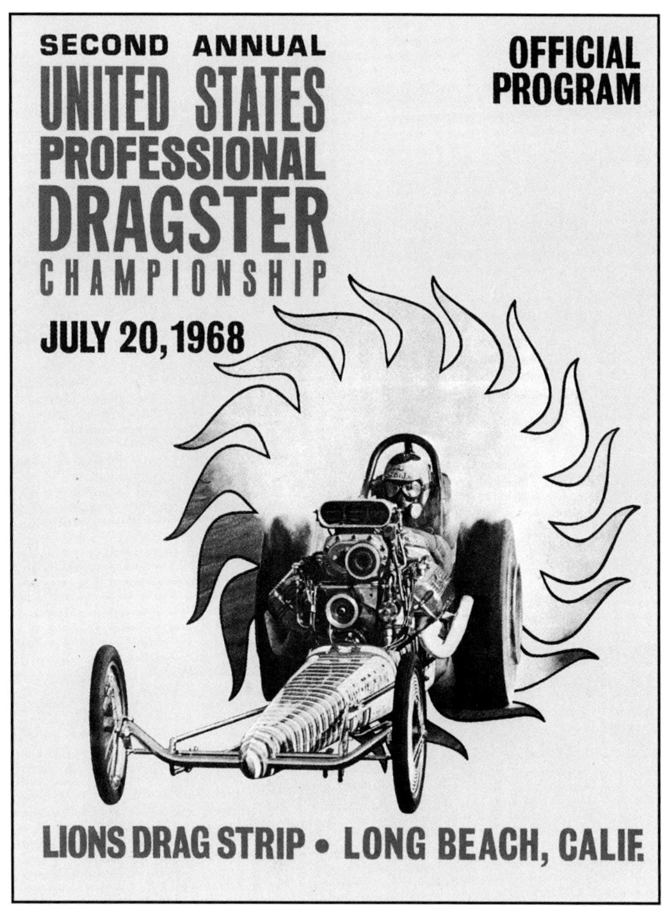
SECOND ANNUAL
UNITED STATES
PROFESSIONAL
DRAGSTER
CHAMPIONSHIP
OFFICIAL
PROGRAM
JULY 20, 1968
LIONS DRAG STRIP • LONG BEACH, CALIF.

CarTech®

LIONS DRAG STRIP

1955 1972

LOU HART

CarTech®

CarTech®, Inc.
6118 Main Street
North Branch, MN 55056
Phone: 651-277-1200 or 800-551-4754
Fax: 651-277-1203
www.cartechbooks.com

Edit by Wes Eisenschenk
Layout by Connie DeFlorin

ISBN 978-1-61325-853-8
Item No. CT701

Library of Congress Cataloging-in-Publication Data
Available

Written, edited, and designed in the U.S.A.
Printed in China
10 9 8 7 6 5 4 3 2 1

DISTRIBUTION BY:

Europe
PGUK
63 Hatton Garden
London EC1N 8LE, England
Phone: 020 7061 1980 • Fax: 020 7242 3725
www.pguk.co.uk

Australia
Renniks Publications Ltd.
3/37-39 Green Street
Banksmeadow, NSW 2109, Australia
Phone: 2 9695 7055 • Fax: 2 9695 7355
www.renniks.com

Canada
Login Canada
300 Saulteaux Crescent
Winnipeg, MB, R3J 3T2 Canada
Phone: 800 665 1148 • Fax: 800 665 0103
www.lb.ca

Contents

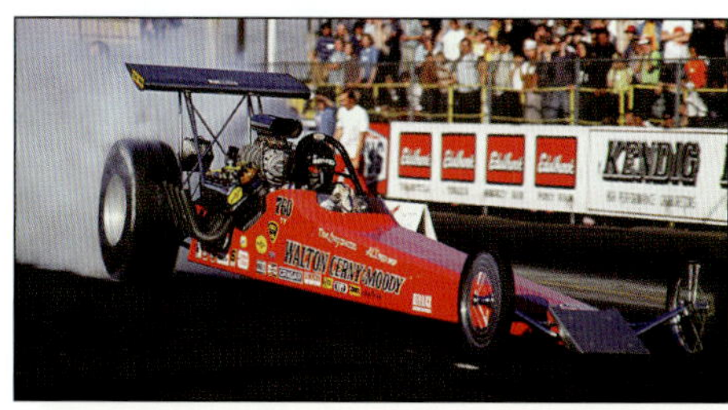

Dedication

This book is dedicated to the 11 original South Bay chapters of Lions Club International. They devoted their time, effort, and resources and made the necessary sacrifices to lay the foundation for Lions Drag Strip (also known as Lions Associated Drag Strip and L.A.D.S from 1955 to 1962) to get unlawful racing off the streets and into organized racing at Lions Drag Strip. The nonprofit organization was operated by the members of Lions Club International, which provides for those who are underprivileged and raised nearly $400,000 in donations for its various charities during the drag strip's 17-year history.

To the participants who competed at Lions Drag Strip.

To the volunteers and the employed staff behind the scenes.

To my peers who are no longer with us. Their lives have left me with lasting memories of their work and words that will always be in my mind and heart. I deeply respect and have learned from their craft. I am forever grateful to the late Tom West, who was my mentor and great friend of many years. He was a brother figure in my life, and it's truly an honor to keep his memory and work alive.

To Mr. Rick Lorenzen, the founder of the Lions Automobilia Foundation and Museum. You have given me the inspiration, drive, and support on this venture.

To my wonderful wife, Dawley, and my family for giving me the space and time for this special project.

Acknowledgments

I would like to express my sincerest gratitude to these awesome friends, coworkers, and everyone who has given me the time and opportunity to collaborate on this book. I'm beyond grateful to Lana Chrisman and the Lions Automobilia Foundation and Museum for their assistance. Photographers Tom West (the photos that he took and are used in this book are part of my collection), Steve Reyes, Jere Alhadeff, Steve Brackett, Darr Hawthorne, John and Don Ewald (J&M Photos), Don Gillespie, Don "the Wavemaker" Prieto, Dick and Rick Bain, Tony Thacker, Tom Walsh, the Chrisman family, and Dave Wallace. An extended thank you goes to Tim Pearl and Paul Johnson for allowing the use of their fantastic image collections to show the history of Lions Drag Strip.

Thank you to the heroes of Lions Drag Strip, whose quarter-mile memories and stories roar to life in this book: Danny Thompson, Carl Olson, Steve Reyes, Don "the Snake" Prudhomme, Jake Johnston, Larry Reyes, Stan Shiroma, Bob Muravez (also known as Floyd Lippencott Jr.), Steven Chrisman, Robert "Bones" Balogh, Larry Sutton, Don Ewald, Tim "Weed" Kraushaar, Donnie Hampton, Jim Shue, Steve Montrelli, and Steve Brackett. This book wouldn't have been possible without you.

Foreword

by Danny Thompson *Mickey Thompson's Son*

My dad was born in Alhambra, California, on December 7, 1929. He was an avid hot rodder during his teen years. When Lions Club International decided to open a drag strip, it was all about getting the kids off the street to race in a safe environment.

The word got out about the search for a manager to run and operate a drag strip, so my dad approached the Lions Club about the job, and he was one of five people who applied to run Lions Drag Strip. He was interviewed by a board that was comprised of Lions Associated Club officers, and he was hired as the drag strip's only paid employee.

At the time, my dad was 26 years old and employed as a press operator for the *Los Angeles Times*. He took on the task to oversee the planning and construction of the facility that began in early 1955. I remember the time when the strip was being built. Interstate 710 was under construction, and various parts of the project were complete.

We lived in El Monte, California, which was 32 miles from Lions Drag Strip. My dad and I would jump on the dirt of the uncompleted interstate and roar down to the drag strip because it was quicker than taking the side streets. He removed barriers that were in the way, smoked it down the completed portions of the freeway, and got off when it stopped. He drove short distances before the road ended, and then he jumped back on when the road began again. When he encountered a bridge that wasn't finished, he exited onto side roads until he was able to get back onto the dirt again. We did this many times without incident.

I distinctly remember taking the first ever lap down Lions Drag Strip—and I never drag raced. Although my dad forbade me to race, he did take me on my first ride down Lions Drag Strip in a Caterpillar grader at 2 mph. It smoothed out the dirt where the strip would be. I was there for that. As a child, this stuff happened all the time with my dad. It wasn't that big of a deal to me regarding what my dad did, but it was the routine of how my life was at the time.

At the time, my dad was a 26-year-old man who didn't know much about running a drag strip, as there weren't any permanent purpose-built drag strips around at that time from which to learn. My dad finished high school, but it was my mom who did all the work for him. She did his homework while he rebuilt engines and other automotive projects for the teachers at the school. He learned by doing.

When Lions Drag Strip opened in October 1955, there were no bleachers—just telephone poles on which people sat. My dad expected roughly a few hundred people, but on opening day, thousands showed up, which was incredible. As time went onward, the attendance slowed down and the track was in danger of closing. He suggested installing permanent lighting and adding an extra day (Saturday) for "hot car racing" and billed it as "date night." Sundays were still dedicated to car clubs and stock cars. Overall, that saved Lions Drag Strip.

My dad had the ability to make things happen and get people involved. He had that kind of personality to get you to work for free and really want to. He'd make things happen, and you just wanted to be a part of it. From the tech inspector to the starter and ticket collector, he made you feel like a part of a family.

My dad got nearby resident Butch Taylor and his daughter Pam (also known as "Popcorn Pam") Taylor to run the concessions stands and make all of the food, including tamales, hamburgers, and hot dogs, which were a delicacy from the opening day to the last drag race. My dad had the quarter-midget track there at the backside of the spectator side and kept all of the parents involved with the strip.

When his parts manufacturing and tire business took off, his other racing interests took off as well. My dad decided he didn't want to run the drag strip anymore, so he resigned as manager in 1963. The Lions Club brought in another Lions Club officer to run it, but he wasn't knowledgeable about drag racing or how to run a drag strip, which caused a major uproar among all of the racers and track personnel. Tom McEwen got my dad to ask C. J. Hart to apply for the position of general manager. C. J. applied for the job, was unanimously hired by the Lions board, and the rest is history.

Foreword

by Carl Olson *Top Fuel Eliminator Champion at Lions Drag Strip's Last Drag Race*

My first memory of Lions Drag Strip was in 1957. My brother was coerced into taking me there with his buddy, who had a little 1932 Ford coupe with a flathead engine that he was going to race. My brother didn't want to take me, but my parents insisted. I had been a motorsports fan from about the age of 3 but had never seen a drag race until that time. I remember seeing a car go about 180 mph, and I was hooked! That was the beginning of my relationship with Lions Drag Strip, and it didn't end until the very last race in December 1972.

Drag racing at Lions Drag Strip fascinated me because of the speed and performance, horsepower, acceleration, and parachutes that were needed to slow the cars before they got to the end of the shut-off area.

The culture of brotherhood that I sensed existed among those who raced and the spectators. Unlike a circle-track race, where the duration is maybe 3 hours from beginning to end, in the early days before Lions Drag Strip had lights, we were there from 8 a.m. Sunday until the sun went down. Something was happening all day. Unlike some of the oval races that I attended, you could go into the pit area at Lions Drag Strip and watch the racers work on their cars doing maintenance, teardowns, and rebuilding engines. You had the opportunity to meet the drivers, and if you had the courage, you could approach them and maybe have a conversation or ask for an autograph.

This was such a contrast to everything I had known as a spectator and enthusiast in other forms of racing. I was so enamored with Lions Drag Strip that I literally decided on that first day there that I was going to be a drag racer and that I'd drive those powerful race cars someday. Coming from a blue-collar family with no economic resources whatsoever, I didn't know how it would happen but had the vision and desire.

I spent a lot of time competing at Lions Drag Strip. My most vivid memory was the first time I ever drove a supercharged, nitromethane-burning, front-engine Top Fuel dragster. I was doing my licensing runs at Lions Drag Strip, running elapsed times (ETs) in the low-7-second bracket at 220 mph. I find it difficult to even describe those experiences. They were so impactful and overwhelming. My passion for drag racing was built on that first experience.

The word that embodied Lions Drag Strip the most was "culture." This included the pungent odors from the oil fields and refineries, the shooting range that was nearby and its odors, and the fog that would roll in late at night along with Lions Drag Strip's rare air. To look at it physically, it wasn't a pretty place, and it certainly couldn't hold a candle to a facility like Orange County International Raceway (OCIR), which was a jewel of a facility. However, it was about the culture, people, and the facts about the place. This was where I met the majority of my close personal friends at the time, and these friendships have lasted a lifetime.

The conditions were perfect. The clean air, temperature, and air density made the ideal horsepower, and the all-important bite of the strip surface made it the most outstanding place to race.

During its entire existence, I felt that Lions Drag Strip was the best drag strip in the world. I certainly wouldn't classify it as the cleanest, fanciest, or the most impressive, but Lions Drag Strip was unquestionably the place where everyone wanted to race and win. The conditions had a lot to do with it. The fact that it was just a few feet above sea level was a huge factor to make a tremendous amount of horsepower at that time. There were only a few drag strips in the country that were at or near sea level and close to having those ideal conditions. Fremont Dragstrip and Half Moon Bay Drag Strip had some similarities.

Mickey Thompson played an instrumental role in how the track was built and oversaw the strip's surface construction. The amount of grade preparation, the track base, and the overall mixture of the asphalt provided far better traction than any other racetrack of that time. The other element was the maintenance of the track. When C. J. Hart took over as manager, he had the track power-washed every week to be ready for Saturday night. When the race cars showed up on Saturday, it was like running on virgin asphalt. It didn't have any oil, fluids, or built-up rubber that was in the process of deteriorating or balling up like at other tracks. The combination of the tuning and weather conditions was unparalleled at that time.

Chapter One

1948–1954

When the Action Roared to Life

The sport of drag racing began in the early 1930s on the dry lake beds in the desert regions of Southern California. In 1938, speed contests gained greater notability after young hot rodders, including a young man named Wally Parks, helped organize the Southern California Timing Association (SCTA).

Around this time, Southern California had become the hub of motorsports with the abundance of the finest speed parts and equipment available. Many creative designers and builders of high-performance vehicles and aftermarket speed parts were from the West Coast and set the table for the advent of a new form of organized motorsport.

When World War II ended on September 2, 1945, many of the rodding veterans returned home and went back to their racing roots. They incorporated new ideas for turning faster speeds and quicker elapsed times (ETs). The increased performance made it even less safe to race stoplight to stoplight on the streets. To avoid accidents, injuries, and any prosecution by the local authorities, car club leaders and activists promoted a safer alternative.

They promoted a location where souped-up jalopies, crudely built contraptions, and hot rods could drag race in a safe environment. At one local car gathering, a young man stood out from the rest and suggested the use of a decommissioned, abandoned military base with flat landing strips. This man was Cloyce Roller Hart (also known as C. J. "Pappy" Hart) from Ohio. He led the charge to find a place to race in a safe, controlled environment.

He led his car buddies on weekends to an ex-Navy installation in Orange County, California, that had a proportioned square-mile concrete surface to race sometimes six to eight cars abreast. On one Sunday morning, the rodders arrived to find a company of armed US Marines with loaded rifles and fixed bayonets, who immediately escorted the dejected racers back to the streets.

After World War II ended, drag racing became a popular motorsport that had grown with the return of soldiers who were eager to jump back into their hot rods and jalopies. Southern California became a hot spot throughout the late 1940s and 1950s, when decommissioned military air stations and abandoned runways were used for racing. A prime example was the United States Marine Corps (USMC) Air Station in Tustin, California, where this pair of modified roadsters prepare to race in front of thousands of spectators, who were lined up for a half mile on each side of the runway.

One day, Hart encountered the manager of the Santa Ana/Orange County Airport (currently John Wayne Airport), who offered an unused runway to race on with the understanding that the group would pay the airport a percentage of the proceeds and provide insurance.

With an investment of $1,000, Hart, his wife, Peggy, and two other investors opened the Santa Ana Drags on June 19, 1950. Hart charged 50 cents for spectators and racers. At the time, he wasn't aware that he created a major American motorsport.

However, there was a need for drag racing to be an organized sport. So, in 1951, Wally Parks formed the

C. J. Hart (pictured), his wife, Peggy, and two other backing partners invested $1,000 to lease an unused runway at the Santa Ana Airport (now John Wayne Airport) in Orange County, California. The Santa Ana Drags opened on June 19, 1950. (Photo Courtesy Lions Automobilia Foundation Museum)

National Hot Rod Association (NHRA). This led to drag racing producing record numbers in interest and participation. Many racers traveled miles to run their cars, which paved the way for NHRA expansion. Drag strips were soon built and flourished in several areas of California, including Pomona, Ramona, Saugus, Paradise Mesa in San Diego, and Bakersfield.

Progress

With a thriving economy (a population increase with new job opportunities, home building, and business expansion) in the Orange County/Santa Ana airport area, the demand for air transportation reached an all-time high. It was only a matter of time before the drag strip shut down and the runway was returned to the airport. The clock began to tick on Santa Ana.

Meanwhile, 29 miles north of the Santa Ana Drags in the South Bay District of Long Beach, hot rodders and cruisers clogged the streets from boulevard to boulevard to determine who had the top machines. However, the public did not look upon them favorably because of their loud cars, high speeds, and reckless driving. These hot-rod hoods posed major safety problems to the community and brought anxiety and fear to the local citizens, who demanded results from law enforcement.

Crucial meetings were arranged by city council members and local businessmen, concerned citizens, and educators, and numerous car-club members were invited to look for solutions and answers to these questions. Many of these meetings ended with decisions being split down the middle.

Hot rodders and racers asked, "What's wrong with hot rods? Why shouldn't teenagers be allowed to race cars if they want to in a safe environment?"

The responses from the council meetings were always the same.

"We don't have the time, place, or resources to have these hooligans speed up and down on our unincorporated streets."

The council decided that hot rods were fine and that the pursuit of speed was an excellent pastime if it was at a safe speed. However, can speed be safe? There was an answer to this dilemma. A permanent drag strip would make high speeds as safe, interesting, and fun as possible.

Meanwhile, municipal courtrooms were overcrowded with the speeding law breakers and hooligans when a noted Long Beach judge, Fred Miller, took notice and examined the need to get racing off the streets. To find a solution, Judge Miller contacted the area service clubs to help form an organized drag strip.

The word about the proposed drag strip spread like wildfire because it had something to do with an unusual background. The idea was first proposed with a motion by the city of Long Beach juvenile department authorities as a means of combating juvenile delinquencies.

Committee Obtains Land

The journey of the Los Angeles drag strip began two years before the gates officially opened for racing on the hallowed grounds of 223rd Street and Alameda Street in the city of Wilmington.

In January 1954, a committee was brought together that consisted of Los Angeles Mayor Norris Poulson, who was instrumental in bringing the Dodgers from Brooklyn to Los Angeles in 1958; Councilman John Gibson; John Chadwick from the Wilmington Lions Club chapter; and local area radio and television newscaster George Putnam. Chadwick, who had recently left his post as president of the Los Angeles Harbor Commission, was instrumental in the group's success in obtaining the commission-owned land that was formerly property of the railroad. Plans were quickly drawn up that included a paved drag strip and a section of permanent bleachers on a 43-acre field. The venue was to be equipped with the latest racing equipment, and plans included two acres for a pit area that would be fenced for safety.

DRAG NEWS

VOL. ONE — NUMBER 3 APRIL 1, 1955 PRICE TWENTY CENTS

Construction To Begin On LAD's Strip

In answer to many queries, as to the location and layout of the new LAD's strip in the west part of Long Beach, we have reproduced a drawing showing the strip and related information. In a venture of this magnitude, there are untold problems that arise but Lions Associated Drag Strip, Inc. Secretary, Bob Jerauld, says that ground breaking ceremonies await only the final signatures of the Los Angeles Harbor Commission. It was from them that the ground was leased and to whom many thanks are due.

These ceremonies will undoubtedly

(Continued on Page Two)

Latest Southern California Strip Rules

Safety Hubs at Santa Ana

All machines, other than cycles and stocks, running at the Santa Ana strip will be required to have some form of a safety hub installed. This is to prevent possible injury to either driver or spectator in case of a snapped axle and consequent loss of a wheel. The need for safety in our sport cannot be over emphasized if its growth is to continue and this is definitely one of the more important precautions.

Watch for a forthcoming feature on safety hubs in this paper describing their importance and installation.

Beginning on page 10 of this issue, you will find the first of a two part series on drag strip rules and regulations as they exist on the Southland strips. The first is the N.H.R.A. Classifications and are in effect at Pomona, Colton and Paradise Mesa. Cycle and sports car classes under this, is at the discretion of the individual strips, but will usually follow this pattern.

Sports cars are broken into two groups: A, over 1500 C.C. (cubic centimeter) and B, under 1500 C.C., with any other

(Continued on Page Twelve)

This issue of **Drag News**, *dated April 1, 1955, provides detailed information of the new Lions Drag Strip. It shows a blueprint rendition of the location and layout of the leased property at the corners of Alameda and 223rd in the west part of Long Beach, California. (Article Courtesy Lions Automobilia Foundation Museum)*

Lions Club International Petitions to Build Drag Strip

Of all of the service clubs that were contacted, only Lions Club International stepped forward with its local chapters and volunteered its services regarding how to help raise the necessary funds to start the drag strip. Representatives of the 11 clubs met for the first time on May 3, 1954, at the home of L. R. Jones, who was the president of the Signal Hill Lions Club. The clubs represented were Torrance, Harbor City–Lomita, San Pedro, Wilmington, Downtown Long Beach, West Long Beach, North Long Beach, Belmont Shores, Los Altos, Signal Hill, and Lakewood. The first and most important task was to negotiate with the Board of Harbor Commissions of the city of Los Angeles for a lease of a suitable location on the south side of the county. Eddie Baker of the Downtown Long Beach Lions Club spearheaded the drive for $45,000.

Second, the intent of the group stipulated that all profits from the operation of the drag strip be donated to charity through the Lions Club groups. All 11 groups in the harbor area formed a corporation known as Lions Associated Drag Strip.

With a window of 60 days to accumulate the funds, Baker accomplished the goal in 30 hectic days and borrowed money from 244 separate sources. Four new car dealerships in Long Beach loaned $2,000 each, several Lions clubs loaned a total of $5,000, and the balance came from individual sources.

Viewing site of drag strip which will stretch 3,500 feet are Val Deaser, left, vice president of Lions Associated Drag Strip and Eddie Baker, finance chairman. A harbor area Lions Club project, the strip will be built west of Alameda between Willow and 223rd Sts.—(Staff Photo)

COMPLETION DUE IN AUGUST

Drag Strip Contract Scheduled July 18

Construction of a quarter-mile drag strip for hot rod car racing will begin soon west of Long Beach.

The builders, Lions Associated Drag Strip, Inc., an organization composed of representatives of 11 harbor area Lions Clubs, expect the strip to be completed by the middle of August. The contract is to be let July 18.

The $45,000 strip, first to be constructed in the harbor area, will be located on a 43-acre site one-half mile west of Alameda St. between Willow and 223rd Sts.

A lease has been negotiated with the City of Los Angeles for use of the land. The area is controlled by the Los Angeles Harbor Board.

anticipated each year. Each contestant will be insured by the corporation for $300,000 liability and $100,000 property damage.

Members of 34 hot rod clubs in this area will use the strip, Deaser said.

Cars will race from north to south on the strip.

This **Long Beach Press-Telegram** *article featured Val Deaser (vice president of Lions Drag Strip) and Eddie Baker (finance chairman of Lions Drag Strip) as they view the plans for the new site of the Lions Club project, which was located on a half mile of Alameda Street between Willow Street and 223rd Street. (Article Courtesy Lions Automobilia Foundation Museum)*

A Matter of Great Importance

The money was placed before the California state commissioner for project approval. The petition was given priority attention by the commissioner's office, and after complying with the state's requirements, the $45,000 was released to Dean Williams, the Lions Club's attorney. The construction of the strip was overseen by Herb Murphy of the Downtown Long Beach chapter.

Chapter Two

1955–1962

Plans for a Roaring Roadway

In February 1955, Lions Club Secretary Bob Jerauld announced the start of construction of a drag strip built between Santa Fe and Alameda streets with a completion scheduled for September 1955. The asphalt strip was 60 feet wide and 3,520 feet long. The dimensions were equivalent to a highway with two lanes of traffic in each direction with room for parallel parking in each direction. Runs were from north to south amidst cool westerly winds. Seven lanes, or chutes, were provided in the staging lanes near the starting line. Permanent timing equipment and electronics were installed.

The plans announced by Jerauld included the hiring of one full-time paid employee, who would be the operating manager and general manager and would draw support from members of the outlining area clubs to assist with operating and maintaining the new facility.

THOMPSON TO MANAGE NEW L. B. STRIP

Mickey Thompson, well known for his Hot Rod activities in Southern California, has just been selected as the manager for the new LAD'S Drag Strip. The strip is to be located between Alameda and Santa Fe just north of Willow in the Wilmington-Long Beach area. Operation of the strip is expected to begin in Sept. and Manager Thompson is to hold an open meeting at the Long Beach Auditorium Aug. 25th at 7:30 p.m. of all interested car clubs to discuss rules, operating procedure, etc. Movies of the Pan American Road Race will also be shown.

Drag racing spectators watch a pair of roadsters compete in a heated start at Lions Drag Strip. The results proved to be a success for the local associated Lions Club chapters, as it moved illegal racing off the streets. Soon, "drive the streets; race at Lions," was coined. (Photo Courtesy Lions Automobilia Foundation Museum)

The ***Long Beach Press-Telegram*** *announced the details regarding the hiring of Mickey Thompson as the new general manager of Lions Drag Strip. Thompson was the only paid employee by Lions Club International, and he assigned duties to a cast of volunteers.*

Mickey Thompson to Manage Lions Drag Strip

On August 16, 1955, Bob Jerauld announced that Mickey Thompson, an innovator who was well-known for his involvement in hot rod activities in Southern California, was selected by a committee to manage and operate the new drag strip. Thompson was paid $400 per month plus 2 percent of the gross revenue.

With operations slated to begin on September 18, Thompson organized and held an open meeting on August 25 at the Long Beach Convention Center. The objective was to discuss the track's rules, operating procedures, and concerns for all interested parties, including area residents, car clubs, and racers.

Thompson announced that the strip would feature modern attractions, such as a multi-light electronic starting system. The staging person and starter would still be present on the starting line, but the new automated colored light system, consisting of yellow, red, and green lights, was activated from a handheld switch. These replaced the customary flag starts and eliminated any potential movement or gesture prior to dropping the flag that would cause a mis-start. The Thompson era had begun.

Lions Associated Drag Strip Scheduled To Open Soon

Colored Lights Replace Starter

Mickey Thompson, manager of the new Lions Associated Drag Strip, announces that the strip will open within the next couple of weeks instead of the Sept. 18th goal, and will feature among other attractions, an inovation new to organized drag racing—no starter.

Actually a starter or staging man will be present on the line but rather than use a conventional flag to give the "go" signal, he will use a set of red, yellow and green lights actuated from a hand carried switch.

This, it is hoped, will eliminate the possibility of an anticipated start due to a particular gesture or movement by the starter prior to waving a flag. (i.e., grab his cap). This should prove to be a big advance in drag racing and shouldn't require much "getting used to" as the technique, in effect, may be observed on practically any street corner.

Car classifications will be in accordance with the National Hot Rod Association except for the addition of a dragster class. O-305 C. I. and 305 C. I. and over are the divisions and all 1, 2, 3 and 4th place class winners will receive weekly point awards, which will be totaled every four months. Weekly trophies will go to the first place winners in addition to the point awards and a choice of a long list of valuable merchandise awards await the top point men at the end of each four month period.

The point award system is as follows: First, 100, 3 cars must run; second, 75, four cars must run; third, 50, five cars must run

Bill Hannon, co-owner of the San Fernando strip, presents special trophy and congratulations to Ray Brown (left) and Mickey Thompson for their world's record performance Sept. 4th. Brown's 300 C.I. Chrysler, powered driver Thompson to new high for the one-fourth mile of 151.26.
—Photo by Dean Vannice.

Russetta Plans Three Drag Meets; Saugus

The Russetta Timing Association will switch its attention from the lake bed of El Mirage to the asphalt quarter mile of Saugus on Sunday, October 2nd, when it launches the first of three scheduled drag meets.

The drag sessions will climax one of the association's best years on the lakes; a season that has seen the inner-club point standings reverse themselves practically every meet and an accumulation of class records so far that undoubtedly will be the highest yet.

Russetta rules and classifications will be used and the association officials will be in charge. The public is cordially invited and guest entries will be accepted. All contestants must file official Russetta entry blanks; entry fee

will receive trophy awards and all contestants will be presented with timing tags. Best appearing car and crew and Top Time of the meet will receive special trophies from strip manager, Bob Corbett.

The lakes safety rules will be enforced by a rigid inspection and suitable flywheel covers are a must. Rail jobs must be in a class of three or more entries to be eligible for a trophy.

Pit gates will open at 8 a.m. with first run at 9. For additional information on the meet, contact R.T.A. president, Ed Pink at

The **Long Beach Press-Telegram** *newspaper was a staunch supporter of Lions Drag Strip and the sport of drag racing. The paper had a strong influence on the community and provided regular updates regarding the strip's proceedings as well as additional information about the other racing venues in the area. This article details the innovative use of an automated colored-light starting system and descriptive car classifications.*

What About the Concessions?

The last meeting of the Lions board was three weeks before the long-awaited opening of the new facility. Mickey Thompson laid out the progress on the racecourse and how much had been spent to get it ready to open for business. Many questions were asked, and Thompson had all of the answers on the tip of his tongue except one.

"What about concessions? Shouldn't there be some food for the participants and the spectators?" a member asked.

Until that point, it hadn't occurred to Thompson to look into concessions, but he was quick to say that he was open to suggestions. Another member, Butch Taylor, a Long Beach Poly High School teacher who also owned a sandwich shop on nearby Santa Fe Avenue, stepped up to provide the means to operate a concession stand. All he needed was space and a location—he would do the rest.

"Done!" replied a sitting board member.

Taylor, with the aid of his family, created a conservative menu for opening day complete with hot dogs, tamales, chili, chips, candy, and soda.

The Roar Heard for Miles

At 9 a.m. Sunday, October 9, 1955, Lions Drag Strip opened its gates to a massive crowd

Starter Danny Lare waves the green flag to signal the start of a race between a pair of motorcycles at Lions Drag Strip. The lanes were filled with all types of vehicles, including stock cars, street cars, sports cars, and motorcycles, that were lined up at the entrance gates near the strip on 223rd Street. (Photo Courtesy Lions Automobilia Foundation Museum)

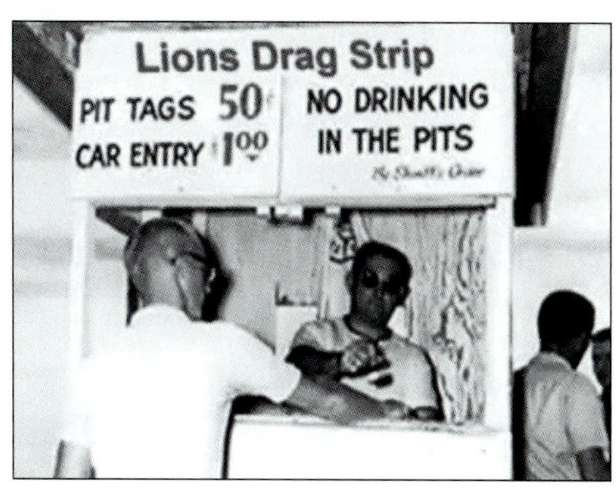

It was such a deal for everyone at the ticket booth, as it only cost $1.50 for you and your car to race all day long. (Photo Courtesy Lions Automobilia Foundation Museum)

The lanes begin to fill up early on a sunny Sunday morning for unlimited racing all day long at Lions Drag Strip. Many members of the local car clubs, motorcycle clubs, and those who were just curious came to Lions Drag Strip to support keeping mischief off the streets. (Photo Courtesy Lions Automobilia Foundation Museum)

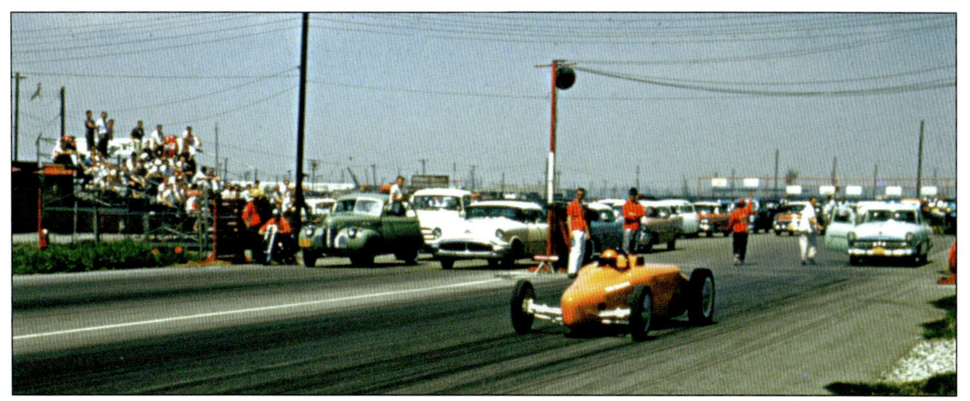

On the opening day at Lions Drag Strip, Gary Lee "Red" Greth and Lyle Fisher compete in the **Speed Sport Special II** *fuel roadster. The Tucson, Arizona, racing team ran a 331-ci blown Chrysler Hemi on 100-percent nitromethane and became the world's quarter-mile record holder for a non-dragster exceeding 180 mph. (Photo Courtesy Don Prieto)*

and hundreds of the area's top drag racing racers and their machines. Admission on opening day was 75 cents per adult, and children under 12 years old were free. Race participants were charged $1.25 each to compete as many times as they wanted.

Racing continued all day until it was dark. The event was proclaimed by many in the media to be the greatest automobile racing spectacle in local history. By 12:30 p.m., officials were forced to close the pit lanes and limit class contestants to fewer runs per vehicle. Parking adjacent to the strip had filled beyond capacity and forced the late arrivals to park in the streets of the surrounding neighborhood.

Many were pleased with the blistering competition and strip conditions, as Ed Losinki led the way with a 12.07 ET at 151.26 mph to set the top speed for the meet in his Chrysler-powered Gas dragster. By the day's end, Fritz Voigt took honors of the first Lions Top Eliminator title. He collected a large trophy and a case of oil for his win. As the popularity grew for the following events, the prizes for all the Top Eliminator winners increased in value. In addition to a trophy and oil, each winner received a Lions jacket and a savings bond.

When Lions Drag Strip opened, there were no frills. The winners were announced over the public-announcement system. Over in the tower, racers picked up their elapsed time (ET) and speed slips that were attached on a card. Then, they sent it down on a line with the use of a clothespin to the timekeeper at the bottom of the tower, who then handed it to the driver. It wasn't the most scientific solution, but it worked.

The success of opening day made headlines in the next day's *Long Beach Press-Telegram* newspaper. It praised the organized racing that attracted more than 10,000 fans and racers without running into major obstacles or garnering complaints. It was also mentioned that the volunteers from the 11 area Lions Clubs were responsible for the Long Beach strip, and their efforts were worthy of any commendations that can ever be given out. These club members were a credit to their respective community.

The utmost goal of Thompson and Lions Club International on opening day was realized, as Lions Drag Strip got racing off the streets and onto the drag strip.

On December 6, 1955, the Harbor City–Lomita and Belmont Shores clubs dropped out, leaving nine active Lions Club chapters.

Make a Date at Lions Drag Strip

Lions Drag Strip operated on a weekly schedule every Sunday in its first year of operation. It was a struggle at first to keep the facility open, but the ingenious Thompson drew up a plan to change sunlight to arc lights when he announced an additional day of racing with "date night" racing at the strip. Thompson's idea to install permanent, ample lightning on the strip and in the pits received unanimous approval from the city and Lions Club board of directors as the popularity of Saturday-night drag racing brought in the crowds.

On Saturday, July 7, 1956, the gates opened at 3 p.m., and the time trials and qualifying began at 5 p.m. The first round of racing commenced at 7 p.m. sharp

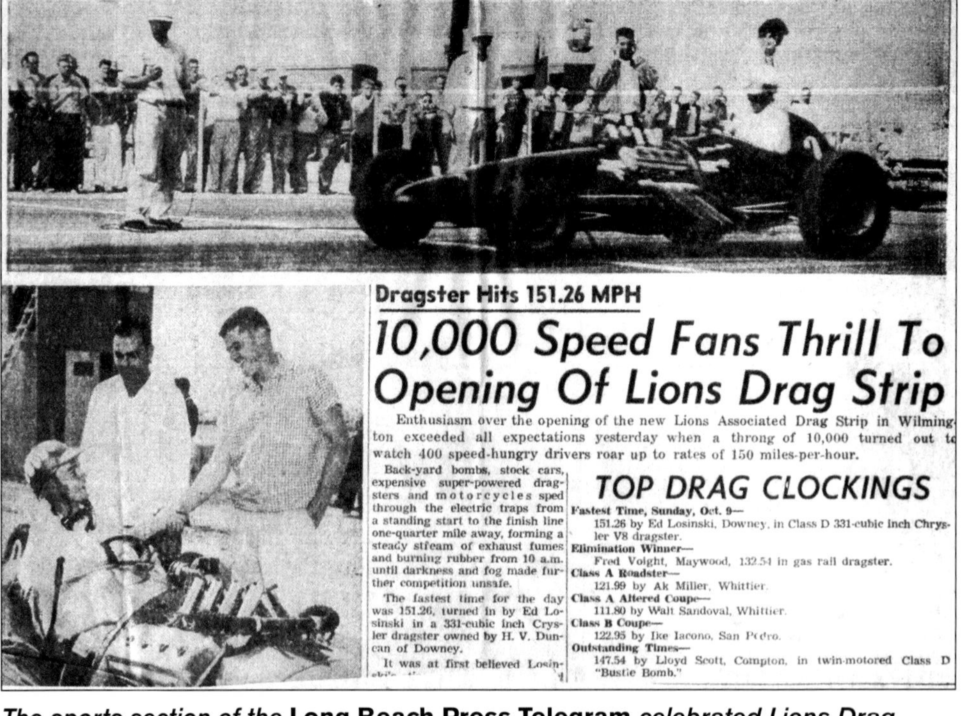

Dragster Hits 151.26 MPH

10,000 Speed Fans Thrill To Opening Of Lions Drag Strip

Enthusiasm over the opening of the new Lions Associated Drag Strip in Wilmington exceeded all expectations yesterday when a throng of 10,000 turned out to watch 400 speed-hungry drivers roar up to rates of 150 miles-per-hour.

Back-yard bombs, stock cars, expensive super-powered dragsters and motorcycles sped through the electric traps from a standing start to the finish line one-quarter mile away, forming a steady stfeam of exhaust fumes and burning rubber from 10 a.m. until darkness and fog made further competition unsafe.

The fastest time for the day was 151.26, turned in by Ed Losinski in a 331-cubic inch Crysler dragster owned by H. V. Duncan of Downey.

It was at first believed Losin-

TOP DRAG CLOCKINGS

Fastest Time, Sunday, Oct. 9—
151.26 by Ed Losinski, Downey, in Class D 331-cubic inch Chrysler V8 dragster.

Elimination Winner—
Fred Voight, Maywood, 132.54 in gas rail dragster.

Class A Roadster—
121.99 by Ak Miller, Whittier.

Class A Altered Coupe—
111.80 by Walt Sandoval, Whittier.

Class B Coupe—
122.95 by Ike Iacono, San Pedro.

Outstanding Times—
147.54 by Lloyd Scott, Compton, in twin-motored Class D "Bustie Bomb."

The sports section of the **Long Beach Press Telegram** *celebrated Lions Drag Strip's successful grand opening and posted the top ETs, top speeds, and winning class results. (Article Courtesy Lions Automobilia Foundation Museum)*

and concluded before the 11 p.m. curfew. That night's racing schedule included 38 competition classes that were opened to include cycles. Trophies for the winners and drivers with top times received 5 gallons of nitro. The overall Top Eliminator received a $500 savings bond and a trophy lamp that was valued at $50. The change to night racing resulted in near-capacity attendance numbers.

Long Beach Draws the Hot Cycles

Drag racing under the lights had caught on like wildfire in Southern California. Saturday night racing united the highly sought-out hot cars, while the long-established Sunday afternoon meets were dedicated to the local street rodders and car clubs. Lions Drag Strip staged its second night drag meet on July 14, 1956, which proved to be a major success. This strategy lifted drag racing to a higher level of the popularity of entrants, including motorcyclists. The motorcycle classes were placed in the capable hands of Gizmo Buerkle, who was a familiar figure to anyone who rode bikes in the Los Angeles and South Bay area. Buerkle established the motorcycle classes and organized the check-ins, trophy presentations, and other incidentals that made up the routine at Lions Drag Strip.

Buerkle's success in the cycle venture was judged by the number and quality of the southland's hottest drag cycles that filled the pits each weekend. The bike boys enjoyed competing at Lions Drag Strip. Some of the top riders were Dewey Merritt's fuel *Thunderbird*, Mike Ward's fuel-burner *Eight Ball* ridden by Bill Johnson, and Tommy Auger riding Bill Martz's gas-burning Vincent Rapide. The *Double Trubble*, owned by Bill Kock and ridden by Bob Thurston, was a twin-engine 1953 Triumph Iron Tiger that had recorded speeds above 142-mph mark and was one of the few bikes in the Southern California area that could match the acceleration of the fastest hot rods.

Other Triumph standouts were Joe "Lucky" Franklin and Bud Hare. The Harley-Davidson contingent was led by local man Shorty Harman, whose 1952 chopped '74s had accounted for 41 trophies in 43 outings in the Gas class. Then, there was Walt Fontaine, who compiled a record of winning 16 straight weeks in a row in the Gas class.

One of the top motorcyclists in Southern California was Tommy Auger. He was a motorcycle drag racing pioneer and a top competitor who made his mark by running either in the Gas class or as a potent Fuel burner. Auger and bike owner and tuner Bill Martz took home more trophies and gold awards at Lions Drag Strip than at any other racing venue around Southern California in the 1950s. The lightweight cycles often ran up against the more powerful V-8 roadsters, coupes, and, occasionally, Top Eliminator dragsters.

The smaller-displacements cycles were well represented, including a Mustang ridden by 14-year-old Steve Brackett. Brackett's Mustang was built by Steve's father, Jay, who was responsible for the milled and fly-cut competition head, a $1^{3}/_{16}$ Amal Monobloc carburetor, and the Potvin 281 cam. Unfortunately for Brackett, the 19-ci machine had to compete in the 30- to 50-ci Gas class, where it was no match for other larger-displacement machines.

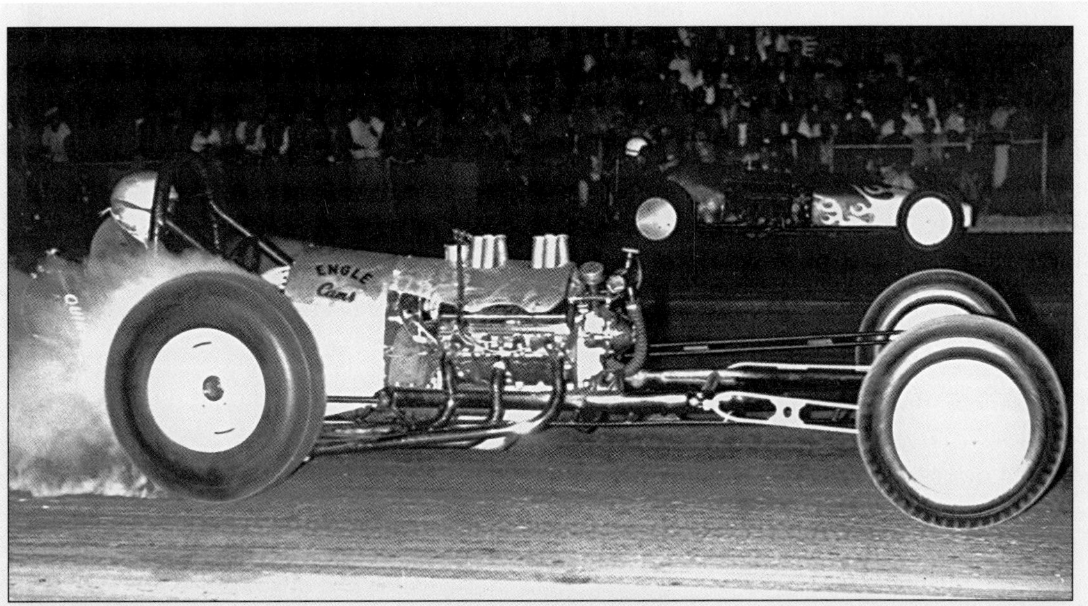

Driver Walt Nichols pitted the **Quincy Auto Parts** *dragster against Fritz Voigt. They raced toward the finish line in the Top Car runoff to determine who would race the motorcycle of Tommy Auger in the finals. Nichols's machine was powered by a 354-ci Oldsmobile, while Voigt's entry relied on the larger-displacement 395-ci Chrysler. (Photo Courtesy Lions Automobilia Foundation Museum)*

The 14-year-old Steve Brackett had been racing his Mustang motorcycle before he could legally obtain a driver's license. Steve raced regularly since the opening day at Lions Drag Strip along with his father, Jay, who built the smaller, highly modified 19-ci engine. Steve rode the cycle for fun because the Mustang wasn't categorized in its own class at the time. (Photo Courtesy Steve Brackett)

Jim "Jazzy" Nelson's Mercury-powered hot rod fell victim to Tommy Auger's gasoline-class Vincent Rapide motorcycle in the semifinal round during the second night race at Lions Drag Strip. Nelson's flathead-powered altered set Lions Drag Strip's ET record at 9.10. Nelson found the flathead to be reliable and saw that it often outran the larger displacement overhead-valve (OHV) threats. (Photo Courtesy Steve Brackett)

As Danny Lares waves the green flag, motorcyclist Tommy Auger takes off against Walt Nichols (in the **Quincy Auto Parts** *dragster) for that evening's Top Eliminator crown. It wasn't uncommon for motorcycles and the heavier rails to compete against each other in the final rounds for the prize money and hardware. (Photo Courtesy Steve Brackett)*

The jam-packed grandstands and a vast turnout of car and motorcycle competitors watched Jim "Jazzy" Nelson's flathead Mercury hot rod win over a Gas-class Vincent Rapide motorcycle that was ridden by Tommy Auger. Nelson, who owned the ET record at 9.1 seconds at Lions Drag Strip, had no problems blowing off all types of the overhead valve (OHV) competition with his outmoded flattie.

Other notables in the Dragster class included the evil-appearing slingshot dragster of the Yeakel Brothers' Experimental Motors Cadillac-powered machine that ran more than 130 mph but experienced mechanical difficulties on the run. Bakersfield's own Ernie Hashim made the 100-mile trek to Los Angeles with his supercharged Chrysler

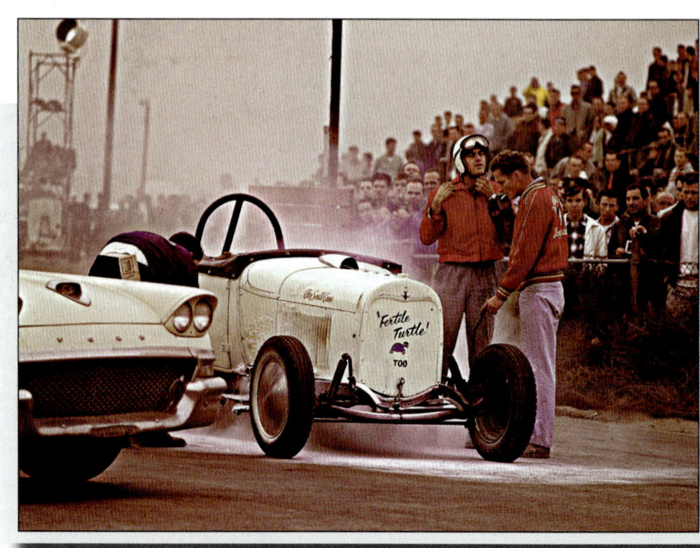

rail that was fitted with a crank-driven blower. Hashim ripped off a record run of 155 mph, but it wasn't enough to take down Nelson in the final car elimination run.

A Man of Action

Mickey Thompson spent his workdays employed as a pressman for the *Los Angeles Times*, but he never stopped brainstorming ways to promote the drag strip and increase attendance. One of his passions was circle-track racing, so he went forward with one of his plans and built a quarter-Midget track in the parking-lot area that proved to be very successful, as the Midgets drew a lot of families. His dedication to drag racing and motorsports, along with his innovative leadership, made Lions Drag Strip the greatest drag strip in the country.

The Lions Drag Strip Family

After a full day or night of racing, Mickey and Judy Thompson gathered with the track volunteers around the starting line and gave them sandwiches, potato chips, and drinks. They'd sit and recap the day's racing activities and then listen to suggestions and ideas from the staff regarding ways to improve the drag strip. This gesture created unity and gave recognition to all who volunteered to operate the drag strip, and it gave the Thompsons the satisfaction of giving back to the community.

Lions Drag Strip Celebrates an Anniversary

Lions Drag Strip celebrated its first anniversary over the weekend of October 27 and 28, 1956. The action-packed weekend concluded as drivers Maurice Richer (in the *Nesbitt Orange Special*) and Calvin Rice matched up in the final. The pressure was too much, and both drivers jumped the starter's signal. They received the red disqualifying flag and ended in a dead heat. It was decided that both drivers would meet in November and race for the title.

Facing page: Several fire extinguishers were emptied on Jerry Norwich's Delta Machine–backed **Fertile Turtle Too** *gas roadster. Norwich, who was from Long Beach, California, unstraps his helmet while the volunteer safety crew surveys the damage. The Chrysler engine erupted into a ball of flames when a ruptured fuel line spewed gasoline onto the hot exhaust. A volunteer safety crew/ Long Beach Car Club member holds the ruptured fuel line while enjoying his Lucky Strike cigarette. After this incident, Thompson hired off-duty firefighters to handle safety issues. (Photo Courtesy Don Prieto)*

A New Age of Timing Technology

The weekend of February 16 and 17, 1957, was the first time in drag racing history that 14 individual timing devices were installed throughout Lions Drag Strip's quarter-mile track that systematically recorded how fast a car accelerated from start to finish. One run saved hours of guesswork and experimentation. To participate in the invite-only, multiple-electronic-timing demonstration, each entrant was offered the chance to fill out an entry blank for $2 on a first-come, first-served basis. O. V. Riley of the Chrondek Corporation supervised the clocking.

The multiple timing part of the two-day program was to give all contestants (from stock cars to dragsters) the opportunity to learn better starting-line techniques and provide knowledge regarding when to shift, the effects of engine changes, gear ratios, and tire sizes. For those who were technical-minded, acceleration graphs were available for each run.

At 9 a.m. Saturday, February 16, the action began with timekeepers in the tower double-checking their clocks and relaying the signal over to the announcers stand. A different official recorded the time, temperature, humidity, and wind velocity on a large information board. Passing the go signal back to the announcer, the starter activated the green light, and both cars rocketed off the starting line. Seconds later, both engines shut off. The first run at Lions Drag Strip's two-way record meet had been accomplished.

This procedure was repeated over the next two days as some of the strongest gas-burning dragsters in the country converged at Lions Drag Strip for this newest drag racing innovation. From an early Saturday morning start until the last run late on Sunday night, the thousands of spectators were treated to one of the top drag racing meets ever hosted by the facility.

Mickey Brown, driving the new Harryman, Brown, and Frank A/Dragster, captivated the sellout crowd with five consecutive runs of 149 mph with ETs of 10.49. Ted Cyr posted the low ET of 9.87 at 144 mph during the meet in the *U-Fab Special* dragster that was co-owned by Cyr and Bill Cooper.

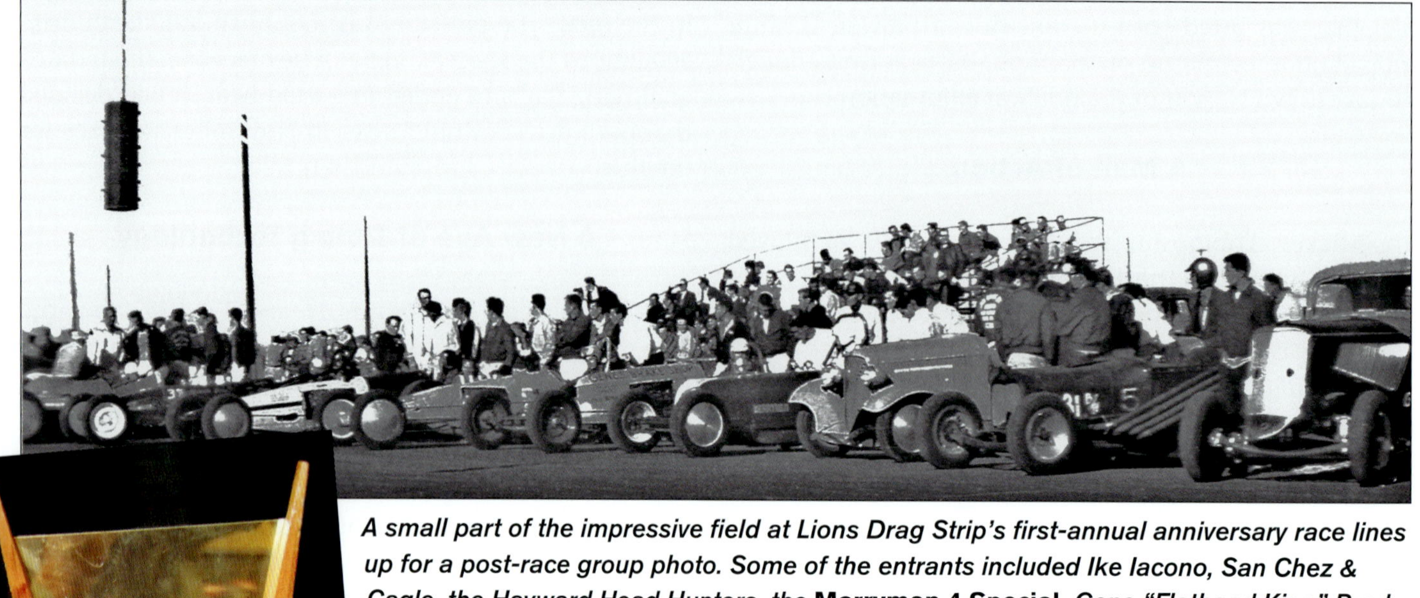

A small part of the impressive field at Lions Drag Strip's first-annual anniversary race lines up for a post-race group photo. Some of the entrants included Ike Iacono, San Chez & Cagle, the Hayward Head Hunters, the **Merryman 4 Special**, *Gene "Flathead King" Bradley's* **Brake Special**, *Maurice Richer's* **Nesbitt's Orange Special**, *Calvin Rice, the Nichols Brothers, Weeks & Nobile, Gus Barks, Lou Baney's* **Yeakel Cadillac**, *Don Cook, Manuel Coelho, and the Transmission Specialists. (Photo Courtesy Steve Brackett)*

A prized memento from Lions Drag Strip's second-anniversary race is this Sports Car class trophy. Along with winning a class trophy, racers could "trade up" their extra trophies and redeem them for a Lions Drag Strip jacket and savings bonds.

"Run What You Brung" Nationals

Lions Drag Strip offered a potpourri eliminator race with all types of competition cars on February 23, 1957, that was dubbed the "Run What You Brung" Nationals. Dragsters, modified coupes, roadsters, and motorcycles were up for the challenge. Leading the way were the entries of Ike Iacono, Mickey Thompson, Mickey Brown, Ted Cyr, and Bill Coburn's *Coburn Glaze Special*, and dozens more attempted to take the $500 bond and trophy. The top honors went to Gene Hamm in the *Delta Machine* dragster.

The NHRA Bans Exotic Fuels

Starting on March 10, 1957, any fuel other than straight gasoline was no longer allowed in any classes from Dragsters to Stocks (including motorcycles) at all NHRA-affiliated drag strips. Mickey Thompson made the announcement to competitors at Lions Drag Strip that any alcohol and special fuels were prohibited.

Dragsters were recategorized into two classes: one for multiple-engine entries and single engines with superchargers and one for single-engine vehicles without superchargers. Reasons for the ban included the skyrocketing cost of participation, insurance costs, adequate stopping distance, and the general desire to return to gasoline. Enforced fuel checks were standard, and violators were suspended from completion for a lengthy time.

Out of the Red

Even with the nitro ban, by August 24, 1957, the attendance rose to record numbers that Thompson and the Lions Club forecasted. Within two years of operation, all outstanding loans and promissory notes owed by the Lions Club would be completely paid off. Financial aid to all nine harbor area clubs started to pour in, which benefitted charities, including helping the blind, local Boys and Girls Clubs of America, the Community Chest, Red

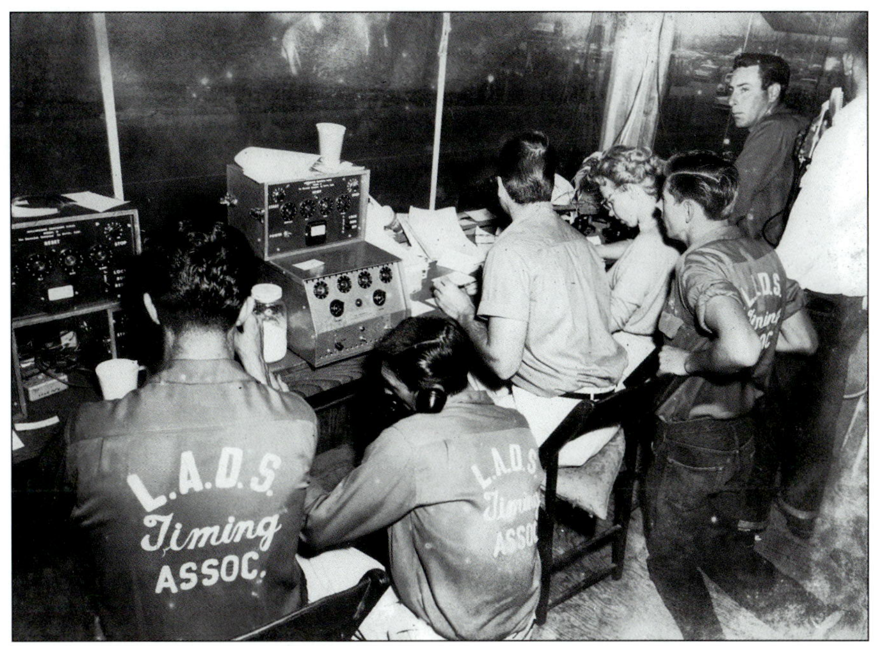

This view from inside the crowded tower at Lions Drag Strip shows the latest sophisticated timing equipment manned by an all-volunteer Lions Drag Strip Timing Association staff. Even the announcer was a volunteer from the Pacers Car Club in Long Beach, California. (Photo Courtesy Lions Automobilia Foundation Museum)

Cross, Exceptional Children's Foundation, Young Women's Christian Association (YWCA), Young Men's Christian Association (YMCA), and the City of Hope. Each received a share of the estimated $75,000.

Lions Drag Strip Opener Sets Five Records

On January 18, 1958, Lions Drag Strip celebrated its New Year's home opener with 2 radical sidewinders, 20 conventional dragsters, and a horde of very fast coupes, sedans, and roadsters. The Cyr & Hooper team (Ted Cyr and Bill Hooper) won Top Eliminator, and five new records were set during the day. Tommy Ivo pushed his A/Street Roadster to a 13.31 ET at 121.45 mph. Next, Al Freeman, driving his A/Modified Roadster became the fastest roadster in the nation with a top speed of 116.42 mph to go with a quick 12.10 ET. John Caulkins's A/Sports Car Volvo set the A/Sports Car record

Ike Iacona's GMC 235-ci 6-cylinder was a solid runner around the Southern California drag strips. Iacona won numerous top awards in Top Gas Eliminator, including a trophy and a $50 bond at Lions Drag Strip's Patriotic Spectacular event on July 4, 1958.

Jack Ewell in the seat of the **Kamboor-Jado Special** *blown Chrysler A/Dragster screamed down the strip with a 9.17 ET at 162.16 mph.*

Bill Coburn, owner and founder of the Coburn Glaze Company, was asked to go to the drag races with his son. Coburn took that opportunity and put several cases of his glaze into the back of the family station wagon to promote his products. He was instantly hooked on drag racing, but it was due to the overwhelming demand of his carnauba glaze wax by the racers. Bitten by the racing bug, Coburn decided to build his first chopped coupe, the **Coburn Glaze Special**. *Waiting to make the next run, Coburn applies another coat of his glaze to the coupe.*

The **Delta Machine** *was a Cadillac-powered dragster fueled on alcohol that collected the trophy and the $50 bond for the Top Gas Eliminator category.*

with a 17.35 ET at 75.30 mph. Lonnie Botts's A/M Fiat reset the record book with a 123.62 mph record and set the unofficial cleanup record for Lions Drag Strip—as his engine threw a rod and piston from the block. The final mark set was by the Bonner Brothers with a new C/Cycle record, running a 12.79 ET at 102.07 mph. This indicated that 1958 would be an epic year at Lions Drag Strip.

Speed Traps on the 1,320

The second-annual multiple electronic timing meet at Lions Drag Strip on February 22 and 23, 1958, was another weekend event organized by Mickey Thompson.

The drag strip featured $15,000 of new Chrondek timing equipment, which was used for the first time to provide 1) trap times for 10 individual 132-foot traps within the quarter-mile distance, 2) standard ET, and 3) top speed.

Unlike the previous year, the multiple timing tests of the two-day program offered all contestants the opportunity to learn better starting-line techniques, when to shift, the effects of engine changes, gear ratios, tire sizes, and acceleration graphs for each run. One of the entrants who took part in the timing experiments was a young Tom McEwen, who found ways to improve the performance of his D/G '57 Chevy.

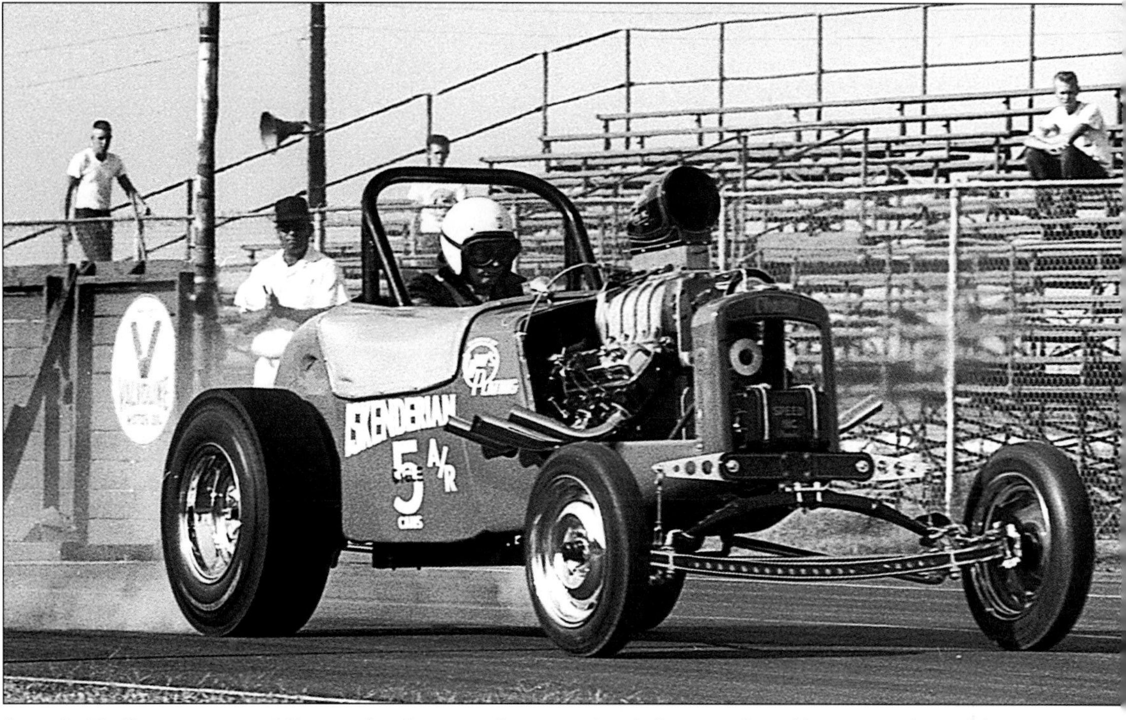

Lonnie Botts was one of the early pioneers in organized drag racing. He campaigned in various racing cars throughout the 1950s, including his A/R entry, which was sponsored by Iskenderian's five-cycle cams. (Photo Courtesy Steve Brackett)

Pittman Brothers and Edwards Slam B/Gas Record

On June 28, 1959, the Santa Ana Drags (the first official drag strip in the country) ceased operations due to the needed expansion and high demand for air travel in the Orange County area. Lions Drag Strip supported Santa Ana's last drag race and donated a 4-foot-tall trophy for the lowest ET of the meet, which Dode Martin claimed in the *Dragmaster* with a 9.42 at 163.53 mph. On the same day, Lions Drag Strip had the pleasure of hosting "gasser wars" in the B/Gas class. The Willys of K. S. Pittman and John Edwards took top honors, the $200 bond, and set the national record in the B/Gas ranks with a 11.19 ET at 119.26 mph, which earned an additional $50 bond.

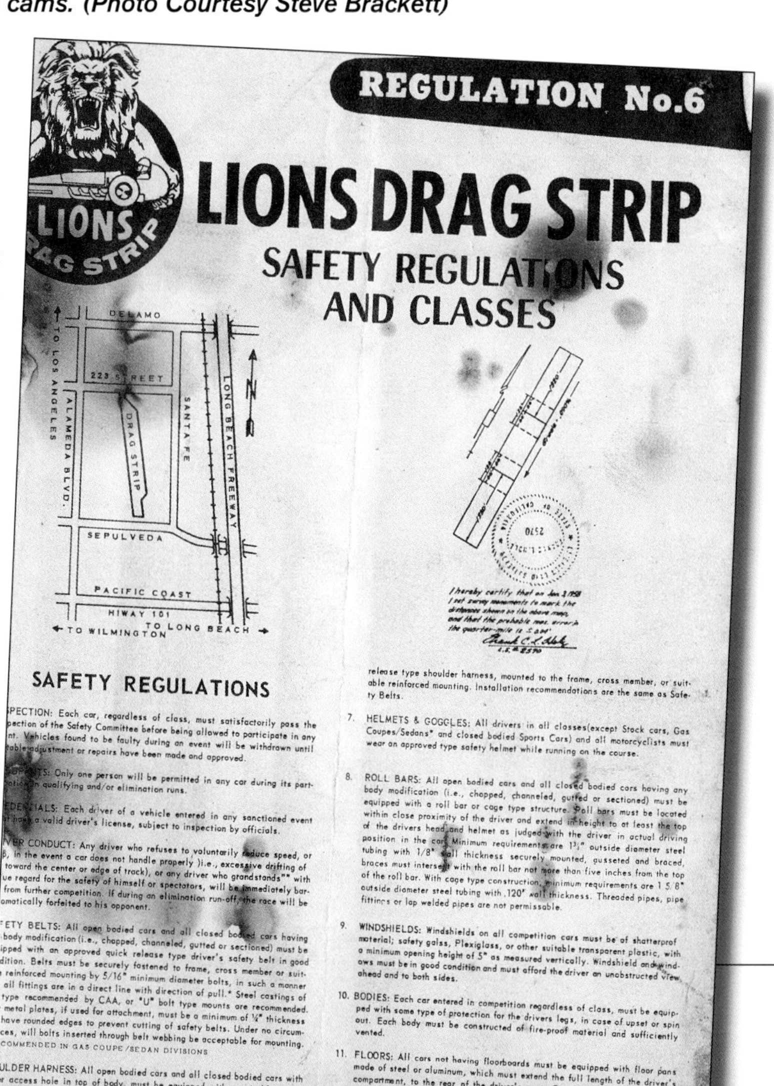

REGULATION No.6

LIONS DRAG STRIP

SAFETY REGULATIONS AND CLASSES

SAFETY REGULATIONS

...SPECTION: Each car, regardless of class, must satisfactorily pass the ...pection of the Safety Committee before being allowed to participate in any ...nt. Vehicles found to be faulty during an event will be withdrawn until ...table adjustment or repairs have been made and approved.

...TS: Only one person will be permitted in any car during its part...ation in qualifying and/or elimination runs.

...EDENTIALS: Each driver of a vehicle entered in any sanctioned event ...t have a valid driver's license, subject to inspection by officials.

...VER CONDUCT: Any driver who refuses to voluntarily reduce speed, or ..., in the event a car does not handle properly)i.e., excessive drifting of toward the center or edge of track), or any driver who grandstands"* with ...ue regard for the safety of himself or spectators, will be immediately bar... from further competition. If during an elimination run-off, the race will be ...omatically forfeited to his opponent.

...FETY BELTS: All open bodied cars and all closed bodied cars having ...body modification (i.e., chopped, channeled, gutted or sectioned) must be ...ipped with an approved quick release type driver's safety belt in good ...dition. Belts must be securely fastened to frame, cross member or suit...e reinforced mounting by 5/16" minimum diameter bolts, in such a manner ... all fittings are in a direct line with direction of pull.* Steel castings of ... type recommended by CAA, or "U" bolt type mounts are recommended. ...t metal plates, if used for attachment, must be a minimum of ¼" thickness ... have rounded edges to prevent cutting of safety belts. Under no circum...nces, will bolts inserted through belt webbing be acceptable for mounting.
...ECOMMENDED IN GAS COUPE/SEDAN DIVISIONS

...OULDER HARNESS: All open bodied cars and all closed bodied cars with ...er access hole in top of body, must be equipped with a suitable quick-release type shoulder harness, mounted to the frame, cross member, or suitable reinforced mounting. Installation recommendations are the same as Safety Belts.

7. HELMETS & GOGGLES: All drivers in all classes(except Stock cars, Gas Coupes/Sedans* and closed bodied Sports Cars) and all motorcyclists must wear an approved type safety helmet while running on the course.

8. ROLL BARS: All open bodied cars and all closed bodied cars having any body modification (i.e., chopped, channeled, gutted or sectioned) must be equipped with a roll bar or cage type structure. Roll bars must be located within close proximity of the driver and extend in height to at least the top of the drivers head and helmet as judged with the driver in actual driving position in the car. Minimum requirements are 1¾" outside diameter steel tubing with 1/8" wall thickness securely mounted, gusseted and braced, braces must intersect with the roll bar not more than five inches from the top of the roll bar. With cage type construction, minimum requirements are 1 5/8" outside diameter steel tubing with .120" wall thickness. Threaded pipes, pipe fittings or lap welded pipes are not permissable.

9. WINDSHIELDS: Windshields on all competition cars must be of shatterprof material; safety galss, Plexiglass, or other suitable transparent plastic, with a minimum opening height of 5" as measured vertically. Windshield and windows must be in good condition and must afford the driver an unobstructed view ahead and to both sides.

10. BODIES: Each car entered in competition regardless of class, must be equipped with some type of protection for the drivers legs, in case of upset or spin out. Each body must be constructed of fire-proof material and sufficiently vented.

11. FLOORS: All cars not having floorboards must be equipped with floor pans made of steel or aluminum, which must extend the full length of the driver's compartment, to the rear of the driver's seat. Cars equipped with bellypans made of fiberglass or other breakable material must contain metal sub-floo...

CONTINUED ON BACK PAGE

This pocket-sized copy of the rules was found in nearly all of the glove boxes of stock cars racing at Lions Drag Strip circa 1958.

First West Coast Appearance

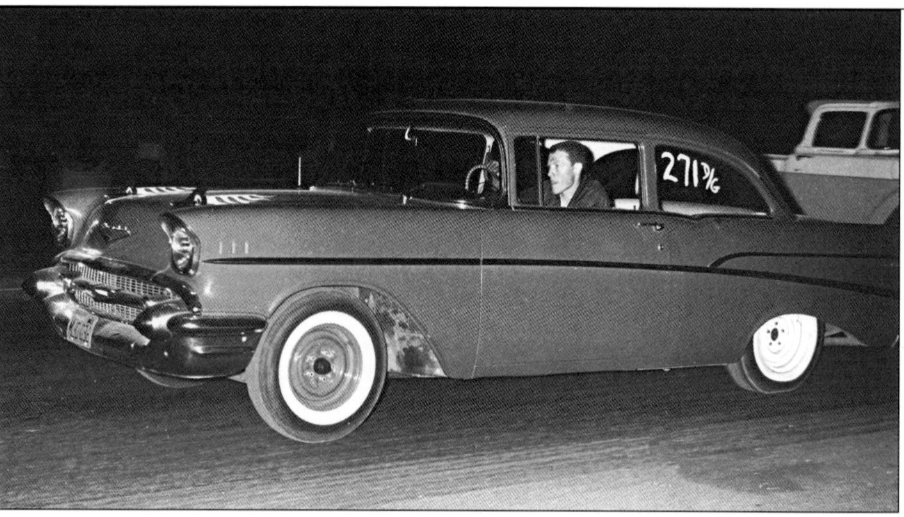

A young Tom McEwen was a weekly competitor at Lions Drag Strip, which was also known as the "Beach." To begin his drag racing career, he raced his mom's 1954 Oldsmobile before stepping into his custom-flamed '57 Chevy and ran in D/Gas. McEwen went on to be one of the most influential drivers and personalities at the Beach.

A crowd of 20,000 people packed Lions Drag Strip from July 18 to 19 and had the opportunity to view some of the most outstanding cars in drag racing. From the slowest stock cars to the hottest dragsters, each had its own concoction of engines, but never had Lions Drag Strip utilized a race car built with an aircraft engine. For its first appearance in Southern California, the *Green Monster* of Walt and Art Arfons used Lions Drag Strip as the venue to debut their 1,710-ci, 1,700-hp, Allison-powered dragster. The goal was to run a 180-mph top speed on pump gasoline. To attain that speed in the allotted space, the dragster was equipped with a parachute.

On hand for the big two-day meet was the *Sidewinder* fuel roadster driven by Jack Chrisman and prepped and owned by Joe Mailliard. Chrisman won both days of the meet and ran consistent ETs in the low 9.00s at speeds of 160 mph.

200-Foot Drags

Lions Drag Strip closed out the racing year with one of the most unusual races ever seen in drag racing. There had been several 1/2-mile, 3/16-mile, and 1/8-mile drags at several drag strips, but never had there been a 200-foot drag. A broken axle kept Arfons out of eliminations. Throughout the history of Lions Drag Strip, racing conditions were rarely unsatisfactory due to the weather or poor conditions left by track officials. Days before this big dragster meet took place on December 6, 1959, Mickey Thompson decided to sandblast the strip's surface. The results allowed the stock cars and motorcycles to compete the whole quarter mile, but the conditions didn't allow for the "hot cars" to run.

With a large crowd anticipated for that evening's meet with the big-name racers, the innovative Thompson gathered the drivers and announced an alternate plan. This plan was to conduct the first-ever 200-foot drag

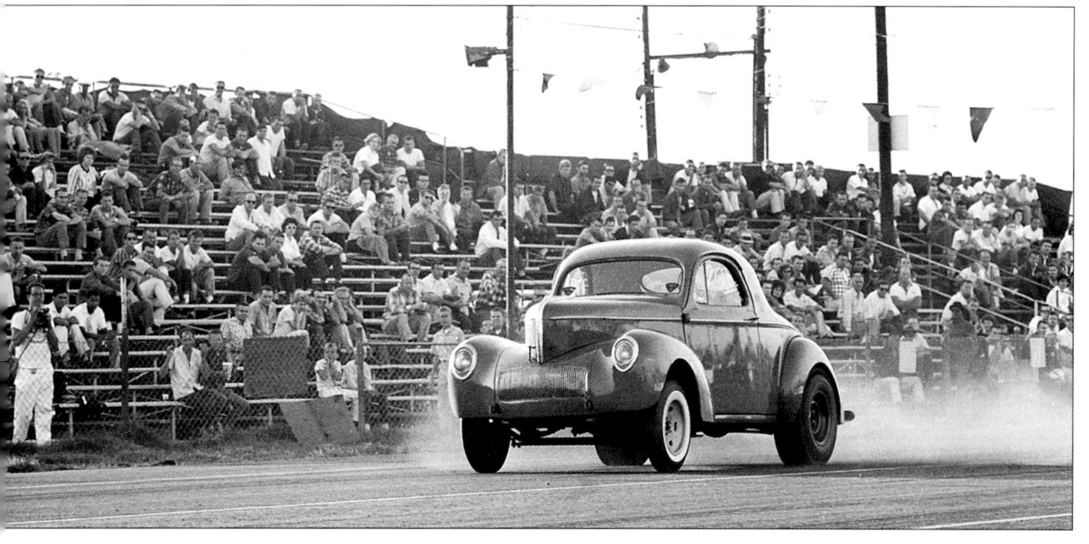

The 1941 Willys coupes were among the favorites of many spectators during the gasser wars, especially at Lions Drag Strip. The list of legends campaigning Willys coupes includes Stone, Woods, & Cook; "Big" John Mazmanian; Jerry and Gary Mallicoat; and the Brown Brothers. Gasser powerhouse K. S. Pittman is shown here at Lions Drag Strip in the new **Pittman & Edwards** *C/Gas Willys with a 327-ci Oldsmobile engine. (Photo Courtesy Steve Brackett)*

The inquisitive Mickey Thompson takes time from his daily routines to get accustomed to the seat of the 1,710-ci, 1,700-hp **Green Monster XI**. *The* **Green Monster** *cars of the Arfons Brothers attracted more than 14,000 spectators when the team made its West Coast debut at Lions Drag Strip. (Photo Lions Automobilia Foundation Museum)*

The unpainted **Sidewinder** *wasn't pretty, but for owner and tuner Joe Mailliard and driver Jack Chrisman, they knew how to make the car perform. On July 18 and 19, 1959, Chrisman drove the* **Sidewinder** *to the Top Eliminator title on both days. The rear-engine roadster was one of the earliest successful roadsters of its time. (Photo Courtesy Chrisman Family)*

UT OF CHAOS: THE STORY OF IONS ASSOCIATED DRAG STRIP

Whoever or wherever you are . . . if you but take the time to do so, I sincerely believe you will find the entire contents of this explanatory pamphlet well worth the reading.

Yours in service
HERBERT MURPHY,
President
Lions Associated
Drap Strip, Inc.

nly a few years back, a speed-thirsty, unorganized, mechanically talented segment of young Americans e creating havoc in our southland communities.

hey were mass drag-racing. They used back streets, ys, even highways at times for these speed clashes. y had no place to race, so they used any place they ld find.

They were flouting the law. They knew it. But worse, se semi-organized rendezvous of speed often left injury, times death — plus always, blazing headlines and conmnatory editorials — in their wake.

Drag racing was becoming a menace. None realized more than those of the traffic patrol and the juvenile visions of the Police Departments.

NEAR GENIUS

Yet many wiser heads among those of this speed fraternity also realized. They also knew that many of these "hot-rodders" verged on mechanical genius. They poured time and talent into putting horse-power and dig into their home-built machines.

But in them was the pent-up fury to speed, to test that equipment. Test it they did, despite hell and high water. But the way of it was all wrong and, knowing this, wiser heads among them asked for help.

It was in 1954 that directors of several harbor area Lions Clubs were approached. They seriously pondered the situation. They knew help was needed, and deserved. Many possibilities were considered, yet the only answer which kept recurring appeared to be "get them a place to do this thing sensibly and legally". But how?

The "if's" confronting were big ones: If a place of sufficient size for a drag strip could be found; if a strip could be built and operated so that all possible safety precautions were present; if the most strict rules of conduct prevailed and were enforced; if a way could be found to amortize the costs, which would be considerable; and finally, if, in the long haul, both these speed-intent young Americans and the public at large would be truly served— then this considerable venture should be made.

TIME DONATED

It was. Thousands of gratis hours have since been given by responsible (Lions Club and other) civic-minded citizens, to help make it all come true.

An area ½ x 3 miles was found, lying between Alameda and Santa Fe Avenues and (north-south), Willow and 223rd Streets. A lease was negotiated with the Los Angeles Harbor Department and work begun.

The first drag meet at Lions Associated Drag Strip (whose nick-name is L.A.D.S.) was held in May of 1955. Since, more than 850,000 spectators have attended more than 250 meets held there.

It can now stand firmly on an admirable record.

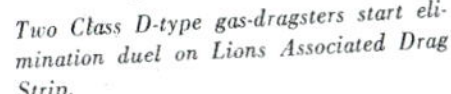

THE COVER

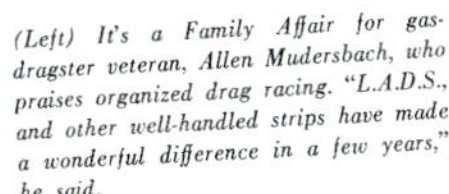

Two Class D-type gas-dragsters start elimination duel on Lions Associated Drag Strip.

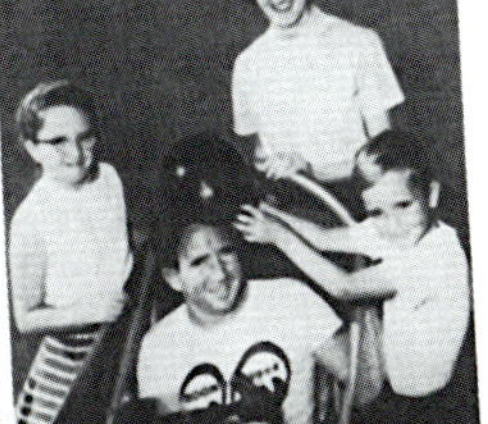

(Left) It's a Family Affair for gas-dragster veteran, Allen Mudersbach, who praises organized drag racing. "L.A.D.S., and other well-handled strips have made a wonderful difference in a few years," he said.

(Right) Any car can drag if it passes inspection. Thousands of stock car owners have discovered what their cars did (or did not) possess, in runs over the Long Beach strip.

MORE THAN 250 DRAG MEETS AND 375,000 TIMED RUNS MADE AT L.A.D.S.

Herbert Murphy, Lions Drag Strip's president, distributed to the local area this informative brochure that explained the story behind the drag strip. In addition, the brochure stated the purpose of the drag strip and how it provided financial aid for those less fortunate in the community. (Brochure Courtesy Lions Automobilia Foundation Museum)

Jack Chrisman teamed with Joe Mailliard to campaign the **Sidewinder** *mid-engine dragster. The history of running sideways-mounted engines was credited to the* **Slice of Pie** *creation by Creighton Hunter in 1955. Mailiard and Chrisman used a blown Chrysler for power. The chain-driven* **Sidewinder** *was a constant 9-second runner with speeds in the 160-mph range. (Photo Courtesy Lions Automobilia Foundation Museum)*

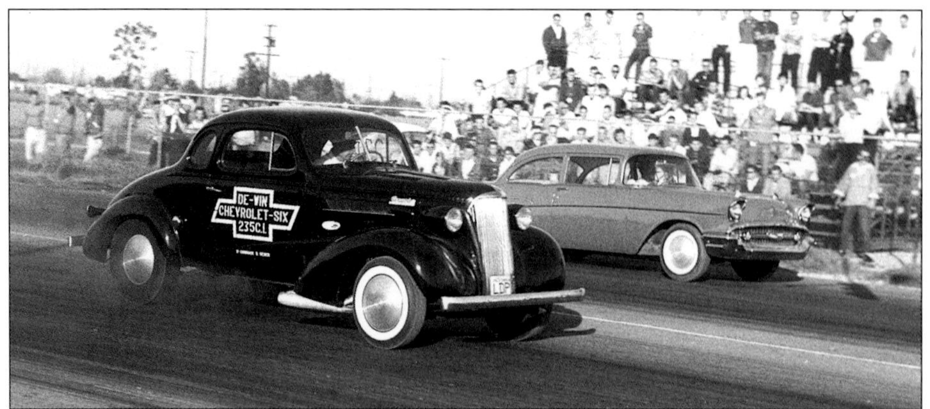

A strong competitor in the Gasser classes at Lions Drag Strip was the **De-Win** *1937 Chevrolet of McCormick & Sedar. The Chevrolet held numerous top speed and ET records, running Chevy's bulletproof 235-ci, 6-cylinder engine. The award-winning 1937 coupe consistently outran many of the heavily favored OHV V-8 competitors, such as Tom McEwen, who is driving his '57 Chevy here.*

race by holding eliminations through the staging lanes without the use of both the timing and speed lights—only flag starts and eyeballing finishes were used. Without any times or speeds recorded, the race ran without any major glitches. Jack Chrisman (driving the *Sidewinder*) outran Thompson in the final round and claimed the title of the first and only 200-foot Top Eliminator champion.

Gary Gabelich's passion for going fast began when he was a teenager attending Long Beach Polytechnic High School in Long Beach, California. He became friends with some of the most influential names in drag racing while in high school. One of Gabelich's earlier dragster rides was in the **Bounty Hunter** *dragster of the Koenig-Pick-Sundin team from Long Beach, California. (Photo Courtesy Steve Brackett)*

On January 3, 1960, Lions Drag Strip brought in the new year with a full field of dragsters led by the twin Chevrolet rails of Mudersbach & Herbert (Allen "Lefty" Mudersbach and Chet Herbert) and Glenn Stokey. Next was Tommy Ivo's twin-engine Buick, Mickey Thompson, Chrisman's *Magwinder*, the *Dragmaster Jr.*, Gary Gabelich, Glen Ward, and the Cook Brothers' *Auto Wrecking Special*.

Tommy Ivo set the low ET at 9 seconds flat in his famous Buick but lost the crankshaft bearings in the right engine, so he was unable to make the run for the record. With Ivo sidelined, Mudersbach waded his way through three rounds of competition and met Glen Ward for the eliminator money. Ward's engine bogged off the line and

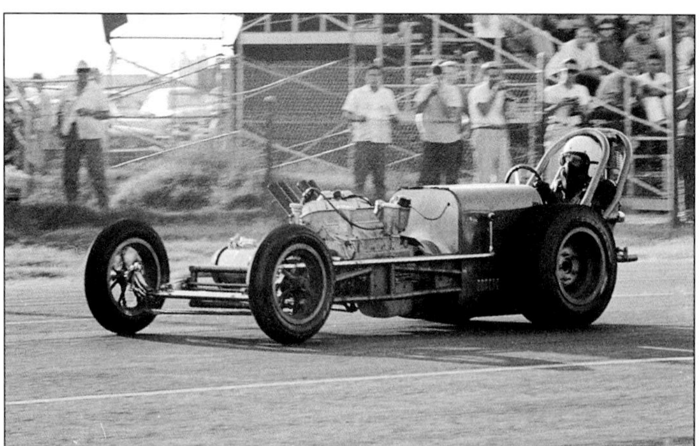

In 1960, Mickey Thompson became the fastest man in history when his **Challenger 1** *streamliner reached 406.60 mph at the Bonneville Salt Flats. The* **Challenger 1** *was powered by four blown Pontiac 8-cylinder engines. When Thompson returned from Bonneville to Lions Drag Strip, he toned it down a bit by piloting his 190-ci, 4-cylinder Pontiac Tempest dragster to a new 1320 class record, topping 151 mph in 9 seconds. (Photo Courtesy Steve Brackett)*

Gary Gabelich was a young, fearless driver. One of his earliest rides in a dragster was this 330-ci DeSoto Hemi-powered B/Dragster machine of Joe Koenig, Steve Pick, and Jim Sundin. The Dosser Motors **Bounty Hunter** *ran on gasoline that fed the downdraft carburetors. Gabelich's best run was a 10.58 ET at 146.57 mph. (Photo Courtesy Steve Brackett)*

The **Quincy Auto Parts Special** *from of Santa Monica, California, was a fan favorite at Lions Drag Strip. In his earlier driving days in drag racing, driver Bob Muravez mastered the handling chores, despite the car being extremely difficult to drive. Notice the missing front air scoop that was destroyed when extreme vibrations cracked and broke the aluminum scoop into pieces. (Photo Courtesy Steve Brackett)*

shut off, and Mudersbach continued onward for the win with a 9.20 ET at 160.14 mph, which was the top speed of the meet.

Smoke and Fire

Another attraction in April that drew spectators to Lions Drag Strip was the Arfons Brothers' *Green Monster Cyclops*. It was amazing to witness the power from the Westinghouse J-47 engine. Not everyone liked the jets, especially the racers, as the J-47 consumed gallons of kerosene during a run and left residue on the strip.

Horse Racing

After four straight weeks of watching the *Albertson Olds* dragster of Gene Adams and Leonard Harris take Top Eliminator honors at Lions Drag Strip, June 18 brought the drag strip into a new phase of racing. Along with the outstanding drag racing, the night included a horse racing a car and a man racing a horse.

Mickey Thompson had been told by quarter-horse enthusiasts for many weeks that a horse could beat a car in a drag race. Thompson, who was not one to shy away from anything, decided to give it a whirl.

With the distance of 1/8 of a mile, a horse was matched against a Chevy. The car won. The second round was once again won handily by the car. For the third round, Thompson called out for a volunteer track star from the crowd to race the horse. Out of the stands came a promising young man who was given a handicap head start. The odds were in the horse's favor, and the win went to the horse—but just barely. The horse seemed to tire before the end. This was another first for Thompson.

Live from Lions Drag Strip

Lions Drag Strip was in the final planning stages of the biggest race of the year when local television station KTTV announced a month-long schedule of televised races that started in July 1960. This was the first drag racing event on live TV. The threating sky over the

Jet dragster pioneers and brothers Art and Walt Arfons's **Cyclops/Green Monster** *jet dragster blasts to a top speed of more than 121 mph at Lions Drag Strip. It was powered by a Westinghouse J-47 engine that consumed 16 gallons of kerosene per minute. Still in the experimental stages, Art and Walt figured that they could hit a top speed of more than 220 mph on the strip and 273 mph on the Bonneville Salt Flats. (Photo Courtesy Lions Automobilia Foundation Museum)*

drag strip wasn't promising, but the weather held out for three rounds before the rain washed out the rest of the race. On the television side of things, the broadcast went without any major difficulties, except when the finish-line camera went out after the fourth race.

Midsummer Championships

On July 30, 1960, Lions Drag Strip hosted the Midsummer Championships, which was one of the largest one-day spectacular meets of the year. Stiff competition between the top dragsters took place. All were focused on stopping the winning streak of the *Albertson Olds* rail. In all, 27 dragsters were on the grounds at Lions Drag Strip to see if they had what it took to win.

As with any big meet, many had their own troubles—from losing complete engines to losing blower drives. Among the casualties in time trials was the blown Chevy dragster of Ed Janke and Bob Muravez when the engine backfired and coughed several rods out of the block. Adding to the list that exited before eliminations began was Curley Cowen in the new dual-Chevy-powered dragster of Quincy Automotive; Ted Cyr; the team of Langford, Koulan, & Brown, and the team of Stokey & Mailliard.

The first round of top eliminations got started with the current C/Dragster record holder, Hayden Proffitt, and the McEwen & Olson (Tom McEwen and Carl Olson) blown Chrysler. Proffitt led McEwen early, and the Chevy held off McEwen with a 9.76 ET at 154.63 mph to McEwen's losing but quicker 9.68 ET at 158.45 mph. Next to the line was Mudersbach & Herbert against the competition coupe of the Rakers car club. Mudersbach got off the line first and led from the start to finish with a 9.34 ET at 169.17 mph, as the Rakers entry got

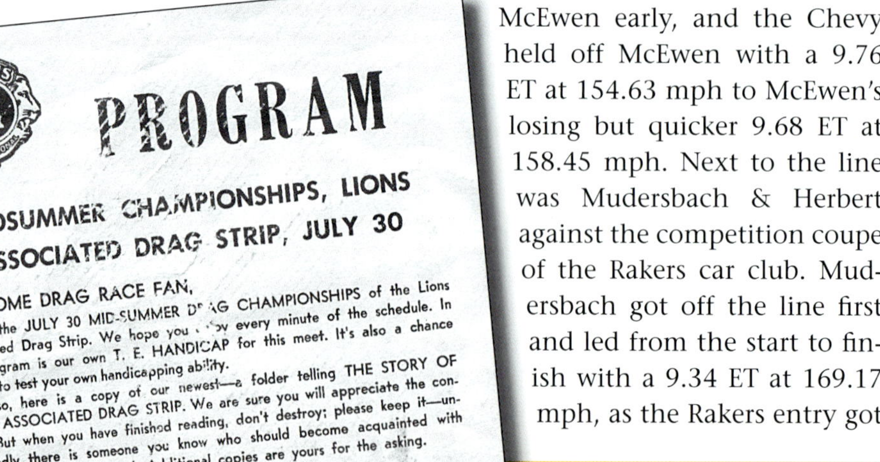

LIONS INTERNATIONAL

PROGRAM

MIDSUMMER CHAMPIONSHIPS, LIONS ASSOCIATED DRAG STRIP, JULY 30

WELCOME DRAG RACE FAN,

To the JULY 30 MID-SUMMER DRAG CHAMPIONSHIPS of the Lions Associated Drag Strip. We hope you [illegible] every minute of the schedule. In this program is our own T. E. HANDICAP for this meet. It's also a chance for you to test your own handicapping ability.

Also, here is a copy of our newest—a folder telling THE STORY OF LIONS ASSOCIATED DRAG STRIP. We are sure you will appreciate the contents. But when you have finished reading, don't destroy; please keep it—undoubtedly there is someone you know who should become acquainted with L.A.D.S. Mail it to a friend. Additional copies are yours for the asking.

EVENTS

1. QUALIFYING RUNS, ALL CLASSES, 3:15 p.m.
2. 30-MINUTE BREAK, 6:30 - 7 p.m.
3. TOP ELIMINATOR HEATS BEGIN 7:45 p.m.
4. INTERMISSION FEATURE—**ONE WHEEL(!)** PREDICTED TIME CONTEST: JIM GOLDSMITH, LONG BEACH vs. DANNY PHILLIPS, LOMITA
5. TOP ELIMINATOR & SUMMER KING OF DRAG, FOR $500 U.S. SAVINGS BOND.

Surprise: Aug. 13

Something new in the history of Drag Racing—

Test Your Picking Powers: See Inside

The Wilmington chapter of the Lions Club printed free weekly program folders, including this one for the July 30 Midsummer Championships. The Lions Club was a staunch supporter of Lions Drag Strip and the South Bay communities.

Curley Cowen, the latest driver in the seat of the **Quincy Auto Parts Special**, *rolls to a stop after a Gas Eliminator win. With the backdrop of the beautiful Palos Verdes Peninsula in the distance, the aroma of burnt rubber and the pungent smells from the nearby Tidewater/Flying A oil and gasoline distribution terminals and refineries were part of the charm and character of Lions Drag Strip. (Photo Courtesy Steve Brackett)*

WHO WILL BEAT THAT OLDS ?

Above are just some of the hottest gas dragster drivers who will tonight go out to (1) pick up a $500 U.S. Savings Bond and (2) beat the "unbeatable" Albertson Olds (pictured), driven by Leonard Harris (right inset). They are (l to r) Glen Stokey Redondo Beach; Dick Lechien, San Diego; Allen (Lefty) Mudersbach, Pico-Rivera.

Lions Drag Strip's weekly program shows the drivers who will compete against the Oldsmobile of Leonard Harris and Gene Adams to win a bounty. However, the **Albertson Olds** *dragster kept its winning streak intact.*

off the line with troubles and shut off.

Next, Leonard Harris competed against Pfaff & Sowins (Paul Pfaff and Dave Sowins). Sowins, in the *Albertson Olds*, fouled off the line and was running on seven cylinders, and Harris completed the win with a 9.45 ET at 151.51 mph.

$500 up for Grabs

The final pair of the round brought up the repaired dragsters of Stokey & Mailliard along with Langford, Koulan, & Brown. Both cars left the line, but then both broke down due to driveline problems that stopped them in their tracks and left the round without a winner.

The final round of the day brought what was beginning to be a common matchup between the *Albertson Olds* and the *Mudersbach & Herbert*

Allen "Lefty" Mudersbach held a firm grip over the competitive field en route to setting a new Lions Drag Strip top-speed record of 184.42 mph, running gasoline in the **Mudersbach-Herbert Cam Special**. *Mudersbach went on to set a world record of 195 mph with an 8.53 ET using twin injected Chevrolets. The Mudersbach-Herbert rail was a constant runner for Drag News Mr. Top Eliminator, and both Mudersbach and Chet Herbert won Bakersfield in 1961. Mudersbach and Herbert's partnership ended in 1963. (Photo Courtesy Steve Brackett)*

Special. As the cars were brought up to the starting line, each gave the okay nod to the starter, and the green was given. Harris was out in front and never backed down. He won Top Eliminator with a 9.14 ET at 164.53 mph to Mudersbach's 9.63 ET at 168.53 mph.

Leonard Harris

The skilled team of Gene Adams, Ron Scrima, and Leonard Harris continued its record-breaking year when it brought the *Albertson Olds* to national recognition through a terrific finish. It won the 1960 A/Dragster class Top Eliminator in a field with more than 35 other entries during Labor Day weekend (September 2 to 5) in Detroit, Michigan, and became the national champion. Harris, also known as the "King of Lions," won a record 12-consecutive Top Eliminator titles when an unthinkable calamity happened on the drag strip.

The* Albertson Olds *gasoline dragster was one the most dominating machines in the early years of Lions Drag Strip. Owned and built by Ron Scrima and Gene Adams, Leonard Harris drove the car to a record 12-straight Top Eliminator wins at Lions Drag Strip. Between the rails was a 462-ci Oldsmobile engine with a 6-71 GMC blower. (Photo Courtesy Don Ewald Collection)

In Memoriam

On October 22, 1960, in what was deemed to be one of the greatest match races of the year a heartbreaking tragedy occurred. Before the match race was underway, the unsinkable *Albertson Olds* split a cylinder wall while the Chrisman-Howard (Jack Chrisman and Howard Johansen) twin-engine beast lost one engine, which postponed the race.

With the second engine damaged, Harris was asked to help another team that didn't have its driver for the evening. Harris agreed to step in to see if he could solve the other team's handling problems. He made a pass, told them it was pulling to the left in the lights, and decided to give it another try. In the first round of Top Eliminator, Harris faced the Quincy Automotive rail. Either the steering arm came off or the front axle broke away from the car, and the car got away from Harris and crashed. It folded into a ball of broken and twisted metal while the stunned crowd watched in disbelief. Harris succumbed to his fatal injuries.

All-Star Meeting

A gathering of the top runners in drag racing converged at Lions Drag Strip on December 3 with several

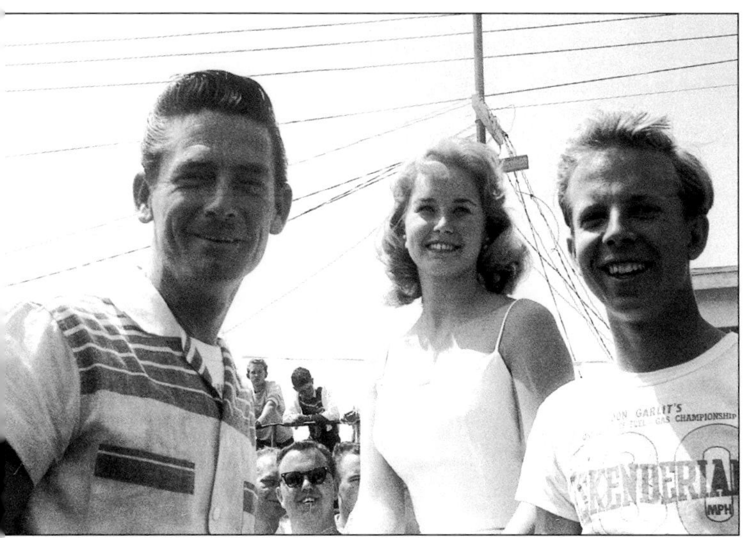

Jack Chrisman and Tommy Ivo were rivals on the strip but close friends in the pits. Here, they share pre-race smiles and festivities with the Lions Drag Strip race queen before their highly publicized match race for Drag News Mr. Eliminator. (Photo Courtesy Chrisman Family)

all-star drivers and their machines ready to claim the winnings in Top Eliminator.

The majority represented the West Coast, as the lone participant east of the Colorado River was the *Guzzler* driven by John Kranenburg.

Recent winners at Lions Drag Strip who participated in the meet included Tom McEwen, Joe Tucci, Hayden Proffitt, Jack Chrisman, Tommy Ivo, and Lefty Mudersbach. The spectators got their money's worth throughout the night, as the action never let up. The final round pitted the McEwen & Adams Oldsmobile against Ivo. What was thought to be a revenge rematch for Ivo wasn't meant to be, as he suffered a flat tire at the line. Ivo had his hands full, and the final round was postponed until the following Saturday, when both Chrisman and Ivo were scheduled to compete in a best-of-three match race. Unfortunately, the outcome was never determined, as wet weather was declared the winner.

McEwen Wins 1961 Opener

Lions Drag Strip returned to competition after the new year on January 8, 1961. Tom McEwen in the Adams & McEwen blown, Oldsmobile-powered rail ran a new top speed of 176.36 mph. McEwen took down the strong D/Gas Chevy-powered dragster of the Tapia-Hoffman team in the first round and defeated Bill Butters in the *Grohs Texaco* entry in the second before he met Keeter & Stewart in the Top Eliminator final. McEwen pulled out first and never surrendered his lead. He ran a 9.56 ET at 168.83 mph to Stewart's 9.83 ET at 159.01 mph.

McEwen versus McEwen

A two-day meet took place at Lions Drag Strip on February 25 and 26, 1961. More than 40 total dragsters from seven states were entered in the single-engine eliminator on Saturday. Tom McEwen pulled double duty and drove

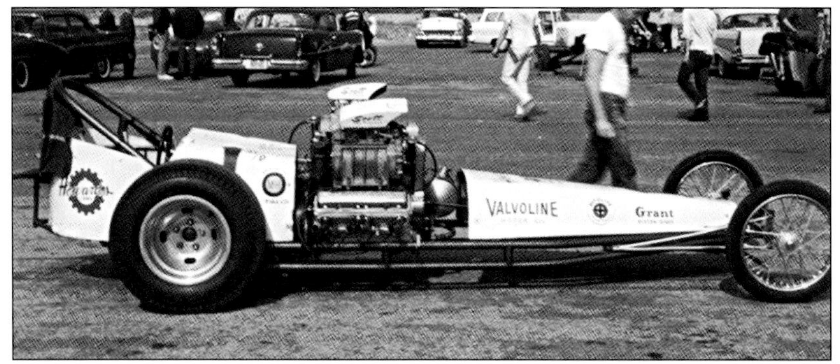

In late 1960, Jack Chrisman took over the driving duties in the Howards Cams* Twin Bear *when Glen Ward crashed the car in Oklahoma City and went to the hospital. Chrisman continued to drive the* Twin Bear *for the 1961 season and won the very first Winternationals with an 8.99 ET at 170 mph. After Pomona, Chrisman hit the road with the* Twin Bear *and toured with an intense schedule. (Photo Courtesy Chrisman Family)

Facing page: ***This elite lineup of dragsters competed at the Lions Drag Strip. From left to right are Tom McEwen, driver of the* Adams & McEwen *Oldsmobile rail; Joe Tucci's* Lynwood Welding Special*; Allen "Lefty" Mudersbach; the Guzler team of Don Mattison, Bud Roche, and John Kranenburg (the driver); the Howards Cams* Twin Bear *and Chuck Jones's* Magwinder*, which were both driven by Jack Chrisman; and the* Mis-Tuned 2 *C/Dragster of Hayden Proffitt and Clyde "Pete" Petre. (Photo Courtesy Lions Automobilia Foundation Museum)***

both the blown *Adams & McEwen* Olds and the *McEwen & Rhea* blown Chrysler.

With both McEwen cars running close for top honors, many of the 14,000 in attendance had thoughts of McEwen drawing McEwen, which would present a problem. Those thoughts turned into reality when three cars were left in Top Eliminator.

One was Bill Alexander in the *Ernie Camera Special* blown Pontiac, and the other two were Tom McEwen entries. A flip of the coin by officials determined which car of McEwen's would run in the final round.

The outcome pitted the McEwen-Rhea entry against Alexander for the title. Both cars ran consistent low-9.0-second ETs, and everyone in the

With the untimely death of Leonard Hughes, Gene Adams brought in Tom McEwen to drive the **Albertson Olds** *dragster. McEwen rose to stardom with Adams as one of the most successful duos in blown gasoline dragsters. The Adams & McEwen machine closed the 1962 season with three straight wins. (Photo Courtesy Steve Brackett)*

Glen Stockey was one of the top drivers in the 1950s and 1960s and one of the pioneers to break the 200-mph barrier in the quarter mile. The **Stockey-McCartney** *rail paired twin supercharged V-8 Chevrolets that frequently propelled Stockey into the winner's circle. It was rumored that he stayed on the throttle and drove through the infamous Willow Street barrier before coming to a complete stop. As Stockey pulled himself out of the car, an elderly man was the first person to come to his aid. The man looked over and around the car, spotted the open parachute and dragster, and asked, "When did they start dropping these out of airplanes?" (Photo Courtesy Steve Brackett)*

Mickey Thompson, Lions Drag Strip's general manager, regularly jumped away from the tower and into one of his dragsters to compete. Thompson pulls the chute at Lions Drag Strip after completing another pass in his **Attempt** *streamliner dragster at the new year opener on January 8, 1961. The innovative Thompson was attributed with designing the first slingshots in drag racing. (Photo Courtesy Lions Automobilia Foundation Museum)*

Jim Nelson and Dode Martin ran Dragmaster, a very successful business that built state-of-the-art chassis for customers and themselves. One example of the company's highly detailed craftsmanship was the **Dragmaster Jr.** *dragster, which was powered by a blown small-block Chevrolet. The* **Dragmaster Jr.** *ran consistent 11.50 ETs at 120 mph on gasoline. (Photo Courtesy Steve Brackett)*

stands thought it would be a close final round. Both cars left exactly on the green, where it was too close to call. As both cars approached the finish stripe, McEwen broke the light beam first with a 9.03 ET at 169.49 mph to the *Ernie Camera Special*'s 9.23 ET at 165.13 mph. The cars were only separated by hundredths of a second, and the winner earned $500.

Sunday's eliminations featured several surprises. Tom McEwen drove the *McEwen-Rhea* blown Chrysler all the way to the semifinals and dropped the *Chrisman-Howard* dual-engine Chevrolet. McEwen got the edge over Chrisman as Chrisman fried the slicks and lost traction off the line. Chrisman buried his foot on the pedal to close the gap, but McEwen lit the win lights with a 9.24 ET at

Tom McEwen played a double role during the weekend of February 25 and 26, when he drove the **Adams & McEwen** *and the* **McEwen & Rhea** *dragsters. An unforeseen scenario unfolded when both McEwen cars advanced all the way to the semifinals, where one was to face "Wild" Bill Alexander for the prize money. A coin toss determined which car would run against Alexander. The blown Oldsmobile of Adams & McEwen won the toss, and McEwen took top honors and the $500 bond. (Photo Courtesy Steve Brackett)*

Tom McEwen stepped up from driving his C/Gas '57 Chevrolet and jumped into blown gas dragsters. One of McEwen's earliest rides was driving Dick Rhea's K-88-chassis, gas-powered rail. McEwen was a natural driver who became one of the greatest drivers and personalities in drag racing. (Photo Courtesy Steve Brackett)

155.70 mph to the twin-engine Chevrolet's 9.23 ET at 168.53 mph. McEwen's luck ran out when he faced the dual-engine dragster of Mudersbach & Herbert. McEwen shut off before the lights with a blown engine.

Nitro Ban Expunged

It had been nearly five years, since February 10, 1957, when Wally Parks and the NHRA banned all exotic fuels, including nitromethane from competition to slow down speeds and save lives, equipment, and engines from exploding. The decision on the ban was reversed by C. J. Hart on January 21, 1962. The first fuel meet took place on January 26 with $500 bonds going to each of the top winners in Top Fuel and Top Gas Eliminator who ran more than 160 mph consistently.

As the smoke cleared out along with the nitro fumes, the safety crew surveyed the whole track and was glad to see the tire mark covered the distance of the 1,320. There was no doubt that nitro racing had returned.

The pits were overflowing with familiar faces who hadn't run in competition for about four years: Art Chrisman, Jim Kamboor, Jack Ewell, Bill Stecker, Chuck Gireth, Gene Mooneyham, and Don "the Snake" Prudhomme were back and ready to compete in nitro classes.

A new fire-up area was in place and worked extremely well. It cut the time it took to push the car down the strip and fire up in half. The average for six fuel cars was less than 3 minutes, which keeps the cars running and gives everyone more time to make more runs. C. J. Hart said that it was great to bring back the fuel cars, but the cars that still run on gas put on terrific shows. A young Don Moody piloted the blown *Davis & Johnson* Oldsmobile-powered Top Gas dragster to the runner-up spot against Gordon Collett. Collett was scheduled to leave for the coast after a run of bad luck but decided to stick around and roll the dice, which paid off. Moody recorded a 8.79 ET at 177.51 mph.

Shark Attack

The *Shark*, the new dragster of owner Gene Adams that was driven by Tom McEwen, made its debut on February 4, 1962, at Lions Drag Strip. The beautiful blown Oldsmobile-powered A/Gas rail was built by master craftsman Kent Fuller and wrapped in a Wayne Ewing hand-formed aluminum body. The debut caused a buzz throughout the pits, but the big news was that McEwen took over the No. 2 spot in Drag News Mr. Eliminator from Connie Kalitta in a best-of-three match race.

Colossal Money Meets

In September 1962, Lions Drag Strip amassed four straight weeks of colossal money meets that brought out the best competition to the venue. Out in force on September 13 were the large fields of Fuel and Gas dragsters and the unpredictable roadsters that brought the spectators to their feet. Bucking stiff headwinds, the reliable and steady Gary Cagle pushed the *Newhouse Special* to pick up the $1,000 bond money for the Fuel Top Eliminator class. The $500 bond for Top Gas Eliminator went to first-time winner Chuck Branham, who drove the Chrysler-powered Pomona Valley Timing Association *Starlight* A/Dragster over another new A/Dragster, the Starbuck-Douglas-Alexander entry from nearby El Segundo, California.

Altereds and Roadsters Run Wild

Altereds and Modified Roadsters brought out the best in the competition, as their unpredictability amazed all who watched in the grandstands and along the fences. Compared to a rodeo rider atop a raging bull, drivers often challenged the power from the engines down to the short-wheelbase ratios to run straight down the strip.

Lonnie Botts in the *Iskenderian 5 Special*, Jim Waldo in the *Hurstfield-Beaver Automotive* Fiat Topolino, and the roadster of Willie Borsch were the favorites in the class. The Don Ratican-Ron Stearns-Ferguson entry claimed the win in A/MR that week at Lions Drag Strip.

Lions Drag Strip Ends Year on a High Note

The final event of the 1962 season was on December 15 and offered the spectators a bit of everything. The variety of the top machines in the Fuel category brought out a new ET record of 8.11 seconds with the blown Oldsmobile of Davis & Moody. Tommy Ivo in the Ivo-Zeuschel machine was right in there with an 8.12 ET and set the top speed at 188.66 mph. Although they were the best runs, not many trailed behind Moody and Ivo. A pair of blown Pontiacs followed the parade.

"Wild" Bill Alexander of Ernie's Camera turned an 8.17 ET at 187.88 mph, and Jack Chrisman's blown

The Chrisman Brothers and the **Cannon** *Fuel dragster attracted curious onlookers in the pits at Lions Drag Strip. The dragster won its share of big events and continuously set top speed and ET records on the West Coast. (Photo Courtesy Don Prieto)*

The **Apricot Coupe** *of Ronnie Rapp and Gary Slusser was popular at Lions Drag Strip. Powered by a 331-ci supercharged Chrysler Hemi on fuel, the coupe ran consistent 160-mph blasts. (Photo Courtesy Don Prieto)*

Lions Drag Strip attracted well-known racers from across the country for the big meets, including Bob and Shirley Sullivan from Kansas City, Kansas. Sullivan's A/F dragster, with a full-aluminum body built by Rod Stuckey, was powered by a 331-ci Chrysler engine with a Chet Herbert cam. In 1956, Bob was the first Midwest racer to break the sought-after 150-mph mark in the quarter mile. (Photo Courtesy Don Prieto)

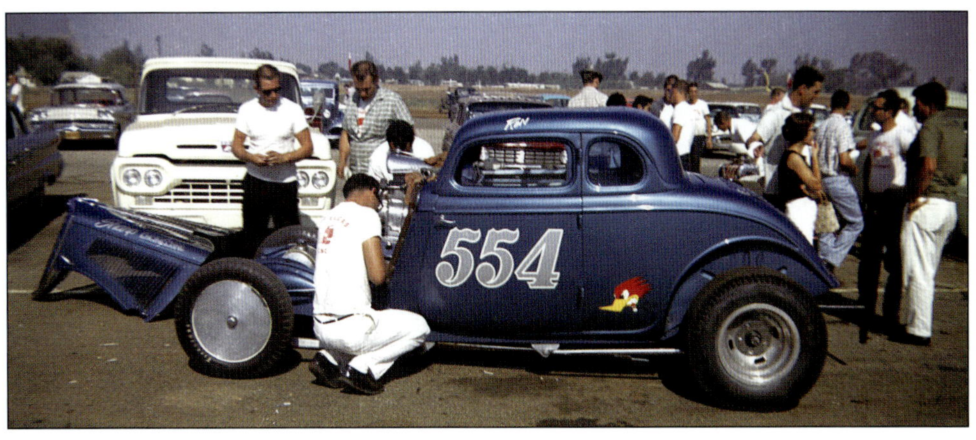

One of the most-feared fuel coupes from the late 1950s to the early 1960s was the steel-bodied 1934 Ford Mooneyham & Sharp **554** *coupe. In its day, the coupe was the king of the Fuel Altereds and ran a 1951 Chrysler 353 Hemi, which was fed by a nitro mix of 60 to 70 percent. The engine was set back 25 percent on the 112-inch-wheelbase frame. (Photo Courtesy Don Prieto)*

Memories

Don "the Snake" Prudhomme

Hall of Fame Drag Racer:
International Motorsports Hall of Fame
and Motorsports Hall of Fame of America Member

"Lions [Drag Strip] was where the names 'Snake' and 'Mongoose' started. I was driving the [*Greer-Black-Prudhomme*] car when one of the guys on the crew, Joel Purcell, started calling me Snake. Ed Donovan started the Mongoose nickname, and it stuck with Tom [McEwen].

"Even the public announcement speaker got into it, calling me Snake and Tom the Mongoose. Joel was a practical joker kind of guy. He kept the guys laughing."

The Chrisman family was one of the original pioneers in all of motorsports. From back to front is Everett, working on Art's **No. 25** *car; Lloyd, checking bearings; and Art, working on the rear-end. (Photo Courtesy Chrisman Family)*

Gary Cagle dominated Fuel Eliminator at Lions Drag Strip's Colossus Meet when he took home the $1,000 bond on September 13, 1960. Cagle's **Newhouse Special** *ran its best numbers at Lions Drag Strip, as the conditions were favorable. (Photo Courtesy Steve Brackett)*

Tom McEwen marched his way to a win over Connie Kalitta in the Mr. Eliminator series at Lions Drag Strip. McEwen drove the beautiful new **Shark** *A/Gas dragster of Gene Adams. The* **Shark** *was powered by a blown Oldsmobile engine built by Adams, the chassis was built by Kent Fuller, and the car was finished with an aluminum fabricated body by Wayne Ewing. (Photo Courtesy Lions Foundation Museum)*

George Cerny ran one of the earliest modified roadsters in drag racing. The roadster was powered by a small-block Chevy and painted burnt orange by Cerny himself. In addition, Cerny fabricated the aluminum body. (Photo Courtesy Steve Brackett)

Leland Kolb travels down the quarter mile during an early afternoon qualifying session at Lions Drag Strip. His rail featured a 78-inch moly square frame with air suspension. Horsepower was provided by a supercharged Lincoln engine fed with a twin-port Enderle injector. Although the blower was belt-driven, Kolb elected to keep the chain guard in place as an extra precaution. (Photo Courtesy Steve Brackett)

Pontiac had an 8.21 ET at 165.56 mph. Martin's Market from Bakersfield occupied the final spot in the field with an 8.41 ET at 178.92 mph. What proved to be the last race of 1962 was between Bill Alexander and Ivo. Although Alexander won the race with an 8.38 ET at 170.77 mph to Ivo's 8.23 ET at 182.53 mph, the ever-ready beam caught Alexander leaving a little too early, and Ivo was declared the winner.

Gene Adams and Tom McEwen dominated Top Gas for the third week in a row and won at Lions Drag Strip for the final meet of the year. McEwen in the Adams & McEwen entry received top honors with the win (an 8.40

Wayne Ferguson was on a mission to get to the finish line first in his Oldsmobile roadster. Ferguson went on to form the Jungle Four Top Fuel team with Gene Mooneyham, Jerry Jackson, and driver "Jungle" Larry Faust. (Photo Courtesy Steve Brackett)

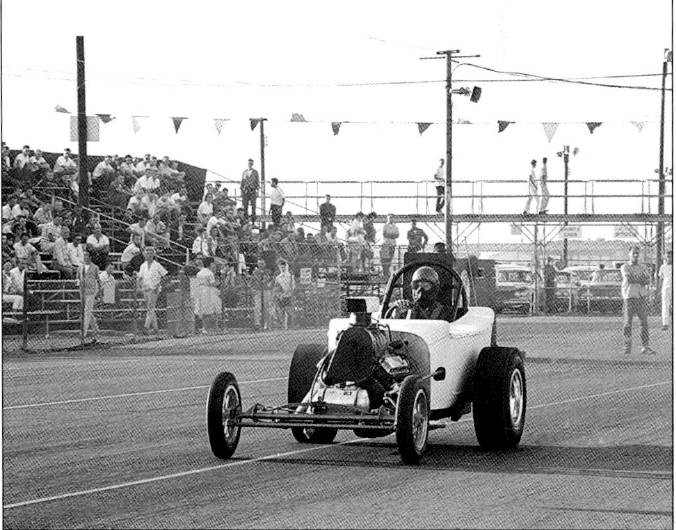

Lions Drag Strip was a hotbed of testing new cars, including this new blown A/Altered. The location of the drag strip featured ideal cool air that created the ideal conditions to create more horsepower. (Photo Courtesy Steve Brackett)

The **Hurstfield-Beaver Automotive** *B/A Fiat of was a regular at Lions Drag Strip with Jim Waldo driving. In 1955, Waldo got hooked on drag racing when he raced down the runway at the Santa Ana Airport. (Photo Courtesy Steve Brackett)*

ET at 179.64 mph) over Earl Canavan. A point of interest in the Gasser class was Robert "Bones" Balogh. He competed in a 1949 Chevrolet four-door fastback and was the one to beat in the D/G class. Balogh's overall win percentage ranked high in the history of Lions Drag Strip.

Not to be overlooked was the special match race between the Fuel dragster of Gary Cagle's *Newhouse Special* and the twin-engine Gas rail *Quincy Auto Parts Special* of the Brissette Brothers. Both cars provided remarkable times, but Cagle took the match and won two straight out of three.

The meet brought closure to a year of racing that was successful in many ways. With attendance and competition,

Gary Cagle quickly realizes the grip of the strip in the **Newhouse Special** *fueler in front of the iconic Lions Drag Strip sign. The absence of guardrails at Lions Drag Strip didn't deter the high-speed action. (Photo Courtesy Steve Brackett)*

Robert "Bones" Balogh

Drag Racer and Lions Automobilia Foundation Hall of Fame Member

"Lions [Drag Strip] was my home track. I won my first trophy in my 60 years of drag racing on the day it opened. That was back in 1955, and it got me hooked.

"It was just a little 1937 Chevy coupe with a Jimmy motor. One thing led to another, and I bought another car—a 1949 fastback with a V-8. Everybody laughed.

"'What are you gonna do with it?' I was asked by my buddies.

"'It's too heavy, it's blah, blah, blah.'

"I was good friends with Ed Iskenderian, and I went down to his shop and told him what I was going to be doing. You know, race it.

"'Yeah, that's good,' Iskenderian said. 'We'll put this camshaft in there, but you gotta have little gears.'

"'We couldn't just go buy those little gears back in those days.' he said. 'We'd go to the junkyard and get them. That Chevy's got a torque-tube driveshaft, and so does a 1953 or 1954 Buick rear-end, and it's got 4.44 gears in it. You go out and buy one of them, take it to Henry's machine shop, and he'll adapt it to your Chevrolet.'

"I didn't have a Chevy transmission. I used the Packard transmission. Everybody says, 'Why Packard?'

"It's because everybody's using a little cell transmission, and Iskenderian said it's got a lower first gear too. So, to get that heavy car moving, I got new tires and a pair of Inglewood slicks. They had just started making slicks. Iskenderian suggested that I go down and get the smallest-diameter tire, take the battery out of the front and put it in the trunk, fill [the trunk] up with some concrete or something, and put a rug back over it.

"That's when I went back out to Lions Drag Strip. Over the years, I won more than 250 races with that car. I was protested so many times. Mickey Thompson was running Lions Drag Strip then, and when he put me through tech inspection and told me to pull the pan, he said that they were going to check it over for everything (the bore and stroke)—you know, everything.

"Well, the second time he did it, he said, 'Oh, just leave half of the pan bolts. We can get it down quicker than I could if I would get the money that people would have to put up.'

"I don't remember what happened to the $25 when they protested, but if you were legal, you got their money. This went on for a while, taking their money. I was living life."

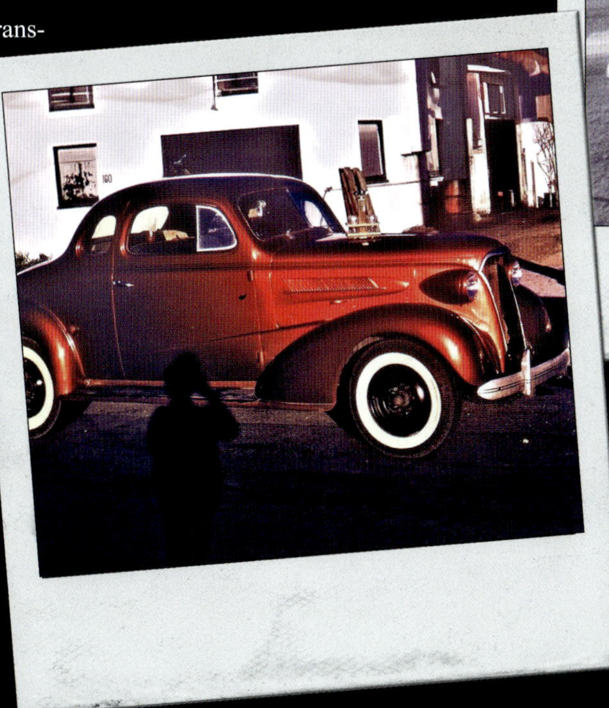

Robert "Bones" Balogh collected his first racing trophy at Lions Drag Strip on opening day (October 9, 1955) in his 6-cylinder Jimmy-powered 1937 Chevy coupe. Balogh had a successful driving career in the Gasser classes from 1955 to 2010. (Photo Courtesy Bones Balogh)

Robert "Bones" Balogh was your typical weekend drag racer who thrived on the competition but raced on a small budget. The only modifications to his stock 1957 283-ci Chevy engine were adding an Isky Z30 cam and kit, an Edelbrock three-carburetor manifold with carburetors, and a set of J&J Headers. The 1950 four-door Chevy fastback weighed nearly 2 tons and dominated the D/G class. Another amazing fact is that Balogh won the 1959 Southern California Championship in D/Gas when he accumulated 55 wins out of 59 starts and set the record of 33 straight wins at Lions Drag Strip against competitive competition. (Photo Courtesy Bones Balogh)

Bob Muravez was a force behind the **Quincy Auto Parts Special** *twin-engine, Chevy-powered dragster that raced with the front suspension raised 10 inches higher than most other twin-engine rails. Muravez drove by instinct, mastering bump steering. His right hand was positioned high up on the steering wheel, which gave him better handling of the car. As the car went up under power, it would veer hard to the left, and when the front end came down, it pulled hard to the right. (Photo Courtesy Steve Brackett)*

Gary Cagle muscles the **Newhouse Special** *through the quarter mile to win another round. Cagle was an active participant and competed in the popular Drag News Mr. Eliminator series. (Photo Courtesy Steve Brackett)*

it was far above the previous six years of operations. The year saw many improvements made at the strip, but most of all, it was a year free of accidents. Roughly estimated, Lions Drag Strip coordinated more than 90,000 timed runs with at least a dozen cars per night. It was a satisfying season, and many of the big meets received national exposure. Lions Drag Strip finished the year as the No. 1 drag strip in the nation.

The Gasser battles were in full swing by 1962 with strong interest after the Gassers were reclassified into three main classes: A/GS, B/GS, and C/GS. Heating up in the wars at Lions Drag Strip was Robert "Bones" Balogh in the **J&J Muffler** *Willys coupe from Inglewood, California. (Photo Courtesy Steve Brackett)*

Chapter Three

1963–1965

Lions Drag Strip Gains National Attention

The most successful year in the history of Lions Drag Strip unil this point was 1962, but Mickey Thompson wasn't looking to celebrate. He looked toward the future to prepare Lions Drag Strip for its most prosperous year yet.

This is an aerial view of the early years of Lions Drag Strip. This 200-acre parcel of land contains the complete area of the quarter-mile drag strip and the quarter-midget oval track located next to the main parking lot. The close proximity of the neighborhood is evident. (Photo Courtesy Don Gilespie)

Thompson thanked everyone for their support in the past year to keep Lions Drag Strip as the best drag strip in the country. He announced that nitro would return to the venue on January 21, and the drag strip would set records with increased bond and cash payouts.

Don Prudhomme dominated the two-day Gigantic All-Cash Meet on February 24 and 25, 1963, at Lions Drag Strip, which drew the nation's elite Top Fuel dragsters. Prudhomme piloted the **Greer-Black-Prudhomme** *dragster to wins on Saturday and Sunday and collected $3,300 for his efforts. (Photo Courtesy Lions Automobilia Foundation Museum)*

Prudhomme Takes Two

Lions Drag Strip hosted its Gigantic All-Cash Meet with two outstanding and competitive days of drag racing (February 24 and 25) that climaxed with a record-breaking run in the final round of Top Fuel Eliminator. Don Prudhomme, driving the blown *Greer-Black-Prudhomme*

Chrysler-powered AA/FD dragster, wrapped up the two days of racing on Sunday and defeated the blown *Porter and Reis Oldsmobile* dragster with an 8.03 ET at 191.48 mph.

The victory gave Prudhomme the Top Fuel Eliminator trophy, and he and the crew were awarded $3,300. The 180-mph bracket was stacked with contenders. Bob Haines, driving the Richter and Masters entry, turned in his best performance on Saturday night and hit 191.48 mph. It was the second car ever to run more than 190 mph at Lions Drag Strip. Then, Prudhomme topped 190-plus mph three times on Sunday.

The low ET (8.33 seconds) on Saturday was a three-way tie among the blown Pontiac of Ernie's Camera Shop (driven by Bill Alexander), Hampshire & Goss, and Don Prudhomme in the *Greer-Black-Prudhomme* car. Instead of splitting the money, the three flipped a coin for it, and lucky Alexander took the loot.

Emergency Role

When eliminations began on Sunday morning, there was an unfamiliar face working the starting line. Ronnie Samuel had worked at Lions for a few years—but not as the official starter. He was quickly initiated into the role, as the regular official starter Danny Lares viewed the races from the stands. Lares was temporarily incapacitated due to a severely broken leg that he suffered during Saturday's eliminations. Assisting Samuel with the starting duties was Altered racer Ronnie Stearns, who did a tremendous job.

Bill Hrosokoski and Tom McCourry took Top Eliminator honors in the Gas class with their little B/Fueler on Sunday. In addition, they shared Gas honors with Jack Chrisman, who took AA/D Top Eliminator.

The out-of-town fuelers had taken top priority, including Connie Kalitta, who set a record 8.34 ET with a top speed of 179.64 mph. "Sneaky" Pete Robinson had a tough go during eliminations on Saturday and bowed out. Gordon Collett ran an 8.61 ET at 174.75 mph on his way to the finals against Jack Chrisman, where he was defeated. Sunday's final round in Top Fuel between Prudhomme and Garlits was another nail-biter. Prudhomme won with an 8.46 ET at 178.21 mph while Garlits ran an 8.60 ET at 185.94 mph.

Garlits Wings It

Don Garlits's *Swamp Rat V* drew electrifying cheers from the spectators as he pushed down the fire-up road with a large, negative-lift-airflow wing attached directly above the blower. For Garlits, his top speed of the meet was a subpar 168.56 mph due to engine troubles on Saturday night. The reason for the trouble was a bad cylinder, and Garlits pulled one of his pushrods out and ran on seven cylinders against Richter & Masters and defeated the healthy rail with an 8.53 ET at 187.10 mph.

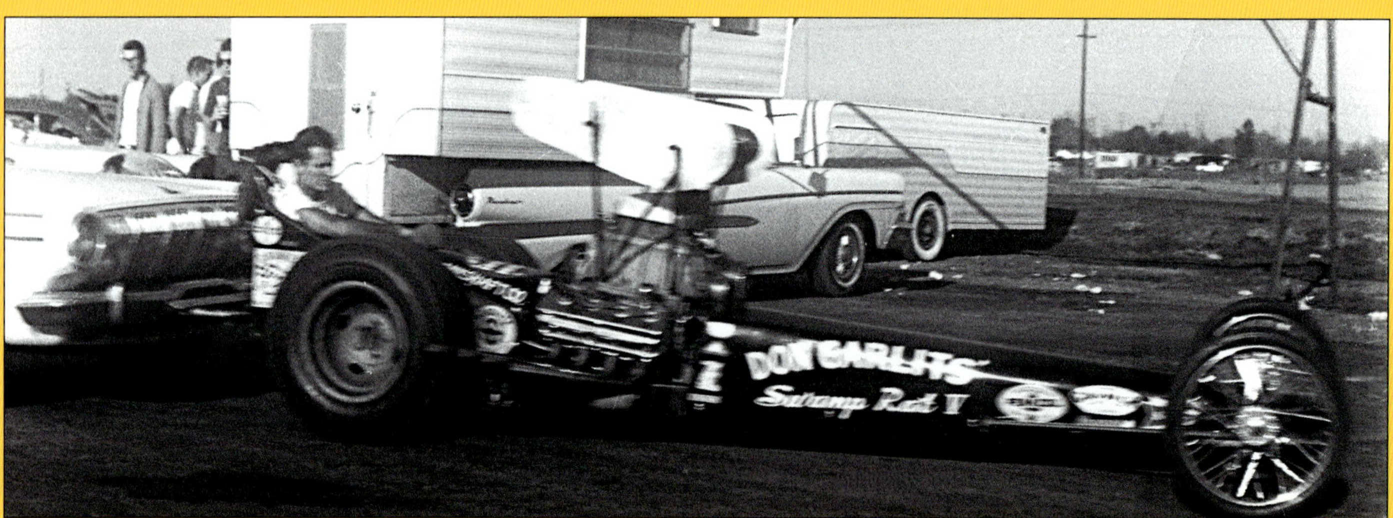

Don Garlits drew rousing cheers and favored glances as he returned to the pits at Lions Drag Strip with this wing attached over the top of the engine. Garlits's top speed of the meet on Sunday was 188.56 mph. He ran almost as well on seven cylinders as he did on eight. After experiencing engine difficulties on Saturday night, Garlits found a damaged pushrod and removed it. He managed to run an 8.53 ET at 187.10 mph against the stronger **Richter & Masters** ***AA/FD.***

There's a mystery surrounding the wing that was mounted above the supercharger on Don Garlits's **Swamp Rat V**, *which is shown at Lions Drag Strip. One week later, at the NHRA Winternationals in Pomona, the wing dimensions were relatively smaller than the one used the prior week at Lions Drag Strip.*

Safety personnel rushed to the aid of a driver who hit the guard rail and rolled over before coming to a stop in the middle of the top end. Racers and spectators had a fantastic view of the majestic Vincent Thomas Bridge, which can be seen in the background of this photo during its construction phase. Notice the missing grid plates between the 6,060-foot bridge. It was the only suspension bridge in the greater Los Angeles area. It opened in November 1963 to link California State Highway 47 from San Pedro directly to Lions Drag Strip. (Photo by Brian Pain/Courtesy Lions Automobilia Foundation Museum)

Humanitarian Role

Lions Drag Strip was one of the top drag strips in the country and was a formidable source of revenue for the nine local Lions Clubs that supported the surrounding communities. With all income derived from the drag strip operations, the charities received the funds to assist underprivileged families and children with proper medical care, clothing, education, and opportunities to live a better life.

The individual contributions of time and hard work by the 500 Lions Club members and volunteers from the nine chapters were vital to the success enjoyed by Lions Drag Strip since its opening in 1955. Their efforts in 1962 alone distributed $33,480 to individual club charities to aid in children's programs, such as the physically handicapped and the underprivileged, Youth Men's Christian Association (YMCA) and Young Women's Christian Association (YWCA) programs, youth camps, and the renowned Toberman Settlement Foundation. The Lions Club directors announced that 307,737 paid fans came through the gates for top-caliber drag racing in 1962 and made Lions Drag Strip one of Southern California's most popular spectator attractions.

All in a Day's Work

Split-second decision-making leads to either success or failure. The difference between making or breaking a driver's chance of winning is the sole judgement of one man: the starter. Lions Drag Strip starter Danny Lares had seen every top name in national drag racing take his "go" signal since he took the job for Lions Drag Strip's opening day in October 1955.

Danny Lares was a member of the Road Kings car club in Wilmington, California, from 1950 to 1956, when he started working at Lions Drag Strip as the lead timer. He became the official starter, and that continued until the resignation of Mickey Thompson on March 11, 1963. Lares belonged to the newly created NHRA and Associated Car Clubs of Los Angeles Harbor (ACCLAH), and he was responsible for writing the safety bylaws that helped change the mindset of the general public. (Courtesy Lions Automobilia Foundation Museum)

Experience is the biggest factor in a starter's decision of when to pull the switch of the starting light. A little-known aspect of the starter's job is the necessity to completely mask any movements or emotions that may tip an alert driver that the flag is immediately coming up.

In one highly touted race, Don Prudhomme sat in his dragster at the starting line against his final opponent of the meet, Steve Porter. There was $3,000 in cash riding on the outcome. At that time, this was the largest cash prize in the history of Southern California drag racing. It all rested on the shoulders of starter Danny Lares to equalize their chances from the starting line.

Standing motionless before them, Lares held a piece of wood in his right hand with a green cloth against a 50-cent electrical switch. He lifted the symbolic green flag a fraction of an inch from the switch to illuminate a 300-watt light bulb over his head, which simultaneously started 2,000 hp to blast Porter and Prudhomme down the track.

With thousands of spectators watching in the stands, it was another great race won by Prudhomme with an ET of 8.03 and a top speed of 191.43 mph. For Lares, this was another big-money race, where the all-important start was perfect. He was now able to take his first breath since both drivers signaled that they were ready by pulling up to the line.

King Jet versus King Dragster

An electrified atmosphere of excitement and enthusiasm unfolded on June 15, 1963, that captivated the spirit of a crowd of more than 10,000 spectators who witnessed two of the top machines in drag racing battle it out for supremacy. This wasn't your average match race between two internal-combustion machines. Instead, it was horsepower against thrust, the roar of fire, the eruption of smoke, and the likes that had never been seen before: a Top Fuel dragster versus a jet dragster.

Don Prudhomme (Lions Drag Strip's ET and top speed record holder in the *Greer-Black-Prudhomme* Top Fuel dragster) and Gary Gabelich (the holder of the national strip record in Bill Frederick's *Valkyrie 1* jet dragster) warmed up for what they hoped to be record runs.

Each driver made warmup runs earlier in the day. Don Prudhomme made his initial run with an 8.05 ET at 187.56 mph that thrilled the crowd. He blasted through the traps on his second run with an 8.14 ET at 187.56 mph. At 6:30 p.m., Gabelich blasted off for his warmup and roared through the lights with a 6.96 ET at 223.88 mph. This gave the crowd a sample of what was in store later in the evening.

It was time to go back to the pits and make the last-minute adjustments needed and discuss the starting procedure for synchronizing the dragster to the jet, which was not an easy task. It was decided that as soon as the jet's nose would drop under power and the afterburner would light, the flag would drop. The discussions lasted for several minutes. The jet was plugged in to be started. The dragster was sent down to the end of the track and pushed toward the starting line, and it fired to life. The

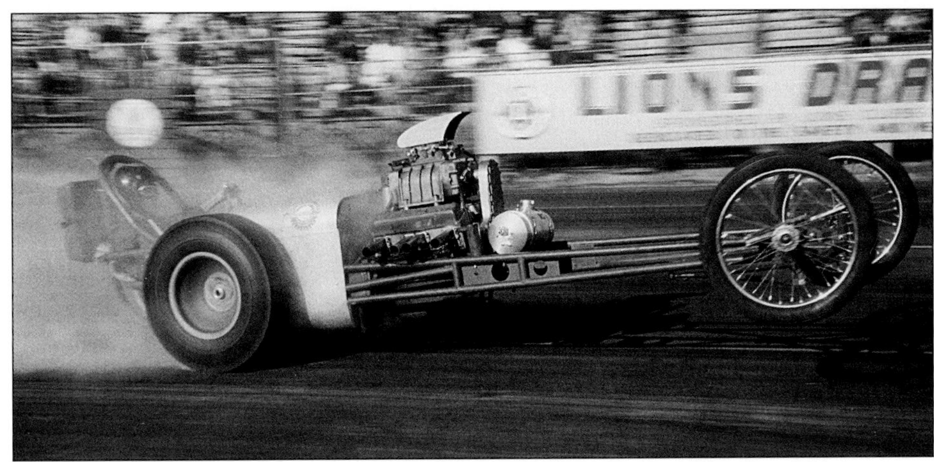

Gary Gabelich takes aim toward the finish line in the **Howards Cams** *gasoline-fueled rail. The dragster's power came from a blown Chevrolet and featured cable steering. Gabelich drove all types of cars—from backyard-built jalopies and land speed rockets to motorcycles and boats. (Photo by Brian Pain/Courtesy Lions Automobilia Foundation Museum)*

Nothing brought the sheer excitement to Lions Drag Strip more than when the first match race of its kind was held between the winningest AA/FD dragster in the country (the **Greer-Black-Prudhomme** *dragster) and the powerful* **Valkyrie 1** *jet dragster of owner Bill Fredrick and driver Gary Gabelich.*

fans in the grandstands emitted deafening cheers. Both cars were ready. The *Valkyrie 1* rolled up to the line, and the *Greer-Black-Prudhomme* dragster rolled alongside the jet. Both were ready to blast down the strip.

At a given signal of the flag (when the jet reached the needed RPM), the flag dropped and the race was on! There was a white, 30-foot flame shot from the back of the jet, and the dragster was in hot pursuit. It was all *Valkyrie*, which took the first race with ease.

Round two was close to a repeat of the previous round, but this time, the start was nearly perfect. The *Greer-Black-Prudhomme* car led by several car lengths, but in the blink of an eye, Gabelich got the lead and took the win over Prudhomme.

They were tremendous runs for tremendous machines, but Prudhomme took it on the chin and lost two straight against Gabelich, who had a 7.22 ET at 213.28 mph and a 7.47 ET at 216.82 mph. Although the dragster dropped two straight to the jet, Prudhomme received cheers from the crowd when he ran his best pass with an 8.05 ET at 189.86 mph. After losing two out of three, the defeat didn't settle well with Prudhomme. He took to the microphone and announced to the crowd that an upcoming rematch was in the works, making the crowd go wild.

Memories

Don "the Snake" Prudhomme

Hall of Fame Drag Racer:
International Motorsports Hall of Fame
and Motorsports Hall of Fame of America Member

"We were one of the first guys to run a Top Fuel dragster against a jet, and Lions wanted to pair the Greer-Black-[Prudhomme] car up against Gary Gabelich in the Valkyrie jet.

"Gary was driving a Top Fuel dragster besides driving the jet. The thought of racing a jet scared the s—— out of me. ET-wise, we could beat him down to the other end, but when Gary came by me, it was like I was parked down there. Man, he was a lot faster. You could hear him coming. I never really enjoyed doing that because I was always worried about the jet getting out of control and running into me or something. But back in those days, we didn't know what danger was. We just went out and did it and got paid for doing it."

Ivo Runs Four Over to Fuel

"Beauty is as beauty does" was the headline at Lions Drag Strip on May 18, when television star "T.V." Tommy Ivo brought out his $20,000 four-engine *Showboat* to make several exhibition runs at the track.

With Ivo under contract with the studio, he wasn't allowed to drive his popular *Showboat*. Ivo showed up at Lions Drag Strip along with costar Cynthia Pepper to watch driver Tom McCourry have his share of problems when Ivo converted to run fuel for the initial run at Lions Drag Strip.

With the intention of setting numerous records on nitro at the venue, the innovative dragster's performance didn't live up to the expectations of Ivo, but to the 8,000 spectators, they were not disappointed. The tremendous amount of engineering and complexity of the four Buick engines and four-wheel drive made it the most complex exhibition dragster of its time. The runs themselves were far from spectacular in setting top-speed and fastest-ET records, but the thrill experienced by the spectators was not dimmed with the haze, rubber burning, and fumes of nitro when the car roared down the strip, which was shrouded in massive clouds of smoke.

The television actor's *Showboat* gave new meaning to the word "exhibition."

Thompson's Exit Leads Lions in a New Direction

When the gates of Lions Drag Strip opened for racing on October 9, 1955, Mickey Thompson's commitment and perseverance made the drag strip a special place to visit. His dedication to running the drag strip and working full-time took up most of his time and kept him away

"TV" Tommy Ivo's original four-wheel-drive **Showboat** *dragster was built with four Buick Nailhead V-8 engines. The two left-hand engines synchronized to power the front wheels, and the two right-hand engines synchronized to power the rear wheels. The engine displacement measured a total of 1,856 ci, which produced an estimated 2,000-plus hp. Due to contractual obligations with movie studios, Ivo wasn't allowed to drive the car, so he put Tom McCourry in the seat. (Photo Courtesy Lions Automobilia Foundation Museum)*

from his other venues. Thompson did *everything* at Lions. He built it and put it on the map as the greatest drag strip in America. He dug the post holes by hand, scrounged up the piping that was used for the fence posts, nailed together the timing tower, and sold pit passes.

In Thompson's spare time away from the drag strip, he ran a machine shop and fabricated speed and high-performance parts for friends and racers. With the high demand for parts, he decided to open a parts business. Mickey Thompson's Speed Shop was located on 1419 Santa Fe Ave. in Long Beach, California. Thompson hired longtime friend Jack Ewell as manager and Dick Malland as head counterman. The open house and grand opening was on April 5. The store carried everything from door panels to mag wheels. The ex-backyard hot rodder now led an organization with 157 employees and manufactured more than 1,100 items. The business skyrocketed to new heights, and it took up most of his time, so it was time for Thompson to start thinking about changes in his life.

When Thompson decided to concentrate more on his business enterprise and other racing interests, he submitted his resignation as manager and general manager to the Lions Drag Strip board of directors.

When Thompson stepped away on Monday, March 11, 1963, the search for a new manager began. Harbor Area Lions Inc. President Dr. Roy M. Stokes appointed Leo Breithaupt as interim manager until Stokes found an experienced applicant to fill the position. Breithaupt was a respected member of a Lions Club, but he had no experience running a facility like Lions Drag Strip and had little knowledge of drag racing.

A few weeks into Breithaupt's tenure as manager, things soured and then went from bad to worse, as racers and personnel nearly pulled off a mutiny. Tom McEwen was summoned by the racers to step in and find a solution. McEwen reached out to Mickey Thompson to help lure C. J. Hart to take the position.

Thompson suggested that the board of directors reach out to C. J. Hart. Hart's resume included that he founded and managed the Santa Ana drag strip and that was currently the manager at the Riverside and Taft (formerly known as Gardner Army airfield) drag strips in the San Joaquin Valley in Kern County, California.

Without hesitation, Hart agreed to become the new manager. The Lions Drag Strip board of directors unanimously voted for Hart to have complete control as both the manager and general manager of the famed drag strip.

After venturing out with his speed parts business, Thompson also became the new owner of Fontana Dragway on June 13, 1964. Everything was basically new at Fontana, including the name. It was now the Fontana International Raceway, and Thompson brought many of his old gang from Lions Drag Strip, including starter Danny Lares.

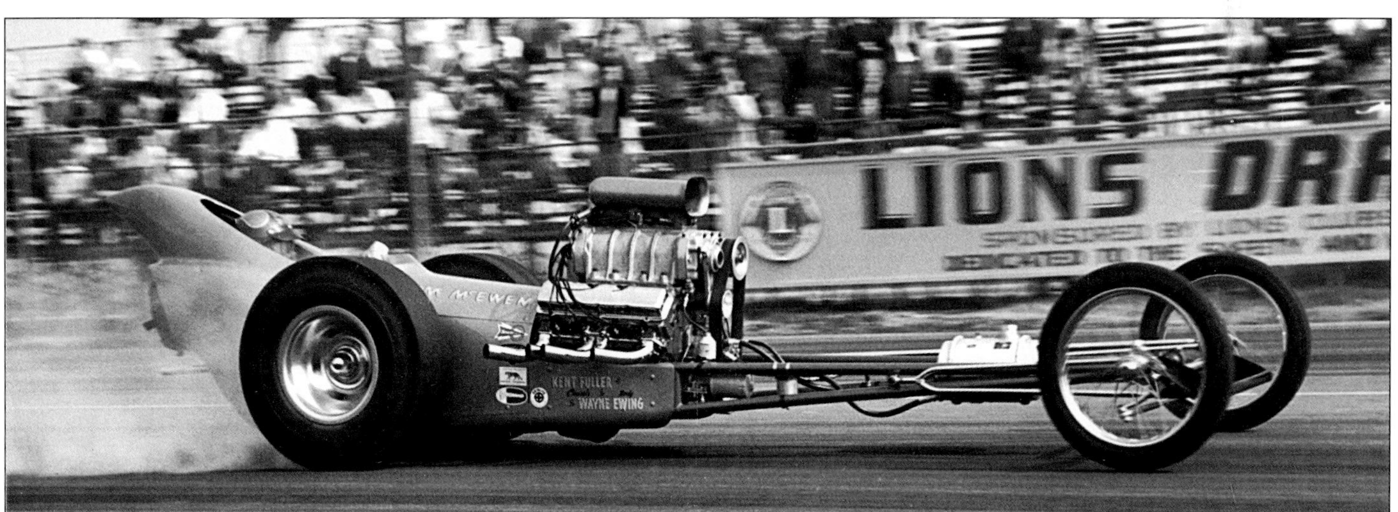

Tom McEwen jumped aboard with Gene Adams after Adams's record-setting driver, Leonard Harris, succumbed to injuries while driving another dragster at Lions Drag Strip. The Adams & McEwen **Shark** *car was one of the best-running gas dragsters in 1962 and 1963. It was mainly powered with a 394-ci Oldsmobile engine, but Adams often dropped in blown Pontiac between the frame rails. The car was built by Kent Fuller and fitted with aluminum panels that were built and painted by Wayne Ewing. (Photo Courtesy Lions Automobilia Foundation Museum)*

Memories

Don "the Snake" Prudhomme

Hall of Fame Drag Racer:
International Motorsports Hall of Fame
and Motorsports Hall of Fame of America Member

"When Mickey was running Lions [Drag Strip], it was around the same time he ran over 400 mph at Bonneville. I recall Lions [Drag Strip] only having three water spigots on a single section of pipe in the pits, way back against the fence. Racers would get in line for their turn to cool down their engines by changing out the water, like we did in our Buicks.

"Well, Tommy Ivo and I were in line waiting, and there was this one guy who kept giving Mickey a difficult time, grinding on him on the fact of having only three faucets. This guy kept going on and on and not letting up on him. It was then when we could see that Mickey finally had enough of the guy. I remember Mickey hauling off and smacking him good, knocking him over the hood of a car, and sending him to the ground. He was knocked out cold.

"Both Tommy and I looked over at each other, and I thought, 'Holy s——.' From that day forward, I was always scared of Mickey Thompson. Scared that I would say the wrong things to him. That sight of Mickey always stuck in my mind."

Mickey Thompson was hired to manage Lions Drag Strip in 1955. (Photo Courtesy Lions Automobilia Foundation Museum)

"I remember Mickey hauling off and smacking him good, knocking him over the hood of a car, and sending him to the ground."

The C. J. Era Begins

C. J. Hart's colorful background began when he ran away from home at a young age and found steady work in a circus. Years later, he operated a still and ran moonshine before the law caught up with him. Later, he was offered a job from Henry Ford to assemble engines at the Ford Motor Company.

Hart and his wife, Peggy, moved to Santa Ana, California, where he met Wally Parks, who hired him to help organize drag races. When Hart was hired to run Lions Drag Strip, he brought a flamboyant style of entertainment to the venue, where his carnival expertise played out in major roles at the drag strip.

Chrysler Brass Brings Factory A/FXers to Lions Drag Strip

Under the bright, sun-filled skies over Wilmington during a midweek winter day in January 1964, several trucks with trailers from Chrysler Racing Division rolled through the gates at Lions Drag Strip with three 1964 Plymouth sedans to test the new race-prepped 426 Hemis.

These new race cars were scheduled to run in the A/FX classes at the upcoming AHRA Winter Nationals and NHRA Winternationals but failed to meet expectations and were excluded from the action.

The entourage included several members of the top Chrysler brass, such as Bob Cahill (Chrysler's drag

Al Eckstrand checks the adjustments on one of the aluminum 4-barrel (AFB) carburetors on the new 426 Race Hemi before test runs. Both Eckstrand and Roger Lindamood played important roles with the development of the performances of the new Race Hemis, which fell short of the projected numbers. (Bob Martin Photo/ Courtesy Darr Hawthorne)

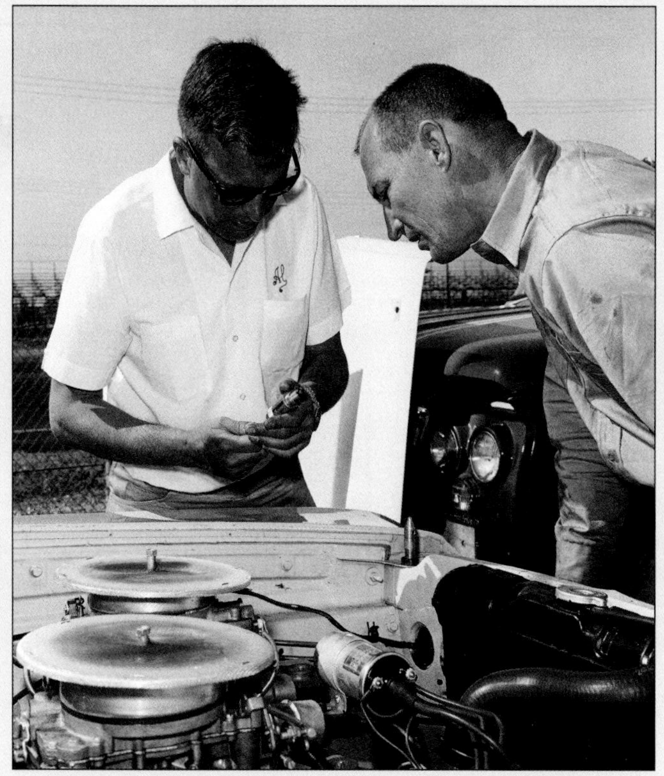

Al "the Lawman" Eckstrand was the driver who was assigned to lead the engine-testing program with underpowered AFB carburetors and an underperforming camshaft. The desired results instantaneously changed when the camshaft was replaced with a more aggressive model and the more power-productive Holley carburetors replaced the AFB Carters. Eckstrand and Roger Lindamood examined the condition of the spark plugs after each test run. (Bob Martin Photo/ Courtesy Darr Hawthorne)

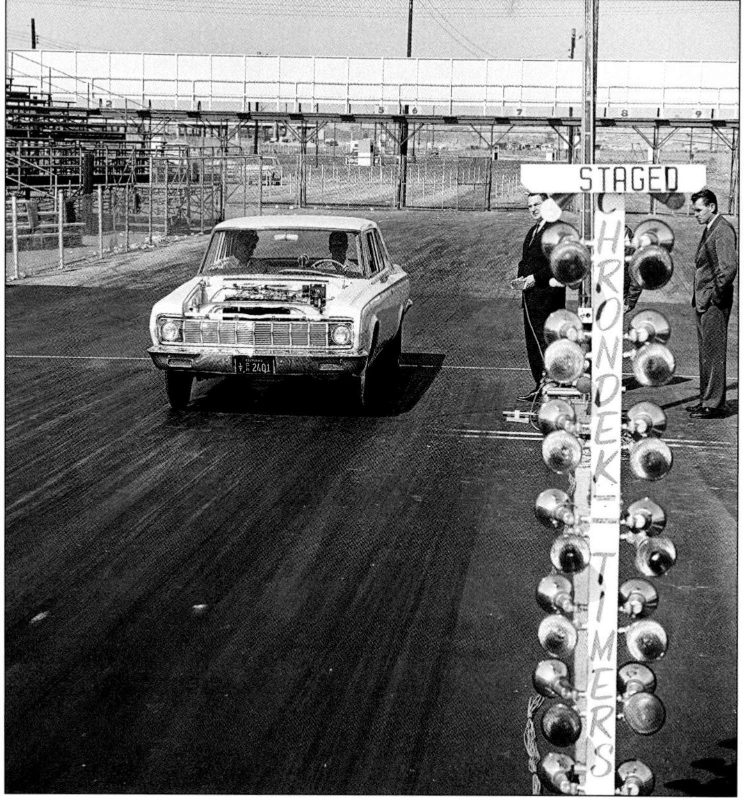

Chrysler's Robert McDaniel (in the dark suit activating the Christmas-tree switches) with Bob Cahill (the man behind and to the right of the tree), and an unnamed Chrysler executive (right) witness Eckstrand coming hard off the line when testing the new Plymouth. (Bob Martin Photo/ Courtesy Darr Hawthorne)

Memories

Larry Sutton

Lions Drag Strip Starter

"When C. J. 'Pappy' Hart was hired as the new track manager (and me being the youngest member of Lions Drag Strip), I was at a meeting they held to announce that C. J. was coming in to discuss what he expected as the new manager.

"C. J. showed up in his familiar 1954 or 1955 Ford station wagon powered by a Cadillac motor. He walked into the meeting at the time everyone was discussing different things, and he stopped them and said he was going to change things. One of the major changes he was going to make was that all the Lions Drag Strip people each would get paid an X-amount of dollars individually instead of the money coming out of the timing association funds. This way, he could hire or fire anyone or keep all of them. This was the way it was going to be.

"The acting leader of Lions Drag Strip went straight over to Hart and said, 'C. J., you don't understand us. *We* run the racetrack, and your job is only to be the business manager—overviewing expenses and handling bookings. That's it!'

"C. J. looked back at him and said, 'Excuse me. I've been hired as the manager, and those are my rules. If you don't like them, you better notify me by Tuesday because by Saturday I will have a whole new crew.'

"Several members said, 'Yeah, right. We [Lions Drag Strip members] had been around, running the strip for all of these years, and there was no way that's going to happen.'

"Come Tuesday morning, C. J. walked into Mickey Thompson's, where I was working, and came into the shop and said, 'Larry, the Lions Drag Strip members decided they were not going to go with my terms so are you going to go with them, or do you want to keep being the starter?' I said, 'C. J., I want to be the starter.'

"Needless to say, that didn't go over well with the members. For roughly two months, they all sat in the front row of the grandstand, harassing me by yelling obscenities, throwing pennies at me, and calling me names. With each weekend that went by, the Lions Drag Strip members showed up less and less until they finally gave up and went away.

"Basically, I was the longest-[tenured] employee ever at Lions Drag Strip. C. J. was genuine, sincere, authentic and, most importantly, my friend. He was like a second father to me."

Tom Jacobson jumps out with the lead over Bob Thompson's 426 Max Wedge–powered SS/SA 1964 Plymouth. The **Old Blue** *1962 Chevrolet Biscayne of Upton & Jacobson relied on the power of a 409-hp, 409-ci engine with dual carburetors that was formally prepped by Hayden Proffitt Enterprises. (Photo Courtesy Darr Hawthorne)*

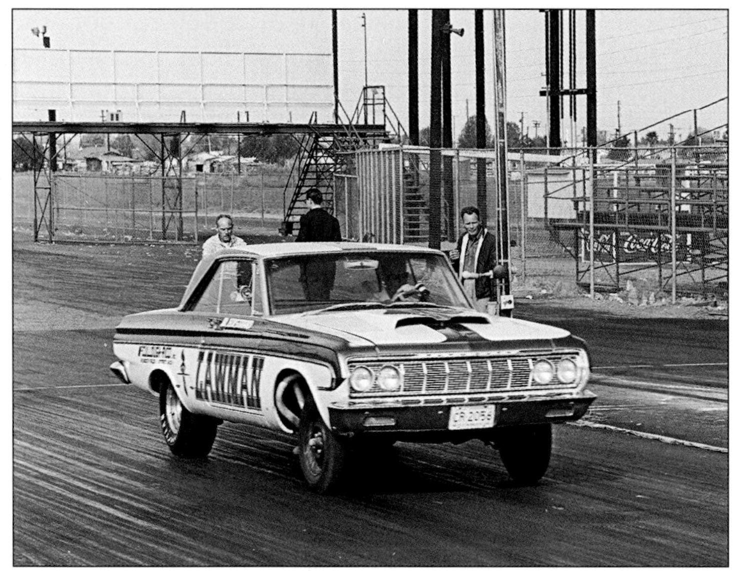

During a break in testing the New Hemi sedans, Al Eckstrand jumped behind the wheel of his 1964 Max Wedge Stage III–powered 426-R Belvedere hardtop to test the conditions at Lions Drag Strip. Satisfied with the Hemi's improved performance, the Plymouth sedans returned to action at NHRA and AHRA national events. (Bob Martin Photo/Courtesy Darr Hawthorne)

racing man in charge), lead drivers Al "the Lawman" Eckstrand and Roger "Color Me Gone" Lindamood, and several top factory mechanics to tune and oversee the performance and expectations of this highly funded project. The three 1964 Plymouth sedans had been preassigned to Tommy Grove (*Melrose Missile*), Jim Thornton (*Ramchargers*), and the team of Bill Jenkins and Dave Strickler.

Eckstrand was assigned to be the test pilot and put the cars through rigorous tests. Along with the plain white sedans, Eckstrand, a well-respected Detroit attorney, made a few test runs in his 1964 Max Wedge Stage III–powered 426-R Belvedere hardtop for future competition.

Prudhomme versus Karamesines

It's common at any drag strip to back off and take it slow before a big meet, but Lions Drag Strip showed no indication of doing that with the huge two-day United Drag Racers Association (UDRA) extravaganza a week away. The strip was booked for February 21, 1964, where the highly popular best-of-three match races

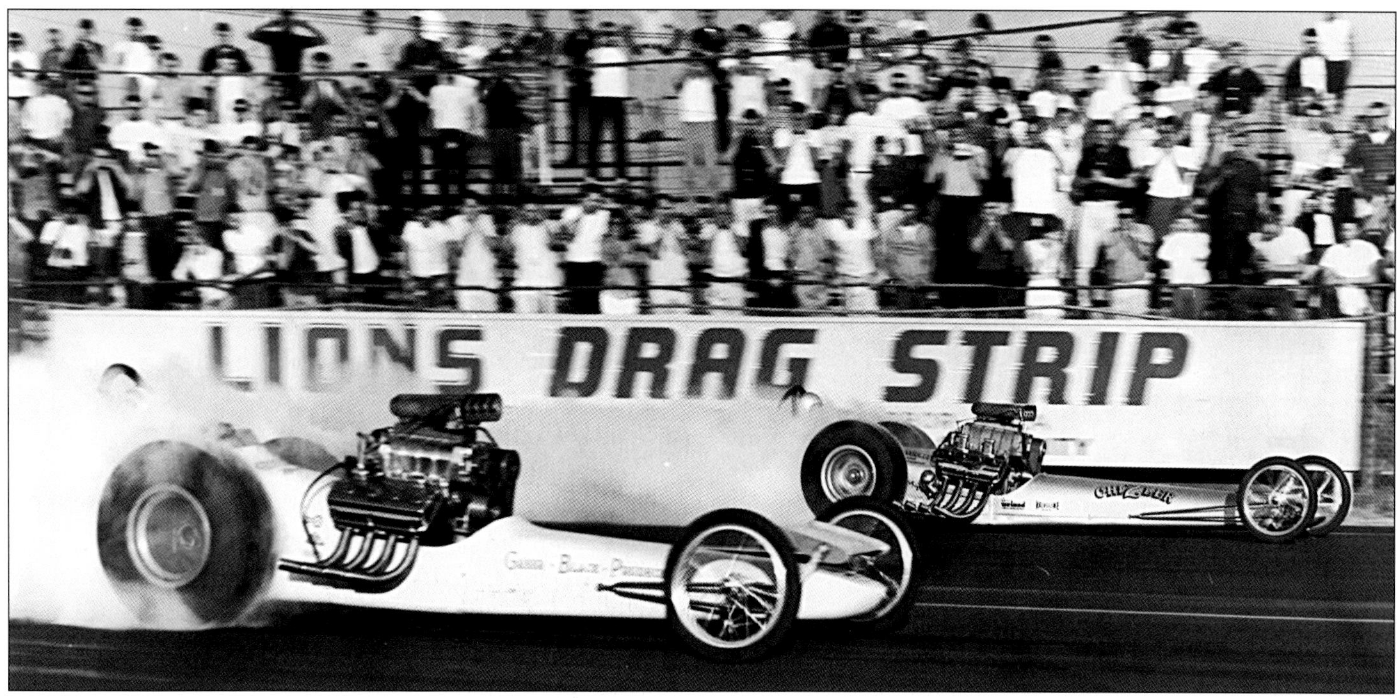

The ***Chizler*** *of Chicago's Chris "the Golden Greek" Karamesines battles Don Prudhomme, the winningest Top Fuel racer on the West Coast, who is shown driving the* ***Greer-Black-Prudhomme*** *digger. Karamesines and Prudhomme split the first two races, which led to the third and final match. Karamesines took an early lead with a holeshot and never let up, running an 8.12 ET at 189.06 mph to beat Prudhomme, who ran an 8.26 ET at 189.46 mph. (Photo Courtesy Lions Automobilia Foundation Museum)*

between Chicago's Chris "the Golden Greek" Karamesines and the South Gate, California, *Greer-Black-Prudhomme* dragster would take place.

For both Prudhomme and Karamesines, it was a critical matchup, as both scored a win in previous meets at Lions Drag Strip, so the third and final match was natural. Karamesines had set the national record with a 7.60 ET the week before the race at Lions.

In the first round of the race, Karamesines got past the up-in-smoke Prudhomme with an 8.05 ET at 181.50 mph. After the second round, it was tied 1-1, as Prudhomme won by a few inches with an 8.13 ET at 190.26 mph to Karamesines's 8.18 ET 188.28 mph.

As darkness fell, the Chicago invader prevailed with an 8.12 ET at 189.06 mph to the *Greer-Black-Prudhomme* dragster's trailing 8.26 ET at 189.46 mph.

Tuller Takes Title

The undercard of the Prudhomme-Karamesines match race featured eight Top Fuel dragsters that took to the strip for qualifying. Orange County Metal Processing's (OCMP's) "Stormin' Norm" Weekly held onto the first slot, and Paul Sutherland in Race Car Engineering's *Charger* was in the number-two slot with an 8.43 ET at 182.48 mph.

Sutherland was followed by Goob Tuller in the Skinner-Crosser-Jobe car with an 8.44 ET at 186.72 mph, Wenderski-Kamboor with an 8.47 ET at 189.66 mph, Porter & Chambers with an 8.64 ET at 180.78 mph, the brand-new rail of the Adams Brothers & Stewart with an 8.68 ET at 182.54 mph, Lefty Mudersbach with an 8.74 ET at 181.13 mph, and Earl Canavan's Lincoln with an 8.89 ET at 176.36 mph.

Top Eliminator got things underway with the Adams Brothers & Stewart running wire to wire for a win with an 8.91 ET at 157.06 mph over Mudersbach & Canavan. John Wenderski took down the number-one qualifier, Norm Weekly, in the *OCMP* digger, who was aided by Dennis Holding and Jim Fox when the blower let go in the lights. Goob Tuller locked horns with Paul Sutherland and won it with a close 8.26 ET at 187.88 mph to Sutherland's 8.36 ET at 184.40 mph. Closing out the round were the Wedge-type powerplants of the world's quickest Oldsmobile of Porter & Chambers and Earl Canavan's 555-ci Lincoln. The huge torque from the 1962 Lincoln Continental engine proved to be too much for the clutch, as Canavan rolled forward past the staging beams, giving him an automatic foul.

For round two, Wenderski and Kamboor were out due to mechanical woes, which in turn gave a single run to Rick Stewart. Goob Tuller hammered the Oldsmobile-powered machine of Porter & Chambers with an 8.36 ET at 187.50 mph. The anticipation of an epic final round never took place, as the Adams Brothers & Stewart discovered a broken blower and were unable to go, which handed the Top Eliminator win to Tuller.

The first round of Top Fuel paired the **Orange County Metal Processing** *car (in the background) of "Stormin' Norm" Weekly, who qualified with an 8.40 ET at 188.45 mph, against number-four-qualifier John Wenderski's* **Black Beauty** *(in the foreground). Both cars left evenly off the line, but Weekly lost the blower before the lights, handing the win to Wenderski. (Photo by John Ewald/Courtesy Don Ewald)*

Hart Creates Jr. Fuel

C. J. Hart always looked out for the little guys who were basically the backbone at the drag strip. When nitro returned to the NHRA in 1963, the rules and regulations were basically the same for the D/Fuel Dragsters with engine displacements under 303 ci. In early 1964, Hart created a new dragster class that brought new life to drag racing when he designed a new unlimited class for the smaller-displacement, non-supercharged engines. It looked much like the D/Class Fuel Dragster class but without any weight restrictions. This unlimited weight class was available for all 301-ci (or less) small-block engines that made it possible to race competitively on a smaller budget. Thus, Jr. Fuel was born. These changes became very popular, so the NHRA created a new A/Fuel class. Hart was considered the father of Jr. Fuel, and the results added up to great drag racing.

Defying the Establishment

C. J. Hart was a direct, no-nonsense type of manager. He managed under stringent safety regulations but always used fair judgements. In one incident, Hart threw out a well-known photographer and banned him for not playing by the rules.

In the first week of June, Hart received a call from NHRA director and chief announcer Bernie Partridge and NHRA founder and president Wally Parks. They wanted him to shut down Lions Drag Strip for the weekend of June 12, 13, and 14, 1964, during the first-annual *Hot Rod* magazine Nationals at Riverside. Hart declined their suggestion and told them that Lions Drag Strip would stay open to run the URDA Top Fuel Challenge the same weekend. Both Parks and Partridge were infuriated with Hart's decision to stay open and threatened to revoke NHRA sanctioning for Lions.

Hart did not back down from Partridge's ultimatum and immediately made a call to Jim Tice, the president of the American Hot Rod Association (AHRA), and requested that Lions Drag Strip become an AHRA-sanctioned facility. Tice instantly (and graciously) accepted Hart's proposal, and the URDA went off as planned under the new sanctioning body.

The UDRA Out-Stages the NHRA

In the next few weeks, the NHRA publicly printed slanted editorials about Lions Drag Strip's safety record, stating that a lack of safety was the reason that the drag strip was no longer being sanctioned by the NHRA. On June 13 and 14, Lions Drag Strip weathered the NHRA's oily smoke screens, as many at Lions felt that the UDRA meet was the best race since Bakersfield.

The UDRA's low eight and second low eight qualifiers were a prelude to Sunday's eliminations. By 7:30 p.m., the stands were filled, and rows of taillights signaled the late arrivals that poured into the parking lots.

Top Fuel honors for the number-one spot for Top Eliminator and $700 cash was awarded to the team of Dave Zeuschel, Joe Purcell, and driver Don Moody, who won over Paul Sutherland. Sunday's Top Fuel Eliminator was captured by Tom McEwen when he drove the *Donovan Engineering Special* past Warren-Coburn-Warren. McEwen took home $1,000 for his effort.

Declaration of Appreciation

Now under AHRA affiliation, C. J. Hart and Lions Drag Strip issued a public statement in the June 20, 1964, issue of *Drag News* to thank all the racers and spectators that attended the successful two-day URDA event. The gesture was received well by all who were at Lions Drag Strip.

Memories

Tim Kraushaar

Lions Drag Strip Starter and Announcer

"The first time that I met C. J. Hart was in 1957. I hadn't been to a drag race until one of my high school pals took me on a drive through the bean and sugar-beet fields to Santa Ana Airport, where the first commercial drag races were being held. Being the bold one, I found the owner/manager [Hart] and introduced myself. That was the beginning of a long and wonderful friendship, and I can assure you that I didn't miss many weekends of racing after that.

"Fast-forward to 1960, and C. J. was running the drag races at Riverside International Raceway. So, one day, I approached him and told him that I wanted to work for him. He asked me what I wanted to do, and I said, 'I want to be the starter.'

"He looked at me like I was nuts. I think that me being a snot-nosed kid who was barely 19 years old was a bit off-putting. He just looked at me for what seemed like forever and said, 'You come with me.'

"He took me to the starting line and introduced me to the starter who worked for him at Santa Ana. His nickname was Hambone, and C. J. informed him that I was his new assistant. Hambone was a mail carrier for the city of Orange, California. After lugging the mail all week, he disliked the drive from Orange County to the far side of Riverside and then standing all day in the desert sun. Three weeks later, he retired, and I became the full-time starter.

"Wow—I was 19 years old, going to college, and the starter at a racetrack! I told my mother what I was doing. Her response was, 'Oh dear,' but she was kind enough to make a set of red and green flags for me, as I had inherited Hambone's old ones."

Big Bash Upset

One of the biggest upsets of the year at Lions Drag Strip (and possibly in all of drag racing) took place on Saturday, June 22, 1964, as jet jockey Gary Gabelich took down the mighty *Swamp* Rat of champion Don Garlits.

Gabelich drew the cheers of thousands in the stands when Gary drove Bill Martin's Herbert-powered *400 Jr.* past the surprised Garlits with an 8.42 ET at 180.72 mph to Garlits's 8.55 ET at 180.72 mph. Gabelich, a comparatively new dragster driver, is best known as the helmsman of the *Valkyrie* jet. He delivered the blow with a lineup of 28 fuel dragsters eager to get a crack at the national champion.

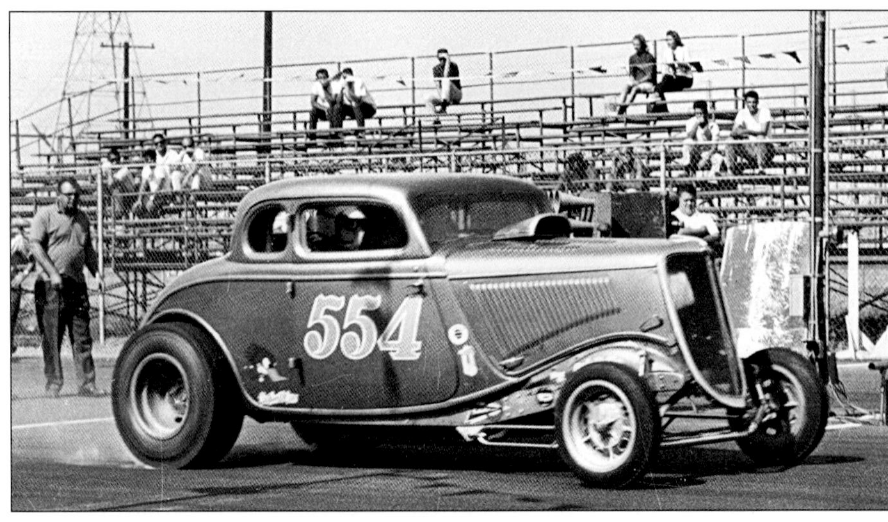

Gene Mooneyham and Al Sharp's **554** *nitro coupe was one of the most-feared hot rods in all of drag racing. "Jungle" Larry Faust wheeled the potent '34 Ford-bodied Altered, which featured a blown 1951 Chrysler 354-ci Hemi. The coupe consistently found the winner's circle with 8.80 ETs at 170 mph.*

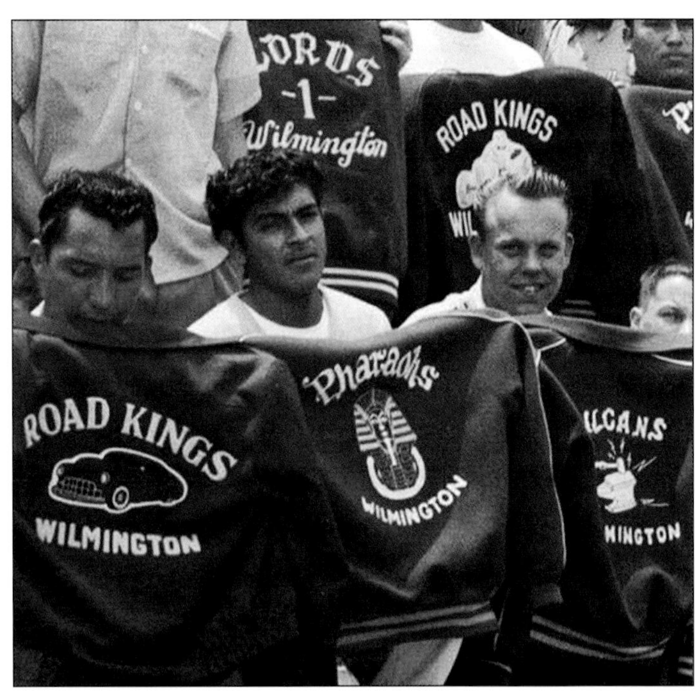

These car club members represented Wilmington and were a portion of the 78 car clubs located throughout Southern California. Many car club members from Wilmington chapters became volunteers and top racers at Lions Drag Strip. (Photo Courtesy Lions Automobilia Foundation Museum)

Ronnie Winkle gives driver John Wenderski some advice before his run in **The Black Beauty** *Top Fuel dragster at Lions Drag Strip. Wenderski recorded an 8.34 ET at 183.66 mph in this qualifying session. Wenderski and Winkle successfully toured nearly every drag strip in California and set multiple strip records from Cotati to Romona. Wenderski was successful in the* **Drag News** *National Fuel list competing among the nation's fuel dragsters. At the age of 24, John Joseph "Sonny" Wenderski lost his life in a racing accident on February 23, 1964, at San Diego Raceway in Romona, California.*

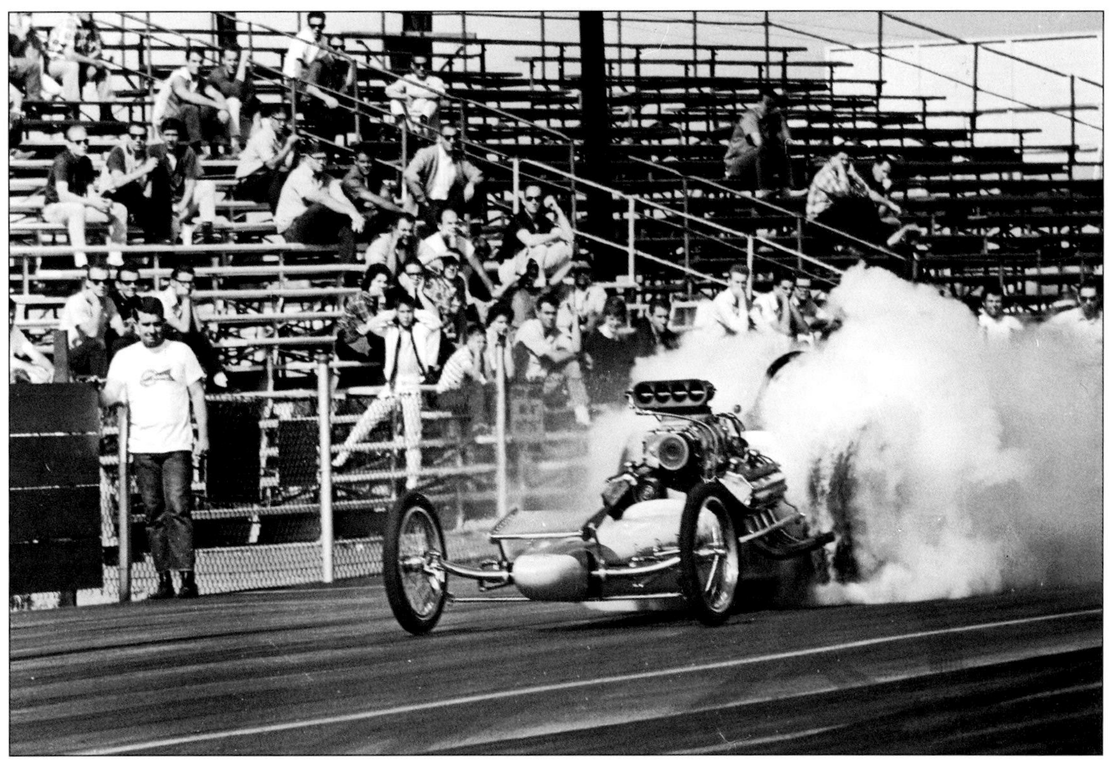

Since its first race on June 17, 1962, the team of Greer-Black-Prudhomme proved its supremacy. In 25 big meets, it recorded 22 out of 25 low ETs, 17 out of 25 top speeds, 17 out of 25 Top Eliminator titles and set 11 records at five different strips. (Photo Courtesy Paul Johnson Collection)

Garlits swamped the rest of the competition with consistent runs in the high 180s (mph) with ETs in the 8.20s all weekend. The best pass for the touring Floridian leading up to the grand finale was an 8.16 ET at 190.66 mph.

The lead-up to the amazing Garlits-Gabelich run was the greatest series of events seen at Lions Drag Strip so far that year. The stiffest competition was from the *OCMP* (Orange County Metal Processing) dragster from nearby Fullerton with George Van in the seat against the *Lefty's Speed Shop* entry driven by Mike Quigley. Van wasted no time against the Chevy with an 8.59 ET at 188.28 mph to Quigley's 8.92 ET at 161.87 mph.

Don Yates in the *Gross & Yates* machine lost to Jeep Hampshire in the *Stellings & Hampshire* rail in a close run of 8.55 at 185.94 mph to Hampshire's winning 8.27 ET at 185.18 mph. Bill Martin's Chevy came to the line with driver Gary Gabelich running against his first competition of the evening against Jack Williams in the *Hilton-Crossley-Williams* entry out of Bakersfield. Williams made a valiant effort against Gabelich with an 8.26 ET at 186.7 mph, but Gabelich got him off the line and outdistanced

Jack Chrisman made his presence known at the two-day Big Bash Meet during Sunday's Eliminations on June 22, 1964. He out-muscled the competition behind the wheel of Mickey Thompson's Pontiac Hemi-powered AA/G dragster to take Sunday's Top Eliminator for the gas dragsters. Chrisman dropped Tom McCourry and Bill Hrosokoski in the finals with an 8.70 ET at 175.78 mph. In September 1962, Chrisman won Top Eliminator and at the U.S. Nationals at Indianapolis in Thompson's Pontiac Hemi-powered AA/Dragster. (Photo Courtesy Lions Automobilia Foundation Museum)

Gary Gabelich tries to play catch-up against Don Yates in the Prieto, Cagle, & Yates fuel rail. Don "the Wavemaker" Prieto is one of the leading historians in drag racing. (Photo Courtesy Don Prieto)

The Willie Borsch-Jim Harrell **Red Hot Roadster** *was a holder of many records in the A/FR class, running consistent 9.0 ETs at 180 mph in early 1963 at Lions Drag Strip. The Altered's blown 392 Chrysler Hemi was built by owner Jim Harrell, who was the proprietor of Jim's Auto Parts. The 23T fiberglass body was molded by Cal Automotive. The first* **Winged Express** *debuted in 1960.*

Lefty Mudersbach was one of the great drivers who ran regularly at Lions Drag Strip. Mudersbach and Chet Herbert made a formidable team that often outperformed many of the nation's top drivers. In 1961, Mudersbach and Herbert pulled a miracle that was never duplicated again. At the Fuel & Gas Championships at the Famoso Drag Strip in Bakersfield, California, Mudersbach won Top Fuel Eliminator while running on gas. (Photo Courtesy Paul Johnson Collection)

Williams for the win with a slower 8.42 ET at 180.72 mph, which sent Williams back home to Bakersfield.

Jack Warye, in his blown Pontiac, squared up against the *Broussard, Purcell, Davis, & McEwen* Chrysler-powered rail. McEwen wasted no time in downing the Pontiac when he topped out with a fast 188.66 mph run with an 8.30 ET.

Another team out of Bakersfield was James Warren in the *Warren-Coburn-Warren* dragster of the Hashim Automotive against Steve Sturgeon in the *Martin's Market* dragster. Sturgeon got out ahead of Warren, but Warren was able to catch up and reel in Sturgeon with an 8.26 ET at 187.88 mph to Sturgeon's 8.73 ET at 174.41 mph.

The next pair to the line was the Adams Brothers & Stewart against Lloyd Banks driving the Boyd-Banks Chrysler from Culver City. Off the line, Banks ran into trouble and shut off with a 9.10 ET at 159.57 mph to Stewart's winning 8.57 ET at 184.42 mph. The dragster of Bolthoff & Hampshire with Bolthoff in the seat behind the blown Chevrolet advanced into the next round when the *NKG Special* of Dwayne Wilcox crossed over the centerline at mid-track, tried to correct the steering, and ended up rolling in the lights.

The final pair of the round was between Frank Cannon and Don Garlits. These two heavyweights alone were well worth the price of admission. The shining black *Swamp Rat V* of Garlits (a national champion) and Cannon (a fan favorite at Lions Drag Strip) had the spectators, drivers, and crews standing at attention. It was dead even at mid-track when Cannon's engine exploded while Garlits sailed through the traps and stopped the clocks with an 8.30 ET at 190.66 mph.

In round two, Garlits took care of McEwen in the *Broussard, Purcell, Davis, & McEwen* car when Garlits stepped it

Doug Rose began his racing career in 1959 by racing a 1951 Ford Victoria at Great Lakes Dragaway. He spent time behind the camera as the track's photographer and he introduced himself to Walt and Art Arfons, who were jet dragster pioneers. During conversations with the Arfons, Rose's Navy career came up, where he had served as a jet mechanic. His jet experiences launched his driving career in the seat of the Arfons's **Green Monster** *during late 1962. (Photo Courtesy Paul Johnson Collection)*

up with an 8.21 ET at 189.46 mph to McEwen's 8.38 ET at 187.88 mph.

Gabelich was next up to the line with Dick Stewart in the other lane. Both took off for the finish line, and Gabelich won with an 8.42 ET at 180.72 mph to the Adams Brothers & Stewart's 8.57 ET at 181.44 mph. George Bolthoff and George Van's *OCMP* entry were the next pair up to the line, and Bolthoff's Chevy once again took care of business with an 8.42 ET at 177.51 mph to Van's losing 8.69 ET at 187.18 mph. Warren, Coburn, & Warren and Stellings & Hampshire closed out round two with James Warren heading to the semifinal round when he put Hampshire on the trailer with an 8.25 ET at 185.56 mph to the Jeep's 8.47 ET at 180.36 mph.

Ronnie Sox made a trip from Greensboro, North Carolina, to enjoy the warm California sun and seize the win in A/FX class with his 427-ci side-oiler racing engine. The **Brinsfield Lincoln-Mercury** *car was one of the factory Comets that was modified with dual Holley 4-barrel carburetors and a hi-riser intake manifold. The engine was backed by a 4-speed transmission. (Photo Courtesy Paul Johnson Collection)*

The semifinal round in Fuel Eliminator pitted George Bolthoff against James Warren. Bolthoff continued his winning streak when he beat Warren with a close 8.38 ET at 177.51 mph to Warren's 8.40 ET at 183.66 mph.

In an instant, the anticipation reached its peak for the evening when the Chrysler of Don Garlits and the Chevrolet of Gary Gabelich rolled up to the line for the run of the night. Garlits, the 31-year-old dragster champion who already took top speed and top ET of the event, was ready to add the 22-year-old Gabelich to his list of victims. In 8 seconds, the news hit the drag scene like a meteor hitting the ground. Gabelich's reaction from off the line was the difference in the race. Gabelich won with an 8.32 ET at 181.44 mph to Garlits's 8.28 ET at 186.44 mph.

Suicide Split

With all of the big names in Top Fuel and Top Gas up the freeway in Pomona for the NHRA Winternationals, C. J. Hart reached into his bag of tricks and pulled out a one-of-one show that was only fitting for Lions Drag Strip—the Ace of Clubs motorcycle club. The precision drill motorcycle team consisted of 12 riders led by Gerald Pecor, the Ace of Clubs drill captain who guided the precision motorcycle riding group through its paces during the dinner break. Most of the spectators stayed glued to their seats and forgot to eat till later due to the show that was performed by these uniformed guys and gals.

Crossover maneuvers, such as the cartwheel, double eight, and single eight, were followed by "thread the needle." The group stole the show with "the swan" and "the single roman," where one girl rode between two cycles. They closed their set with the ever-dangerous suicide split, where the cyclists ride into columns 6 inches apart while a single rider hurtles toward them at speed. The columns part at the last possible second to avoid mayhem and open up an escape path.

Second-Annual UDRA Draws 200 Fuel Dragsters

By 8 a.m. on Saturday, February 21, 1964, there was a legion of Top Fuel dragsters waiting in line, (double file) for the second-annual Lions UDRA Grandnationals.

More than 100 single runs began at 8 a.m. and concluded at 5:15 p.m. This extended past the stated time due to clearing debris from the track after the *U.S. Speed Sport* roadster's tragic accident.

Many had a sinking feeling upon witnessing this, where parts from a once-proud race machine were strewn across the track during a turmoil of somersaults. The roadster was barely visible through the dust and shower of metal pieces. Two ambulances were there within seconds.

Driver Jerry "Gory" Goure of South Whittier, California, came out of it with a possible broken shoulder and arm. A 20-foot-long crease down the Lions Drag Strip safety board fence broke off where Goure lost it past the

Don Prudhomme beats Kenny Safford in the Safford, Gaide, & Ratican **Sour Sisters** *rail with a 7.76 ET at 191.88 mph during the United Drag Racers Association's two-day extravaganza, which attracted more than 200 big-name cars to Lions Drag Strip. Safford ran a 7.83 ET at 187.10 mph. The only name missing was Don "Big Daddy" Garlits, who had another commitment at Amarillo, Texas. (Photo Courtesy Lions Automobilia Foundation Museum)*

The A/FX class was in full swing Saturday at the UDRA meet, as the two Yeakel Plymouths of Hayden Proffitt (right) and Roger Caster (left) were the last ones to fight it out for the win. Caster's 1964 Plymouth ran an 11.79 ET at 120.88 mph to Proffitt's 11.92 ET at 120.48 mph. (Photo Courtesy Lions Automobilia Foundation Museum)

lights. The roadster was so broken up on the spot examination that it was difficult to determine whether a possible structure failure caused the accident.

Saturday night's final was between Logghe-Steffey and the *Frantic Four* Plymouth Hemi-powered dragster. It was 10:30 p.m., and the halfway point on the strip was covered with dew and fog. Both machines were readied. In a scene that was unprecedented in Lions Drag Strip history, after conferences between the two racing teams, they elected to split the top prize of $1,750 and the runner-up prize of $500 instead of running the next morning.

"That was the first time I'd ever been fogged out," Maynard Rupp said. "This machine is a fog cutter from way back. We have the same conditions at Detroit Dragway."

On Sunday morning, 92 more fuelers gave spectators high hopes of something to write home about. The Grand Nationals featured 24 cars running for Top Fuel, including a match race between Stone, Woods, & Cook versus K. S. Pittman as well as exhibition runs by Tom McCourry in the *Bismarck of all Dragsterdom*, which was Tommy Ivo's four-engine, four-wheel-drive, Buick-powered creation. With the smoke from McCourry breaking in the four new Goodyear slicks, it was difficult to determine whether the fog had lifted from the previous night. The quad-Buick-powered dragster turned an 8.54 ET at 166.97 mph.

Final Round of Two Winners

In the semifinal round, Tom McEwen (in the *Yeakel Plymouth*) faced Red Lang, Spider Razon, and Joe Anahory, who were known as the "Dead End Kids" from Brooklyn, New York. With McEwen carefully manipulating the big Chrysler, the Dead End Kids (and driver David Jeffers) were running on only seven cylinders to keep the lead against McEwen. Before the traps, it looked as if an atom had split and a halo of orange briefly engulfed the motor, as both the supercharger and injectors were blown clear over Jeffers's head.

When the smoke cleared, the Dead End Kids had won the race, but their return to the starting line for the final against Wayne "Peregrine" King and the *Donovan Engineering* car seemed improbable due to engine damage.

Razon, Anahory, and a team of eager helpers got to work in a blur of flying tools. In a matter of seconds, Sid Waterman offered to loan them the top end of his engine. They installed it with 4½ minutes to spare. Cooling water soothed the 392 Herbert-cammed Chrysler, and after the fastest checklist in history, Jeffers buckled into the untested machine, which fired up easily.

However, it was to no avail, as fire fanned alongside the right bank of the wounded mill. As Jeffers popped the clutch, the motor had finally consumed itself. Fire extinguishers doused the flames, and Jeffers exited the cockpit as a loser—yet a winner.

In the final, King raced down the strip with an engine note of crisp, clear authority.

In the closing moments of the 1965 UDRA Grand Nationals, a great bond existed between the drag racers that showed their power to beat the odds.

A/FXer Rules the Day

Each week, local publications took turns jabbing at all of the fun and excitement that the spectators and racers experienced at certain West Coast drag strips. Lions Drag Strip extended its gratitude to various Hollywood reporters for their beneficial but biased editorials that

Don't underestimate the fury of a stock car versus a Top Fuel dragster. Don Prudhomme got off the shoulder and into the grass and had to lift, which gave the win to Jim Barnes's* Snorkasaurus *with a 9.24 ET at 129.46 mph.

were entertaining and helped the attendance increase to new levels.

One Top Fuel meet at Lions Drag Strip that raised eyebrows was the match race between the *Greer-Black-Prudhomme* Fueler and Bill Hanyon's A/FX Plymouth.

The *Greer-Black-Prudhomme* entry returned to Lions Drag Strip with authority by posting an off-the-trailer 7.99 ET at 195.64 mph to let everyone know they were serious in taking down the Hemi-powered Plymouth.

As the 7,000 fans scurried to their seats, the announcer blared, "Here it comes! The first stock car versus the G-B-P challenge."

"I feel I have a pretty good chance," Hanyon said sarcastically during a pre-race starting line interview. "He's *only* going 65 mph faster and a whole second quicker. It's going to be a wild ride to the other end."

The crowd watched Prudhomme as he returned to the starting line, fired up, and prepared to run. Hanyon was at the pit gate warming up the Bourgeois & Wade–prepped white 1964 Mopar. Hanyon put the pedal to the wood, and a blur of white passed the line and tower before Prudhomme hammered down in a cloud of smoke and headed toward the finish line. As Prudhomme pulled even with the stocker, Prudhomme shut off and ran a 10.07 ET. Hanyon won with an 8.90 ET at 125.87 mph, but it was costly, as the engine suffered cylinder damage that put the Plymouth on the trailer.

To keep the show going, the call rang out to Bakersfield's Jim Barnes, who was the driver and owner of the Barnes Core Drilling *Snorkasaurus III* (a Hemi-stocker Dodge), to race Prudhomme for A/FX supremacy. As the *Snorkasaurus III* screamed from the pit gate and past the tower, Prudhomme stood on the gas pedal and freewheeled into an eruption of white tire smoke and nitro. He was nearly invisible, but two dark tire marks that veered to the right of the strip into the grass shoulder were visible. Prudhomme regained control but lifted to give the long-shot *Snorkasaurus III* the round win with a 9.24 ET at 129.46 mph.

In the last chance for redemption for Greer-Black-Prudhomme, Prudhomme earned a win and passed the *Snorkasaurus III* at the lights to take the third round with an 8.54 ET at 189.06 mph to the Dodge's 9.34 ET at 129.68 mph.

Memories

Don "The Snake" Prudhomme

Hall of Fame Drag Racer:
International Motorsports Hall of Fame
and Motorsports Hall of Fame of America Member

"When you went to Lions [Drag Strip], you went to race the best that drag racing had to offer. It was all the Chrisman-Cannons put together. All the fast guys were there, you know. That was the place to go.

"Once I started to drive the Greer-Black[-Prudhomme] car, that was our home racetrack because Keith [Black] was right there in Downey, California. It was a stone's throw from the racetrack. It was the premiere drag strip. We'd run the Greer-Black[-Prudhomme] car there at pretty much every meet they had for a long time. It was the racetrack that Roland [Leong] crashed and where I started driving his Hawaiian car.

"If you won at Lions, that was the news of the weekend, according to *Drag News*. You'd wind up being on the cover of *Drag News*. It was just a great racetrack."

10th-Anniversary Race Jamboree

On September 26, 1964, Lions Drag Strip hosted its 10th-Anniversary Jamboree, which was an enormous success. Qualifying bursts down the quarter mile began at 10:30 a.m. and concluded at 5:45 p.m. Right out of the gate, Northern California's Bay Area Muffler's *Pegasus* entry grabbed the number-one spot with an unreal 8.10 ET at 197.80 mph, but the flying red horse couldn't stick around due to another track commitment.

Moving up the ladder into the number-one slot was Donovan Engineering's Tom McEwen with a near-perfect 8.11 ET at 191.48 mph. Behind McEwen was his archrival, Don Prudhomme, who made a spectacular run with an 8.14 ET at 191.88 mph in the *Greer-Black-Prudhomme* rail.

Dode Martin and Jim Nelson of Dragmaster built a trio of steel-bodied promotional Polara 330 exhibition cars using Dodge Chargers with supercharged 426 Wedge engines that ran on pump gasoline. The cross-country tour of the factory-backed match racers began in California and went to Lions Drag Strip in March. The S/FX Dodges averaged ETs of 11.40 at 140 mph.

A monumental pairing in the first round of eliminations was the big blue *#44* dragster of Mooneyham-Ferguson-Jackson and driver Larry Faust against the famous *#33* entry of Greer-Black-Prudhomme. As always, Don Prudhomme, Keith Black, Don Culp, and the crew received a deafening ovation on the push down.

With the crowd anticipating the race of the year, Faust left too early, tripped the light, and blasted through the lights with an 8.03 ET at 193.12 mph. For Prudhomme, the Hemi exploded near the lights and knocked the team out of contention. Unknown to the drag racing community, including partner Tom Greer and driver Don Prudhomme, this was the moment when Keith Black decided to concentrate more on his engine and parts business and park his record-setting dragster.

The anniversary celebration included $3,000 in spectacular prizes for the spectators who had supported the drag strip during the past decade. Prizes included two color television sets, two portable television sets, six transistor radios, toasters, griddles, broilers, vacuum cleaners, one 6-hp Mercury outboard motor, a surfboard, and many other outstanding prizes.

Opportunity Knocks in a Most Unusual Way

On Saturday, October 3, 1964, the long-awaited debut of the *Hawaiian* Top Fuel dragster of Roland Leong made its debut a memorable one at Lions Drag Strip. Accompanying

*The **Jungle 4** Top Fueler of Gene Mooneyham, Wayne Ferguson, and Jerry Jackson had driver Larry Faust crack the pedal at Lions Drag Strip's 10th-anniversary race. For the **Jungle 4**, Faust's encounter with Don Prudhomme signaled the end for one of the most dominating fuelers in the history of drag racing. Faust tripped the red light against Prudhomme, who destroyed the Keith Black mill in the lights, which eliminated the **Greer-Black-Prudhomme** rail from advancing further. This was the moment when Keith Black decided to devote his time to manufacturing racing parts and building engines. (Photo Courtesy Paul Johnson Collection)*

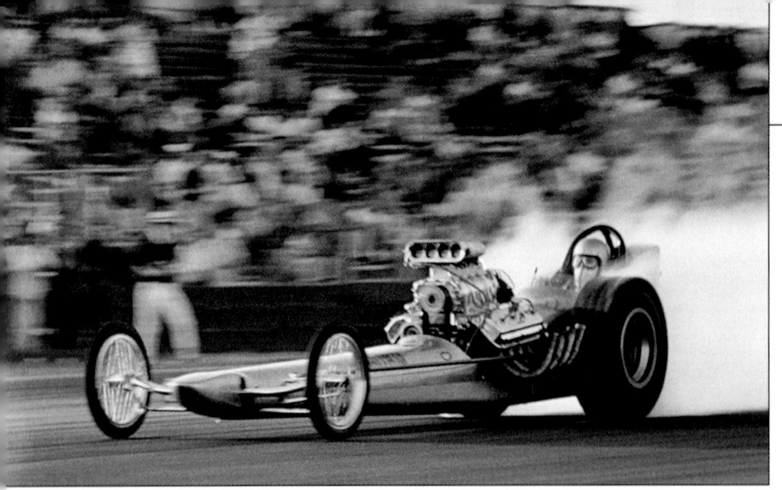

Roland Leong was one of the most respected owners and tuners in drag racing history. His driving career in Top Fuel fell short of his expectations, as he crashed his new **Hawaiian** *AA/FD on its maiden voyage. His accident rewrote drag racing history, as Leong and Keith Black put Don Prudhomme (shown) into the seat of the* **Hawaiian** *and won both the 1965 NHRA Winternationals and the prestigious U.S. Nationals in the same year. (Photo Courtesy Don Ewald Collection)*

Leong were Keith Black, Don Prudhomme, and crewman Wes Hanson. They were there to get Leong accustomed to his new car.

Leong thought the transition from driving his gas-powered dragsters over to nitro would be a cinch. As the team was busy preparing the car for Leong's Top Fuel licensing run, Black thought it would be conservative to run straight alcohol in the tank for Roland and the fueler's first run.

Leong thought, "What a waste."

Knowing the power provided by nitromethane, Black and Prudhomme decided to be cautious. They set a limit of a 40-percent nitro load to use on the run. Using a hydrometer, Leong came up with three different percentages, and they finally settled on a 47-percent mixture that Black agreed to put into the fuel tank.

While Black performed the final adjustments, Prudhomme buckled Leong securely into the seat of the car. Leong was instructed by Black, Prudhomme, and starter Larry Sutton to get familiarized with the new car and instructed Leong to make a half-pass run and shut off. Leong nodded and agreed.

The car was pushed down toward the end of the strip and made the turn back up the push-off road, and the Keith Black Hemi came to life. The idle was set too low and the engine stumbled and died.

Hanson added more fuel into the tank, and Black made adjustments. Sutton went over to Leong and instructed him once again to make only a half-pass and shut off.

The car was pushed back down the strip for the repeat trip and turned back around and headed back toward the starting line. The car came to life before Leong made the sweeping turn toward the starting line. He rolled the car into the staging beams and increased the revs. At the green, he launched off the starting line like a missile with his foot buried to the floor.

As instructed, he let off the throttle at the 300-foot mark. In Leong's mind, he was on a decent run, so he decided to replant his foot back into it and headed toward the finish line under full power. Leong entered the traps at over 190 mph, and he started to drift to the left. He drifted farther left, and then it appeared that Leong jerked the steering wheel in search of the chute release.

In what seemed like slow motion, Leong drove off the end of the track, turned around, and became airborne. As the dirt, gravel, and debris filled the air, Leong landed right side up when he finally came to rest on a set of railroad tracks.

Rushing their way toward the wreck, both Prudhomme and Black were visibly shaken and thought the absolute worst had happened. When they got to Leong, he was conscious, dazed, and smiled through the heavy bath of sand and dirt.

For Leong, this was the first and only attempt at driving a Top Fuel dragster. The NHRA banned him for life from obtaining a Competition Fuel driver's license. Leong vowed to repair his $10,000 rail and promised that the *Hawaiian* would return in weeks—this time with his new driver, Don Prudhomme!

Greatest Promotion of Lions Drag Strip

C. J. Hart booked Jack Chrisman's astounding Sachs & Sons *Super Cyclone* Mercury Comet to run at Lions Drag Strip on Saturday, October 24. It would be Chrisman's first Southern California appearance. His Comet was advertised over the radio airwaves as going 0 to 160 in 10 seconds, having 1,200 hp (advertised), guzzling nitromethane for fuel, and being "fun to drive while making men quake and women faint."

Chrisman's Comet made every eastern exhibition stop a sellout, so when Hart booked the advertised 160-mph Stock car, he knew that he had something special. He also brought in the fuelers to come out to witness

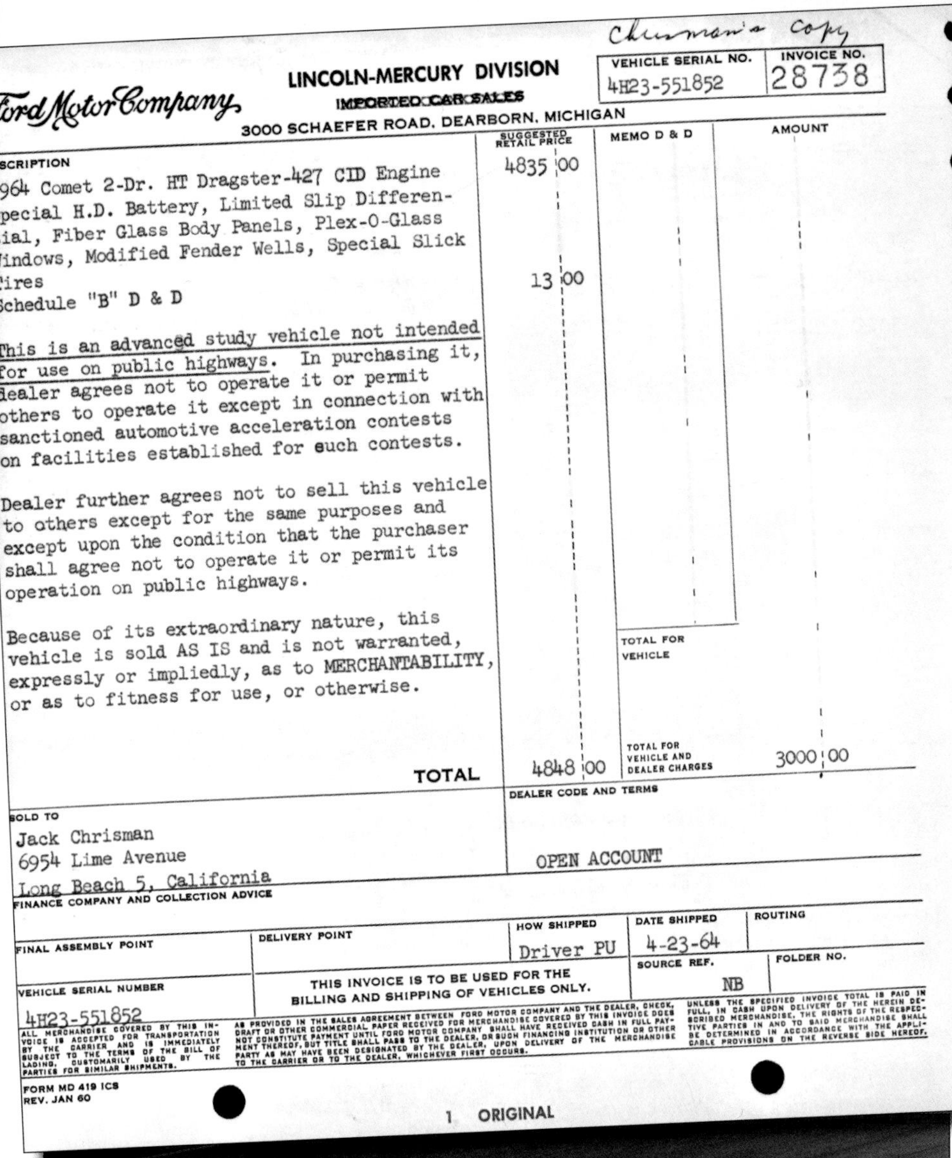

Chrisman's Copy

Ford Motor Company
LINCOLN-MERCURY DIVISION
~~IMPORTED CAR SALES~~
3000 SCHAEFER ROAD, DEARBORN, MICHIGAN

VEHICLE SERIAL NO.	INVOICE NO.
4H23-551852	28738

DESCRIPTION	SUGGESTED RETAIL PRICE	MEMO D & D	AMOUNT
.964 Comet 2-Dr. HT Dragster-427 CID Engine Special H.D. Battery, Limited Slip Differen-tial, Fiber Glass Body Panels, Plex-O-Glass Windows, Modified Fender Wells, Special Slick Tires	4835 00		
Schedule "B" D & D	13 00		
		TOTAL FOR VEHICLE	
TOTAL	4848 00	TOTAL FOR VEHICLE AND DEALER CHARGES	3000 00

This is an advanced study vehicle not intended for use on public highways. In purchasing it, dealer agrees not to operate it or permit others to operate it except in connection with sanctioned automotive acceleration contests on facilities established for such contests.

Dealer further agrees not to sell this vehicle to others except for the same purposes and except upon the condition that the purchaser shall agree not to operate it or permit its operation on public highways.

Because of its extraordinary nature, this vehicle is sold AS IS and is not warranted, expressly or impliedly, as to MERCHANTABILITY, or as to fitness for use, or otherwise.

SOLD TO
Jack Chrisman
6954 Lime Avenue
Long Beach 5, California

DEALER CODE AND TERMS
OPEN ACCOUNT

FINANCE COMPANY AND COLLECTION ADVICE

FINAL ASSEMBLY POINT	DELIVERY POINT	HOW SHIPPED	DATE SHIPPED	ROUTING
		Driver PU	4-23-64	

VEHICLE SERIAL NUMBER		SOURCE REF.	FOLDER NO.
4H23-551852	THIS INVOICE IS TO BE USED FOR THE BILLING AND SHIPPING OF VEHICLES ONLY.	NB	

ALL MERCHANDISE COVERED BY THIS INVOICE IS ACCEPTED FOR TRANSPORTATION BY THE CARRIER AND IS IMMEDIATELY SUBJECT TO THE TERMS OF THE BILL OF LADING, CUSTOMARILY USED BY THE PARTIES FOR SIMILAR SHIPMENTS.

AS PROVIDED IN THE SALES AGREEMENT BETWEEN FORD MOTOR COMPANY AND THE DEALER, CHECK, DRAFT OR OTHER COMMERCIAL PAPER RECEIVED FOR MERCHANDISE COVERED BY THIS INVOICE DOES NOT CONSTITUTE PAYMENT UNTIL FORD MOTOR COMPANY SHALL HAVE RECEIVED CASH IN FULL PAYMENT THEREOF, BUT TITLE SHALL PASS TO THE DEALER, OR SUCH FINANCING INSTITUTION OR OTHER PARTY AS MAY HAVE BEEN DESIGNATED BY THE DEALER, UPON DELIVERY OF THE MERCHANDISE TO THE CARRIER OR TO THE DEALER, WHICHEVER FIRST OCCURS.

UNLESS THE SPECIFIED INVOICE TOTAL IS PAID IN FULL, IN CASH UPON DELIVERY OF THE HEREIN DESCRIBED MERCHANDISE, THE RIGHTS OF THE RESPECTIVE PARTIES IN AND TO SAID MERCHANDISE SHALL BE DETERMINED IN ACCORDANCE WITH THE APPLICABLE PROVISIONS ON THE REVERSE SIDE HEREOF.

FORM MD 419 ICS
REV. JAN 60

1 ORIGINAL

This is the window sticker from when Jack Chrisman picked up the full-race 1964 Mercury two-door hardtop Comet **Super Cyclone** *from Lincoln-Mercury. The Comet was equipped with a dragster 427 Wedge V-8. The suggested retail price of $4,848.00 included a special heavy-duty battery, limited-slip differential, fiberglass body panels, Plexiglas windows, modified fender wells, and special slick tires. Because of its nature, the vehicle was sold "as is" and not warrantied with the order. The vehicle was not intended for use on public highways. (Image Courtesy Chrisman Family)*

the *Super Cyclone* and to race in a special eight-car Top Eliminator show for their choice of $500 cash or a brand-new RCA color television.

From all appearances, it was the day of the Mercury Comets, as three white machines arrived behind Bill Stroppe's racing van. The avid crowd of spectators gathered around to catch glimpses of the phenomena. The main attraction of the day was the A/FX *Super Cyclone*, but you couldn't ignore the mystery unlettered Comet that seemed out of place and looked like it had an undersized 289-ci, 271-hp motor.

Fran Hernandez, the director of Mercury Racing, worked out a one-of-a-kind arrangement for Jack Chrisman to take possession of a 1964 Mercury two-door hardtop Comet equipped with 427 Wedge V-8 that Chrisman could compete with in the NHRA's B/Dragster and Exhibition classes. Chrisman's Dragster was deemed by many as being the first true nitromethane Funny Car. (Photo Courtesy Tony Thacker)

The Super Cyclone *Takes Center Stage*

As the final notes of the national anthem faded out, all eyes were fixed on the white 1964 Comet, which appeared under the bank of floodlights that surrounded the starting line. Lying in wait was the blown, Hilborn-injected, 427 ci of Ford power that was ready to wreak havoc on the strip.

Before Jack Chrisman gave the crowd the thumbs-up signal to fire, 10,000 eager fans went to a dead silence as the 427 roared to life with the crackling sounds of a fuel car. The Comet shot off the starting line with sound wailing from the quad exhaust that built up to unheard-of levels—especially when compared to the *Mooneyham & Sharp* 1934 coupe and Lyle Fisher's *Speed Sport* roadster.

As the Comet crossed half-track, the decibel levels and power dropped off to a dead silence. Groans of disappointment greeted the Comet's subpar performance—an 11.20 ET at 137.19 mph. The *Super Cyclone* dropped a valve on the right-hand bank that forced the Sachs & Sons crew into a race against time to install a new reverse head.

Round Two Repeat

When the famous Lions Drag Strip fog began to roll in, the crowd chanted, "Down in front—sit down." It wasn't difficult to determine that it was time for the *Super Cyclone*'s second round. With another storming exhibition off the line, the promising run quickly turned to disappointment when another valve dropped, this time on the left-side engine bank. The Comet ran an 11.27 ET at 131.77 mph, but the dejected Chrisman vowed to return for round three.

Late into the show, Chrisman made a valiant attempt to make a run to the traps on seven cylinders, but he shut down the big Mercury at the 1/8-mile mark. Most of the faithful stayed around to the finish to see the mighty *Super Cyclone*'s fury, but Chrisman wasn't satisfied. He returned to the pits for answers. A crew member noted that it was another valve.

"The engine we ran here tonight is the same one we've run on tour but all fresh," Chrisman said. "I know one thing—I'm gonna keep running it here if it takes all year."

True to his word, Chrisman returned in a few weeks for the highly touted match race against Stone, Woods, & Cook.

Jack Chrisman brought the curious crowd to its feet for its first glance of the famed **Sachs & Sons** *supercharged Mercury Comet. Chrisman was drag racing's equivalent to a rock star. He sold out drag strips across the nation and captivated the mass crowds with loud noises, bellowing clouds of smoke, and excitement. (Photo Courtesy Paul Johnson Collection)*

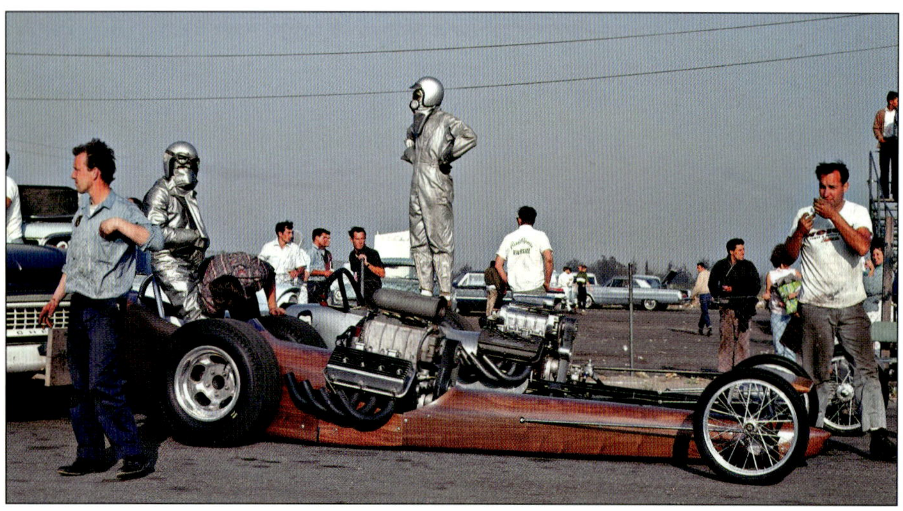

Dragster pilots Dave Babler (wearing a silver helmet near the driver's seat) of the California Woody, Wayne King (wearing a silver helmet in the middle of the photo), and Jack Chrisman (in the foreground near the front wheels of the dragster) attempt to catch a glimpse of Jack Chrisman on his first visit with the blown Mercury Comet to Lions Drag Strip. The dragster guys were not impressed with the Comet, which blistered the slicks down the entire quarter mile on the shakedown pass, but the fans went crazy! (Photo Courtesy Don Prieto)

Four-Day Wonder

With the majority of the regular Top Fuelers away at a UDRA meet, a few brand-new fuelers took to the strip to test out the famed asphalt of Lions Drag Strip. The AA/FD entry of Bateman-Shingleton-Slusser made its return to the dragster wars with driver Don Rackemann, who made easy runs.

The Dead End Kids from Brooklyn tuned their new Race Car Specialties factory car (running a blown 480-ci Chrysler), but the story around the pits was the Jim Dugan Enterprises *Four-Day Wonder Special*. Dugan and his crew began construction on the fueler on Tuesday morning and completed it in time for Saturday's race.

Dugan's chassis and body made a perfect fit for the Frank Pedregon–prepped Chrysler that completed the car.

"We wanted to see how fast it could get done," said Dugan. "It's just like the thing of how many guys you can put into a phone booth. We now hold the A/Fuel Dragster construction record."

Top Fuel qualifying got off with a bang, as the Babler & Harbert's *Bay Area Muffler* entry secured the number-1 spot and set the low ET of the meet with an 8.17 at 191.87 mph. Lions Drag Strip starter Larry Sutton buckled into the *Butters & Girard's* Chrysler-powered entry and took hold of the number-2 position with an 8.25 ET at 189.84 mph.

The list continued with Schubert & Herbert's 8.29 ET at 189.36 mph, the *Mangler* of Broussard-Davis-Garrison driven by Danny Ongais with an 8.37 ET at 197.37 mph that set the top speed of the meet. Next were the Beaver Brothers and Clark with an 8.43 ET at 177.11 mph, Phaff & Sowins's 8.54 ET at 187.50 mph, and Leroy Goldstein driving the Abbott & Lee's *Lenco Engineering Special* rail with an 8.55 ET at 191.48 mph. Occupying the last slot in the field went to Steve Sturgeon, who ran an 8.60 ET at 181.08 mph.

Top Fuel eliminations got underway as fog and dew moved over the strip. Larry Sutton motored past the Beaver Brothers and Clark's Chevy engine that went silent 200 feet out. Zane Schubert faced newcomer Goldstein in the *Lenco Engineering Special*, but Goldstein's car sprang forward and came to a mechanical halt.

Dave Babler's *Bay Area Muffler* cruised to a victory as the *Phaff & Sowins* rail experienced handling problems and, in good judgement, shut off. Danny Ongais demonstrated the prowess of the *Mangler* through the dampness with an 8.37 ET at 194.80 mph over Steve Sturgeon's 9.13 ET at 174.08 mph when the Chevrolet blew a spark plug.

Round two was led by Larry Sutton. As a starter himself, he was foiled by the foul and gave the automatic win to Zane Schubert. Dave Babler punched his ticket to the final round with a holeshot on Ongais as the *Mangler* was late off the line. Babler-Harbert had an ET of 8.58 at 191.08 mph to Ongais's quicker ET of 8.43 at 185.94 mph. For many racers, the motto of "red lights are for stop signs" rang true, as Dave Babler lit the lazy light and gave the automatic win to Schubert & Herbert.

It's a Gas

"Big" John Mazmanian campaigned one of the most legendary 1941 Willys in drag racing. Not only were Mazmanian's candy apple red cars his trademark but his Willys was also one of the toughest cars to beat in the gasser wars. The Willys wars with Mazmanian against Fred Stone, Leonard Woods, and Doug "Cookie" Cook and their rivalries and cam feuds between camshaft manufacturers Ed Iskenderian and Jack Engle brought a whole new meaning to drag racing.

With all the attention focused on the Comet of Jack Chrisman on Saturday, October 24, at Lions Drag Strip, Hart put together a surprise match race with the Willys Gassers of K. S. Pittman and "Big" John Mazmanian. Drivers "Bones" Balogh and Pittman put on a highly competitive show as Balogh took the win and defeated Pittman in the best-of-three encounter.

Match Race of the Year: The *Super Cyclone* Returns to Lions Drag Strip

November usually indicates that the racing season is gradually grinding to a halt and the holiday season is around the corner, but at Lions Drag Strip, the headliners continued with the most anticipated match race of the year. This race featured the supercharged AA/GS Willys of Stone, Woods, & Cook and the blown Sachs & Sons nitro-fueled 1964 Mercury *Super Cyclone* driven by Jack Chrisman.

Extreme interest brought the onlookers to the strip for the year's most requested match race at Lions Drag Strip.

Billed as the world's loudest match race, both Jack Chrisman and Doug Cook took to the microphone before the first race, as Chrisman explained that the 427 blown

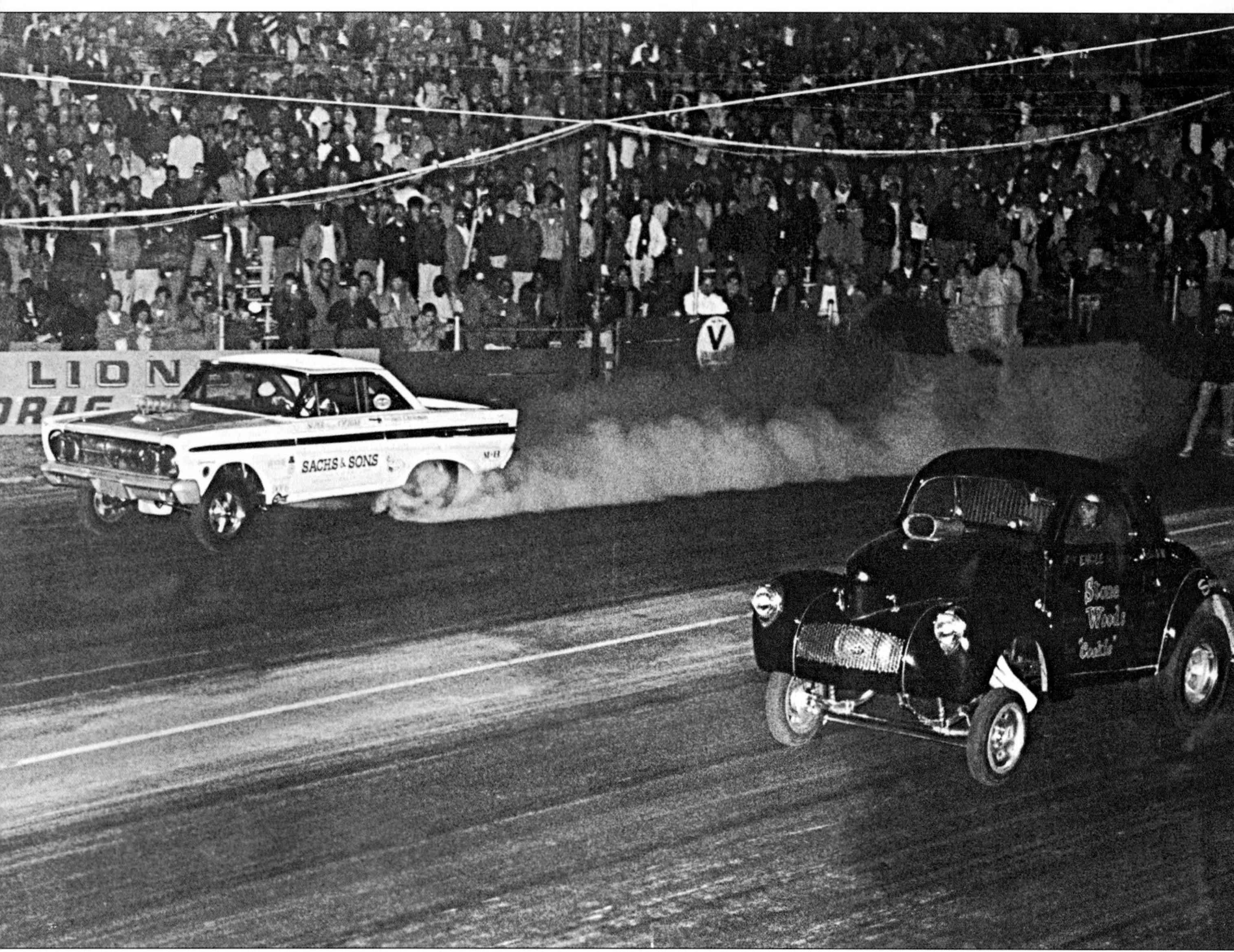

The match race of the year at Lions Drag Strip was between Jack Chrisman in the* Sachs & Sons *blown Mercury Comet and the Willys of Fred Stone, Leonard Woods, and Doug "Cookie" Cook. The match race set a new all-time attendance record for a one-day event. (Photo Courtesy Lions Automobilia Foundation Museum)

Mercury engine woes were resolved after the embarrassing valve issues that took place weeks before. He also explained that the race was to give the fans an unforgettable drag spectacular rather than a wheel-to-wheel grudge race.

Chrisman also noted that the Comet never ran alongside side anything but a dragster and pointed out that Cook often ran under 10 seconds on numerous occasions, whereas the Comet's ET of 10.15 was Chrisman's best to date.

Cook spoke to the crowd that the 440-ci Willys had a career run (a 9.57 ET) the week before at Carlsbad, so "we know the track's pretty slippery tonight and we're going to play it cool—looking to take two straight tonight."

Advantage Cook

With the matter of having a fair race, Cook was given a running handicap start that began at the staging-lane gates. As soon as Cook crossed over the starting line, the Comet catapulted off the line in the attempt to run down the Willys. The *Super Cyclone* made the strong charge, but Cook was declared to be the winner in the lights with a 10.14 ET as the Comet slowed down when the 427 Wedge cracked the front blower plate.

Memories

Robert "Bones" Balogh

Drag Racer and Lions Automobilia Foundation Hall of Fame Member

"One of the last times I was on tour with my Corvette in the summer of 1963 was at Aquasco Speedway, which was the first quarter-mile drag strip on the East Coast. It was built in the mid-1950s and was home to the East's largest meet: the President's Cup Nationals. I didn't know it at the time, but I singed a piston when the engine leaned out, so I packed up and left for home.

"I came back home and got everything cleaned out. I went to Lions [Drag Strip] and saw "Big" John [Mazmanian]. He was out there racing, doing well again. I told myself, 'I've gotta go knock him down.' Well, he beat me. Oh my God, I was stunned. I was looking at my spark plugs down in the pits, and here came John.

"'What happened?' he asked.

"I said, 'You wouldn't have beat me John, but I burned a piston.'

"Anyhow, he said, 'Uh, Bonesy, don't worry about it. Look at this car you got. You have duct tape on the front fender. Look at mine over there. It's brand new.'

"Then, he asked, 'How would you like to drive that car?'

"'Nope! That's got a 4-speed in it,' I said.

"'No, no—I got a proposition for you,' he replied. 'I'll buy your motor and transmission, and we'll put it in my car. We'll go racing.'

"'Sounds good, John,' I said.

"That's the start. That's how I teamed up with 'Big' John. We went out and raced it a bunch of times, and of course, he wanted to go into the gas classes. That's how one thing led to another, and we built the Willys, and that's the history on that stuff.

"At Lions Drag Strip, we raced there many times. We had many races with Stone, Woods, & Cook at Lions. That's one place Doug didn't beat me. We always seem to come out ahead over there. He beat me at the Winternationals the first time he ran it with a Chrysler motor in it.

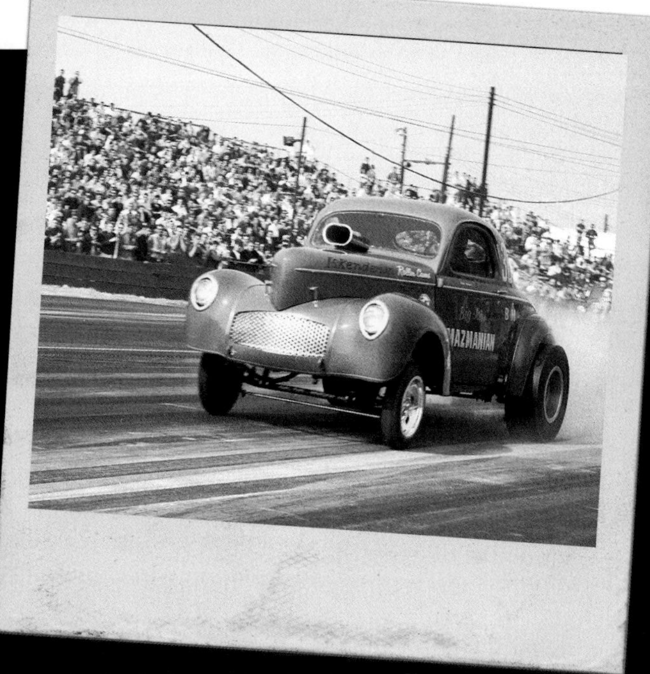

Bones Balogh drove "Big" John Mazmanian's blown 1941 Willys to many wins at Lions Drag Strip in the AA/Gas Supercharged class. The Willys Gassers of Mazmanian and the team of Stone, Woods, & Cook were the top rivals on the strip and in print with the fierce cam wars of Iskenderian and Engle Cams in* Drag News. *(Photo Courtesy Paul Johnson Collection)

"So, that's the story. We put my motor in his Corvette, and then it went into his Willys. It was the same motor out of the '49 that was in all three cars. Then, John wanted to go big time. "'You know Doug Cook is out there with that big Oldsmobile," John said. "Why don't we drop in an Oldsmobile too?'

"'I don't know anything about Oldsmobiles,' I said. 'A Chrysler motor sounds good, but I don't know if we can fit it in there or not, but I know how to build them.'

"You know, I'm working at Iskenderian's and all that. We were going to put a Chrysler in there and go show them. That's it—that's what started it all. It had a lot of horsepower but was difficult to handle until we got some better tires and just started hooking up. And, that's how it was with 'Big' John."

Chrisman Evens the Score

With the crowd chanting "We want Cook," it was time to see if Cook's prediction of two straight wins would occur. With both gladiators assembled on the starting pad, the start was nearly identical to the previous round. Cook was off with a sizeable lead, when at mid-track, the Willys started to drift sideways. Cook corrected but came within 2 to 3 feet of contacting the guardrails at 131 mph and backed off the pedal. Chrisman shot past the Willys, won the race, and shut down before the lights as the Comet began to freewheel.

Ends With a Draw

The time was 10:30 p.m. with 20 minutes until curfew. Chrisman and Cook headed up to the line when Zane Shubert fired up his fueler to make a single run in hopes of taking home the money for the evening's low ET.

Instead of grabbing the cash, Shubert buried his foot to the pedal, drifted hard, and plowed his race car tail first into the fence 100 feet before the push-off road. The crash took out the lights on the starting line, and they could not be replaced before curfew. So, the match race between Chrisman and Cook was considered a draw. They shook hands, and the show was over.

Manager of the Year

In Lions Drag Strip's brief history, 1964 was the most successful. If drag racing handed out recognition awards, C. J. "Pappy" Hart would have hands-down been the Manager of the Year. He guided Lions Drag Strip away from the great NHRA and cut strings from the establishment. Hart refused to give in to the demands of the NHRA that resulted with the AHRA's "How the West was Won" movement and new methods of publicity.

Tinseltown at Lions Drag Strip

Lions was well-known for having some of the quickest (ET) and fastest (top speed) runs in all of drag racing, but it also held a chapter in the entertainment industry. Hollywood took a huge liking to Lions Drag Strip for its close proximity. It was common for production companies to rent the strip from Wednesdays to Fridays to shoot commercials, documentaries, and television series, including *The Tycoon*, *Adam-12*, and the show about everyone's favorite iconic monster family, *The Munsters*.

In 1972, Lions Drag Strip featured actors Martin Milner, who played Officer Pete Malloy, and Kent McCord, who played Officer Jim Reed in the TV series *Adam-12*.

In a season 4 episode titled "Who Won," which premiered on March 1, 1972, and was written with the theme of the reason why Lions was built, Officers Malloy and Reed were summoned to remove illegal drag racing from the streets and onto a regulated drag strip. After working with various racing organizations, they finally met the requirements to build a drag strip. They also required the drivers to keep the noise down in the streets surrounding the strip. This goes back to the time when street racing dominated. Racers found themselves ridiculed for their passion for speed, and loud cars and were targets of local law enforcement.

In the television series *Mad Men*, Lions Drag Strip is mentioned in the episode "The Mountain King." The Lions-Hollywood pop culture continued long after the closure of Lions Drag Strip with the 2019 movie *Once Upon a Time in Hollywood*, which featured actor Brad Pitt, whose character, Cliff Booth, is seen wearing a Lions Drag Strip T-shirt.

That's a Wrap

Seven Second Love Affair was a 1965 documentary film directed by Bob Abel that covered the racing exploits of Rick "the Iceman" Stewart, who became NHRA's chief starter decades later. Filmed from a camera mounted to the top of the roll cage of Stewart's *Beacon Auto Special* Top Gas dragster, Stewart gave a view of the excitement and danger of driving a Top Fuel dragster.

The onboard camera caught Stewart during his qualifying record run—a 7.30 ET at 219.65 mph. However, at the finish line, the engine pushed out a gasket, which saturated him and his goggles with hot oil and obscured his vision. As he attempted to keep the race car straight, Steward veered hard to the right and ran off the track, crashed through the fencing, barrel-rolled several times, and broke up into several sections before coming to a stop. The accident sent him to Long Beach Memorial Center with considerable injuries.

Lions Drag Strip was also featured on the big screen back in 1971 with the film *Drag Racer* that highlighted the West Coast drag racing scene with the legendary racers "Lil' John" Lombardo, Norm Wilcox, Larry Dixon, and Bill Schultz. Orange County International Raceway and Irwindale Raceway were also shown in the film.

Lions Drag Strip Takes on a New Look

When Lions Drag Strip opened in October 1955, the property at 223rd and Alameda was a long, narrow strip of land with a few amenities that served the purpose of great side-by-side racing for racers and spectators. Ten years later, Lions Drag Strip somehow lacked depth and size. To fix this, Lions leased an adjacent parcel of property east of the original boundary lines that quickly received new direct-access roads into the facility that funneled in parking for 30,000 additional cars.

Other updates included a fully illuminated and fenced-in pit area, wider return and fire-up roads, and new ticket booths with turnstiles, providing spectators with convenience and speed of entry to the grandstands.

A new, elevated timing tower was constructed behind the starting line with an added pedestrian crossover bridge that gave spectators easy access to the grandstands on both sides of the strip. The bridge guaranteed spectators an open view of the whole quarter mile.

Brand-new Chrondek clocks and telewriters were installed in the new tower that simultaneously flashed results to the old tower, where timing slips were handed out. A new direct phone system provided instant communications from the new tower to the old tower, the starting and finish lines, and the pits to the entrance gates to replace the traditional walkie-talkie system.

Announcers Bernie Mather, Bob Lavelle, and Jerry Hart no longer performed dual roles in setting, reading, and resetting the clocks and calling the race. The estimated $60,000 spent on the renovations rivaled both Riverside's and Famoso's useful areas and was considered one of the largest facilities in the world that was dedicated to drag racing. The project took place over a three-month period that began in May and concluded in early August. It didn't interrupt weekly racing meets.

Jim Lytle created one of drag racing's most creative machines: the flip-top fiberglass-bodied Funny Car. Lytle invested $2,000 into his 1934 Ford Tudor* Big Al II *project, which was powered by a military surplus Allison V-12—a water-cooled aircraft engine. The engine produced varied power numbers, ranging from 2,300 to 3,200 hp. Lytle fabricated the chopped-top body entirely by hand. With no classes to compete in,* Big Al II *ran only a few times in 1964 at Lions Drag Strip before it was retired. (Photo Courtesy Lions Automobilia Foundation Museum)

C. J. Expedites Racing

One of the top stories in August 1965 for the surrounding area of Lions Drag Strip was the outbreak of the Watts Rebellion, which was a series of riots that broke out on August 11 that shut down the city of Los Angeles. With tensions high in Los Angeles and the surrounding areas, the there were concerns for the spectators, racers, and track personnel for the upcoming Saturday night meet on August 14. Hart hired 17 additional security guards and hastened the racing agenda with a shutdown curfew of 9 p.m.

The shortened eight-car Top Fuel show was won by Tom McEwen in the *Yeakel Motor Special*. The highly

Memories

Steve Chrisman

Son of Drag Racing Pioneer and Lions Drag Strip Legend Jack Chrisman

"Probably the biggest moment for me was in 1964 when I was just 10 years old. There was this big match race between the *Stone, Woods, & Cook* Willys and my dad driving the *Sachs & Sons* blown Mercury Comet.

"I remember the place was packed—completely sold out. The mood was like seeing the Beatles. There had to be 13,000 people there just to watch those two cars going down the racetrack. It was quite a memorable deal for me at least.

"I have thousands of memories of Lions Drag Strip. I grew up there as a little kid, and that was my playground, so I have a lot of good memories."

The Chrismans were racing's first family, and Lloyd, Art, Everett, and Jack were hot rodding icons from the early days. They raced on the dry lakes of El Mirage and sped down the quarter-mile asphalt in drag racing. Jack pioneered the first nitromethane-fed Funny Car coupe that started a drag racing revolution. Chrisman's first visit to Lions Drag Strip on October 24 with the* Super Cyclone *Comet was a monumental one, and the racing venue drew more than 10,000 fans to catch history in the making. (Photo Courtesy Chrisman Family)

touted grudge match race between the fuelers of Mooneyham-Ferguson-Jackson-Faust's *Jungle 4* and San Francisco's "Terrible" Ted Gotelli with driver Denny "the Wolverine" Milani's *Gotelli's Speed Shop Special*. Mooneyham advertised a revolutionary Beach Motor and other secret changes in the valvetrain. Both cars spilt rounds, and the third and final round was not without controversy. With one lane and ET lights taken out in the Top Fuel finale, a trio of judges were dispatched to the finish line to determine the outcome.

A coin flip determined the choice to race on the tower or spectator side. Both machines left evenly on the green, but it was determined that Faust crossed the line first, running 209 mph with no ET. The Frisco phenom, Milani, made a go of it and ran a 7.65 ET at 205 mph. Gotelli smiled and thought there would be another time and place where these two would meet again.

Altereds Times

Four Fuel Altereds running in Competition Eliminator, including the *Beaver Hunter* of Thomas & Pritchard, Harrell & Borsch, Jim Miles's *Magic Muffler* Fiat, and Hyder & Koulan, shared time with the Top Fuelers.

Kaboom!

At Lions Drag Strip, the Fuel Altereds were a major draw that Hart advertised heavily, due to their unpredictable runs. When Jim Miles brought his *Magic Muffler* AA/FA Fiat Topolino to Lions Drag Strip, crewman Gary Essman occupied the seat instead of Miles.

The Topolino fired up and rolled up into the staging beams. Essman staged, stabbed the pedal, and *kaboom*! The entire bottom end of the Chrysler Hemi unloaded its entire inner contents onto the strip. It was determined that Essman didn't properly torque the bottom end. Instead of "letting the genie out of the bottle," it was more like "the genie puked out of the block."

The* Beaver Hunter *AA/FA of Joe Thomas and Nolan Pritchard with driver Don Hicks (foreground) leads the* Wingless Express *of Harrell & Borsch (background) in a match race at Lions Drag Strip. Painter and pinstriper Ed "Big Daddy" Roth painted and lettered the* Beaver Hunter*, which ran a 392-ci blown Chrysler for power. The top run for the Altered was an 8.76 ET at 187 mph. (Jere Aldereff Photography/Courtesy Lions Automobilia Foundation Museum)

Hot Cars Set 20 New Records

The first day of the AHRA World Championships for the hot cars kicked off on Saturday, September 4. This was primarily set up for qualifying and record runs for Top Fuel and Gas Dragster contenders. By midday, Kerry Clark, who was the head of the Lions Drag Strip record certification crew, was busy trying to keep pace with the record runs and verify 20 new track records in 12 different classes.

Most notable was Mike Snively, driving the *Beacon Auto Parts* A/Gas dragster, who set an impressive 8.20 ET for the record and earned the coveted top spot in qualifying.

In the Top Fuel class, Tom McEwen, driving the *Yeakel Plymouth Center Special*, made his first appearance

The engine of Jim Miles's blown Hemi in his* Magic Muffler *AA/FA exploded at the starting line at Lions Drag Strip. Occupying the driver's seat that evening was crewman Gary Essman, who experienced the mishap when he didn't properly torque down the main caps to the proper specifications on the crankshaft. (Ron Lahr Photography/Jere Aldereff Collection/Courtesy Lions Automobilia Foundation Museum)

The Munsters Ascend to "Mockingbird Heights Drag Strip"

Lions Drag Strip was converted into the fictional "Mockingbird Heights Drag Strip" for *The Munsters* episode "Hot Rod Herman," where the loveable Herman Munster, who is played by Fred Gwynne, loses the family car (the *Munsters Coach*) on a dare made by his son Eddie, who is played by Butch Patrick.

Eddie told his friend that his dad could beat his friend's dad in a drag race—not knowing that Eddie's friend's dad is a professional drag racer named Leadfoot Baylor. Herman is duped and loses the race.

Not to be outdone, Herman, with aid from his father-in-law Grandpa Munster, played by Al Lewis, builds his own coffin rail, the *Drag-U-La*, to win back the family car and beat Baylor at his own game. The episode aired on May 27, 1965.

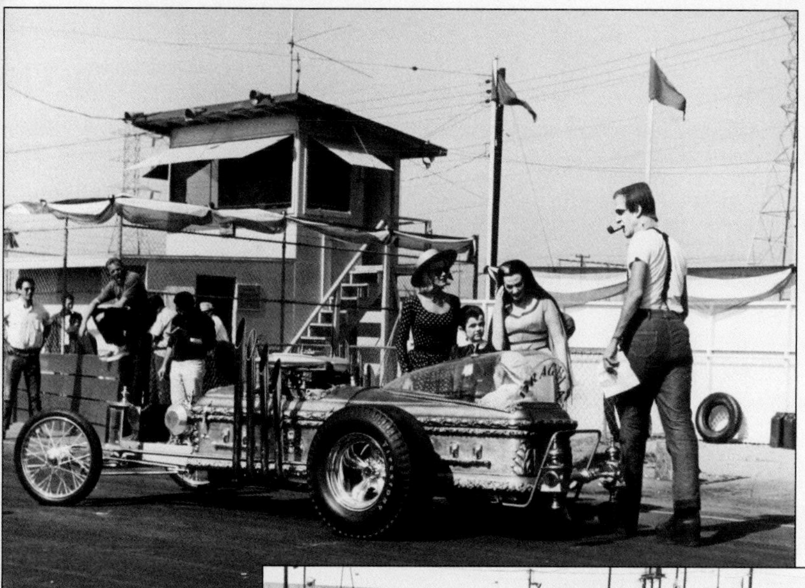

Actors Pat Priest (Marilyn), Yvonne De Carlo (Lily), Butch Patrick (Eddie), and Fred Gwynne (Herman) from the TV show **The Munsters** *inspect George Barris's* **Drag-U-La** *with driver Al Lewis (Grandpa) in the "coffin." (Photo Courtesy Don Gillespie)*

From left to right, Hal Minyard (the 1964 CRA Champion), Fred Gwynne (actor), and Louie Senter (president of Ansen Automotive) stand behind Bill Martin's **400 Jr.** *dragster. Martin was one of the members of the U.S. Drag Racing Team that competed at the 1965 British International Drag Racing Festival. Martin and his dragster were on location at Lions Drag Strip during the filming of an episode of* **The Munsters.** *(Photo Courtesy Don Gillespie)*

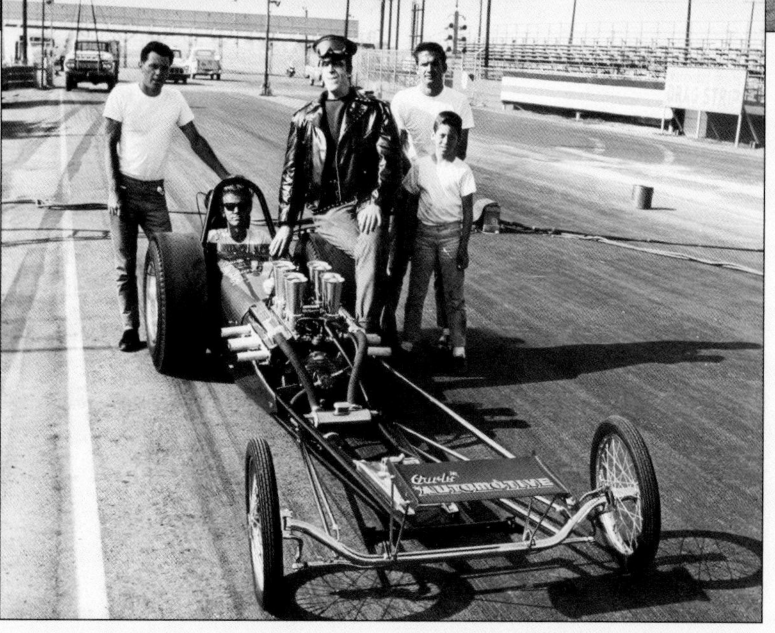

Actor Fred Gwynne takes the time to talk drag racing and pose for photos with the crew of this Junior Fuel dragster that played a part in the episode "Hot Rod Herman" of **The Munsters.** *(Photo Courtesy Don Gillespie)*

The Munsters Ascend to "Mockingbird Heights Drag Strip" *continued*

Fred Gwynne (Herman) and Butch Patrick (Eddie) play with a basketball during a break on the set of the television show, **The Munsters**, *which was shot on location at Lions Drag Strip. (Photo Courtesy Don Gillespie)*

The loveable character Herman Munster, played by Fred Gwynne, graced the cover of the February 1966 edition of Pete Millar's **Drag Cartoons** *magazine. Millar, an avid drag racer, illustrator, and artist, was a cult figure among the drag racing crowd with his cartoon creations of drag racing's stars. (Photo Courtesy Robin Millar)*

Tom McEwen, in the **Yeakel Plymouth Special** *AA/FD, tests a newly designed pancake Scott injector at Lions Drag Strip. After failed attempts to start the dragsters on the rollers, it was determined by Tom McEwen and John Garrison that not enough air was entering the scoop to fire up the engine. The decision was made to drill a hole in the back of the scoop to allow more air in, and the plan worked.*

of the afternoon and posted the first run of the day in the 7s (a 7.99 ET at 204.54 mph). When the day concluded, 15 cars qualified in the 7-second bracket, and James Warren, driving the *Ridge Route Terrors* Warren-Colburn-Miller rail, held onto the top spot with a 7.70 ET at 207.84 mph.

Jack Wayre, Glen Ward, and John "the Zookeeper" Mulligan combined to form one of the premiere Top Fuel teams. The chassis was a Woody car with a shorty Hanna body that was originally finished in black. After some repairs, it was returned to George Cerny's paint shop and repainted in various shades of blue with stripes placed from the front to the back. The paint scheme was beautiful but ordinary. (Photo Courtesy Don Prieto)

James Warren lights up the staging-lane beams and concentrates on the Christmas tree countdown. Warren began as a dirt track racer and compiled a 17-year career behind the wheel of a Top Fuel dragster. He stockpiled countless achievements and won several Big Meets at Lions Drag Strip. (Photo Courtesy Don Prieto)

The **Cook Brothers & Jahns** *C/FD sidewinder ran a blown Dodge powered by nitro. Jeff Jahns of the Jahns Quality Piston family drove the dragster, which used a jack-stand starting system. With the engine running, the car was raised up on jacks and the crew pushed it to the starting line. With the RPM running at near full throttle, the jacks dropped as soon as the flag did, and off he went. (Photo Courtesy Don Prieto)*

The Junior Fuel class ran some of the coolest intake systems that were unique in own their way. The class was the brainchild of C. J. Hart and an unlimited class for the smaller-displacement engines to run competitively and have fun on a limited budget. Chevrolet engines were the favored choice of the class. (Photo Courtesy Don Prieto)

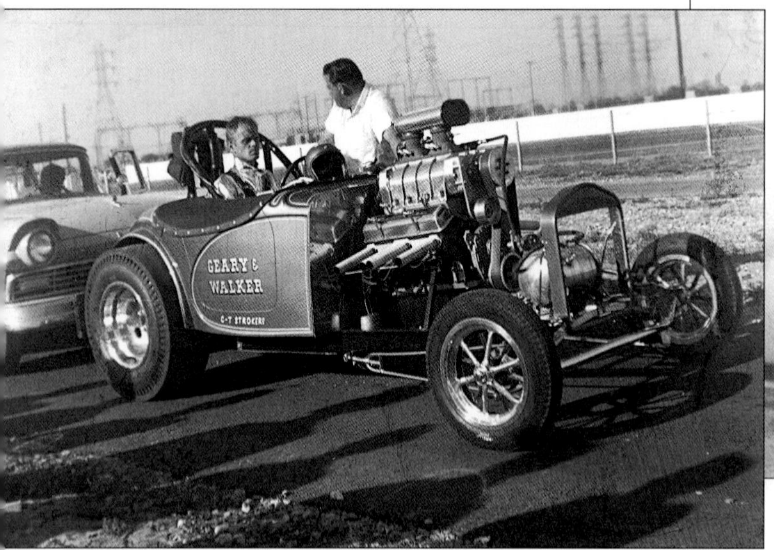

Depending on which side of the drag strip you were on, the **Walker & Geary** *or* **Geary & Walker** *AA/Fuel Altered '32 Austin Bantam roadster was one of the strongest runners that utilized Chevy power. Here, driver Bob Walker and owner Bud Geary wait for the call to push off at the AHRA Nationals. (Photo Courtesy Lions Automobilia Foundation Museum)*

Doug "the Fat Man" Robinson hailed from Pasadena, California, which was home to the popular KRLA radio station. Robinson's 1965 yellow AA/FD was sponsored by KRLA and Horsepower Engineering and was powered by a supercharged 392-ci Chrysler with direct drive. KRLA played top-40 music and had some of the biggest disc jockeys on the airwaves. (Photo Courtesy Lions Automobilia Foundation Museum)

Last Chance to Dance

Sunday morning, September 5, was the last chance for both nitro and gas dragsters to make it into the high-dollar-purse eliminations rounds. The first round of eliminations for all classes kicked off at noon, and several of the top contenders fell to the wayside with mechanical woes or left the line too early. Most of the lower hot classes ran their final elimination runoffs before inclement weather put everyone on the trailers. It was determined in a driver's meeting that the finals would conclude the following morning.

AHRA President Jim Tice and C. J. "Pappy" Hart were able to pull out a remarkable finish at the 11th-annual World Championships. It combined the 16 Top Fuelers that were held over from the previous weekend's washout with the regular show, which was the Drag News Eliminator meet with Top Fuel and Top Gas slingshots and modifieds.

The AHRA Top Fuel Championship was won by Paul "the Kid" Sutherland in the *Sutherland-Brissette* machine. Sutherland drove past Tom Dyer in the *Dyer-VanLuven* entry when Dyer lost the engine at the green.

In the Top Gas final, Fred Lear won with an 8.35 ET at 188.00 mph.

Other noted winners at the Nationals were Dave Beebe (Competition Eliminator), Sush Matsubara & Joe Mondello's A/FA (Middle Eliminator), Mike Mitchell (Little Eliminator) and Manuel Herrera (Street Eliminator).

The Drag News Mr. Fuel Eliminator race for the best-of-three match races for the number-two overall spot pitted titleholder Bobby Tapia (in the *Stellings & Tapia* fueler) against the challenger, Doug "the Fat Man" Robinson (in his *KRLA-Horsepower Engineering* dragster). After both cars split the first two rounds, Robinson earned the upset win with an 8.06 ET at 157.34 mph to Tapia's losing 8.37 ET at 161.29 mph.

Metropolitan Bompera House

For six intense days leading up to the celebration of the 11th anniversary of Lions Drag Strip, local rock-and-roll radio station KFWB 98 "the Good Guys" had Lions Drag Strip owning the station (commercial-wise). The week-long advertising campaign flooded the airwaves. New potential fans were introduced to drag racing with a "two for the price of one" promotion from the Coca-Cola Company.

The marketing incentive brought more than 16,000 spectators to Lions Drag Strip for their chance to win many door prizes and to witness the action of the multiple-car fields. Sixteen Top Fuelers, eight Top Gas and Jr. Fuel dragsters, and four Competition and Altered Eliminator cars made up the fields to compete for the prize money.

LIONS INVITES YOU TO CELEBRATE WITH US THE 11th ANNIVERSARY OF SUPERVISED DRAG RACING IN WILMINGTON!

COMING SATURDAY NIGHT, OCTOBER 2nd

LIONS - KFWB RADIO - COCA COLA

ANNIVERSARY DRAG - BOMP

TOP MONEY MEET FOR THE RACERS

Admission $2.00 - 2 for 1 to Bomp Club Mem.
Gates Open 11 A.M. - Eliminations 6:30 P.M.

$2500 IN DOOR PRIZES TO SPECTATORS

2 Color TV's, 2 Portable TV's, Car Stereo, Top Name Surfboard

A poster was created to advertise the celebration of the 11th anniversary of organized drag racing at Lions Drag Strip. Local radio station KFWB and Coca-Cola co-sponsored the anniversary with tons of giveaway prizes.

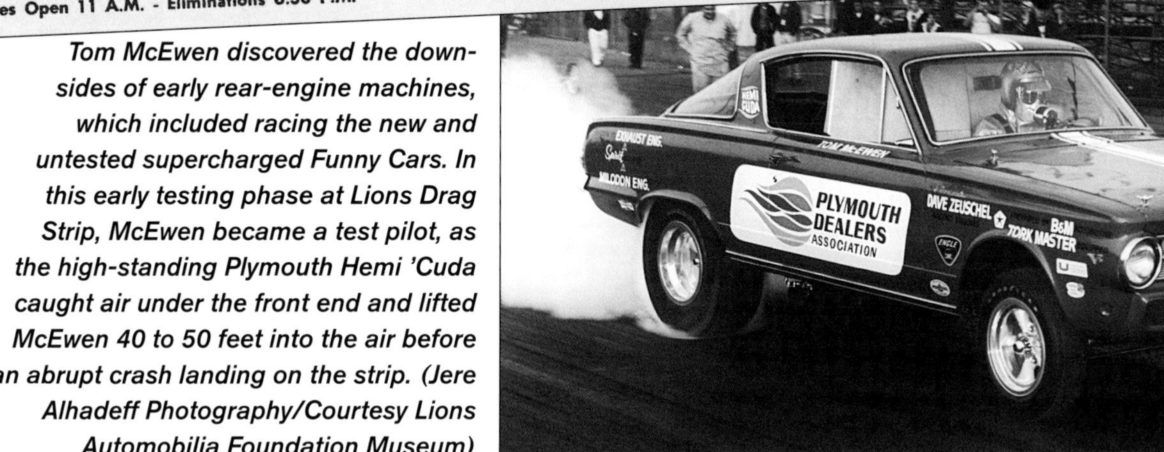

Tom McEwen discovered the downsides of early rear-engine machines, which included racing the new and untested supercharged Funny Cars. In this early testing phase at Lions Drag Strip, McEwen became a test pilot, as the high-standing Plymouth Hemi 'Cuda caught air under the front end and lifted McEwen 40 to 50 feet into the air before an abrupt crash landing on the strip. (Jere Alhadeff Photography/Courtesy Lions Automobilia Foundation Museum)

Door prizes included two Motorola color TVs, two portable Motorola black-and-white portable TVs, one Dewey Weber surfboard, two car stereos, and more.

Mongoose Takes Flight

On October 4, 1965, an unsuspecting Tom "the Mongoose" McEwen took flight in the rear-engine Plymouth Hemi Barracuda at Lions Drag Strip. The Barracuda flew an estimated 30 to 40 feet through the air before it crashed down around the 900-foot mark of the drag strip.

Drag racers were modern-day test pilots or crash-test dummies. They didn't know the dangers and risks involved with new concepts and designs. They would drive anything and get paid without knowing how the aerodynamics worked or how it was supposed to work. It always looked

Memories

Carl Olson

Top Fuel Dragster Driver and Lions Automobilia Foundation Museum Board Member

"C. J. Hart was a wonderful individual. He was a people person, a visionary, and he worked harder than anyone I knew in the sport of drag racing. He was there at the sport's very beginning at Santa Ana, and he virtually wrote the book on how to organize and conduct drag races. The knowledge and experience he brought to Lions [Drag Strip], along with his personality and his people skills, was absolute magic the entire time he was there.

"C. J. understood that drag racing was more than just cars going down the track. It was entertainment. He was very skilled at creating a program that would appeal both to the racers from a competition perspective and spectators as entertainment. The combination of those skills was very rare at the time. His work ethic was so productive that he was well respected by all. When he proposed something, people were likely to go along with him because they knew he was sincere.

"C. J. was one of the most honest people I ever met. Unlike some of the other promoters who were often a bit slippery with the facts and the truth, C. J. Hart was as honest and straightforward as a human being can be. People knew they could count on him when they showed up at Lions [Drag Strip], and they would get the same treatment and the same opportunities that everyone else got. In that day and age, that was very rare."

Tom McEwen is assisted from the wreckage of Lou Baney's **Plymouth Dealers Association** *Hemi 'Cuda after the car took flight at mid-track on October 4, 1965, during test runs for the media. Although McEwen wasn't hurt, the car was a mangled wreck. Baney and McEwen built a newer and lower version that was later sold to Fred Goeske, who ran it with limited success. (Photo Courtesy Paul Johnson Collection)*

good on the drawing board, but that is drag racing. You live and learn with it.

The Snake Upsets the Golden Goose

"Snake's going down in two straight 'cause we got a party going on tonight, and we're leaving early," Tom "the Mongoose" McEwen said this before one of his best-of-three match races with Don "the Snake" Prudhomme.

McEwen and Prudhomme, who were archrivals and friends, traded pre-race barbs in the publicized match race that was held on Saturday, December 4, at Lions Drag Strip. McEwen's *Yeakel Plymouth Special* had been plagued with starting issues with the three-week-old, redesigned Scott injector and would not start for two runs in the match race. After identifying the injector problem, McEwen finally pulled out a win over Prudhomme. Unknown to many, this was the last race in which Prudhomme drove Roland Leong's *Hawaiian*.

Year-End Blast-Off

On December 18, Lions Drag Strip hosted its Year-End Blast-Off, which was a four-stage, match-race booster show, to end the 1965 season on a high note.

The *Red Turkey* B/F Dragster of Jimmy Boyd took on Hayden Proffitt's fuel-burning Mercury Comet. A best-of-three match race took place between the new Ford Mustang of Hubert Platt and Doug Torley's *Chevy Too Much*

WHAT SAYS THE MONGOOSE?

1. "I am the World's Record Speed holder at 214.78 m.p.h.--"
2. "I'm not gonna red light, just leave on the early green!"
3. "I'll blow him off in two straight and run faster & quicker than he does"
4. "Prudhomme has had a very successful year, he's done done everything important but beat me"
5. "I started off a good year by shutting down the Snake, I'm gonna end it the same way!"

WHAT SAYS THE SNAKE?

1. "I am the top speed king at 215.m.p.h., have a better E.T. record of 7.40"
2. "My Lions track record of 7.53 has not been touched in a year"
3. "The Snake is interested only in national events - sometimes we leave the smaller, less flashy meets to McEwen"
4. "I ended his year about 8 months ago, he must realize, it's the year of the Snake!"
5. "Tell the Mongoose to read one of the latest drag magazines, the Snake is polled number one on the West Coast"

Don "SNAKE" Prudhomme and the Leong- Prudhomme "HAWAIIAN" will race.....

Tom "MONGOOSE" McEwen and the Yeakel Plymouth Special

AT

223RD & ALAMEDA, WILMINGTON
$2.00 ADMISSION
PHONE 424-09F1
AHRA SANCTION

SAT. NITE DEC. 4th

To preview an event at Lions Drag Strip, this advertisement shows quotes from Tom "the Mongoose" McEwen and Don "the Snake" Prudhomme, who were friends and rivals.

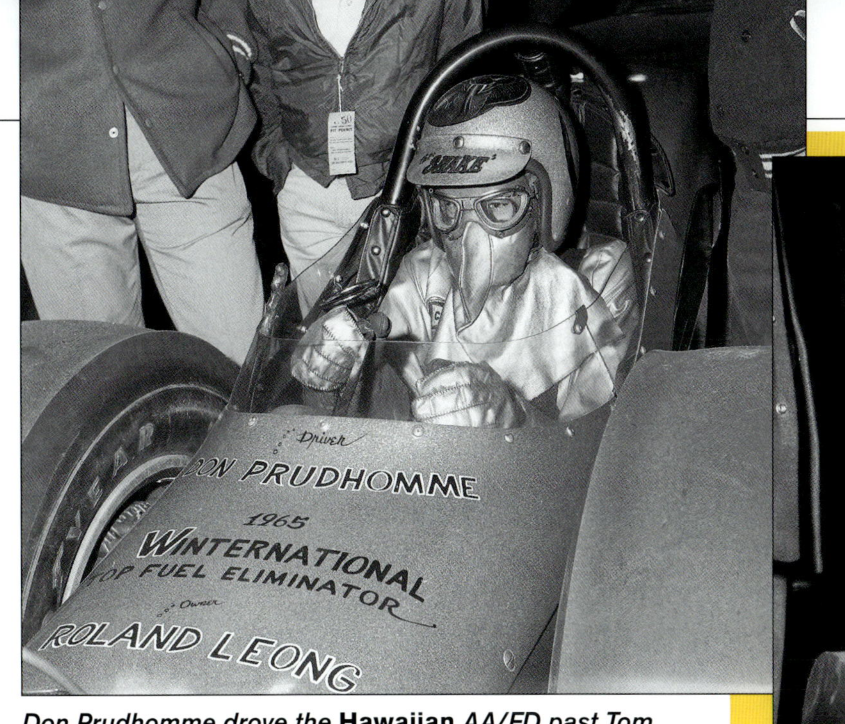

Don Prudhomme drove the* Hawaiian *AA/FD past Tom McEwen, who encountered difficulties when he failed to leave from the starting line in two straight runs. For Prudhomme, this was his swan song with Roland Leong and the* Hawaiian*. He later announced he would venture out on his own for the 1966 season. (Jere Alderef Photography/Courtesy Lions Automobilia Foundation Museum)

Tom McEwen waits attentively on the starting rollers for starter Larry Sutton to bark the command to start the* Yeakel Plymouth Special *for the finale of his match race with Don Prudhomme. McEwen encountered problems all evening long with the three-week-old Scott injector. (Jere Alderef Photography/Courtesy Lions Automobilia Foundation Museum)

Chevy II. There was a contest of who could stay up longer on the rear wheels between Preston Honea (driving Bill Craft's Hemi-powered Rambler Marlin) and Bill Shrewsberry (driving the *Hurst Hemi Under Glass*). The king of the stock car drivers, "Dyno" Don Nicholson, took on the *Melrose Missile* (the new number 7) campaigned by Cecil Yother from Oakland, California.

Hart's drag racing event resembled the combined crews of P. T. Barnum and the Ringling Brothers under one tent. Some of the diehard racers viewed it as a circus and grew hostile, while others judged the crowd's reaction to the acts and were saddened.

The meet winners included Yother's *Melrose Missile,* which beat the Nicholson's heavily favored Mercury Comet and won three in a row. Honea took two out of three wins when the *Hurst Hemi Under Glass* Barracuda was grounded and forced out from contention when it mashed both castor wheels and the replacements never made it to the strip.

C. J. Hart and writer Terry Cook took up their positions at the 1/8 and 1/16 mile markers to judge the Proffitt and Boyd matchup. In typical fashion, Proffitt put the fuel-injected Comet up on the rear bumper in all three rounds, while Boyd's *Red Turkey* took charge and made the clean sweep.

It was now up to Hubert Platt, from the Deep South, to put the Mustang in the win column after his wild ride in round one, when he got out of shape, crossed up at mid-track, shut off, and called it a round. Platt was "loaded for bear" in round two. He added more horsepower, adjusted the shocks, put more weight into the trunk, and hoped the tires were broken in. However, it was all for naught, as Thorley made it two straight with a 9.60 ET at 143.94 mph, as the *Georgia Shaker* scraped the rear bumper with a 7-foot wheel-stand and eased off.

Gearing Up for 1966

Hart's Year-End Blast-Off wrapped up another successful racing season at Lions Drag Strip. Attendance figures reached new heights, and new improvements were planned. One of the new improvements for 1966 began immediately when the current asphalt surface was removed and replaced. In addition, new self-starters replaced push startups for the hot cars, which caused displeasure among some spectators.

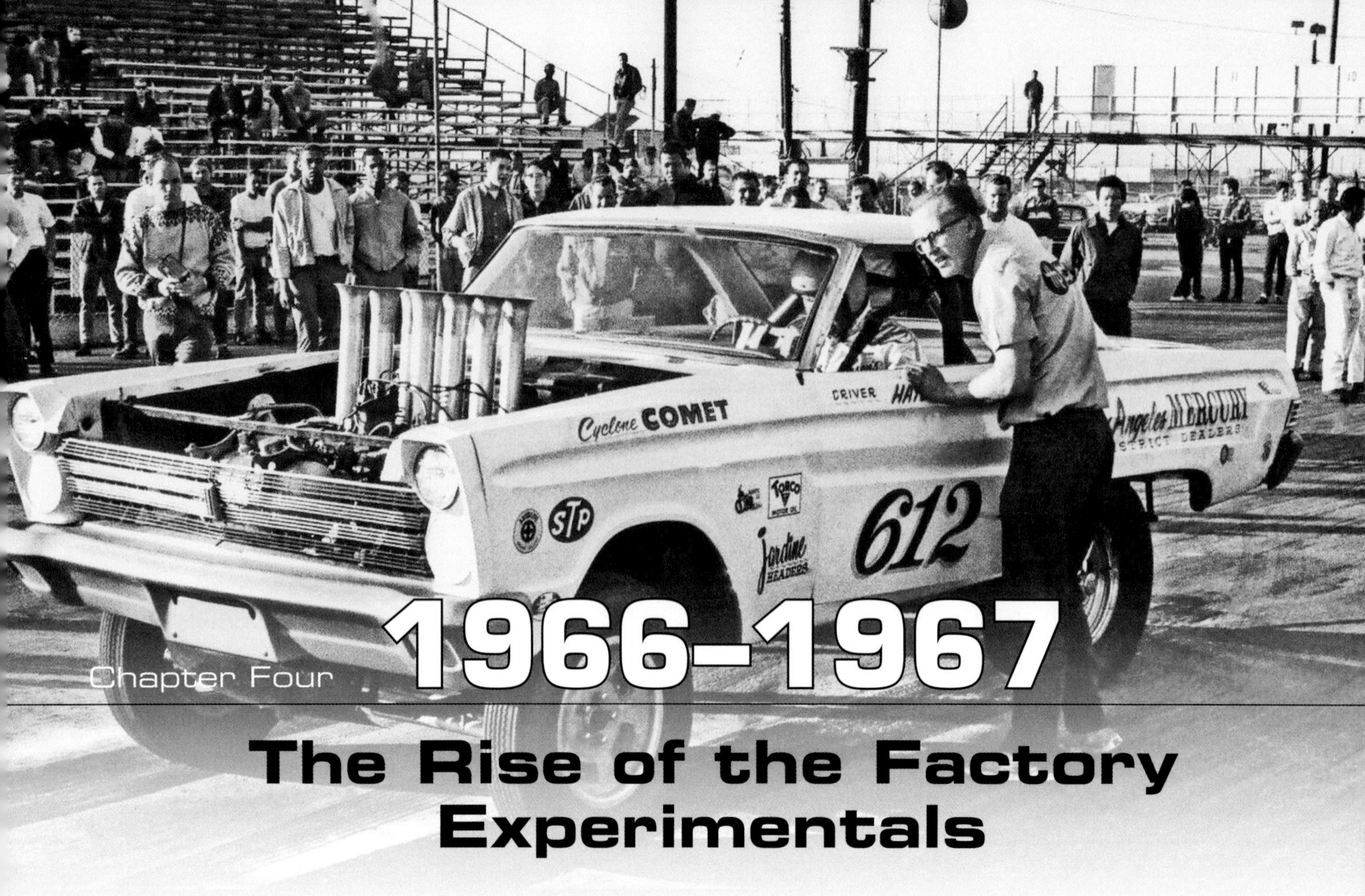

Chapter Four

1966–1967

The Rise of the Factory Experimentals

At the beginning of the 1966 season, Lions Drag Strip was the only drag strip in the United States with a new Sure-Fire starter system and a freshly paved Octo-Vise track surface. The self-starting system eliminated the need for push starts for the hot cars, but many fans felt that it took away the excitement of having the cars fire when they were coming up the strip in front of the grandstands.

UDRA Winternationals

The annual meet for spectators who enjoy championship non-partisan (regarding sanctioning bodies) racing was the UDRA's Winternationals. The third-annual event was planned for February 5 and 6 but racing was delayed after rain plagued the event. The meet was rescheduled to be one day only on Saturday, February 26. More than 100 200-mph Fuelers competed for a spot in the 32-car field.

Registration and tech inspection opened at 9 a.m., and the gates to the public opened at noon. Qualifying runs were from noon to 4 p.m., and eliminations started at 6:30 p.m. Qualifying times that were recorded on February 5 and 6 before the rainouts were counted as good.

The voice of drag racing, Jon "Thunderlungs" Lundberg, sent the crowd into the stratosphere with the announcement that Hayden Proffitt switched from his 1965 Mercury Cyclone to a 1966 Chevrolet Corvair with a 427-injected Rat engine for power. Here, Proffitt lines up his 1965 427 Mercury A/FX Comet for a run. (Jere Aldereff Photography/Courtesy Lions Automobilia Foundation Museum)

Unfortunately for the fans (but gratifying to the racers), Don Garlits, Chris Karamesines, and Jimmy Nix were unable to appear due to other commitments.

Representing both coasts and all parts in between were Connie Kalitta, Don Prudhomme, Pete Robinson, Ed Pink's *Old Master*, Tom McEwen, Leong-Snively's *Hawaiian*, Chicago's Ken Patterson, George "the Bushmaster" Schreiber, Warren-Coburn-Miller, Creitez & Greer, and 90-plus more.

Eliminations consisted of 32 Top Fuel, 16 Top Gas, 16 Jr. Fuel dragsters, 8 Fuel Altereds, 8 Competition cars, and 8 A/GS entries. A special attraction of 10 exhibition Funny Cars were added to one of the largest meets of the new year. The low ET of the meet (7.38 seconds) was set by Brissette & Sutherland, and the top speed of the meet (210.76 mph) was recorded by the Beebe Brothers

GET YOUR RACING KICKS IN '66 AT

LIONS DRAG STRIP

EARLY 1966 SCHEDULE OF EVENTS

JAN. 8th GRAND OPENING FUEL MEET – NEW PAVING – NEW "SURE-FIRE" SELF STARTERS FOR DRAGSTERS!
16 TOP FUEL QUALIFIERS, 8 TOP GAS, 8 JR. FUEL, 4 A/A, 4 COMPETITION ELIMINATORS, 4 A/GS, 10 E.T. BRACKETS. TOM IVO'S FUELER AND 4 ENGINE "SHOWBOAT" IN SPECIAL APPEARANCE.

JAN. 9th "FUNNY CARS" – DICK LANDY vs. BUTCH LEAL
ALL STOCKER, GAS, & MOTORCYCLE CLASSES.

JAN. 15th DETROIT DRAGSTER BATTLE! FORD vs. PLYMOUTH!
CONNIE KALITTA'S O.H.C. FORD vs. CHRIS KARAMESINES' "CHIZLER" PLYMOUTH – PLUS - 8 JR. FUEL, 8 TOP GAS, 4 A/A, 4 A/GS, 4 COMP. ELIMINATORS, 10 E.T. BRACKETS.

JAN. 16th ALL STOCKER, GAS, & MOTORCYCLE CLASSES.

JAN. 22nd "THE SNAKE" vs. "THE GOLDEN GREEK"!
YES, DON PRUDHOMME MEETS CHRIS KARAMESINES FROM CHICAGO PLUS - 8 JR. FUEL, 8 TOP GAS, 4 A/A, 4 A/GS, 4 COMP. ELIM., 10 E.T. BRACKETS.

JAN. 23rd ALL STOCKER, GAS, & MOTORCYCLE CLASSES.

JAN. 29th 1ST TIME ON WEST COAST! ARNIE BESWICK'S BLOWN, FUEL PONTIAC "FUNNY CAR". – ALSO TOM HOOVER'S "HOOVER WHEEL ALIGNMENT SPL." AA/FD. – 8 JR. FUEL, 8 TOP GAS, 4 A/A, 4 A/GS, 4 COMP. ELIM., 10 E.T. BRACKETS.

FEB. 5th & 6th 3RD ANNUAL U.D.R.A. NATIONALS, A $15,000 + MEET!
FUEL: DON GARLITS, CHRIS KARAMESINES, CONNIE KALITTA, MAYNARD RUPP, TOM HOOVER, PETE ROBINSON.
GAS: HIRATA-HOBBS, GORDON COLLETT, RON COLSON, KEN PETERSON.

BIG EASTERN CARS!

YOU MUST SEE! MAYNARD RUPP'S NEW REAR ENGINE CHRYSLER, BLN. FUEL CHEVY "FUNNY CAR"! – THE "HEMI-CUDA", DICK LANDY, SHIRLEY SHAHAN, BUTCH LEAL, DON PRUDHOMME, JERRY RUTH, GOTELLI SPL., BRISSETTE-SUTHERLAND (219 M.P.H.), KENNY SAFFORD, GEO. BOLTHOFF, WARREN & COBURN, GAS RONDA, TONY NANCY, "FRANTIC FOUR", STONE-WOODS-COOK, OTIE'S AUTOMOTIVE A/-HOT ROADSTER & AA/FD FROM AKRON, OHIO, HORSE POWER ENGR., ADAMS & WARYE, DONOVAN-TAPIA!

This "Get Your Racing Kicks in '66 at Lions Drag Strip" flyer features an early schedule with big-name drag racing on tap.

and Vincent & Sixt. Unfortunately, rain began Saturday evening and didn't let up before the race was called at 11 a.m. on Sunday.

On a sad note, Joe "the Jet" Jackson spun the *Cook Auto Wrecking* dragster into the retaining fence and succumbed to head injuries. Jackson was a resident of Sanford, Maine, and was only 26 years old.

Don Garlits competes in his red **Swamp Rat X** *at the UDRA Winternationals. The car was a revamped version of the* **Swamp Rat VIII**, *which was afflicted with unlucky performances. Looking to change the pattern of ill luck, Garlits sent the car to George Cerny for the color change to red when he was in California. However, the color difference didn't change things for the better on the late-model 426 Dodge Hemi. (Photo Courtesy Paul Johnson Collection)*

*The **Shark** AA/FD of Safford and Milodon made it past the **Ewell-Bell-Stecker** car in the first round of 32 with a 7.68 ET at 200.88 mph. Ken Safford outran Jess Sturgeon in round two with a 7.68 ET at 207.84 mph to Sturgeon's 8.23 ET at 187.00 mph. Round three wasn't in the cards for Safford, as he shut off with no ET against Dunn & Yates. (Jere Alderef Photography/Courtesy Lions Automobilia Foundation Museum)*

*Ed Pink's **Old Master** AA/FD was built by chassis designer Don Long, and Ed Pink supplied a 1957 Chrysler Hemi engine. The dragster's first outing was at a fiercely competitive race at Lions Drag Strip with driver Mike Snively in the seat. Connie Swingle replaced Snively and enjoyed moderate success. This included his biggest win in Pink's dragster at Fontana Drag Strip, when he defeated his longtime friend Don Garlits in the final eliminator round at the Mickey Thompson 200-MPH Club Meet. Swingle won the $10,000 cash purse. (Photo Courtesy Tim Pearl)*

*A standing member from the streamliner phase in the mid-1960s was Ed Roth's **Yellow Fang** AA/FD. Tom Hanna created the skins that covered the frame, which was crafted by Jim Davis. It featured a 392 Chrysler Hemi with a direct-drive unit bolted to the back end of the block. Driver George "the Bushmaster" Schreiber was responsible for the maintenance of the engine. (Jere Alderef Photography/Courtesy Lions Automobilia Foundation Museum)*

C. J.'s Three-Ring Circus: The East versus West Showdown

On March 5, 1966, Lions Drag Strip hosted the top Altered Wheelbase Experimentals at the first-annual Drag Racing Magazine Invitational East-West Championships. The crowd of more than 12,000 screaming and cheering fans (the largest in Lions Drag Strip history) filled the grandstands along with several rows of fans lined up against the fences.

Jon Lundberg, the voice of drag racing, filled the role of master of ceremonies and narrated the highly spirited affair, which featured a series of match races between the top 10 East versus West fuel-injected Funny Cars of each section (as rated by *Drag Racing* magazine). The rules of the shootout were simple. Each car would run three no-holds-barred round-robin rounds regarding fuel, rosin, and no weight limits.

The list of drag racing's elite Funny Cars included Malcolm Durham's *Strip Blazer III* Chevelle, Pete Seaton's *Seaton's Shaker* Malibu, Cecil Yother's

SATURDAY MARCH 5, 1966

The Wildest Show Ever

Over 25 of the Top Stockers in the U.S.

-at-

LIONS DRAG STRIP

The 1st Annual

DRAG RACING Magazine Invitational East-West Championships

See such match races as:

West		*East*
Dick Landy	vs.	"Dyno Don" Nicholson
Butch Leal	vs.	Pete Seaton
Gas Ronda	vs.	Sox & Martin
Hayden Proffitt	vs.	Gene Snow
Shirley Shahan	vs.	Malcolm Durham
"Melrose Missile"	vs.	Kelly Chadwick
Dickie Harrell	vs.	Hubert Platt
"Flying Dutchman"	vs.	"Rattlesnake" Austin
Tom Sturm	vs.	"Temptation"
Les Ritchey	vs.	Houston Platt

Additional backup cars will include:

Tom Grove, Charlie Allen, "Quarterbender", Doug's Headers, Al Eckstrand, Platt-Walters, and possibbly, Bill Lawton, Phil Bonner and Dick Brannan.

Eliminations Start at 6:30 p.m. (only 1½ hours from Bakersfield)

AHRA Sanctioned

Another first at Lions Drag Strip was when C. J. Hart created one of the wildest shows in drag racing with this advertisement that featured more than 25 A/FX stockers at the first-annual Drag Racing Magazine Invitational East-West Championships.

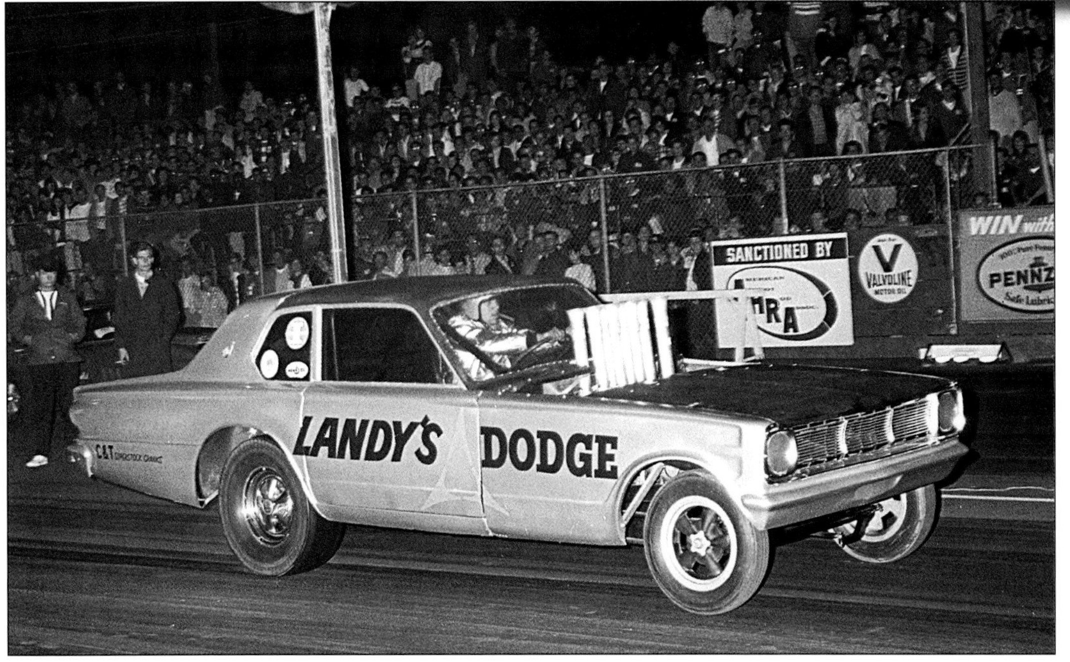

The East versus West match races featured the top 10 Stockers from each section of the country as rated by **Drag Racing** *magazine. The contest featured manufacturer versus manufacturer pairings. "Dandy" Dick Landy wowed them all and set the low ET of 9.62 with his 1966 426-ci Dodge Dart. (Jere Aldereff Photography/Courtesy Lions Automobilia Foundation Museum)*

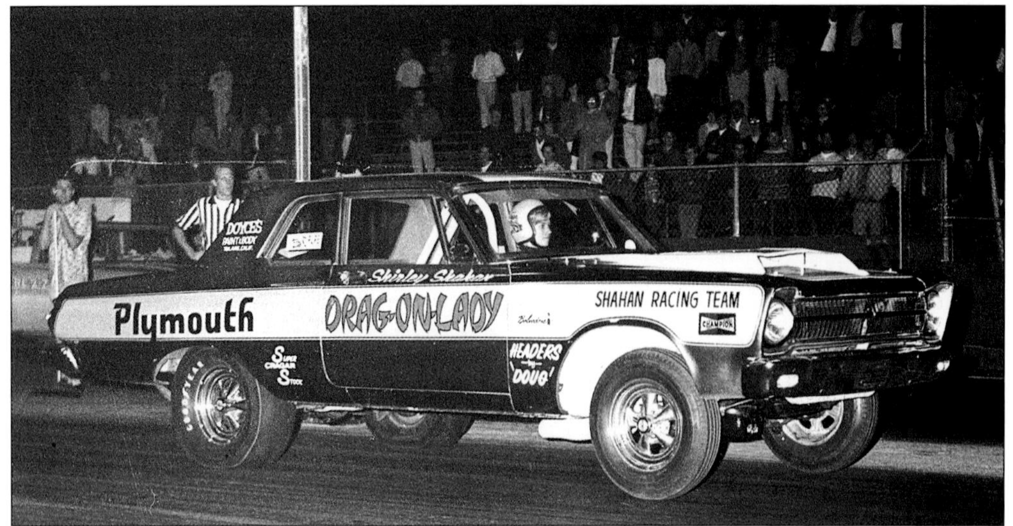

Shirley "Drag-On Lady" Shahan, fresh from her win at the NHRA Winternationals, faced Malcolm "DC Lip" Durham and his Chevy, the **Strip Blazer III,** *in a best-of-three encounter. Shahan powered her Plymouth to the win with an 11.07 ET at 133.13 mph. Durham missed a shift and came up with a 15.00 ET at 126.68 mph. (Jere Aldereff Photography/Courtesy Lions Automobilia Foundation Museum)*

Malcolm Durham's **Strip Blazer III** *1965 Z16 Chevelle was one of the top Stockers at the first-annual Drag Racing Magazine Invitational East-West Championships. Durham was one of the first Black drag racers from Washington, D.C. Nicknamed "the D.C. Lip," Durham made a handful of appearances at Lions Drag Strip. He later teamed with local racer Lee Jones, who ran predominately under Durham's banner. (Jere Aldereff Photography/Courtesy Lions Automobilia Foundation Museum)*

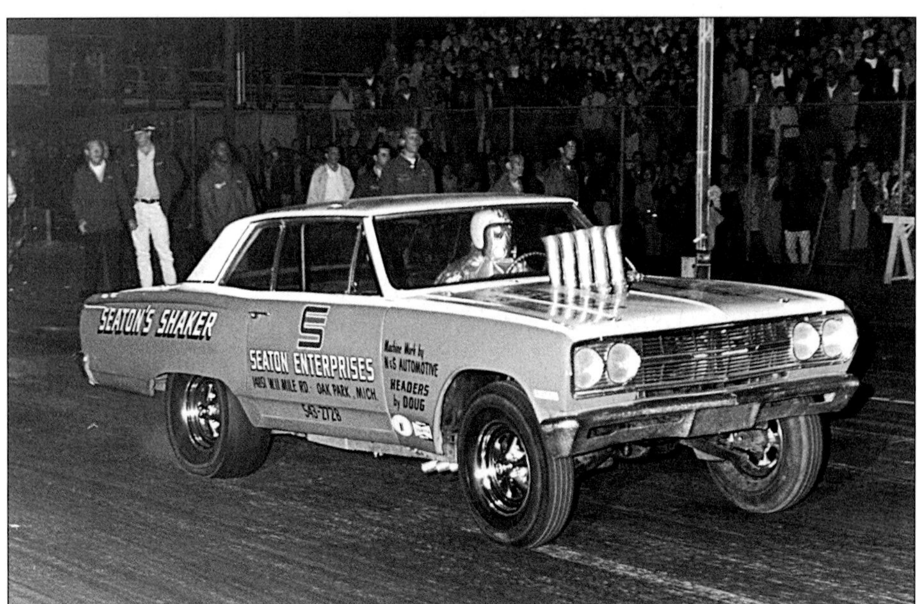

The race between the **Seaton's Shaker** *427-ci Chevelle and the* **California Flash** *of Butch Leal was one of the most exciting races of the meet. Leal's 426 Hemi-powered Plymouth, which ran on gasoline, faced Delmar Heinelt. Heinelt was the driver of the* **Seaton's Shaker**, *which was accented with stock parts and pistons with only the block balanced, and it ran on a 75-percent dosage of nitro. Leal had a two-car-length lead when he missed a shift, and the Chevelle caught up, took the lead, and won with a 10.84 ET at 135.13 mph. (Jere Aldereff Photography/Courtesy Lions Automobilia Foundation Museum)*

Dick Harrell and his **Retribution II** *Chevy II and the* **Georgia Shaker** *Ford Mustang of Hubert Platt performed the best pre-race side show in drag racing. The circus-like high jinks brought laughter and smiles to the fans. (Jere Aldereff Photography/ Courtesy Lions Automobilia Foundation Museum)*

"Mr. 4-Speed" Ronnie Sox and Buddy Martin ran a 1966 fuel-injected, nitro-burning 426 Hemi Barracuda against the Ford of Gas Ronda for their series of races. Sox ran a 9.85 ET at 154.37 mph in the second round but red-lit and handed the race to Ronda, who "smoked the hides" for 800 feet. Both cars set the top speed of the meet in the first round with an identical speed (154.37 mph). (Jere Aldereff Photography/Courtesy Lions Automobilia Foundation Museum)

Melrose Missile VII, Dick Landy's Dodge Dart, Sox & Martin's Barracuda, and Charlie Allen.

As the pre-race introductions and ceremonies wrapped up before the first round of match races, C. J. Hart set the tone by using his unique circus experience by playing "Entry of the Gladiators," which delighted the large crowd.

Out of the gate, Dick Landy's Hemi-powered Dodge 426 Dart set the low ET of the show with a 9.62. Landy was the only driver of the night who ran ETs in the mid-9s all three times (a 9.62 and a 9.71, respectively). The next pair of cars set top speed of the show. Gas Ronda (in his 427-SOHC Ford Mustang) and Ronnie Sox (in the Sox & Martin 426-ci Hemi-Barracuda) recorded identical ETs of 9.91 at 154.37 mph.

Charlie Allen faced Kelly Chadwick, a schoolteacher from Texas. Allen's Hemi Dart, the **Atlantic Flyer II**, *blasted through the rosin and took the win over Chadwick with an 11.07 ET at 133.13 mph to the teacher's 15.13 ET at 126.21 mph, as he missed fourth gear. (Jere Aldereff Photography/ Courtesy Lions Automobilia Foundation Museum)*

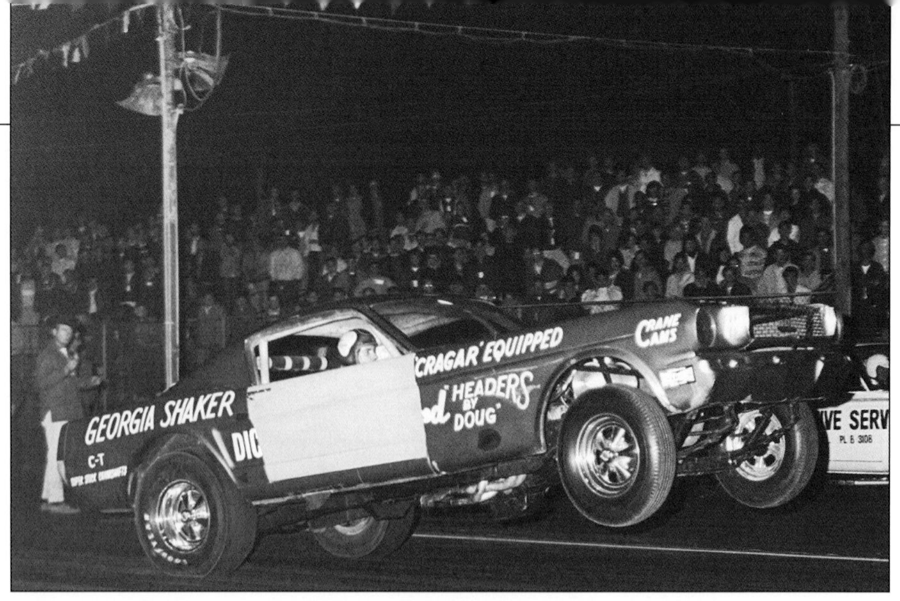

When Dick Harrell snapped both axles during a first-round wheel-stand against Hubert Platt's **Georgia Shaker**, Harrell returned the favor by driving past Platt's out-of-shape Mustang. The third round brought in Shirley "the Drag-On Lady" Shahan to face Harrell while Platt faced off with Mack Young in the **Thweatt's Automotive** Hemi Plymouth. The meet's highest wheel-stand took place when both Young and Platt moved out together. Platt's giant wheel-stand measured more than 10-feet high, came down off to the side, and slid sideways in the dirt. Young ran a 10.23 ET at 139.34 mph to Platt's 11.46 ET at 85.12 mph. (Jere Aldereff Photography/Courtesy Lions Automobilia Foundation Museum)

Carefree Antics of the Funny Car Circus

Up next were the self-proclaimed "Funny Car Clowns," the two strongest cars in the country and drag racing's most entertaining stars of the quarter mile: Hubert "Huey Baby" Platt in his *Georgia Shaker* Mustang and Dickie Harrell in his 427-ci Chevy II.

With both cars out on the starting pad, both crews spread rosin dust for maximum traction. To the delight of the fans, each driver jumped out of the race car and into the other driver's car—albeit for just a moment.

Platt gave Harrell a cigar, climbed into the stands, and told the fans he wanted to watch this race. As Harrell climbed back into his car to clear up a cylinder that was full of fuel, Platt returned to his mount. Both drivers strapped themselves into their cars, fired up, and moved to the starting line. They pulled off the line evenly, but Harrell snapped an axle shifting into second gear that allowed Platt to streak past for the win with a 10.34 ET at 140.40 mph.

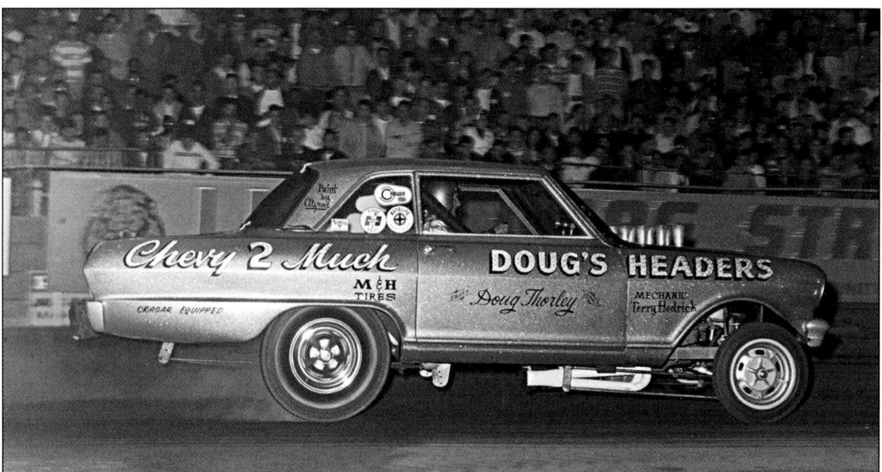

The hard luck award of the meet went to Doug Thorley's **Chevy 2 Much**, *which packed a whopping 481 ci under the hood for this race. Thorley made a full pass against the Dodge of Dick Landy, as the Chevy lost a rod off the starting line. (Jere Aldereff Photography/Courtesy Lions Automobilia Foundation Museum)*

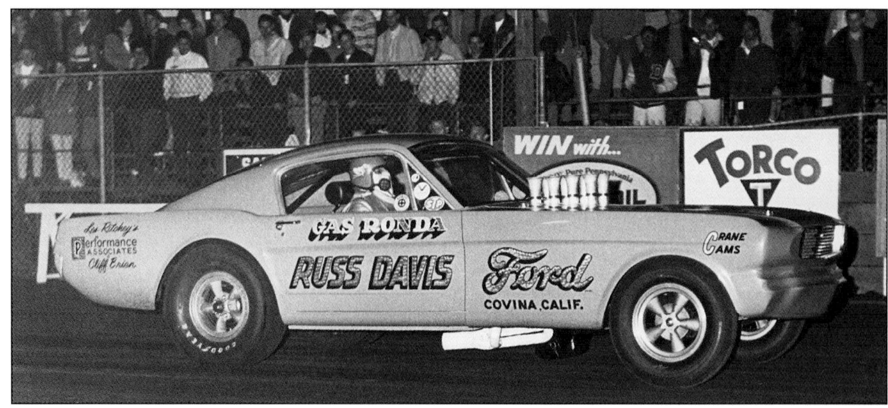

Former dance instructor Gas Ronda waltzes down the drag strip. Ronda captured top honors at the first annual Drag Racing Magazine Invitational East-West Funny Car Championships for the top Stockers and won all three rounds of competition. In addition, he set the top speed of the meet in the last round against Sox & Martin at 154.37 mph. (Jere Aldereff Photography/Courtesy Lions Automobilia Foundation Museum)

Amusing Times of the AHRA

AHRA President Jim Tice welcomed the carnival-type atmosphere of colorful cars and drivers with open arms. Instead of putting the cars into a regulated obscure class, the AHRA turned them loose. It offered incentives of increased cash payouts at all of its major events for appearance, round advancement, setting event low ET, setting event top speed, and being the event champion (record cash purses).

Not only did the drivers and owners reap the benefits, AHRA facilities from the East Coast to the West Coast heavily promoted the premiere Funny Car events to gather the top manufacturers and bring in driver rivalries that had announcers screaming over the public address system to fire up the crowds.

The AHRA realized that the fans would be loyal if you catered to them and gave away more than their money's worth with door prizes (color and black-and-white TVs, surfboards, radios, hair dryers, minibikes, concessions food, and tickets for future events). You name it—they gave it away! At larger venues, the AHRA converted the starting-line area into a music festival for an after-racing bonus event that was aimed toward the younger crowd. The remaining spectators and race crews enjoyed the psychedelic rock band concert that featured brightly colored and radiant lights and sounds as they danced and sang into the early morning hours.

The Great Dragcast of 1966

On May 7, two great events took place at Lions Drag Strip as part of the Great Dragcast of 1966.

Goodwin Play-by-Play

This new, live, weekly radio program was broadcast directly from the strip and was a first in drag racing. Lions Drag Strip and Los Angeles radio station KFWB 98 brought in broadcaster Hal Goodwin, who called the play-by-play action as it unfolded.

Goodwin's tasks included calling the hot round-by-round action in Top Fuel for several match races, including an unusual one-round minibike race between *Cycle News* versus *Drag News*.

The Kid Derails the Freight Train

The top advertised billing of the night was the "Great Train Robbery" match race featuring 17-year-old Billy "the Kid" Scott and the twin-Chevrolet-powered *Freight*

The Great Train Robbery was a well-advertised match race between 17-year-old Billy "the Kid" Scott and engineer Goob Tuller, who drove the twin-engine Chevrolet **Freight Train** *of John Peters. Scott was the driver of the* **Beacon Auto Parts** *Top Gas dragster. Here, Tuller and Scott act out a wild West robbery scene for the crowd. (Jere Aldereff Photography/Courtesy Lions Automobilia Foundation Museum)*

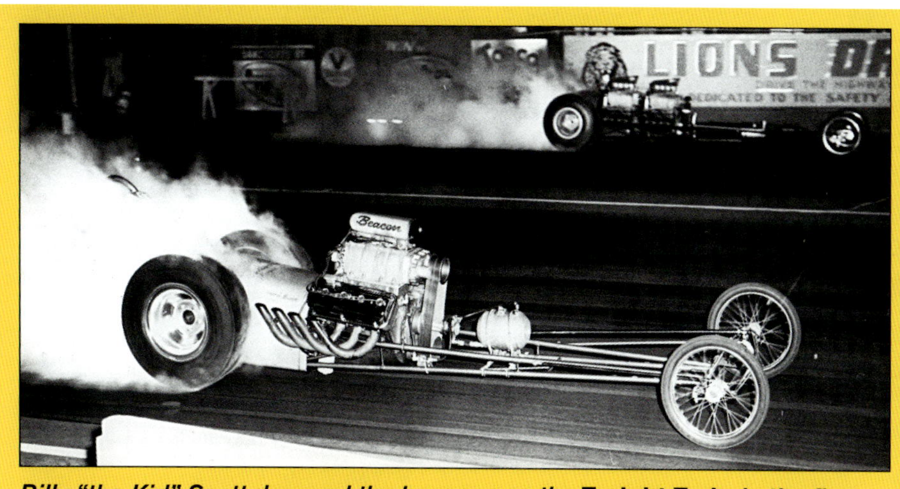

Billy "the Kid" Scott dropped the hammer on the **Freight Train** *in the first round with a 7.94 ET at 189.06 mph to Goob Tuller's 8.00 ET at 179.64 mph. (Jere Aldereff Photography/Courtesy Lions Automobilia Foundation Museum)*

Train of Tuller & Peters. The *Freight Train* made it to the starting line first with engineer Goob Tuller in the seat. In 8 seconds, the first round was over, as Scott's 7.94 ET at 189.06 mph gave his *Beacon Auto Parts Special* the win over Tuller's 8.00 ET at 179.64 mph. The Kid derailed the *Freight Train* in two out of the three rounds.

The Gathering of the Monsters

With 18 years in the drag racing fraternity, Mickey Thompson was one of the nation's most respected names in the speed automotive manufacturing industry. To show his appreciation for the racers who had supported his products, Thompson organized and promoted an exclusive club of dragsters that could run more than 200 mph. Lions Drag Strip hosted the second-annual Mickey Thompson 200-MPH Club Meet on November 12.

More than 100 Top Fuelers, Top Gas, and Jr. Fuel Dragsters were on hand from across the country, including New York, Oklahoma, Florida, and Texas. During the one-day event, they competed for a share of the $20,000 in cash prizes. Not to be overlooked, two of the top nation's Funny Car drivers, "Dyno" Don Nicholson from Georgia and Arnie "the Farmer" Beswick from Illinois, highlighted this premiere marquee match race.

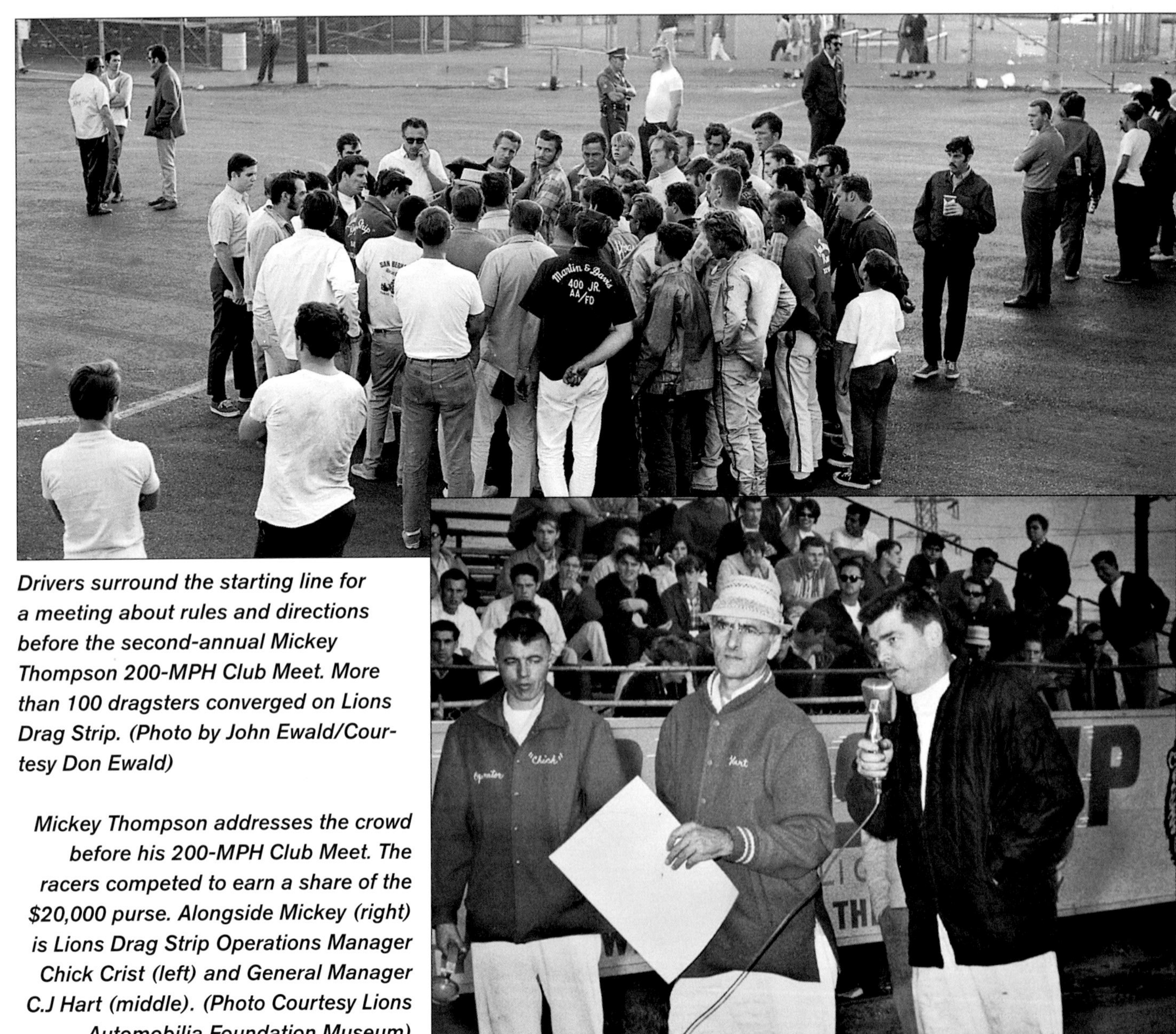

Drivers surround the starting line for a meeting about rules and directions before the second-annual Mickey Thompson 200-MPH Club Meet. More than 100 dragsters converged on Lions Drag Strip. (Photo by John Ewald/Courtesy Don Ewald)

Mickey Thompson addresses the crowd before his 200-MPH Club Meet. The racers competed to earn a share of the $20,000 purse. Alongside Mickey (right) is Lions Drag Strip Operations Manager Chick Crist (left) and General Manager C.J Hart (middle). (Photo Courtesy Lions Automobilia Foundation Museum)

Bob Muravez accepts the celebratory handshake from Mickey Thompson after he won Top Fuel Eliminator at the second-annual Mickey Thompson 200-MPH Club Meet at Lions Drag Strip. Muravez, also known as Floyd Lippencott Jr., drove Don Johnson's AA/FD past Neil Leffler in the **A&W Root Beer Special** *with a 7.32 ET at 195.22 mph to Leffler's 7.80 ET at 212.26 mph. Some of the members partaking in the festivities are (left to right) Johnny Seagraves, car owner Don Johnson, Muravez, Mrs. Don Johnson, Ed Pink, "Famous" Amos Satterlee, and Thompson. (Jere Aldereff Photography/Courtesy Lions Automobilia Foundation Museum)*

Funny Car Weekend

The second-annual Drag Racing Magazine Invitational East-West Funny Car Championships expanded to a two-day event on November 26 and 27. It featured more than 60 Funny Cars of the injected and fuel-burning types.

Saturday night's affair featured the stars of the A/FX injected match racing from the best of the East versus the best of the West in 14 best-of-5 match races.

The East roster included the powerhouse Mercury Comets of Eddie Schartman and "Dyno" Don Nicholson, Pete Seaton's *Seaton's Shaker*, Sox & Martin, the *Bronco Buster* Ford Bronco, and Roger Lindamood's *Color Me Gone* Dodge Charger. The West team was anchored by Hayden Proffitt, the *Melrose Missile*, Gas Ronda, Dick Landy, and Charlie Allen.

West Sweeps Championships

The race attracted a record crowd of 23,000 fans for the two-day weekend that featured round-robin match racing with added circus music from a steam-powered calliope (a musical instrument with large whistles that uses steam to make sound). The Saturday afternoon and evening show opened the round-robin East versus West competition, and the stars from the East prevailed with five wins over the West's two, and each team split two ties.

Memories

Bob Muravez

Second-Annual Mickey Thompson 200-MPH Club Meet Winner

"There were 117 Top Fuel cars that entered at that time. Mickey said any car that ran over 200 mph anywhere on this planet was prequalified, so there was no qualification at all. When you came in through the gates, you were basically put on a roster or a ladder of sorts. There were seven rounds of eliminations. The bad part of that was no one knew a lot of guys towed with their buddy in another car behind them, so many of them raced against their buddies in the first round. Had they known they were put on a ladder or without qualifying, they would have come in separately.

"After we won the ADRA Winternationals race in Vegas against McEwen and McCourry, we showed up at Lions [Drag Strip] with a brand-new car built by Roy Fjastad of Race Car Specialties. The car had never made a pass down the drag strip, and Ed Pink was doing the motor work. We won the race going through the seven rounds of eliminations. I wrenched my back in the third round, so I couldn't get out of the race car. My dear friend Johnny Seagraves, who ended up being the godfather to one of my children, always packed my parachutes. Through all of the racing I've done throughout my career, Johnny always packed my parachute.

"I made enough money driving for Don Johnson for the six or seven months to buy a house. I got 25 percent plus expenses for every race, and I think that my part for winning the 200-mph race was $3,000. I bought my house with a $5,000 down payment, so if the circumstances fall into place, you can win money in racing."

SIXTY SIXTY SIXTY SIXTY SIXTY SIXTY SIXTY SIXTY SIXTY SIXTY SIXTY SIXTY

THESE ARE THE  FUNNY CARS

Appearing this SATURDAY and SUNDAY at

DRAG RACING MAGAZINE'S

EAST–WEST STOCKER CHAMPIONSHIPS....

AT LIONS

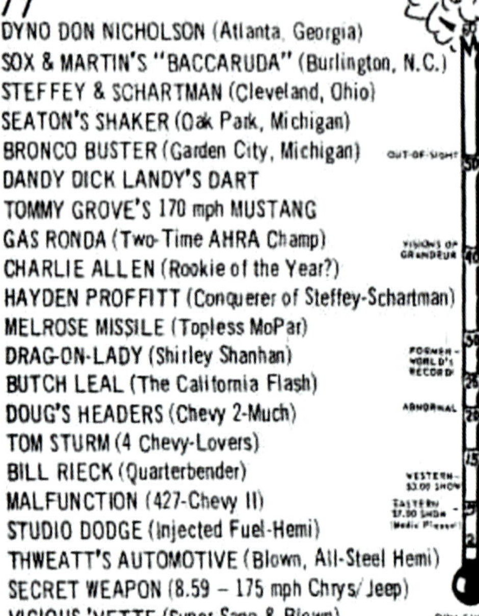

DYNO DON NICHOLSON (Atlanta, Georgia)
SOX & MARTIN'S "BACCARUDA" (Burlington, N.C.)
STEFFEY & SCHARTMAN (Cleveland, Ohio)
SEATON'S SHAKER (Oak Park, Michigan)
BRONCO BUSTER (Garden City, Michigan)
DANDY DICK LANDY'S DART
TOMMY GROVE'S 170 mph MUSTANG
GAS RONDA (Two-Time AHRA Champ)
CHARLIE ALLEN (Rookie of the Year?)
HAYDEN PROFFITT (Conquerer of Steffey-Schartman)
MELROSE MISSILE (Topless MoPar)
DRAG-ON-LADY (Shirley Shanhan)
BUTCH LEAL (The California Flash)
DOUG'S HEADERS (Chevy 2-Much)
TOM STURM (4 Chevy-Lovers)
BILL RIECK (Quarterbender)
MALFUNCTION (427-Chevy II)
STUDIO DODGE (Injected Fuel-Hemi)
THWEATT'S AUTOMOTIVE (Blown, All-Steel Hemi)
SECRET WEAPON (8.59 – 175 mph Chrys/Jeep)
VICIOUS 'VETTE (Super-Sano & Blown)

DRM FUNNY CAR THERMOMETER

MR. NORM (Chicago-Charger & Dodge)
ARNIE BESWICK (2 Illinois Pontiacs)
TEXAS DON GAY (Infinity II)
BRUTUS (West Coast Champ!)
JACK CHRISMAN'S COMET
LIBERMAN-COYLE CHEVY II
CORVETTE AUTO PARTS (Gypsy)
STEVE BOVAN (Blair's Chevy II)
FLYING DUTCHMAN
TERRIFYING TORONADO
STINGER II (192 mph Chrys/Astra)
WAGONMASTER (4-Engine Wagon)
CONNERS' VW (Wheelie-Wagen)
CHUCK POOLE (Chuck Wagon)
PRECISION ENG. (Chevy-VW)
C&O-CIAMBELA (Navy Jeep)
FEROCIOUS FROG
BLUE HELL 'VETTE
MR. PICKETT 'VETTE
SUPERSEDAN
DALE ARMSTRONG'S "CANUCK"

Plus! 1st. Time Anywhere; Stone–Woods –Cook's All–New '67 Funny Mustang!

WARNING! THIS WILL BE THE ONLY WEST COAST APPEARANCE OF THE FOLLOWING CARS...

HUBERT PLATT
HUSTON PLATT
THE VIRGINIAN
KELLY CHADWICK
BILL IRELAND
CLESTER ANDREWS
KINGFISH—REYES

COLOR-ME-GONE
GENE SNOW
DICK LOEHR
AMT/PIRANHA
BILL SHREWSBERRY
NICKEY CAMARO'S
—IN—
SPECIAL MATCH RACES

CONTINGENCY AWARDS
Not Previously Mentioned

DOUG'S HEADERS – Custom-Built

FAT FOSTER – $200 Merchandise

CYCLONE SALES – Special Drawing

KEYSTONE MAGS – Set of Four

MICKEY THOMPSON – $500

FLASH—WORLD'S PREMIERE: DICKIE HARRELL'S NEW FUNNY CAMARO!!!

DRAG RACING MAGAZINE CAR OF THE YEAR AWARD TO BE GIVEN TO ? SUNDAY

LIONS DRAG STRIP
223rd & ALAMEDA, WILMINGTON
PHONE 424-0961

$3.00 ADMISSION EACH DAY

IMPORTANT: NO E.T. BRACKETS WILL BE RUN THIS WEEKEND! NO HYDRAZINE!!

DON'T BE FOOLED. NEVER BEFORE AND NEVER AGAIN...60 CONSTANT FUNNY CARS

This flyer advertised the largest Funny Car show to date, which featured 60 injected and blown fuel entries at Lions Drag Strip. C. J. Hart had the knack for promoting events that the fans loved.

Saturday's match races during the two-day Drag Racing Magazine Invitational East-West Stocker Championships featured "Dyno" Don Nicholson and "Fast" Eddie Schartman. Here, Nicholson waits in the staging lanes for the command to fire up the Mercury Comet. (Jere Aldereff Photography/Courtesy Lions Automobilia Foundation Museum)

These two protestors use a sign to show their displeasure regarding the Funny Car movement. The popularity and demand for the circus cars swept across the country like wildfire and drew crowds. (Photo Courtesy Don Prieto)

Before he had the nickname "Jungle," Jim Liberman was a young, up-and-coming Funny Car star. Liberman displayed his driving abilities at the Drag Racing Magazine East-West Stocker Championships. His blown Chevy II gave "Dyno" Don Nicholson the best races of his West Coast trip with an 8.69 ET at 163.93 mph and an 8.44 ET at 167.91 mph to Nicholson's 8.99 ET at 163.00 mph and an 8.65 ET at 165.44 mph. (Jere Aldereff Photography/Courtesy Lions Automobilia Foundation Museum)

Bob Davis's 1965 Chevrolet Impala wasn't your average family car, and it sure made noise in the quarter mile with ETs in less than 8 seconds and thundering speeds around 170 mph. Davis's **Jolly Green Giant** *began as an A/S car before it made the transformation to run a blown big-block Chevrolet and compete on the West Coast as a match racer. Expert driver Denny Savage spent time behind the wheel of Davis's Impala and the* **Jolly Green Giant** *Corvette. (Jere Aldereff Photography/Courtesy Lions Automobilia Foundation Museum)*

The **Kingfish** *Barracuda was driven by Larry Reyes and ran under the Bill Taylor Racing Enterprises banner in Memphis, Tennessee. (Jere Aldereff Photography/Courtesy Lions Automobilia Foundation Museum)*

Hayden Proffitt drove a 1965 Mercury Comet earlier in the year and received backing from the factory. He was then released by Mercury Racing Executives Al Turner and Fran Hernandez. So, Proffitt raced in a Chevrolet as an unsponsored independent. The decision by Mercury proved to be profitable for Proffitt, as he got his revenge at the second-annual Drag Racing Magazine Invitational East-West Championships. The Ford-backed Mustang of Gas Ronda failed to start, which gave Proffitt the win.

Sunday's Mr. Factory Stock show featured the 2,500-plus-pound cars running both injectors and superchargers. Gas Ronda, Don Gay, Dick Landy, Roger Wolford's *Secret Weapon* Jeep, Hayden Proffitt, Jim Liberman driving both his Chevy II and Lew Arrington's *Brutus* GTO, Arnie Beswick, the *AMT Piranha*, and dozens more entertained the fans.

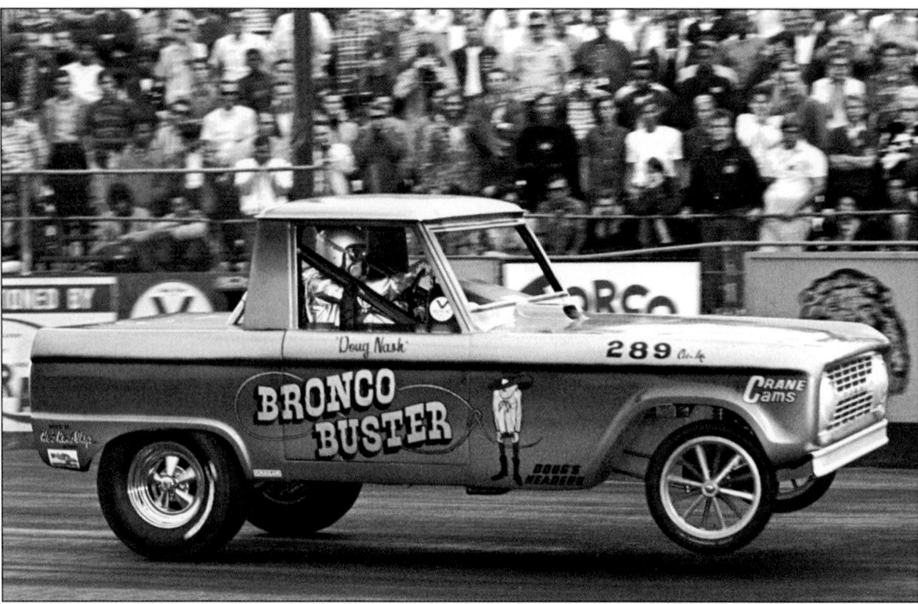

From Garden City, Michigan, Doug Nash's 1966 Ford Bronco* Bronco Buster *ran the smallest-displacement engine at the Drag Racing Magazine Invitational East-West Championships. The stock-block 289-ci Ford engine was fitted midyear with a blower that was shoehorned into the all-aluminum chassis. The Bronco was in high demand on the match-race circuit, but its erratic handling made the Bronco top out around the 8.30 ET at 180 mph range. (Jere Aldereff Photography/Courtesy Lions Automobilia Foundation Museum)

Revenge of the Old Man

Saturday's racing was ruled by the "Old Man" Hayden Proffitt. His performance at this event was his all-time career best. He soundly disposed of Charlie Allen's *Atlantic* Dodge Dart in the first round with an 8.63 ET to Allen's 8.83 ET.

Proffitt earned a single run in the second round with the quickest ET from the previous round (an 8.49 ET at 161.57 mph) in his Corvair. In round three, he met his toughest adversary yet: Ronnie Sox.

Proffitt opened a four-car-length holeshot against the Sox & Martin Barracuda and never looked back, posting an 8.52 ET at 160.11 mph. Archrival Gas Ronda met Proffitt in the final round.

This classic Ford versus Chevy finish had an interesting twist that unfolded several months earlier when Proffitt was dropped by Al Turner and Fran Hernandez (the leading men on the Mercury Comet program), leaving Proffitt without sponsorship. When Proffitt came up to the line, he requested the microphone from announcer Jon Lundberg, and, over the public-announcement system, he dedicated the race to Turner and Hernandez.

The standing-room-only crowd screamed and yelled with delight. Lundberg played up the crowd of the Ford and Chevy rivalry for the final run, but it was anticlimactic when Gas Ronda's Mustang failed to start. Proffitt seized the moment with a single run by producing a giant, 7-foot wheel-stand while waving to the crowd.

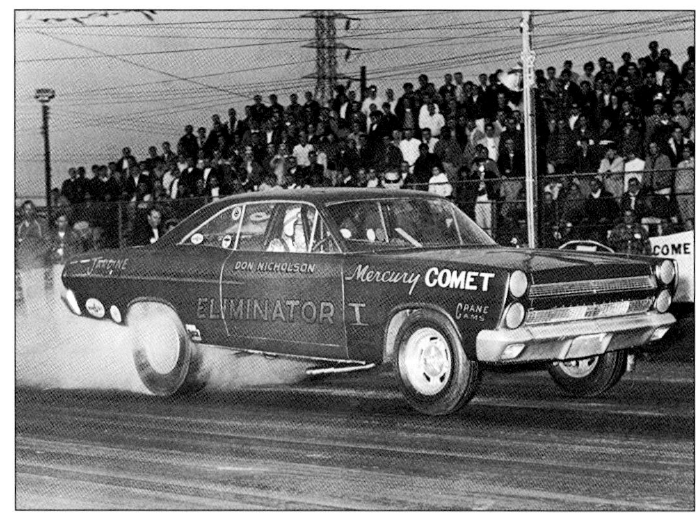

In the second round in the match race of the Comets, "Dyno" Don Nicholson would have beaten Eddie Schartman with a 8.35 ET at 170.13 mph, but he set off the red light. (Jere Aldereff Photography/Courtesy Lions Automobilia Foundation Museum)

Supercharged Phenomena

Sunday's Supercharged Eliminator featured a selection of the nation's top blown nitro Funny Cars, including Mr. Norm's new Dodge Charger, Jack Chrisman, the *Kingfish* Barracuda driven by Larry Reyes, Don Gay's *Infinity II* GTO, Arnie Beswick, the *Secret Weapon* Jeep, Jim Liberman, the *Flying Dutchman* of Al Vanderwoude,

Don Gay's 1966 Pontiac GTO **Infinity** *gave the crowd a reason to stand up and cheer, as Lions Drag Strip's track bite produced 4-foot wheelies. The young Texan gunslinger competed in the UL Fuel class and lost in the second round to Roger Wilford's* **Secret Weapon** *Jeep. Wilford ran an 8.81 ET at 171.02 mph to Gay's quicker-but-losing 8.69 ET at 179.12 mph. (Jere Aldereff Photography/Courtesy Lions Automobilia Foundation Museum)*

Lew Arrington pumps a stream of gas into the injectors to fire up his Hemi-powered **Brutus** *Funny Car with driver Jim Liberman in the seat. The West Coast blown Funny Car champ drew Hubert Platt and his* **Georgia Shaker** *Mustang as an opponent for a best-of-three match race. Liberman's chance for victory was slim, as the GTO had been hampered with engine problems throughout the weekend, and he bowed out after round one, which gave two straight wins to the* **Georgia Shaker***. (Jere Aldereff Photography/Courtesy Lions Automobilia Foundation Museum)*

"General" Roger Wilford and "Private" Lenarth's **Secret Weapon** *Hemi-powered Jeep pulled off a near impossible win in Sunday's Fuel Eliminator and defeated Al Vanderwoude's* **Flying Dutchman** *in the finals. Wilford set the top speed of the meet for Funny Cars against Vanderwoude with a 176.81-mph run to capture the prize money. (Jere Aldereff Photography/Courtesy Lions Automobilia Foundation Museum)*

Hubert Platt, and Lew Arrington's *Brutus* GTO.

Also included was the return of Saturday's match race cars to run head-to-head in eliminations. Lions Drag Strip was one to enforce the strip's strict rule policies, especially for this race. A maximum of 100-pound ballast was used to make class, no hydrazine fuel was allowed, protective shields were required for all transmissions, and rigid tech inspections were conducted by Jay Howell.

The featured match race of the one-offs saw the versatile Connie Swingle take two of the three clashes in the AMT **Piranha** *against Gary Southern in the Akins & Hardcastle* **Stinger II** *Astra. Swingle's third-round run in the fish was the quickest and fastest pass (an 8.29 ET at 196.92 mph) at the Drag Racing Magazine Invitational East-West Championships. (Jere Aldereff Photography/ Courtesy Lions Automobilia Foundation Museum)*

Pow! Bang! Boom!

From Gotham City, the most famous car on television was the *Batmobile*, which was created by George Barris. The *Batmobile*'s only visit to Southern California was at Lions Drag Strip, with "Wild" Bill Shrewsberry filling in for Batman.

Sharing the card with the Barris creation was a pair of eight-car fields of Fuel Altereds and A/Gas Supercharged race cars. Leroy Chadderton won the AA/FA class with an 8.76 ET at 136.00 mph to defeat Bob Walker, who broke at the starting line.

The last run in A/GS was the wildest race of the evening. It was between the *Herrera & Sons* Austin and Gary Densham's *Agitator* Willys. Both cars pulled giant wheel-stands, and the Austin landed down first—roughly 50 feet out of the gate. When the Austin landed, its right front wheel broke off and landed behind the Willys. The fans were lucky to get out of the way without being hurt. Densham, on the other hand, won the race, but it was costly, as he hit hard when he came

Sunday's program had three special match races: 1) the number-one showdown of the Comets between "Dyno" Don Nicholson and the team of Roy Steffey & "Fast" Eddie Schartman, 2) AMT's *Piranha* against the *Stinger II*, and 3) "Wild" Bill Shrewsberry and Chuck Poole's *Chuckwagon* in a battle of wheel-standers.

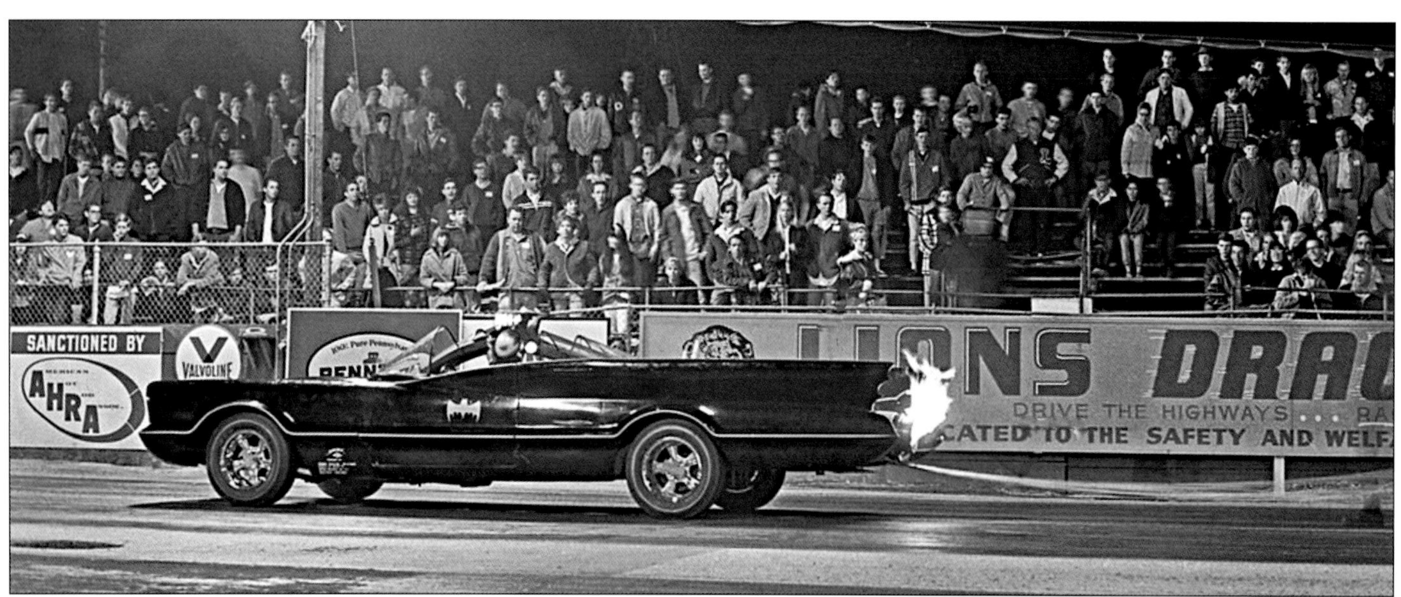

"Wild" Bill Shrewsberry picked Lions Drag Strip to showcase George Barris's **Batmobile** *for its only appearance on the West Coast. The car was powered by a Holman & Moody–prepped 500-hp, 428-ci engine connected to a Ford C-6 transmission. Shrewsberry made a total of three runs at Lions Drag Strip and operated all of the bells and whistles, including running the blue, red, and yellow police lights; shooting 10-foot flames out of the afterburner; emitting clouds of smoke from the bat tires; and deploying the bat chutes on the return trip up the strip after the last run.*

down from his wheelie and damaged the front end.

The sound system blared the *Batman* theme song when the *Batmobile* and a custom El Dorado assist rolled to the line. Shrewsberry lit up the police lights, and the afterburner shot out a steady flame with clouds of smoke. He was off to solve a crime!

United States Professional Dragster Championships

Dragsters were the real deal when promoter Doug Kruse organized and operated the first-annual United States Professional Dragster Championships at Lions Drag Strip on July 15, 1967. More than 16,200 fans shoehorned their way through the gates and witnessed one of the greatest Fuel shows ever staged.

Top Fuel, Gas, and Jr. Fuel cars pulled off the most successful all-dragster, one-day meet at Lions Drag Strip. More than 125 dragsters from as far away from New York packed the pits for a share of the $28,000 purse. The event featured nonstop action that began early in the morning.

The action was at a rapid pace, as all of the top pros gathered, including Chris Karamesines, Don Prudhomme, Chuck Kurzawa's *Ramchargers*, Pete Robinson, Roland Leong, Bob Creitz, Jerry Ruth, Tom McEwen, Danny Ongais, Pete Robinson, Jeep Hampshire, and roughly 50 more in Top Fuel alone.

After the smoke cleared from qualifying, the break ratio left a total of 60 dragsters. They began the quest up the ladder for the $5,100 cash prize for winning Top Fuel Eliminator. The number of cars represented the highest number and the most competitive field since the early days at Bakersfield, and it was the fastest 60-car field ever assembled for the single-day meet.

"Our focus in the beginning was to prove that dragsters alone could still put on a top professional

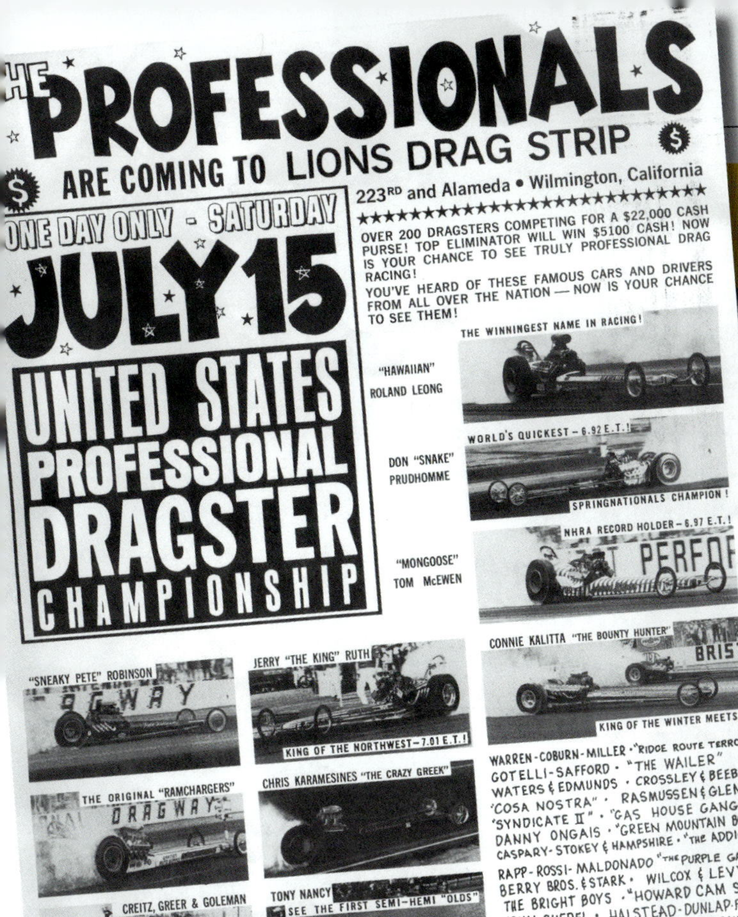

The largest one-day dragster event on the planet featured more than 100-plus Top Fuel, Top Gas, and injected machines at Lions Drag Strip.

Don Prudhomme (left) and Tom McEwen stare down each other in this promotional photo for the United States Professional Dragster Championships at Lions Drag Strip. Prudhomme and McEwen were both primed to win Top Fuel at the one-day championship meet. Promoter Doug Kruse (middle) fulfilled his dream with his first attempt of organizing and operating the one-day super meet for all dragsters, which was a first in drag racing history. (Jere Aldereff Photography/Lions Automobilia Foundation Museum)

Dave Beebe ended Jerry Bivens's hopes to move forward into round four when Beebe reeled off a 7.05 ET at 205 mph against Bivens & Fisher's up-in-smoke run that forced Bivens to shut off early. (Jere Aldereff Photography/ Courtesy Lions Automobilia Foundation Museum)

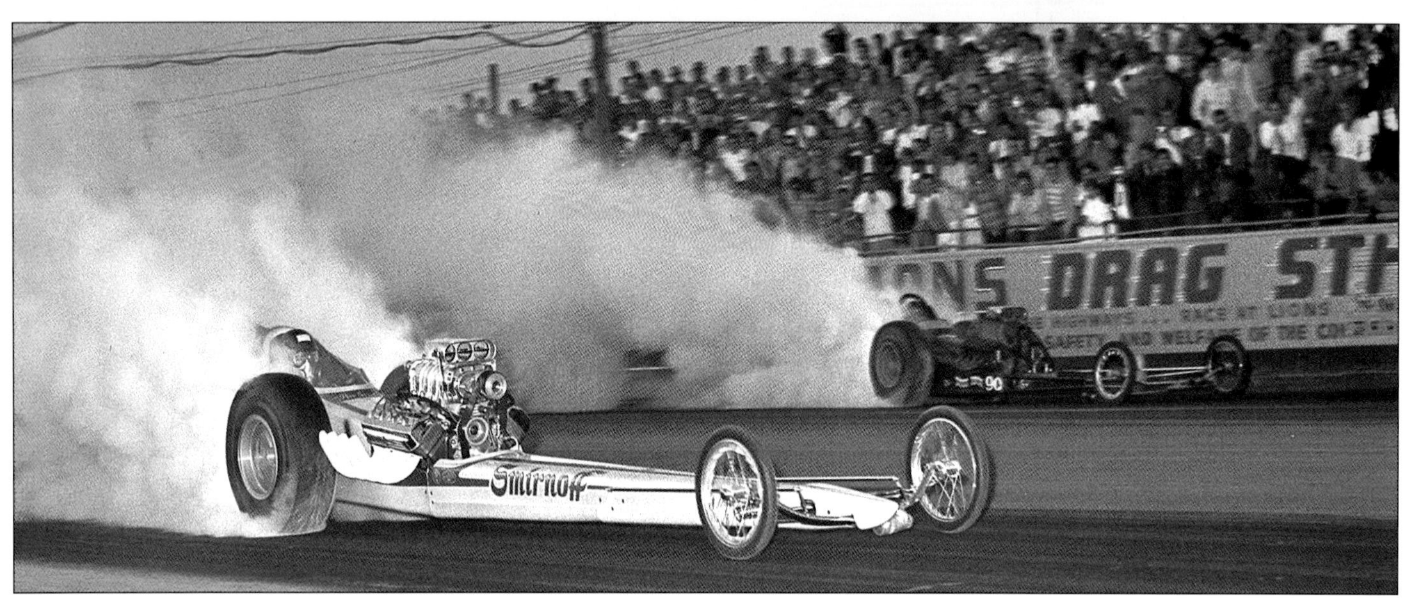

Larry Dixon tied James Warren with a 7.01 run that was the low ET of the meet. With a 7.57 ET, Dixon drove the **Smirnoff Special** *of Darryl Greenamier past the Bob Brooks & Doss Brothers' lone Chevrolet entry. (Jere Aldereff Photography/ Courtesy Lions Automobilia Foundation Museum)*

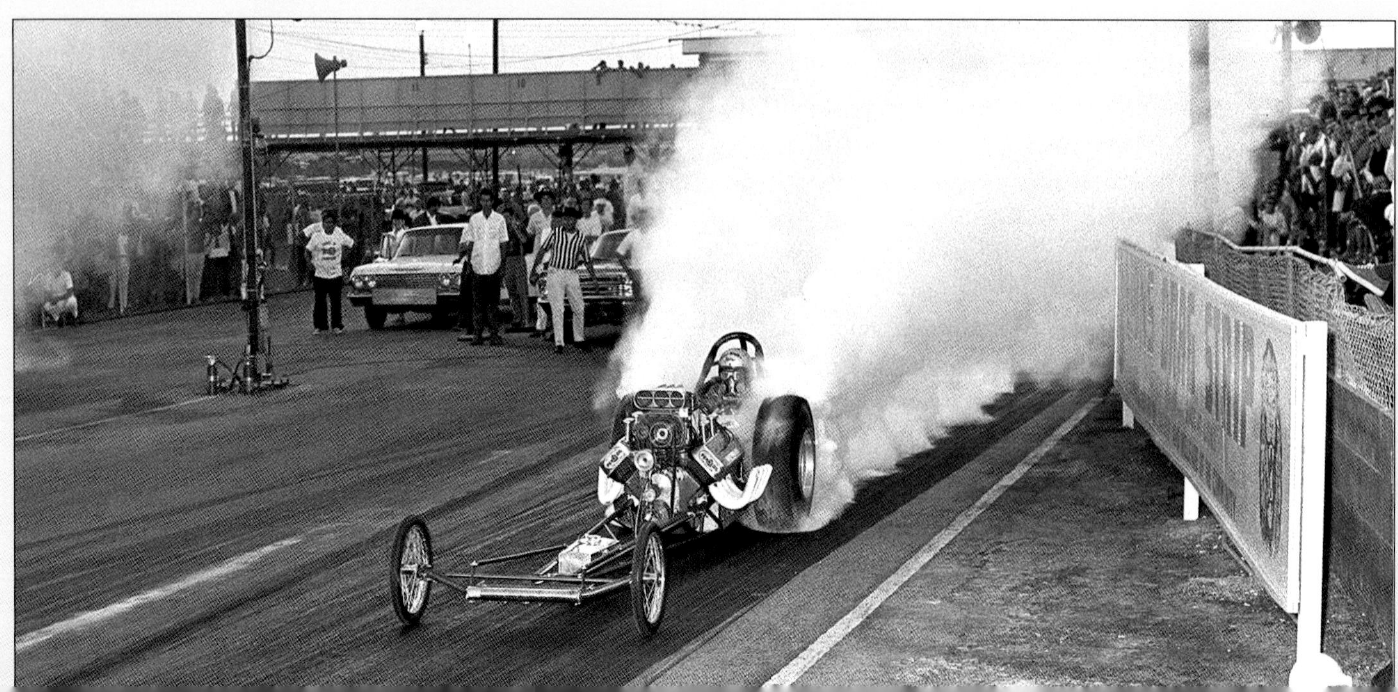

Memories
Bob Muravez
Second-Annual Mickey Thompson 200-MPH Club Meet Winner

"I have many, many memories at Lions Drag Strip. My first pass down the strip was in my 1953 Corvette in 1955 or 1956. Later, I partnered with Don Gaide, where I put my first motor in a dragster and Ed Janke's #3 Fuller car. Finally, I was hired to drive the *Quincy Automotive* car, which later became the *Freight Train*.

"I just got back into driving the #2 *Train* in 1967 before going to Bristol, Tennessee, for the NHRA Springnationals, where we won Top Gas. The following week, we went to Lions Drag Strip, where we met up with Tom McEwen and Marvin Richen of M&H tires. At that time, we were sponsored by Goodyear. Richen gave [me] a set of M&H slicks to try out on the *Train*. In the first round, I let the clutch out, and the car incredibly hooked up and made a pass (a 7.31 ET at 201 mph) that broke my old record (a 7.70 ET at 192 mph). Because of the new tires, the car ran light-years faster than it ever had before. It was almost as fast as the Top Fuel cars."

show," said Kruse. "And the fans agreed that it's well worth it to continue."

Nitro and Smoke

Records were set and reset throughout the course of the event. One of them took place in the first round with Tom McEwen's 7.09 ET at 222.79 mph. However, James "the Ridge Route Terror" Warren, soon bested McEwen with a 7.01 ET at 227.50 mph for his best run of the evening. Warren followed with runs of 226 and 225 mph in the second and third rounds before being ousted by eventual runner-up John Mulligan.

The real surprise was in Top Gas when Bob

The **Freight Train** *of John Peters and driver Bob Muravez had everything lined up perfectly with the stars at the United States Professional Dragster Championships. Muravez won Top Gas Eliminator, set low ET and top speed for the meet, and was the first gas dragster in drag racing to top 200 mph with an unbelievable 7.34 ET at 201 mph. For their efforts, Peters & Muravez netted more than $5,000. (Jere Aldereff Photography/Courtesy Lions Automobilia Foundation Museum)*

Facing page: The Ridge Route Terrors of Warren, Colburn, & Miller shared the low ET of the meet with Larry Dixon with a 7.01 and set the top speed at 227.50 mph. Dark horse James Warren lost to Beebe & Mulligan in the fourth round when Mulligan wowed the crowd with a holeshot and a 7.50 ET at 216.44 mph to Warren's 7.38 ET at 225.00 mph. (Jere Aldereff Photography/ Courtesy Lions Automobilia Foundation Museum)

Muravez (also known as Floyd Lippencott Jr.) drove John Peters's *Freight Train* to a 7.34 ET at 201 mph. Muravez returned in the following round with a run of 7.51 ET to back up his earlier run for the record. Muravez rolled onward to defeat two of the class's toughest competitors: Tony Nancy and Tom Larkin.

The meeting had something for everyone, including controversy. One incident was that the break rule was removed for this event only. In the semifinal round, John "Zookeeper" Mulligan defeated Don Prudhomme, but Prudhomme was reinstated to run in the final round in a rematch against Mulligan. Prudhomme turned the table and won his second match against Mulligan and took the championship title.

Freight Train *Whistles for Win*

Twenty-four entries attempted to make the 16-car Top Gas Eliminator field, and Bob Muravez led the way from start to finish.

In the first round of eliminations, Muravez eased the clutch, produced no tire smoke, and ran the world's quickest ET and top speed for a gas-power dragster (7.34 at 201.34 mph) over Rick Ramsey, who was driving for the Porsche Brothers. Ramsey opened a small lead off the line against Muravez, but the *Freight Train* caught up to and passed its opponent well before mid-track and went on to cross the finish stripes to set the record. This was the second big victory of the year for the *Freight Train*.

Pink versus Black

C. J. Hart, the mastermind who organized the most unique attractions in drag racing, brought together Keith Black, Ed Pink, and their most compatible virtuosos in the sport. The team of Roland Leong, Mike Snively, and Mike Sorokin were with Black, while Tom McEwen and Don Prudhomme joined Pink in the match race of the year.

Keith Black's name was synonymous with consistency and durability, while Pink had a highly reputable knowledge for his engine performance that produced low elapsed times and tremendous top-end velocities.

Leong's Hemi-powered *Hawaiian* and *Hawaiian II* represented Black, while Lou Baney's Ford-powered SOHC 427 Cammer *Super Snake* was piloted by Prudhomme. McEwen filled the seat in the *Bivens & Fisher* entry that was powered by an Ed Pink Hemi.

Not only was it the battle of the engine builders but it also drew the representatives from the Goodyear and M&H tire companies as well as chassis builders Kent Fuller, Don Long, and Woody Gilmore.

The race was a measure in the tire theories between Goodyear and M&H regarding who could best handle the tremendous output of horsepower of these fuel-burning beasts. Both tire companies felt that they had the best product. Both *Hawaiians* and Baney's *Super Snake* rode on Goodyear tires, while McEwen was the only M&H representative.

While the engine-builder and chassis-builder competitions were entertaining and competitive, the racing ended in a tie. However, the Goodyear tires posted more wins than M&H.

Lions Drag Strip had a history of promoting the top names and stars for the high-profile match races, but this one beat them all. Rivals Tom McEwen and Don Prudhomme teamed up with the "Old Master" Ed Pink to counter Roland Leong's **Hawaiian** *and* **Hawaiian II** *Top Fuelers. Here, Mike Snively accelerates off the line. (Jere Aldereff Photography/ Courtesy Lions Automobilia Foundation Museum)*

Don Prudhomme replaces a section of 200-mph duct tape on Lou Baney's **Super Snake** *Top Fuel dragster. Weaving the tape through the front spokes secured the aluminum disc ring so that it would trip both staging and timing beams.*

East versus West

The conclusion of the NHRA U.S. Indy Nationals on Labor Day signaled the start of the migration of the big cars to the West Coast for what is considered to be the second racing season of the year (September through November).

Lions Drag Strip was a favorite stop for many Midwestern and Eastern high-profile All-Stars who drew spectators while they made their bids to scoop up the large cash payouts.

One notable annual event at Lions Drag Strip was the third-annual East versus West Funny Car Team Championships. This year's event was on November 4 and had a total of 27 nitro entries with 10 seeded cars on each team's roster. An additional seven cars were added as standbys that were ready to fill the void if one of the team cars couldn't make the call to the line.

The East team was anchored by captain "Dyno" Don Nicholson along with Terry Hendrick, Dick Harrell, the Farkonas-Coil-Minick's *Chi-Town Hustler*, "Fast" Eddie Schartman, Kelly Chadwick, Roger Lindamood, Clester Andrews, Pete Gates, Dick Loehr, and Ron O'Donnell's *Chapman Automotive* Camaro.

The West squad was mostly comprised of California cars led by captain "Jungle" Jim Liberman along with Don Sappington, Clare Sanders, Jack Chrisman, Butch "the California Flash" Leal, Charlie Allen,

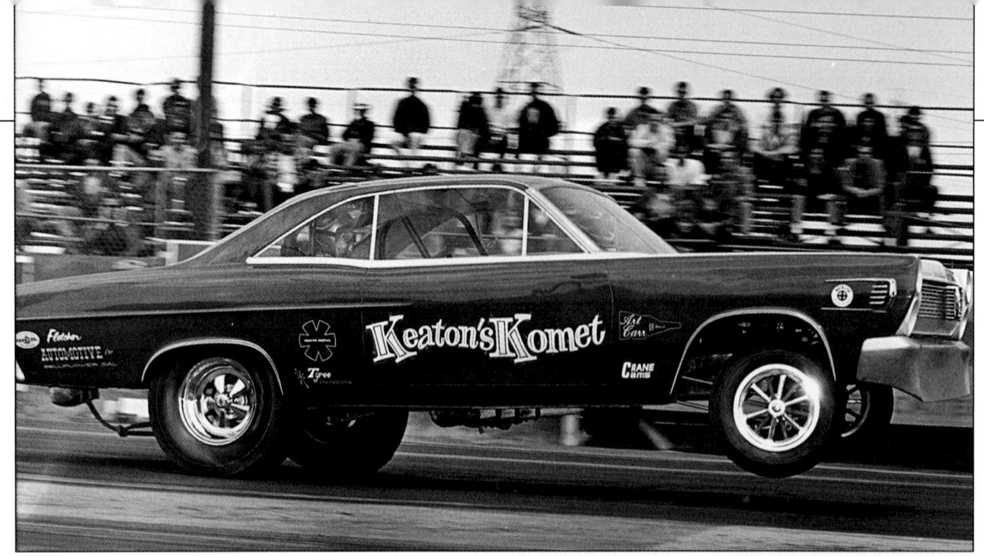

Dee Keaton found that the bite at Lions Drag Strip was a little too aggressive for his flip-top Comet, as he pulled a giant wheel-stand against the "Professor" Kelly Chadwick. Keaton recorded no ET or top speed after landing hard and stopping before the time trap lights. (Jere Aldereff Photography/Courtesy Lions Automobilia Foundation Museum)

Cecil Yother, Tommy Grove, Lew Arrington, and Al Vanderwoude. The standbys consisted of Dee Keaton, the team of Montrelli-Williams-Barrett, Fred Goeske, Ronnie Runyan, and Clyde Morgan.

C. J. Hart set the tone at the third-annual East versus West Funny Car meet and proclaimed, "We're going to run them until they drop."

During the hours before the three rounds of match races commenced, thousands of Funny Car fans backed up the traffic on the San Diego Freeway for more than three miles and forced a half-hour delay of the 7 p.m. starting time. Approximately 13,000 highly spirited fans packed the bleachers to capacity when the first pair of the 24 cars fired up.

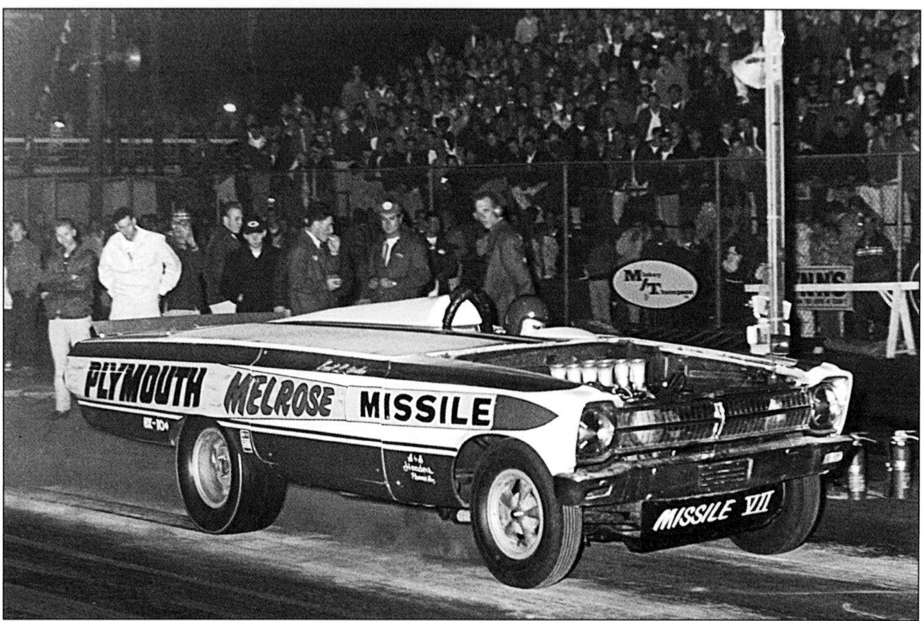

Exiting from out of the rosin, Cecil Yother, who was from Oakland, California, won the #2 Eliminator in his **Melrose Missile** *Plymouth roadster with an ET of 9.59. Yother's opponent was Roger Lindamood, whose* **Color Me Gone** *Dodge Charger headed straight toward the guard rail and shut off. (Jere Aldereff Photography/Courtesy Lions Automobilia Foundation Museum)*

Round 1

Dick Harrell, running under the East banner, was up against the West's Al Vanderwoude's *Flying Dutchman*

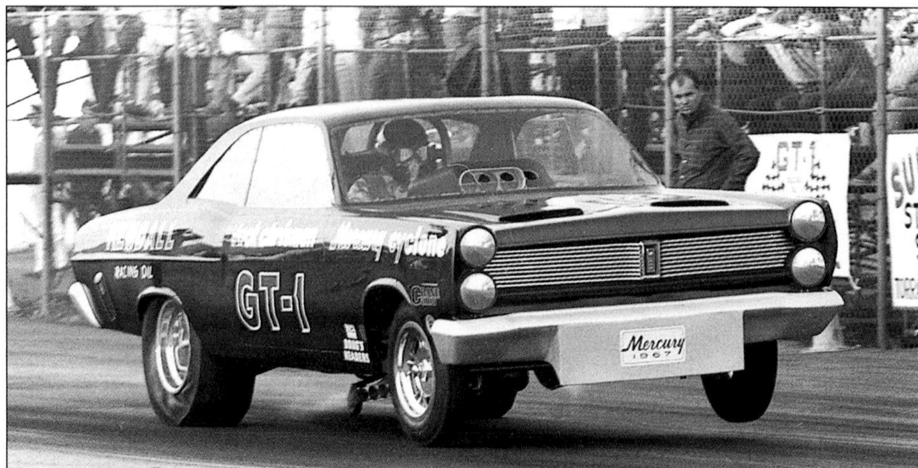

Trading opponents and broken components, Jack Chrisman took an early lead over Dick Harrell and never looked back to earn a point for the West squad with a 8.30 ET at 182.92 mph to Harrell's 8.50 ET at 181.08 mph. Harrell's second week of running a blower was a work in progress. (Jere Aldereff Photography/Courtesy Lions Automobilia Foundation Museum)

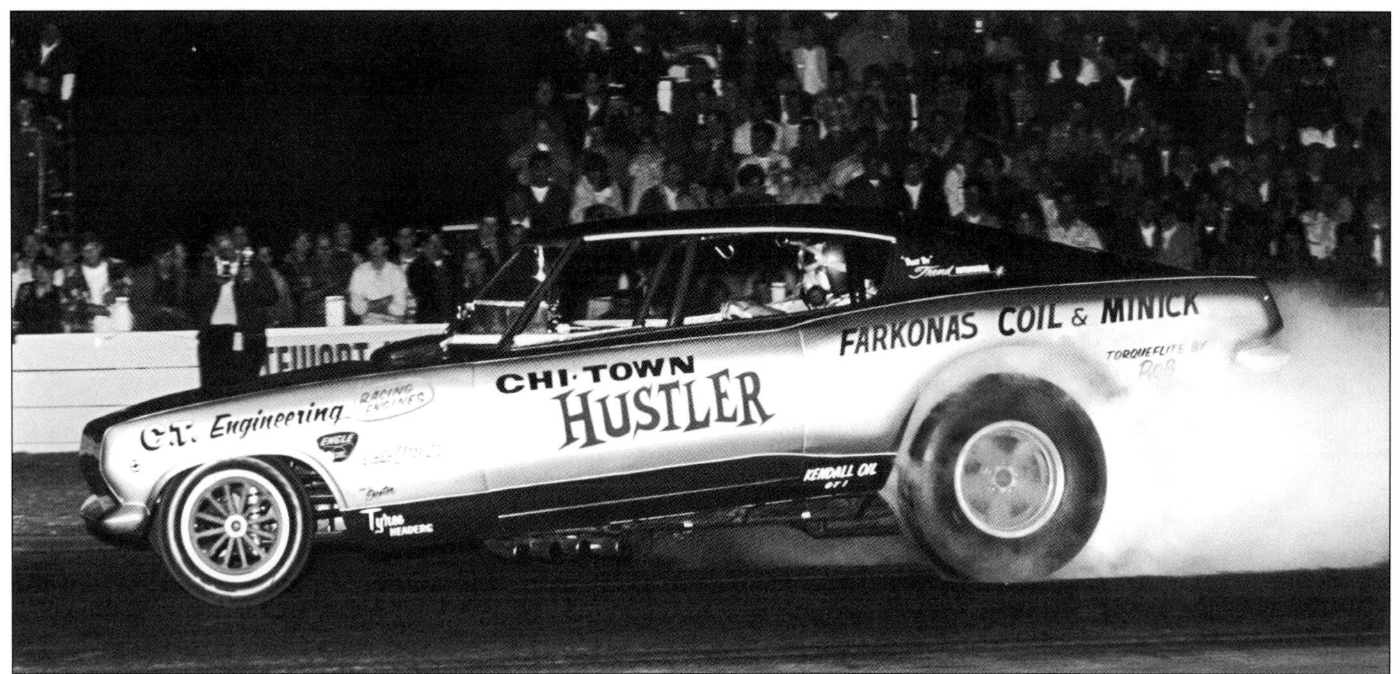

Chicago was home to some of the greatest racers in drag racing, including Chris Karamesines, Ron Colson, Don Schumacher, Bobby Vodnik, Gary Dyer, Norm Kraus, and Ron "Snag" O'Donnell. However, the most legendary name from Chicago was the* Chi-Town Hustler *of John Farkonas, Austin Coil, and Pat Minick. The* Chi-Town Hustler *was famous for its 600-foot burnouts commanded by Minick, who knew how to apply enough pressure to smoke the tires without damaging parts. (Jere Aldereff Photography/Courtesy Lions Automobilia Foundation Museum)

Dodge Dart in the first race of the 10 pairings. Harrell, in only the second week of running a blower, easily outdistanced the crossed-up Dart of Vanderwoude with an 8.58 ET at 172.03 mph for the win. Vanderwoude shut off with a 9.22 ET at 158.17 mph.

The next pair at the line was the Chevrolet of Texan Kelly "the Flying School Teacher" Chadwick, who faced Charlie Allen's blown Dodge Dart. Allen evened up the score when he ousted the teacher with an 8.45 ET at 115.00 mph to Kelly's 9.17 ET at 155.17 mph.

Cecil Yother's newest 1,700-pound, lightweight, injected Plymouth Barracuda whipped the *Bardahl Ford* of Clester Andrews with a 9.18 ET at 127.24 mph to Andrews's 9.97 ET at 150 mph. "Fast" Eddie Schartman and the *California Flash* of Butch Leal faced each other next. With the burnouts completed and both cars in the staging beams, they leaped from off the line in a dead heat when Schartman's 427-ci Cammer coughed up a valve and blew the supercharger off the intake manifold. The engine damage removed Schartman from contention.

Lew Arrington's *Brutus* GTO kept the spectators on the edge of their seats when he executed not one but two 360-degree angle spinouts at mid-track and crossed over the line before he regained control. Arrington kept the GTO off the guardrails and avoided contact with the *Chi-Town Hustler*. Driver Pat Minick drove the *Windy City* Dodge Charger around the sideways *Brutus* to a win with a 9.05 ET at 154.86 mph.

Terry Hendrick piloted Pete Seaton's *Seaton's Shaker* Chevy Corvair to a round win and earned a point for the East team when he defeated the Mercury Comet of Jack Chrisman on a holeshot. Hendrick stopped the clocks with an 8.09 ET at 178.57 mph to Chrisman's quicker 8.03 ET at 189.96 mph.

The *Limefire* Barracuda, driven by Clare Sanders, utilized the 400-ci Chrysler Hemi power to take down the napping Chapman Automotive's *Outa Site* Camaro with an 8.55 ET at 148.32 mph to the Chrysler-powered Chevy's 8.31 ET at 170.45 mph.

Roger Lindamood gave the automatic win to Tommy Grove when Lindamood jumped too early and illuminated the red light. Fortunately for Grove, his Mustang almost got sideways right at the start, which would have given the win to Lindamood's *Color Me Gone* Dodge Charger.

The excitement reached its peak when the announcer screamed, "Ladies and gentlemen, remain standing. Here come your team captains: 'Dyno' Don Nicholson and 'Jungle' Jim Liberman!"

This pair of superstars alone would generate a top-billed match race at any drag strip in the country.

Nicholson, in his second week running a blower, and Liberman, driving his new supercharged Chevy II, rolled into the staging beams. Both cars were practically inseparable when Liberman brought the Chevy II up on its rear bumper with a towering wheel-stand that allowed Nicholson to cross the finish line alone as the winner with an 8.13 ET at 177.86 mph.

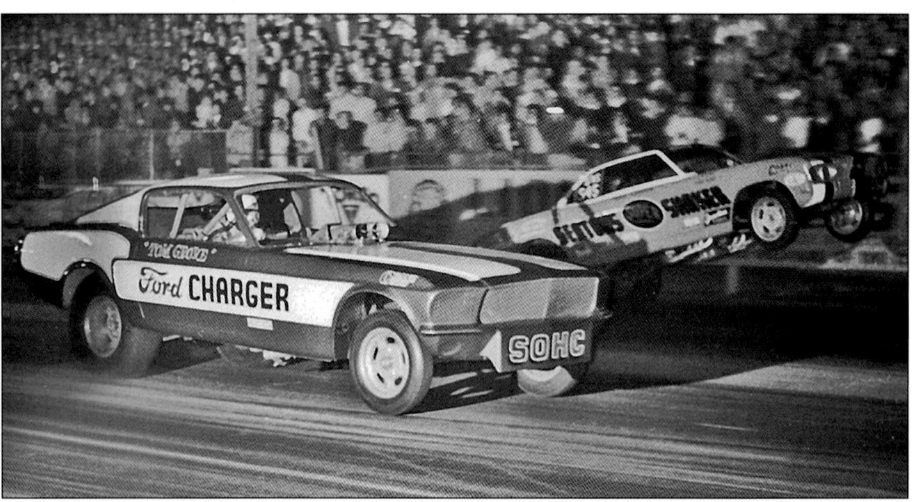

Ford versus Chevy matchups were always thrilling. Tommy Grove and Terry Hendrick provided one of the most exciting match races of the night. Grove regained some Western prestige when he dipped his Ford Mustang into the 7-second bracket as Terry Hendrick pulled the biggest wheel-stand ever seen for a Funny Car at Lions Drag Strip. Hendrick lifted all four wheels off the ground and teetered the Corvair perpendicular to the strip on the left rear corner of the bumper. (Photo Courtesy Steve Reyes)

Next up, by way of Lansing, Michigan, was Dick Loehr, whose Chrysler-powered Mustang faced Don Sappington's *Candid Camaro*. Sappington surprised many, including Loehr, when he cut a quick light. Sappington opened a substantial lead before Loehr started to reel in the Camaro, unleashing the Ford's 1,200 hp. However, the *Candid Camaro* kept its lead and held on for the win with an 8.17 ET at 167.74 mph to Loehr's 8.13 ET at 183.66 mph.

Pete Gates's *Gate Job* Comet and the Montrelli & Barrett *New Breed* Firebird were the next pair to the line. Both cars experienced severe handling problems 300 feet from the starting line that required precise pirouette movements and then shut off, turning the race into a coasting match. The momentum went to Montrelli & Barrett, as the Firebird crossed the finish line with a 17.29 ET at 45.00 mph to "no time" for Gates. The last pair of the first round were the cars of "Fearless" Fred Goeske and Dee Keaton. Goeske's Hemi 'Cuda recorded the win on a single run with an 8.34 ET at 162.31 mph when Keaton failed to fire.

The point tally after the first round tipped in favor of the East team 6-3.

Round 2

With both "Fast" Eddie Schartman and the *Limefire* forced to the sidelines due to breakage from round one, round two brought two new backup cars into the mix: Ronnie Runyan's *Blue Hell* Corvette and Dee Keaton's flip-top *Keaton's Komet* Mercury Comet.

Wins by Jack Chrisman, Charlie Allen, "Jungle" Jim, Tommy Grove, and Cecil Yother brought the West's point count one step closer to the East, while Dick Loehr, Kelly Chadwick, "Dyno" Don Nicholson, and Roger Lindamood topped their adversaries.

The highlight of the second round featured two undefeated drivers: Tommy Grove and Terry Hendrick. At the green light, Grove dropped his Mustang into the 7-second bracket with a 7.98 ET at 177.16 mph. His counterpart, Hendrick, performed the largest wheel-stand ever seen by many in a Funny Car. Hendrick pulled all four wheels off the ground and teetered at a precarious 90 degrees (perpendicular to the strip). Unfortunately for Hendrick, his acrobat act knocked the potent Corvair out of the third round.

Round 3

Round three brought more suspense on the strip when Lew Arrington and Dick "Mr. Chevrolet" Harrell gave the fans more than they expected. As both cars accelerated off the line, all eyes switched over to Harrell, who was performing one of his coveted rear bumper wheel-stands. Arrington's *Brutus* almost met a near tragedy when the GTO exploded into a ball of flames that engulfed the entire car.

Memories

Steve Reyes

Photographer

"I used to take an 8- to 10-hour Greyhound bus ride from Northern California just to be at Lions [Drag Strip]. The other photographers at Lions would make fun of me because all I had was an old Pentax 35-mm and a $10 flash fan that used flash bulbs because I couldn't afford a strobe.

"They stopped laughing when I was the only one who shot the transmission exploding on the *Brutus* GTO with my trusty Pentax and flash fan. The *Brutus* was racing Dickie Harrell, but Lew Arrington was a friend of mine, so I stayed on his side of the strip while everyone dashed over to Dickie's side. At the green light, Harrell went into a 5- or 6-foot wheel-stand. Meanwhile, the *Brutus* GTO exploded, and I got the photo."

If Lions Drag Strip gave an award for being the most exciting at the East versus West Funny Car Championships, the unanimous choice would be Lew Arrington. The adventure started in the first round when Arrington performed a masterful job regaining control after he executed two complete 360-degree rotations with Pat Minick in the next lane. In the third and last round against the wheel-standing Dickie Harrell, Arrington's Chrysler-powered GTO erupted into a ball of flames that engulfed the entire car with Arrington still strapped into the seat. (Photo Courtesy Steve Reyes)

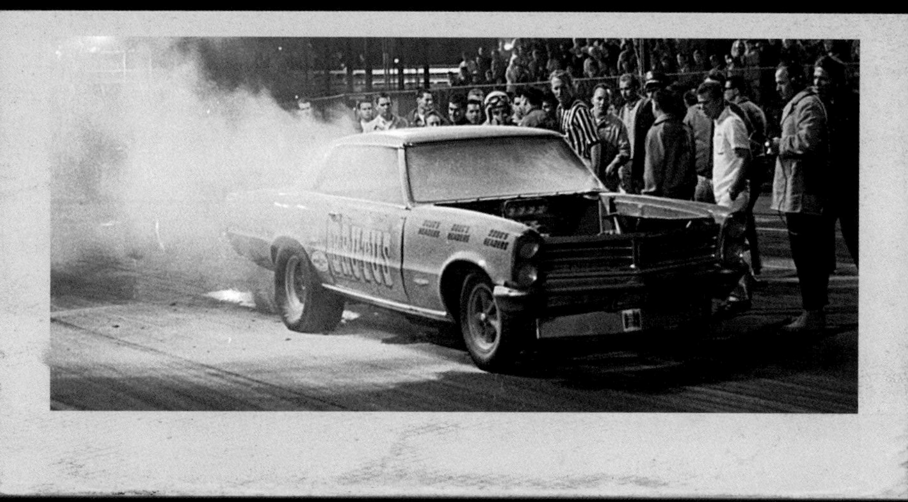

Left: This is the carnage and debris left behind from **Brutus** *when the planetary assembly of the TorqueFlite transmission disintegrated as the car came off the line at Lions Drag Strip. Several bags of rice ash sweep were used in the cleanup, and racing was delayed for an hour. (Photo Courtesy Steve Reyes)*

Two starters, Larry Sutton and Bill Kee, respond quickly with fire extinguishers to douse the flames and remove the shaken Arrington from the GTO. Racers at Lions Drag Strip always had ample safety due to the team of Sutton and Kee. (Photo Courtesy Steve Reyes)

With Arrington helplessly swallowed by the fire, split-second reactions by Lions Drag Strip starters Larry Sutton and Bill Kee extinguished the flames. The shaken Arrington got out of the car without serious injury.

After the lengthy cleanup of the transmission shrapnel and debris, more broken parts and cars took their toll on the Eastern team. Standby cars filled the void for the remaining final round-robin matches. Racing continued when Don Sappington's *Candid Camaro* benefited from the red-light start of the *GT-1* Comet of Jack Chrisman. The *Vicious Vette* of Charlie Wilson and driver Clyde Morgan bombarded the *Bardahl Ford* of Clester Andrews with an 8.85 ET at 157.61 mph, as both cars secured the needed points.

Next up to the line was "Jungle" Jim Liberman, who singled in his 2,080-pound Chevy II when Ron O'Donnell's *Chapman Camaro* fell to engine woes. Liberman's time slip was punched with an 8.35 ET at 179.28 mph.

Two of the quickest injected floppers in the show, Roger Lindamood's *Color Me Gone* and Butch Leal's *California Flash*, locked horns in a do-or-die round. Both drivers resembled prize fighters. Lindamood, in the East corner, weighed in at 2,050 pounds on 98-percent nitro, while over in the Western corner, Leal balanced the scales at 1,800 pounds on 100-percent nitro. When the smoke and rosin settled, the title easily went to the *California Flash*, as Leal knocked out the blue and white Dodge with a 7.97 ET at 177.51 mph.

Kelly Chadwick stormed past the subbing Hemi 'Cuda of Fred Goeske, while Dick Loehr went the ballistic route and took down Cecil Yother's *Melrose Missile* with an 8.07 ET at 183.28 mph to an 8.51 ET at 164.83 mph.

Memories

Larry Sutton

Lions Drag Strip Starter

"Lew Arrington's *Brutus*, an all steel-bodied Pontiac GTO, was entered at Lions [Drag Strip] as a member of the West team at the third-annual East versus West Funny Car Team Championships.

"When Lew came to the starting line to make a test run, he wasn't wearing gloves. I signaled for him to shut off the car. After two situations I had before with drivers, C. J. always backed me up 100 percent. Lew got out of the car and started to call me every name under the sun.

"Just then, C. J. walked up and said, 'What's going on?'

"I said, 'Well, I told this gentleman that he had to have gloves on—otherwise, he doesn't run.'

"Lew continued to swear when C. J. turned around to him and said, 'You take your car and go back into the pit area. Either you find a set of gloves or put your car back in the trailer and leave the racetrack, and you're not going to get paid."

"So, Arrington went around the pits, borrowed a pair of gloves, and put them on. He said that he never wore gloves. He had raced across the country and never wore them before!

"[Arrington] pulled up to the starting line to make his run, and when he hit the throttle, the transmission exploded.

"I always have the fire extinguishers on the starting line with the pins already pulled before the day starts because a situation like this could happen. When it blew up, I instantly grabbed one of the extinguishers. As a matter of fact, if you look in the photo of the car on fire, you see that the rest of them are standing and I'm already moving. I grabbed one of the extinguishers and ran over to the car. Luckily, the car didn't have any side windows, so I kept spraying inside the car until the extinguisher was completely empty.

"Lew got out of the car and calmly took off his helmet, unzipped his fire suit, and turned around. He took off the fire suit, looked at me, and said, 'Okay, you can kick my ass now.'

"Thirty years later when I was at Pomona. I walked over to see my good friend John Force. I was checking out the work on his car between rounds when one of his crew members stopped what he was doing and walked over to me and asked, 'Excuse me, are you Larry Sutton?'

"I said, 'Yes, I am.'

"He proceeded to thank me.

"I said, 'For what?'

"He said, 'I was in my mom's belly when my dumbass father ran at Lions and you saved his life!'

The young man's name is Lew Arrington Jr."

With the stands still full at 10:45 p.m., the final race of the East versus West Funny Car Team Championships pitted a pair of Ford products against each other: Tommy Grove's Mustang versus the Mercury Cyclone of "Dyno" Don Nicholson. With both cars running into the 7-second bracket during the evening, each looked for the takedown. They left the line in unison before a burst of power put Nicholson in front as he crossed the finish line. Nicholson ran a 7.97 ET at 174.08 mph to Grove's 8.10 ET at 167.59 mph. (Photo Courtesy Steve Reyes)

The final race of the evening pitted the undefeated Funny Cars of "Dyno" Don Nicholson and Tommy Grove against each other. With both Ford products producing more than 1,200 hp at 11,000 rpm, each SOHC Cammer lit up the candles at the hit. Both frantically looked to take advantage of the bite of the strip. Nicholson appeared to haze the tires at half-track to give Grove the slight edge. Then, a phenomenal burst of speed powered Nicholson to the win with a 7.97 ET at 174.08 mph to Grove's losing-but-respectable 8.10 ET at 167.59 mph.

For Nicholson, he captured the overall eliminator crown and set the low ET of the meet, but it was the West team that came from behind in the third and final round to earn enough points to upset the East team.

Live from Lions

Imagine driving around Southern California, listening to the radio, and getting the current racing results and the latest happenings at the strip. The radio station KDAY in Santa Monica, California, and the Lions Drag Strip management teamed up to make local broadcasting history with the first live drag racing program from the strip, which aired at 1 p.m. Sunday, November 5. Frank Thompson of KDAY was the announcer at the racing venue, and the broadcast was a regular weekly feature from Lions Drag Strip every Sunday.

Each show had three segments: live interviews with track personnel and racers, taped highlights and interviews from the previous night's racing event, and a live feed of the Lions Drag Strip announcers over the sound system.

Among the first guests on the inaugural broadcast were Lions Drag Strip officials C. J. Hart and Larry Sutton as well as supercharger expert Mert Littlefield. The racers on hand who competed on the strip and shared the microphone were Dick and Mike Landy (with their 1968 Dodges making test runs); bracket competitor Dick Sinclair (driving his C/Gas '56 Chevy to a class win), and the South Bay Racing Association's Mike Blodgett (winner of the bracket three class in his 2-speed GTO).

Not only did they share their happiness of winning their class but they were also given the chance to be interviewed and heard over the local radio waves by their friends, family, and club members. That's something they'll always remember.

As the commentator closed the show, he said, "If you can't make it to the races, listen every Sunday afternoon from 1 to 4 p.m. on 1580 on your AM radio dial for KDAY live from Lions."

Chapter Five

1968–1969

Banzai at the Beach

"Jungle" Jim Liberman captured the Fuel/FX class when he singled in the final round against "Dyno" Don Nicholson's **Eliminator II** *Mercury Comet after Nicholson scrambled to replace a broken transmission. The repair was all for naught when the Comet failed to start. (Jere Alhadeff Photography/Courtesy Lions Automobilia Foundation Museum)*

Lions Drag Strip's nonprofit organization started the 1968 season on a good note with donations of more than $5,000 to various charities. Some recipients included the Long Beach Retarded Children's Fund, the John Tracy Clinic, the YMCA, the Psychiatric Clinic for Children, the Eye Foundation, and the Children's Benefit League.

Being philanthropic was the core mission of the Lions Drag Strip, but drag racing was its heartbeat, and its biggest event was always at the forefront of the new year.

Thirteenth-Annual AHRA Winter Nationals

On January 28, 1968, Lions Drag Strip opened with the 13th-annual AHRA Winter Nationals for Factory Experimentals. Due to rain on Friday and Saturday, the entire meet took place on Sunday, but everything ran relatively well without delays.

1968 AHRA WINTER NATIONALS

Stock Cars and Funny Cars
JANUARY 27 AND 28
LIONS DRAG STRIP

STOCK CAR PURSE (Plus Contingencies)

FUEL FUNNY CARS	
WINNER	$2,000
Runner-Up	$1,000
4th Round Losers (2 - $400 ea.)	$800
3rd Round Losers (4 - $300 ea.)	$1,200
2nd Round Losers (8 - $200 ea.)	$1,600
1st Round Losers (16 - $100 ea.)	$1,600
GAS FUNNY CARS (Injected – 2400 Lbs. – Qualify 16)	
WINNER	$1,000
Runner-Up	$500
3rd Round Losers (2 - $200 ea.)	$400
2nd Round Losers (4 - $150 ea.)	$600
1st Round Losers (8 - $100 ea.)	$800

SUPER STOCK	
WINNER	$600
Runner-Up	$175
TOP STOCK	
WINNER	$400
Runner-Up	$150
MIDDLE STOCK	
WINNER	$300
Runner-Up	$150
LITTLE STOCK	
WINNER	$200
Runner-Up	$100

This is a flyer for the two-day 1968 AHRA Winter Nationals for Stock Cars and Funny Cars.

More than 40 Fuel and Gas Funny Cars were pre-entered, and qualifying was allotted to two hours for the revised schedule. All cars were allowed to make a second run if needed.

When eliminations were underway, 32 Fuel cars were in the running, and 4 alternates waited for their chance to jump into the action. Don Nicholson ran the low ET of 7.63 at the Winter Nationals, while Doug Thorley posted the top speed of 191.43 mph.

Liberman Tames Lions

"Jungle" Jim Liberman made it through four rounds of exhilarating racing. He was supposed to face "Dyno" Don Nicholson in the all-important Fuel-FX final, but Nicholson was late getting to the line after replacing his transmission, as he couldn't fire up the car, which left Liberman to make a single run. Liberman still made it interesting (as he always did), when he left on the green. He twisted and skated his way toward the finish line like a bandit running with the loot. The blue Chevy II stopped the clocks with a 7.75 ET at 189.08 mph.

Super Sox

The three cars in the Super Stock bracket that were indicative of the recent surge in popularity of these cars were those from Sox & Martin, Dick Landy, and the Corvette of Mr. Bardhal and Bill Hielscher.

In the semifinal round, Ronnie Sox ran an amazing 10.55 ET at 133.77 mph to thrash the Bardhal Corvette's 11.43 ET at 120.64 mph. After Landy made a single pass of 10.58 at 131.96 mph, both cars were geared up for the final. Expectations fell short for a great final when Sox tripped the light. Landy's victory was assured with a 10.49 ET at 132.15 mph to Sox's 10.53 ET at 132.53 mph.

United States Professional Dragster Championships

The management of Lions Drag Strip, along with Professional Dragster Association (PDA) organizer Doug Kruse, successfully combined the essential ingredients to create a recipe of the most tantalizing, successful one-day

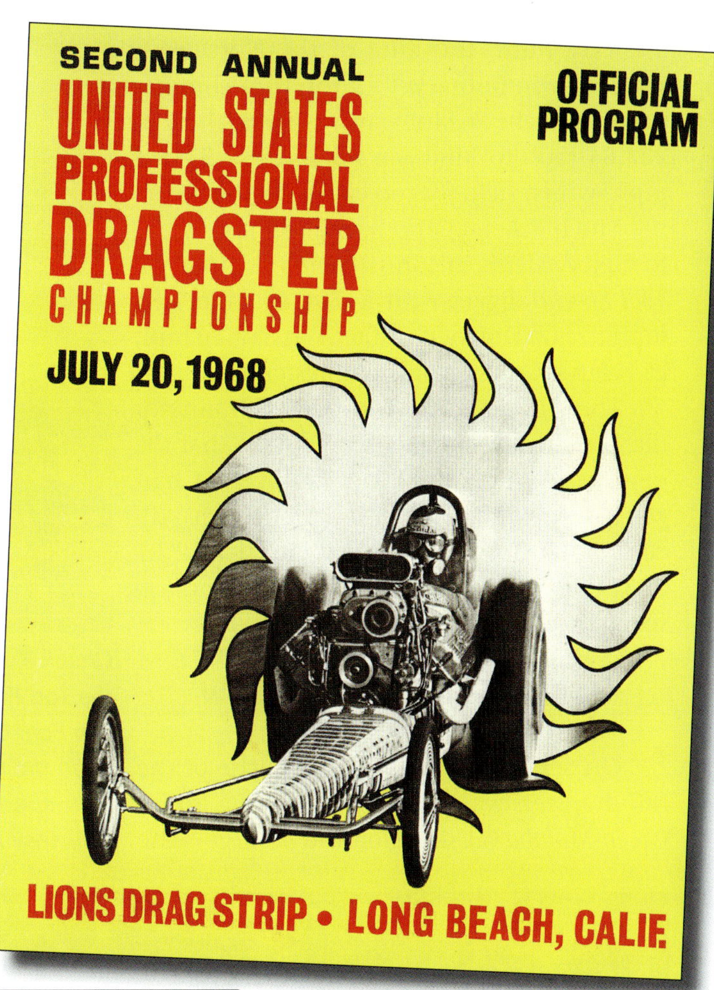

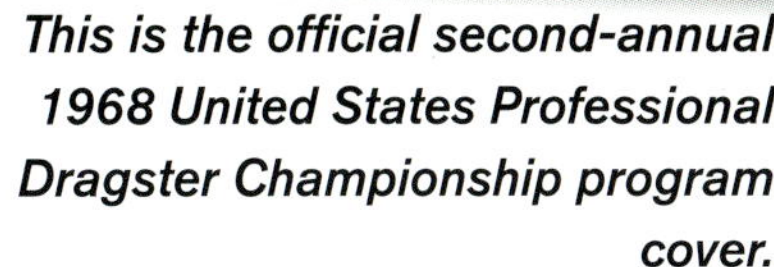
This is the official second-annual 1968 United States Professional Dragster Championship program cover.

One half of the semifinal round featured Ronnie Sox in the **Sox & Martin** *Plymouth GTX against Bill Hielscher's* **Mr. Bardhal** *Corvette. Sox won with a 10.55 ET at 133.77 mph to the Corvette's losing 11.43 ET at 120.64 mph. (Photo Courtesy Steve Reyes)*

drag racing event on the West Coast on July 20, 1968, at the second-annual PDA Championships.

A crowd of 18,472 enthusiasts broke turnstile records and caught the action of 64 AA/Fuel Dragsters that were qualified and placed into four groups of 16 cars based on their qualifying times. The eliminators (number one, two, three, and four) were launched at staggered intervals.

Jerry Ruth, the King of the Northwest, took the win in bracket #1 Top Fuel Eliminator over Beebe & Mulligan with a 6.91 ET at 227.84 mph to Mulligan's 6.97 ET at 231.54 mph, which held for top speed for the meet.

The bracket #2 Top Fuel Eliminator went to Gerry Glenn in John Bateman's *Atlas Oil Tool Special* digger with a 6.86 ET at 211.85 mph to Bob Downey's 7.06 ET at 212.26 mph in Leland Kolb's beautiful dragster.

The bracket #3 Top Fuel Eliminator marked the first time in competition that the new team of Dan and Leon Vanluven's Charger Top Fuel dragster (with driver Norm Wilcox) grabbed overall honors with a 7.12 ET at 211.76 mph. This was the low ET and top speed of the bracket.

1968 Big Top Wonder Show

On September 7, 1968, the battle of the rail dragsters was headlined by Doug Rose's *Green Mamba* jet dragster and George "The Stone Age Man" Hutcheson's *U.S. Turbine 1* in Lions Drag Strip's Big Top Wonder Show. The show also featured five more match races that included Funny Cars, Gassers, and Jr. Fuel.

Hutcheson had already shot down two of the monster jets in Northern California and looked to defeat his latest opponent, the *Green Mamba*, which wouldn't

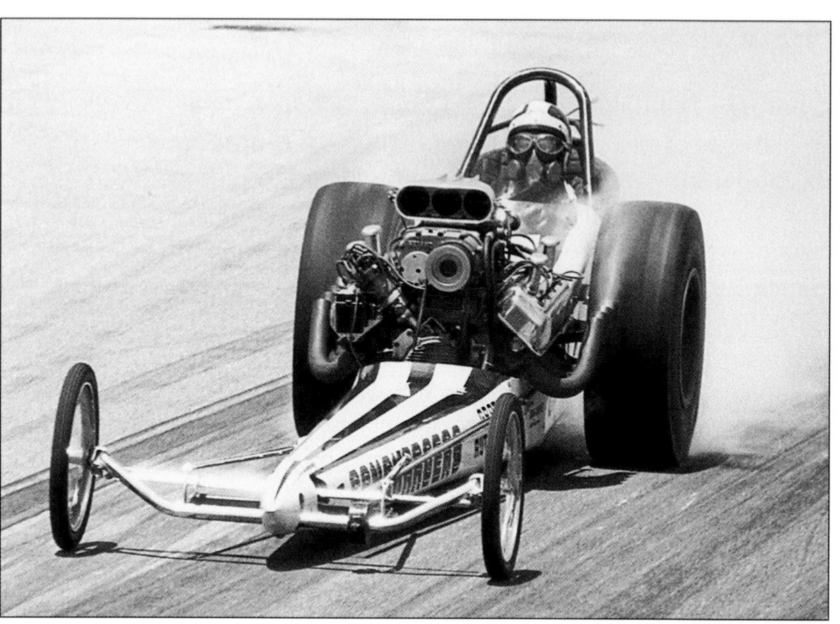

Chuck Kurzawa and the Ramchargers made it into the third round in the Top Fuel bracket before coming up short against the **Up in Smoke** *Top Fuel dragster. Kurzawa won a challenge from Ewell, Bell, & Steckler in the first round, as a rear slick inner liner went flat and caused a high-speed wobble for Steckler. (Jere Alhadeff Photography/ Courtesy Lions Automobilia Foundation Museum)*

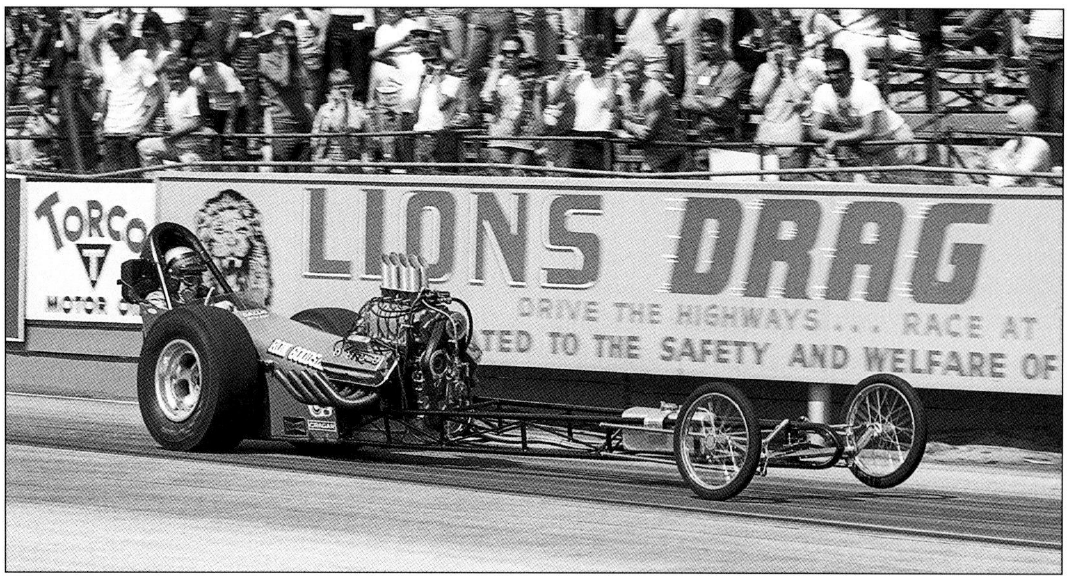

Ron Goodsell's **Earthquake** *Top Fuel dragster suffered a setback when a port nozzle stuck, but he still managed to win in the first round. In the second round, Goodsell was on a mission before his Crower-equipped, rear-end suspended machine ran over debris and took out the top-end lights. (Jere Alhadeff Photography/Courtesy Lions Automobilia Foundation Museum)*

Gerry Glenn in John Bateman's **Atlas Oil Tool Special** *gained an uncontested bye win with a 6.86 ET at 204.04 mph when Leland Kolb and Bob Downey were unable to appear in the money round in bracket #2. (Jere Alhadeff Photography/Courtesy Lions Automobilia Foundation Museum)*

be as easy. Weighing the differences, Hutcheson's *Turbonique* dragster, with a tiny, 84-pound turbine engine that was nearly the size of a watermelon, was up against Rose's Westinghouse J-46 engine that propelled the *Mamba* to speeds averaging 253 mph. This unique match race was supervised by starter Larry Sutton, who donned a flame suit and used flags to start the races.

Before the first round of the turbo jet versus the turbine car, the ground rules on the start were determined by George Hutcheson and Doug and Stephaine Rose. Hutcheson received a handicap with a 1-second advantage.

In the first round, Hutcheson shot off the line just as the *Mamba* hit the afterburner and took chase after the *Turbine 1* and caught and passed him between the first- and second-time lights. Rose stopped the clocks with a 7.12 ET at 229 mph, even while Hutcheson recovered from a mid-track drift and slowed to an 8.64 ET at 137.61 mph.

In round two, both had nearly the exact launches and times, but Hutcheson kept the *Turbonique* dragster out front and took the win light. The third round went to the *Mamba*, as Rose averaged three consecutive runs at 229.00 mph to win the best-of-three match.

Match Races of Different Breeds

An all–American Motors Corporation (AMC) match to determine who was Mr. All-AMC featured Hayden Proffitt and Doug Thorley. Both were represented by Grant, and the AMC public relations brass was there to see the best-of-three match race.

Bill McNealy from AMC distributed "Happiness is a Hot Rebel" buttons and other AMC merchandise, while Phil Bellomy of Grant raffled off a selection of Grant safety products, steering wheels, and T-shirts.

When the smoke cleared, Proffitt claimed the title of Mr. AMC.

A few new race cars made their debut during testing and time-trial runs, including Richard Day's new *Screamer* Chevy Corvette roadster. Lions Drag Strip supported family teams in all classes and proved that racing on a budget was some of the closest and most entertaining competition.

The world's only steel-bodied Cadillac Eldorado Funny Car of Dave Zachary and the Snodgrass & Mahnken's blown 427 Wedge *Psycho* Mustang were the other top headliners at Lions Drag Strip. The mighty *Psycho* Mustang from Glendora, California, bested the amazing, one-of-a kind Cadillac (complete with a supercharged 500-ci Chevrolet engine) with consecutive wins.

A short delay in round one occurred when Zachary couldn't see the starting lights. The upper windshield was mounted too low, and the starting lights were hung too high. After alterations were performed, both cars annihilated the tires in a smoke-fest that was won by Larry Barker, the driver for the Snodgrass & Mahnken team.

During the burnout in round two, Zachary blew the transmission in the Cadillac. He quickly found a reliable replacement, but the repairs were completed right when the curfew fell, which gave the automatic win to the Mustang.

Top-End Tragedy

Jack and Tim Lichty's new J-65-powered jet dragster came to Lions Drag Strip from San Diego, California, and made several test runs before disaster struck.

The home-built dragster was an unusual design manufactured from square tubing that was originally fitted

This is a two-sided adhesive sticker that would be folded around a car's antenna, providing free advertising for the United States Professional Dragster Championship at Lions Drag Strip.

with a Funny Car body. After an easy check-out run of 60 mph, driver Jack Lichty boosted up the runs to an 8.82 ET at 137.91 mph and an 8.02 ET at 191.48 mph before he made the fourth run under full power when misfortune struck. The parachute ripped off the car at more than 200 mph, and the car plowed through the sand trap and into the first sand barrier. Jack was critically injured and rushed to the hospital. Thankfully, he recovered from the accident.

Kenny Safford piloted "Terrible" Ted Gotelli's Speed Shop fueler at the Professional Dragster Association (PDA) Championships. Gotelli's Auto Supply was located in South San Francisco and opened on May 1, 1962. It offered the best speed and high-performance parts for decades. (Photo Courtesy Don Prieto)

Doug Rose lifts the front end of the **Green Mamba** *after pulling the chute at the end of a run against the* **U.S. Turbine 1** *Turbonique dragster of George Hutcheson. Rose defeated the* **U.S. Turbine 1** *dragster two out of three times, and Hutcheson requested a rematch. (Photo by John Ewald/Courtesy Don Ewald)*

George Hutcheson's **U.S. Turbine 1** *dragster lights up the starting line in a storm of blue and white exhaust, tire smoke, and cinder-like sparks created by balls of rubber flying off the spinning tires.*

Memories

Tim Kraushaar

Lions Drag Strip Starter and Announcer

"When C. J. became manager of Lions Drag Strip, he called to see if I wanted to be a starter. I said sure—but he'd have to pay me a hell of a lot more than he did at Riverside. After some back-and-forth, we reached an agreement. Although, I never told him I would've done it for free. I was likely the last starter in California to use only flags, standing 20 feet ahead of some seriously dangerous cars. That bit me more than once.

"When C. J. took over, Larry Sutton became the head starter, and he was as skilled as they came. With the need for an additional announcer, C. J. and I negotiated again, and I moved to the tower to announce races. I held that role until Lions Drag Strip closed in December 1972.

"I thought I'd give it a shot and headed up to the tower to get a feel for it. After calling a few Stock races, Jerry Hart, the head announcer, asked me to cover a match race between Doug Rose's jet car, the *Green Mamba*, and George "the Stone Age Man" Hutchinson's *U.S. Turbine 1*. Although I had never previously called a jet match at that time, I'd seen plenty at Fontana.

"The new tower at Lions Drag Strip, which was directly behind the starting line, offered a great view. As the *Green Mamba* and *U.S. Turbine 1* rolled up, Rose's crew primed the engine with kerosene. Suddenly, everyone in the tower got up and left, abandoning me. I hadn't realized why they bolted—until the *Green Mamba* fired up. The engine wailed, spewing smoke and fire. Then, Rose gave it a little "burp," and a massive cloud of smoke erupted alongside 15-foot flames.

"I sprang up, dashed outside to shut the tower windows, and then went back inside, peering out the side windows. I kept announcing, hyping up the crowd. Then, Rose burped the afterburner—boom! boom! boom!—sending the thick shutters fluttering like butterfly wings.

"This time, I took cover behind the clocks, half-crouched in the doorway. The air reeked of jet fuel. I couldn't see a thing, but I kept calling the action. When both cars launched, their engines engaged, and they vanished into the haze. I couldn't even see them, but I kept announcing, making it all up until the smoke cleared and I could name the winner.

"There were so many incredible racers, but Doug Rose stood out. He was a true 'bucks-down' jet racer who had lost both lower legs in a crash. He recovered, built his own car, and toured with his girlfriend Stefanie (later his wife), who was part of his pit crew. Wherever the *Green Mamba* ran, Rose would visit a veteran's hospital and spend time with amputees.

"I was lucky enough to join him on one visit to Long Beach Veterans Hospital, where he worked his magic. A talented dancer, he glided through the ward like he was on *The Lawrence Welk Show*, sharing stories, signing autographs, and lighting up the room. Eventually, he'd sit on a bed, remove his prosthetics, rub his stumps, put his legs back on, and thank everyone for their time before trotting off. He believed it was his duty to show amputees that life goes on—no matter what.

"Life, however, ends for all of us, as it will for those of us who raced and worked at Lions Drag Strip. A hundred years from now, I hope that someone will read this and think, 'Man, Lions Drag Strip must've been something'—because it was."

Doug Rose's interest in jet engines began after spending four years in the Navy as an F7V Cutlass fighter jet mechanic. He had been driving jet dragsters since the early 1960s when he got his start driving the* Green Monster *jet dragster for brothers Walt and Art Arfons. In an unfortunate accident on a rainy July 4, 1966, Rose hydroplaned on the wet surface, crashed into the guard rail, and severed both legs below the knees. The setback didn't deter him, and he was back in the seat within three months with new artificial legs. In 1968, Rose and his wife, Stefanie, built their successful* Green Mamba *jet dragster. He became quite the showman.

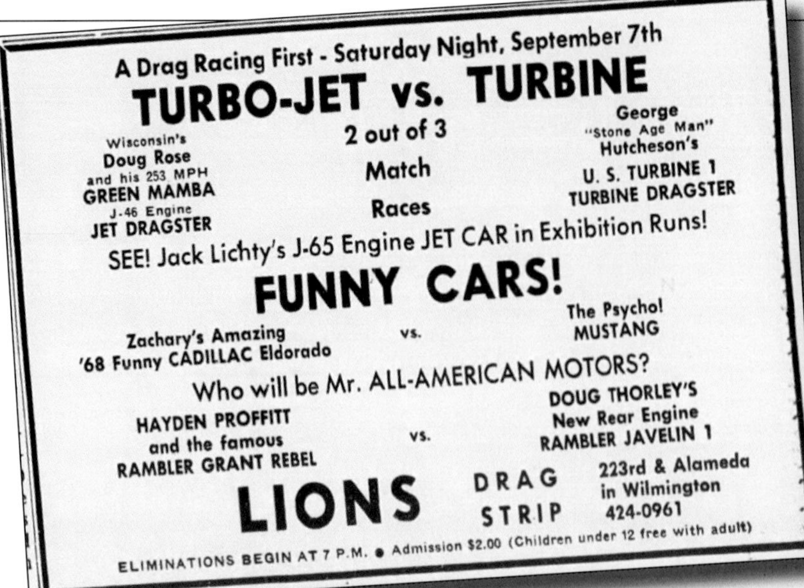

A Drag Racing First - Saturday Night, September 7th

TURBO-JET vs. TURBINE

Wisconsin's Doug Rose and his 253 MPH GREEN MAMBA J-46 Engine JET DRAGSTER

2 out of 3 Match Races

George "Stone Age Man" Hutcheson's U. S. TURBINE 1 TURBINE DRAGSTER

SEE! Jack Lichty's J-65 Engine JET CAR in Exhibition Runs!

FUNNY CARS!

Zachary's Amazing '68 Funny CADILLAC Eldorado vs. The Psycho! MUSTANG

Who will be Mr. ALL-AMERICAN MOTORS?

HAYDEN PROFFITT and the famous RAMBLER GRANT REBEL vs. DOUG THORLEY'S New Rear Engine RAMBLER JAVELIN 1

LIONS DRAG STRIP 223rd & Alameda in Wilmington 424-0961

ELIMINATIONS BEGIN AT 7 P.M. • Admission $2.00 (Children under 12 free with adult)

The Saturday 7, 1968, edition of **The Register** *circulated in Santa Ana, California, and announced the featured match races scheduled for Lions Drag Strip. Last-minute additions like this ran in newspapers the day of the show to hopefully round up a few more spectators for the evening's festivities. (Image Courtesy* **The Register***)*

Fourteenth Lions Anniversary

On September 28, 1968, Lions Drag Strip, the "Giant of the West," celebrated its 14th anniversary of serving the racing and non-racing communities.

The nine Harbor Area Lions Clubs, who were operators of the AHRA racing facility, saw the strip surpass its original goals of getting racing off the streets and donating adequate profits to Lions Club charities. More than $300,000 had been raised over the past 14 years, and all if it went to organizations to help the underprivileged.

Goose Gets Loose

C. J. Hart orchestrated unique ways to make each anniversary meet somewhat different from the previous anniversary meets. For 1968, Hart asked track rivals Tom McEwen and Don Prudhomme to host the annual party for a nitro free-for-all that matched them against the selected field of 14 low qualifiers during "Dragspan." All pairings were selected out of a hat and divided into two groups of eight cars: the "Snake" bracket and the "Mongoose" bracket.

Bob Downey's latest ride, *The Black Plague*, won the top honors in the Snake bracket, while the Mongoose pulled off a first in drag racing history when he won a championship named after himself. McEwen collected $800 when he defeated the *Dean Engineering* rail in the finals with a 6.96 ET at 222.22 mph to a 7.48 ET at 176.81 mph. The top speed of the meet went to Norm Wilcox at 223.88 mph.

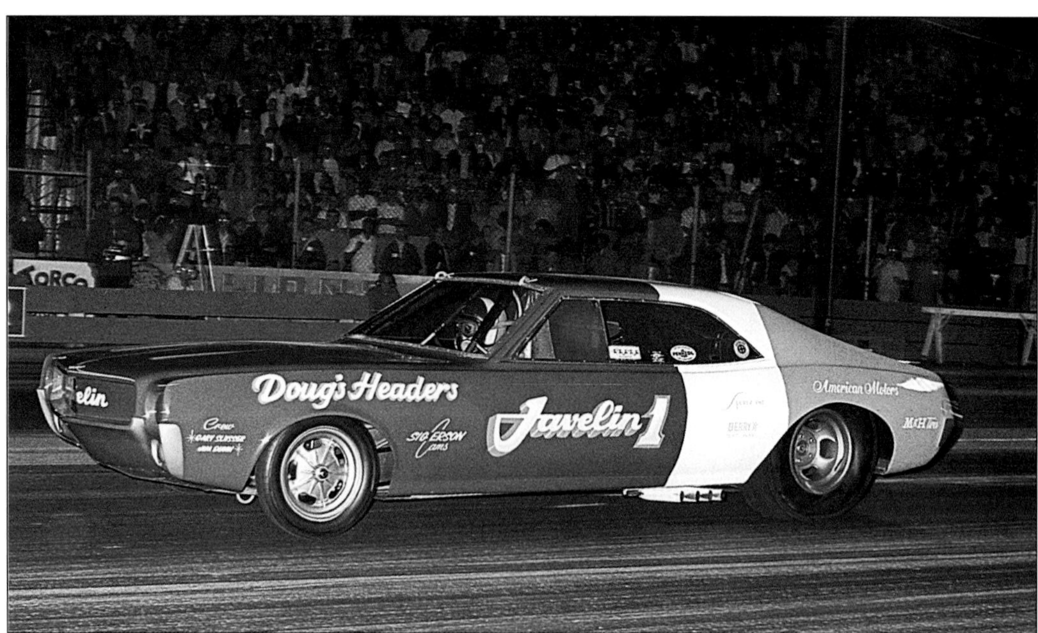

Doug Thorley's revolutionary rear-engine **Javelin 1** *American Motors Corporation (AMC) Javelin used a blown 390-ci AMC engine for power at the Mr. All–American Motors match race against Hayden Proffitt's* **Rebel SST***. With the only two pure AMC-powered Funny Cars in drag racing competing, AMC's top brass was on hand to witness this first dedicated race between the two superstars.*

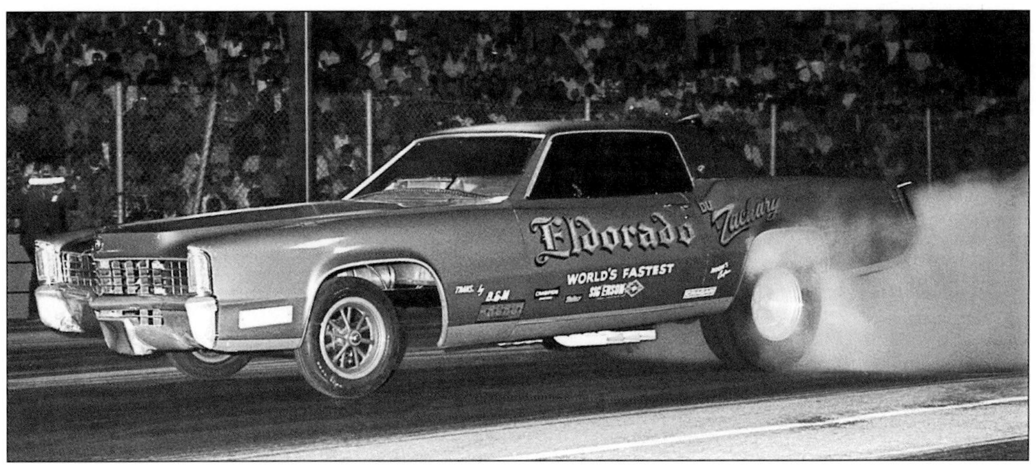

The match race between Dave Zachary's **World's Fastest Eldorado** *and the 1966 fastback* **Psycho** *Mustang of Ralph Snodgrass and Pat Mahnken was regarded as one of the most unusual match races of its day. Larry Barker drove the altered-wheel-based Mustang with a blown 427 Wedge Ford engine bolted to a direct drive transmission.*

C. J. Hart was a staunch supporter and believer of family participation at the drag strip. From full-time professionals to the weekend racers, he showed his utmost respect for family. The debut of Richard Day's **Screamer** *B/A Corvette Roadster was a fine example of family and friend involvement. Richard's wife, Carolyn, and crewman Roger Peterson focus on the Corvette's performance.*

Jack and Tim Lichty's J-65-powered jet dragster was towed from San Diego to Lions Drag Strip for exhibition runs without the aid of the Funny Car body. Jack drove the homebuilt dragster with a fabricated square frame.

Jack Lichty made his unplanned final run of the night in the Lichty Brothers' new jet dragster. It turned to tragedy after Jack blasted to a 200-mph run that resulted in the parachute burning off. The jet entered the sand trap at full speed and continued into the sand barrier before coming to a stop. Jack was taken to the intensive care unit at Long Beach Memorial Hospital.

GIANT 14th ANNIVERSARY MEE

Saturday Night, September 28

TOM 'Mongoose' McEWEN

AND

DON 'Snake' PRUDHOMME

CHALLENGE 14-CAR FIELD

The following AA/FD's waged a 15-week battle to qualify for a chance at McEwen & Prudhomme:

HOWARD CAM RATTLER 6.85 □ DEAN ENGINEERING SPL. 6.95 □ THE CHARGER 6.96 □ WARREN-COBURN-MILLER 6.99

RED MOUNTAIN BOYS 7.05 □ BLACK PLAGUE 7.06 □ CASPARY & HAMPSHIRE 7.07 □ MOONLIGHTER 7.11

BEEBE & FEDAK 7.13 □ CROSSLEY & EDMUNDS 7.13 □ LARKIN & GERMANN 7.14

MR. ED 7.14 □ HOWARD CAM SPL. 7.15 □ FIRESIDE INN 7.16

Alternates: WATERS & KING 7.19 □ EWELL-BELL-STECKER 7.20

LIONS DRAG STRIP

admission $3.00

CHILDREN UNDER 12 FREE WITH AN ADULT

223rd & ALAMEDA, WILMINGTON Call 424-0961

Posters such as this were found on telephone poles in the local area to announce the 14th anniversary of Lions Drag Strip. There was a 15-week battle to qualify for a chance to face Tom McEwen and Don Prudhomme.

Tom McEwen celebrated winning the 14th-annual Lions Drag Strip anniversary meet when he soundly defeated the **Dean Engineering** *dragster in the final round with a 6.96 ET at 222.22 mph to a losing 7.48 ET at 176.176.81 mph.*

All the Smoke You Can Eat

Smoke was definitely expected when those wild and unpredictable AA/FAs invaded Lions Drag Strip on October 26. These beasts with super slip-slider clutches demonstrated that the sun still sets in smoke over the Altered empire. Altereds were the throwback of the evolutionary ladder to drag racing 1963, and the crowds loved it.

The top qualifier in the eight-car field was Leon Fitzgerald's Chevy-powered *Pure Heaven II* with an 8.27 ET at 184.43 mph. A surprising number-two qualifier was the car of Bill and Butch Thurmond with an 8.33 ET at 187.10 mph. Rounding out the field was Mike Sullivan with an 8.42 ET at 174.71 mph, Mondello & Matsubara with an 8.46 ET at 172.08 mph, the Horcher Brothers with an 8.66 ET at 168.93 mph, Leroy Chadderton's *Magnificent 7* with an ET of 8.79 at 187.50 mph, Lee LeBaron's

Between Heaven & Hell with an 8.90 ET at 179.20 mph, and "Wild" Willie Borsch with an 8.92 ET at 181.00 mph.

Jr. Fuel occupied eight slots. Cotton & Tidwell earned the number-one position with a 7.83 ET. George Wong followed with a 7.83 ET and was followed by Allison-Crow-McCarrell (7.88), the Bright Boys (7.91), Gustin & Kramer (7.96), *Special K* (7.97), Frank Britt (7.99), and Holly & Dietz (8.02).

Pure Heaven *Prevails*

Both top qualifiers, Leon Fitzgerald and Bill Tidwell, took down all opponents in their respective fields.

Before the final round between the Thurmond Brothers and Leon Fitzgerald in the winning *Pure Hell,* the Thurmonds ran a one-of-kind race car: an all-steel 1932 Ford roadster–bodied altered with the original stock frame. Even though the 1932 Ford was well past its prime, it still punished the competition.

The Boycott Invitational

The fall months usually indicate when the racing season is done for the year, but on the West Coast, the mild-year-round weather conditions are considered to be a second season for many touring professionals. Many strips in California were booked with high-caliber meets that featured the Eastern stars with the many eager spectators and fans wanting to catch a glimpse of their favorite cars and drivers.

One so-called incident unfolded at Lions Drag Strip with the annual East versus West Funny Car Championships that were slated for November 2, 1968. This was one of the most popular and successful meets at the drag strip.

With the Eastern cars already locked in weeks before and under contract for the invite-only race with guaranteed money, the management at Lions Drag Strip rescinded the 16-car invitational Funny Car East versus West race with little to no notice to the racers involved. The meet was abruptly changed to an open meet with a "John Doe" 32-car open competition, where all cars needed to be qualified.

Both the East and West teams under contract considered it a breach of contract, and a verbal war of words ensued. Both sides exchanged heated barbs and insults, and the East versus West Championships were ultimately canceled.

Drags Strips Collide

Lions Drag Strip issued a challenge to the original group of "fraidy" car owners, drivers, and sponsors to see if they were afraid of the open competition with a purse of $14,000 that was up for the taking. Nearby Irwindale

This full-page advertisement in **Drag News** *provides details about the upcoming October and November Funny Car Meets. Lions Drag Strip always had a major event each weekend for the die-hard drag-racing fan who looked for value and entertainment.*

"Jungle" Jim Liberman took home the prize of $1,000 for winning Top Funny Car Eliminator of the John Doe Funny Car Championships on November 2. Liberman also took the bonus cash when he set the low ET and top speed to make it a clean sweep. Liberman was the lone representative who crossed over the invisible picket line when the closed Drag Racing Magazine Funny Car Invitational East-West Championships event was changed to an open meet.

Raceway held its own East versus West festival two weeks earlier and brought back the same East-West stars from Lions Drag Strip to run the East versus West Re-Challenge. The rematch took place on the same day as the Lions John Doe Open on November 16.

Revitalized Gasser Wars

The days of the gasser wars were highlighted by the Willys of "Big" John Mazmanian, and Stone, Woods, & Cook had been long gone for several years due to the more modern Gassers of Ford Mustangs, Barracudas, and something named an Opel Cadet.

On Saturday, March 1, 1969, the world premiere of Jr. Thompson and John Mazmanian's new 1969 Opel Cadet Gasser made its debut at Lions Drag Strip in a match race against the 1968 Ford Shelby Mustang GT *Swindler A* of Fred Stone, Leonard Woods, and driver Bones Balogh.

Instead of supercharged Oldsmobile engines lurking under the hood, 448-ci big-block Chrysler Hemis occupied the space. The evening's debut of Thompson's

Starter Larry Sutton attempts to muffle out the sounds made by the Hemis of Junior Thompson and Bones Balogh during a throwback match race that featured Gasser legends "Big" John Mazmanian and Stone, Woods, & Cook. Although the Willys coupes were replaced with more compact and modern bodystyles, the high level of rivalry stayed the same. (Photo by John Ewald/ Courtesy Don Ewald)

Opel Cadet had its share of the new car bugs, as the Stone & Woods and Balogh swept the candy-red Cadet.

Drag News Nationals: Top Fuel Surprises and Upsets

On Saturday, August 30, 1969, Lions Drag Strip hosted the Drag News Nationals with 16 Top Fuelers and 16 Fuel Funny Cars vying for the prestige and prize money. By 6 p.m., qualifying was completed and both fields were set as 15,673 racing fans made their way to their seats.

In Top Fuel, John Collins, who was driving Dave McKenzie's *Blue Streak Special*, dropped Bob Hightower, who was driving Jesse Perkins's *Cow Palace Shell*. Last year's Drag News Nationals winner, the *Atlas Oil Tool Special*, chalked up a win over the Beaver Brothers and Dave Condit. James Warren won over Moore & Blanchard. Moving on to the next round were the teams of Joe Lee and Denny Fitt (driving *The Addict*), Caspary and Hampshire, and Hippo and Brissette.

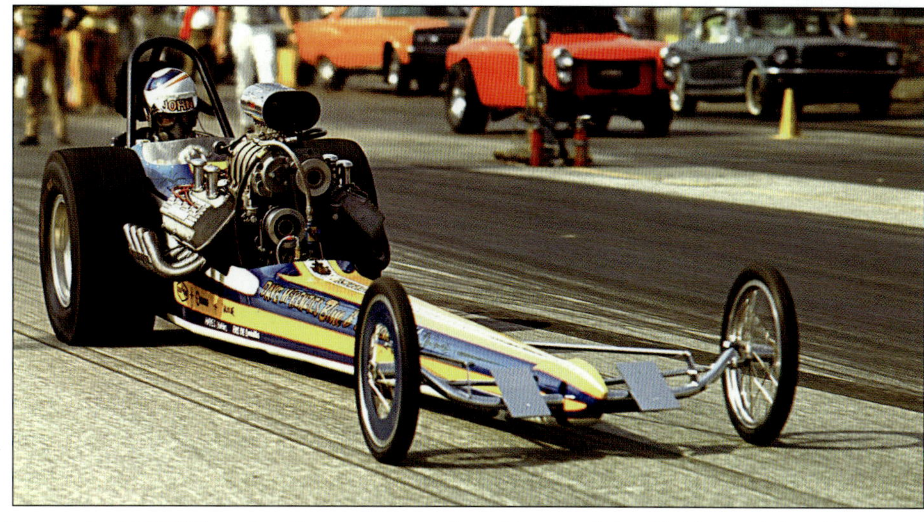

A crowd of 15,763 racing fans were on hand to see John Collins driving Dave McKenzie's **Blue Streak Special** *past the competition at the Lions Drag Strip Anniversary Nationals. Collins's route to the finals went through Bob Hightower in* **The Addict** *(the reinstated* **Cow Palace Shell***) before meeting James Warren in the final round. (Photo Courtesy Don Prieto Photography)*

Dave Condit blasts the hides in the **Beaver Bros. & Condit** *AA/FD at the Drag News Nationals. Gene Beaver maintained the Keith Black Hemi, which ran a 6.92 ET at 209.79 mph during qualifying. However, it overpowered the track in the first round against the* **Atlas Oil Tool Special** *when Condit lost traction. (Photo Courtesy Don Prieto Photography)*

Bikini-clad Carolyn Williams poses with the **Beaver Brothers & Condit** *AA/FD to advertise the upcoming Drag News Nationals on August 30, which featured Top Fuel Dragsters and Funny Cars with $13,000 in prize money. Williams was Lions Drag Strip's public relations gal and race queen, and she did the same thing at Bakersfield. (Photo by John Ewald/Courtesy Don Ewald)*

In round two, the *Atlas Oil Tool Special* retired Caspary and Hampshire. Collins drove past Denny Fitt, and the *Cow Palace Shell*, which lost in round one, was back in when the ailing Abbott & Lee couldn't make the call. Once again, Hightower was eliminated. This time, it was by the Warren-Colburn-Miller entry with a 6.86 ET at 221.76 mph to a close 6.90 ET at 196.93 mph. The last pair in round two featured the *Howards Cams Special* and Hippo & Brissette with the *Howards Cams Special*'s 6.87 ET at 221.13 mph winning over Brissette's up-in-smoke 7.70 ET at 128.56 mph.

The semifinals pitted James Warren, driving the Ridge Route Terrors (Warren-Colburn-Miller) entry, against Bob Downey in the *Howards Cams Special*. Downey's eagerness brought on the red light, trying to gain the advantage over Warren off the line.

Would the saying "third time's the charm" be enough for Bob Hightower's *Cow Palace Shell* to advance to the final round? Once again, Hightower was reinstated into the show when J. W. Bateman's *Atlas Oil Tool Special* broke, and he couldn't make the call to face John Collins. As fate had it, the charm wore off as fast when the race started. Collins sent the *Cow Palace Shell* and Hightower back to San Francisco with a 6.74 ET at 220.04 mph to the losing 6.94 ET at 211.26 mph.

In the fourth and final round of Top Fuel, crowd favorite James Warren and John Collins lined up for the $1,500 ride. With the pre-stage burnouts completed, it was time for the race. This time around, it was Warren who jumped early and drew the red light to send the underdog Collins to the winner's circle.

Funny Cars Go Better with Coke

In its first and only West Coast appearance of the 1969 Coca-Cola Cavalcade of Stars, Lions Drag Strip hosted the series finale of the popular 25-race series of the traveling all-stars on October 18.

Lions Drag Strip always displayed flair and creativity to attract big crowds, so when Ira Lichey of the Gold Agency booked the Cavalcade show at Lions Drag Strip, C. J. Hart and his public relations manager, Jerry Tice, assembled a team of marketing experts to concentrate exclusively on the younger, soft-drink-loving generation.

The team pulled out its playbook and ran with the idea of using an advertising innovation directly from the Goodyear Blimp. The staff hired a helicopter equipped with a custom neon billboard that was fixed to the bottom of the helicopter. The bright neon lights spelled out messages that could be seen for miles in the night sky. It drew the attention of everyone who glanced upward.

Advertising from the Heavens

Friday evening before the culmination of the Cavalcade of Stars, the helicopter took off and flew around Southern California. Seen by thousands, it flew for hours and focused on the cities of Long Beach, Wilmington, Santa Monica, Venice, Hollywood, Pasadena, and greater Los Angeles. It flashed messages from the colorful lights that announced the big race Saturday night at Lions Drag Strip.

With fuel to spare, the pilot made the turn south into Orange County where the helicopter was observed flying over the beach communities of Newport,

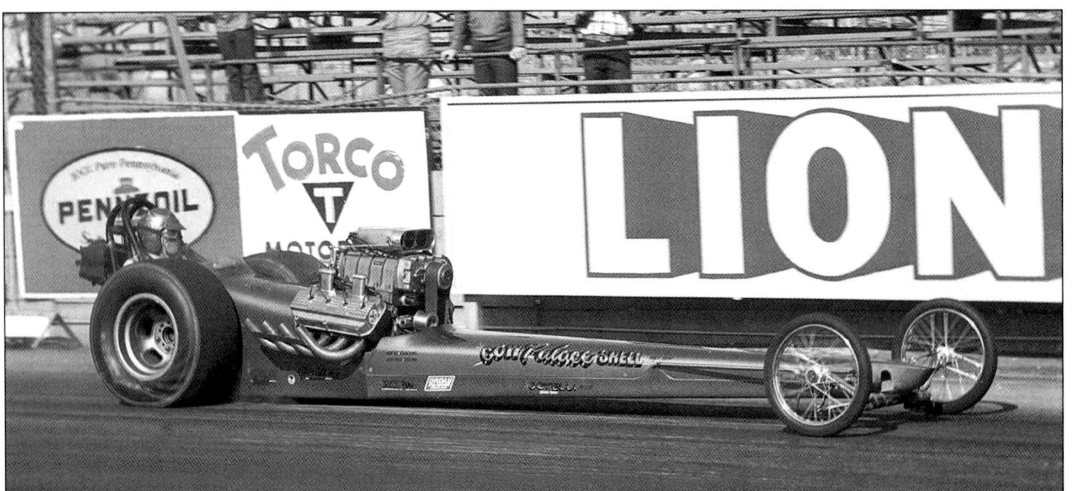

Bobby Hightower was the luckiest/unluckiest driver at the Drag News Nationals. Hightower, driving the **Cow Palace Shell,** *lost in the first round against John Collins. Hightower was reinstated in the second round when Abbott & Lee broke, but once again Hightower was eliminated by James Warren. In round three, Hightower was called back once again to replace the* **Atlas Oil Tool Special** *and face the* **Blue Streak Special.** *Then, in a rematch of the first round, Hightower ran a 6.94 ET at 211.26 mph to Collins's winning 6.74 ET at 222.04 mph.*

James Warren and John Collins met in the fourth and final round with $1,500 on the line. Pre-stage burnouts were completed, and both rolled up to the line. James Warren jumped the gun and left the red light staring him down in his lane.

John Collins flashes the victory sign in reaction to the foul start by James Warren. After a steady diet of running 220-plus mph runs all night, Collins was satisfied with an off-pace 10.96 ET at 94.24 mph.

Dave McKenzie (third from right), John Collins (third from left), Miss Nationals Carolyn Williams, and the crew celebrate good times and $1,500 in the winner's circle after winning Top Eliminator at the Drag News Nationals. (Photo by John Ewald/Courtesy Don Ewald)

Huntington, and Laguna. The pilot turned north and made a few passes over Disneyland when he noticed a heavy concentration of bright lights a few miles away. When the pilot flew to have a closer look at the lights, he came upon Angel Stadium. Evangelist Billy Graham was on stage in front of the capacity crowd inside the venue. Thousands of worshipers were in prayer with closed eyes when Graham cried out, "Lift your hands and cast your eyes toward the heavens."

When the crowd gazed up to the sky, low and behold, there was the helicopter hovering overhead, flashing its message of the upcoming event, "Tomorrow night, Saturday, October 18. Come see and hear the refreshing sounds of real soul music—the loud, 8-cylinder music at Lions Drag Strip!"

Memories

Jim Shue

Hell Fire *Corvette Funny Car Owner*

"In my early days, I made a decent living, but I wanted to go racing and build a Funny Car. I put aside a certain amount of money that went into building the car, but we still scrimped and saved almost every penny, just spending only on the necessities needed for my wife and small daughter. We collected every soda can we found and cashed them in.

"One day, I went to Stardust Raceway in Henderson, Nevada, and met Johnny Wright, who was driving another car. I approached him and said that I was building a Corvette Funny Car, *Hell Fire*. I asked Johnny if he'd be interested, as I wanted to get him involved. We hit it off and exchanged numbers. Johnny was driving another car at that time but on a different strip. He was on a full-throttle pass when the car's engine blew up which led to the car burning to the ground. With no commitment, Johnny came aboard to help finish the car.

"Engine expert Steve Montrelli came into the deal, so we now had the ingredients of a good driver and tuner. I supplied the money and creativity, while Johnny and Steve did the rest.

"Wright wanted to be conservative, and Montrelli wanted to go crazy, so we met somewhere in the middle and were able to be successful without damaging many parts. Together as a team, Johnny, Steve, and I won three meets in row at Lions [Drag Strip] with the *Hell Fire*. Over the years, Steve and I have remained very good friends."

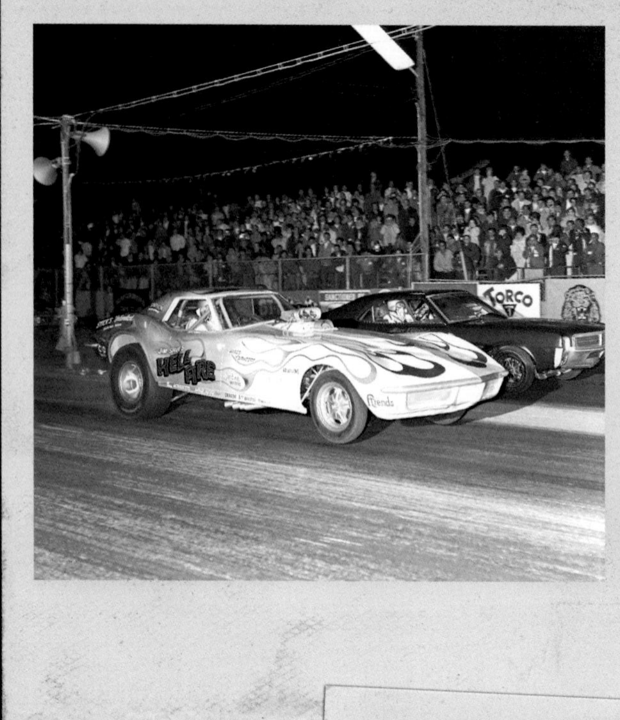

First-round eliminations had Johnny Wright in the **Hell Fire** *Corvette and Rusty Delling driving Marv Eldridge's* **Fiberglass Trends** *candy-red AMC Javelin. Delling had a wild fishtailing ride down the strip with a 9.70 ET at 176.12 mph to Wright's winning 7.82 ET at 186.33 mph.*

The **Hell Fire** *Corvette posted a win over "Flash" Gordon Mineo in round two with a 7.74 ET at 193.54 mph to Gordon's quicker 7.72 ET at 186.72 mph. Wright advanced to the final round to face the* **New Breed** *Firebird of Pete Everett.*

Coca-Cola Stars Refreshed Crowds

Eight of the nation's top fuel-burning Funny Cars were featured in the Coca-Cola Cavalcade of Stars. It got underway with chilly temperatures but some of the hottest action, as every race was loaded with excitement.

The round-robin racing had all eight cars race three complete rounds.

Jon Lundberg, the voice of drag racing, was on hand as the official announcer for the round-by-round excitement. The lineup of the cars from the first to eighth positions was Kelly Chadwick, Bob Smith in the *Un-Cola Invader* Corvette, Marv Eldridge, Dick Bourgeois, Kenny Safford, Fred Goeske, Jess Tyree, and Jack Chrisman.

Memories

Steve Montrelli

Hell Fire *Corvette Crew Chief and Engine Builder*

"Jim Shue and Johnny Wright approached me when I was at Mickey Thompson's place and asked me if I would like to get involved and be a part of the *Hell Fire* [Corvette] team. Jim told me that my job was to build the motors and maintain them.

"During the first few months together, we had our growing pains and had trouble trying to get the car down the track without having something happen. I just couldn't put my finger on it, but it wasn't due to the lack of power. Something wasn't synchronized with the car.

"I went to Mickey's shop and asked if I could borrow his scales from the shop and put them under the race car. Checking the numbers, I figured out what was wrong, made the necessary changes to the chassis, and fixed it.

"The following Saturday, we headed over to Lions [Drag Strip] and got the car to the line. Johnny did the burnout, backed up, and launched it. At the hit—*bang*! The car rolled the rear-end out of the car and snapped the driveshaft into pieces. Wright got hit on the butt by the pieces of the driveshaft, and he went to Long Beach Memorial Hospital to get examined. Other than a few bruises and contusions, he was fine and returned to race.

"Mike Case, who built both the *Hell Fire* and *Invader* Corvette chassis, was at the track and noticed what took place. He told us to load the car onto the trailer and get it over to his shop, which was only a few blocks away. Mike looked over the chassis and found that the damage wasn't too serious. He made the necessary repairs and had the car back to the track within a few hours. Wright returned for qualifying, which started at 6 o'clock. I didn't hold back and hopped that baby up, and Johnny went out and ran 203.61 mph! That was something else."

Johnny Wright brought the $1,500 check to his boss, Jim Shue, after he won at the Drag News Nationals. Wright drove the **Hell Fire** *Corvette past "Doc" Leroy Hales in the* **New Breed** *Firebird with a 8.26 ET at 162.16 mph to Hales's 8.56 ET at 144.69 mph. Shown celebrating the* **Hell Fire's** *victory is (from left to right) crew chief/tuner Steve Montrelli, Carol Wright, Johnny Wright, Miss Drag News Nationals Carolyn Williams, car owner Jim Shue, Judy Shue, and Bridgette Shue. (Photo by John Ewald/Courtesy Don Ewald)*

Alternate Steve Bovan in the *Mister T* Camaro replaced Chrisman in the second round when the roof blew off his Mustang when the blower backfired in the lights. When the racing concluded, Kelly Chadwick was declared the race winner, and Gary Dyer won the Coca-Cola/Sprite Series first championship.

PDA Funny Car Nationals

There were 8,600 Funny Car fans in attendance on Saturday, December 21, 1969, for the first day of the Professional Dragster Association (PDA) Funny Car Nationals. They watched a competition of 40 Funny Cars battle for the top 8 positions during qualifying. The remaining cars went at it for two rounds of hard-charging racing for a remaining spot in the 16-car field that would run on Sunday.

Leading the top eight in the field was "Jungle" Jim Liberman, who posted an unreal 7.08 ET at 192.71 mph. Next in line was Pat Minick in the *Chi-Town Hustler* with a 7.21 ET at 186.33 mph. Larry Reyes driving Roland Leong's *Hawaiian* ran a 7.24 ET at 190.67 mph for third, and Richard Siroonian followed with a 7.28 ET at 198.23 mph. Rounding out the fifth through eighth spots were Tommy Grove (a 7.42 ET at 194.79 mph), Dick Bourgeois driving Don Cook's Corvette (a 7.44 ET at 187.11 mph), "Fearless" Fred Goeske (a 7.44 ET at 194.80 mph), and Danny Ongais piloting the 427 SOHC Mach 1 Mustang of Mickey Thompson (a 7.44 ET at 194.79 mph).

Paula Murphy was considered by many as the first female licensed Funny Car driver when she made a splash in a strong, supercharged Chrysler-powered Mustang. Murphy's previous racing experiences were with Indy Cars, NASCAR stock cars, and other forms of racing that included her most outstanding accomplishment on the Bonneville salt flats.

Murphy set a new women's record in her first-ever jet-powered ride with a top speed of 243.44 mph, which bested her year-old record of 161.29 mph in a Studebaker Avanti. She also set A/SA, F2, and F6 AHRA records while driving an Oldsmobile.

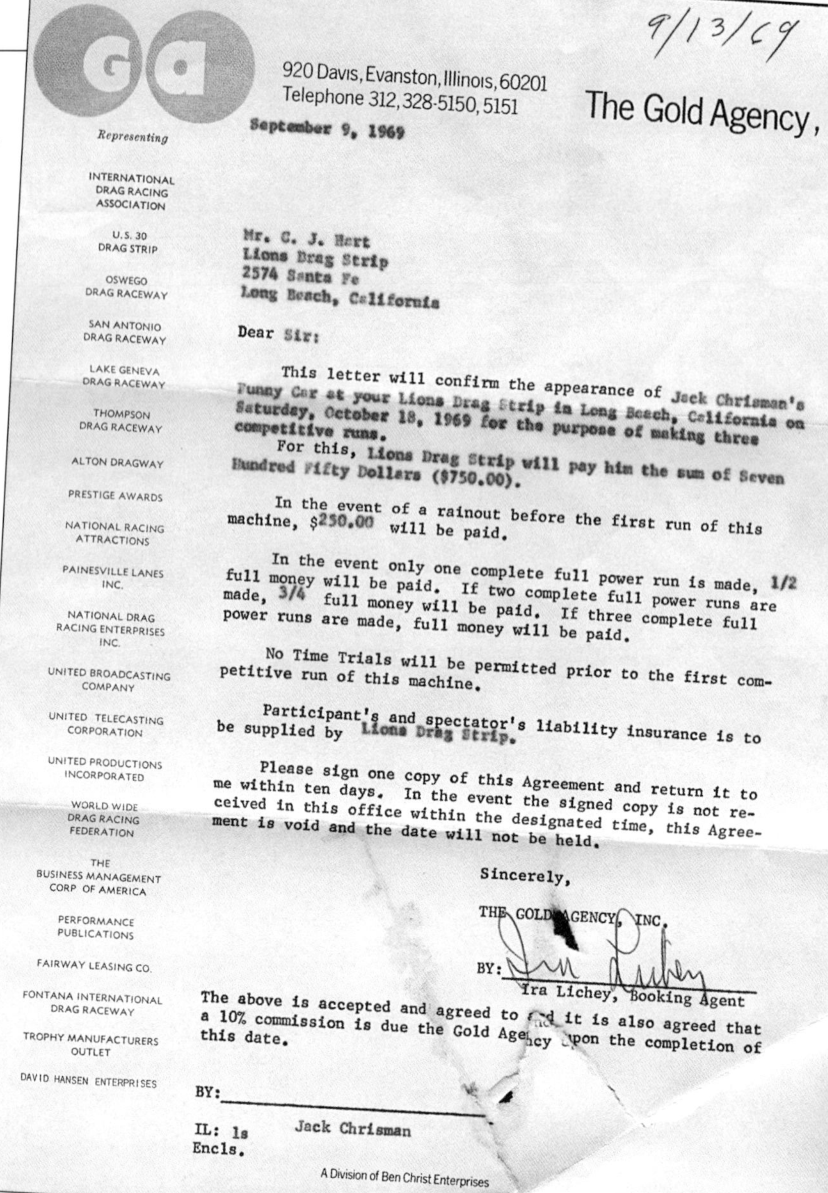

9/13/69

Ga

920 Davis, Evanston, Illinois, 60201
Telephone 312, 328-5150, 5151

The Gold Agency, Inc.

Representing

INTERNATIONAL DRAG RACING ASSOCIATION
U.S. 30 DRAG STRIP
OSWEGO DRAG RACEWAY
SAN ANTONIO DRAG RACEWAY
LAKE GENEVA DRAG RACEWAY
THOMPSON DRAG RACEWAY
ALTON DRAGWAY
PRESTIGE AWARDS
NATIONAL RACING ATTRACTIONS
PAINESVILLE LANES INC.
NATIONAL DRAG RACING ENTERPRISES INC.
UNITED BROADCASTING COMPANY
UNITED TELECASTING CORPORATION
UNITED PRODUCTIONS INCORPORATED
WORLD WIDE DRAG RACING FEDERATION
THE BUSINESS MANAGEMENT CORP OF AMERICA
PERFORMANCE PUBLICATIONS
FAIRWAY LEASING CO.
FONTANA INTERNATIONAL DRAG RACEWAY
TROPHY MANUFACTURERS OUTLET
DAVID HANSEN ENTERPRISES

September 9, 1969

Mr. C. J. Hart
Lions Drag Strip
2574 Santa Fe
Long Beach, California

Dear Sir:

This letter will confirm the appearance of Jack Chrisman's Funny Car at your Lions Drag Strip in Long Beach, California on Saturday, October 18, 1969 for the purpose of making three competitive runs.

For this, Lions Drag Strip will pay him the sum of Seven Hundred Fifty Dollars ($750.00).

In the event of a rainout before the first run of this machine, $250.00 will be paid.

In the event only one complete full power run is made, 1/2 full money will be paid. If two complete full power runs are made, 3/4 full money will be paid. If three complete full power runs are made, full money will be paid.

No Time Trials will be permitted prior to the first competitive run of this machine.

Participant's and spectator's liability insurance is to be supplied by Lions Drag Strip.

Please sign one copy of this Agreement and return it to me within ten days. In the event the signed copy is not received in this office within the designated time, this Agreement is void and the date will not be held.

Sincerely,

THE GOLD AGENCY, INC.

BY: Ira Lichey, Booking Agent

The above is accepted and agreed to and it is also agreed that a 10% commission is due the Gold Agency upon the completion of this date.

BY: ______________________
Jack Chrisman

IL: ls
Encls.

A Division of Ben Christ Enterprises

This contract from the Gold Agency outlines the pay structure for Jack Chrisman. It has been signed by booking agent Ira Lichey. (Document Courtesy Chrisman Family)

Starting off in the first round was "Fearless" Fred Goeske (driving a Plymouth Road Runner in the far lane) against Bob Smith (driving the **Invader** *Corvette in the near lane). The* **Invader** *came on strong for the win over Goeske with a 7.41 ET at 183.67 mph to the Road Runner's losing 7.84 ET at 160.57 mph. (Photo by John Ewald/ Courtesy Don Ewald)*

Jack Chrisman and Marv Eldridge came off the line in the first round to make their burnouts, but Jack lost fire. Eldridge patiently shut off the **Fiberglass Trends** *Corvette and waited for Chrisman to refire. Both cars restarted and moved into the staging lanes. Eldridge got out with the lead and took the win with a 7.84 ET at 180.72 mph. Chrisman turned an 8.13 ET at 177.51 mph and lost the race along with the roof of the car. The input shaft broke out of the transmission, which broke the blower and blew the roof off the car. (Photo by John Ewald/Courtesy Don Ewald)*

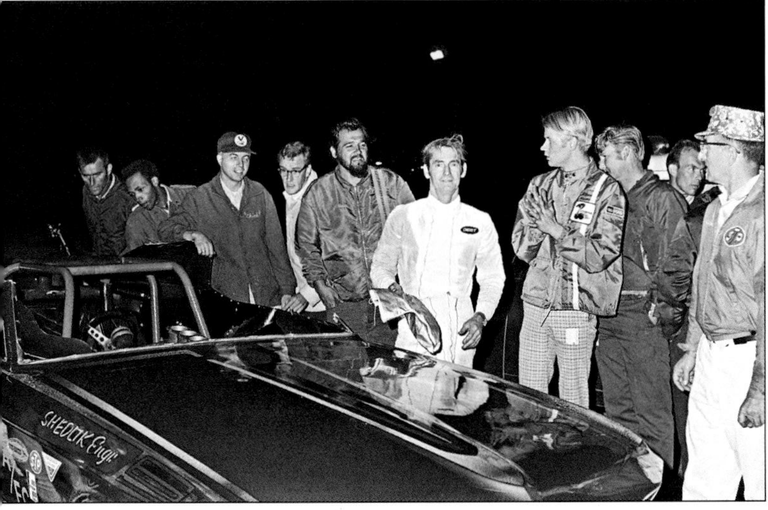

Lions Drag Strip officials C. J. Hart and Chuck Crist survey the damage done to Jack Chrisman's Mustang after the roof became disconnected from the body. The damage was severe and kept Jack from returning to the show. (Photo by John Ewald/Courtesy Don Ewald)

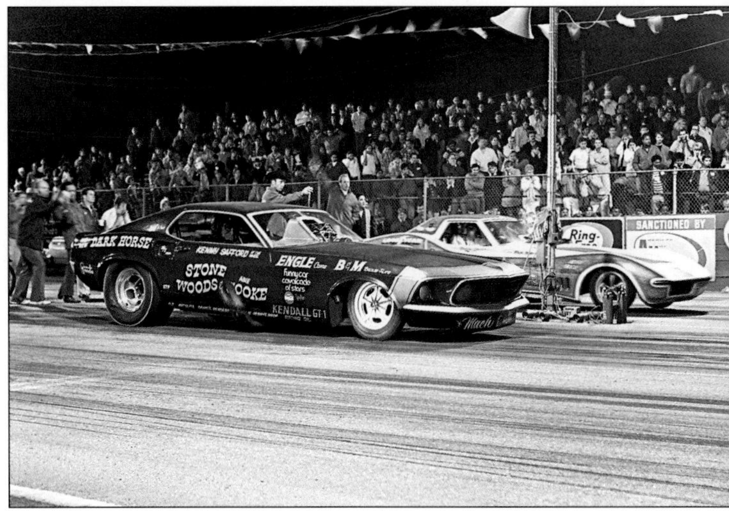

In round two, Bob Smith and the **Invader** *(not taking any burnouts) ran a 7.28 ET at 196.07 mph to shut down Kenny Safford's* **Stone, Woods, & Cooke** *Mustang with a 7.95 ET at 171.75 mph. (Photo by John Ewald/Courtesy Don Ewald)*

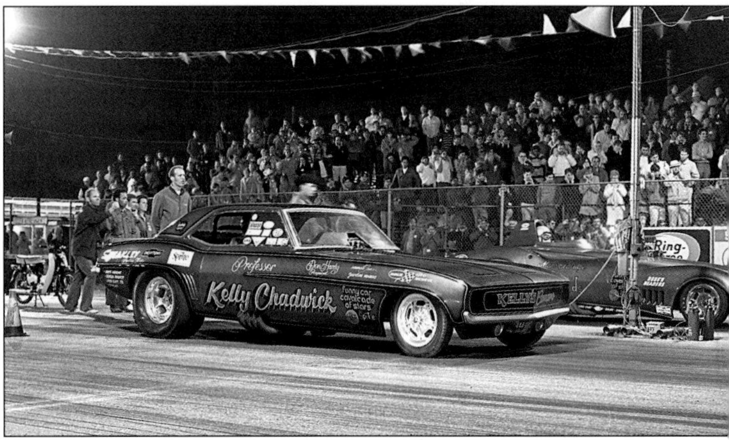

Kelly Chadwick found the strip conditions to his liking when he captured the top honors and the Coca-Cola bucks at Lions Drag Strip. Chadwick won all three of his rounds and set the low ET of the meet. (Photo by John Ewald/Courtesy Don Ewald)

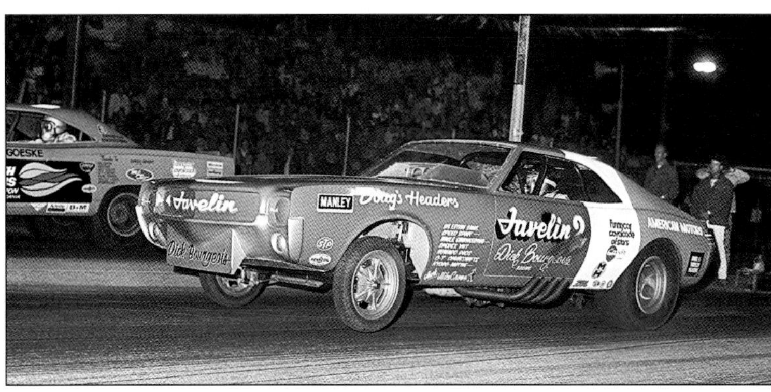

Fred Goeske (far lane), in his 1969 Road Runner Funny Car, takes on Dick Bourgeois in his AMC **Javelin 2** *machine during a rare Plymouth versus AMC matchup.*

Pontiac legend Jess Tyree has always followed the phrase that he coined with Chief Wampum, "I'd rather fight than switch," regarding his loyalty to Pontiac. Tyree ran the Coca-Cola Circuit for several years.

A portion of the Coca-Cola Cavalcade of Stars group gathers at the base of the Lions Drag Strip tower after the race of the popular touring stars. From left to right are the Stone, Woods, & Cooke **Dark Horse** *Mustang with driver Kenny Safford; the* **Fiberglass Trends** *Corvette with Marv Eldridge, his crew, and fans; the Camaro of the "Professor" Kelly Chadwick (the* **Un-cola**)*; the* **Invader** *Corvette driven by Bob Smith; and "Mr. Pontiac" Jess Tyree. (Photo by John Ewald/Courtesy Don Ewald)*

Memories

Steve Chrisman

Son of Drag Racing Pioneer and Lions Drag Strip Legend Jack Chrisman

"I was there in 1969 with my dad when he ran his Mustang for the last time at Lions Drag Strip in the Coca-Cola Cavalcade of Stars. He had already sold the car to Frank Oglesby.

"My dad raced Marv Eldridge in the third race in the first round, and when he got down right by the finish line, the input shaft broke out of the transmission and blew the roof off.

"I remember that Frank was going to come by either Monday or Tuesday to pick the car up. My dad had to call him and say, 'Frank, we have to literally repair the roof that blew off the car.'

"The roof was all scratched up from hitting and dragging along the strip. When Frank came to pick it up, the body was all in primer."

Day 1: Round 1

With the eight seeded cars already planted in the show, the first round of eliminations featured the remaining 32 cars vying for one of the remaining eight slots.

Gene Conway opened with a 6.62 ET at 128.75 mph to win against a troubled Ray Alley's 13.29 ET at 55.18 mph. Roger Wilford soloed in the *Mako Shark* Corvette with a 7.68 ET at 181.09 mph when Junior Brogdon's *Phony Pony* wouldn't fire. Johnny Wright, driving Mickey Thompson's Boss 429 Mustang fell to "Lil' John" Lombardo, who ran an 8.99 ET at 163.68 mph to the Mustang's 9.87 ET at 172.68 mph.

Rusty Delling advanced the *Fiberglass Trends* Javelin into the second round with an all-out single run of 7.73 at 185.56 mph when Don Hampton's *Too Bad* twin-engine Corvette broke on the line.

Bob Pickett's *Mr. Pickett* Javelin was next to advance to the second round when the Javelin drove past the *Proud*

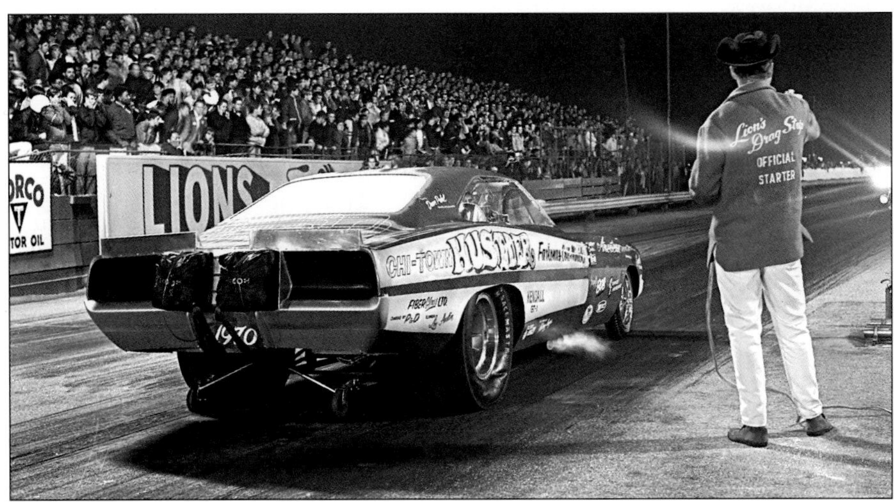

Flames shoot out the exhaust of the **Chi-Town Hustler** *without the smoke clouds from the burnouts that made Pat Minick and the* **Chi-Town Hustler** *the most recognizable Funny Car in drag racing. (Photo by John Ewald/ Courtesy Don Ewald)*

Two Chevy stalwarts, "Jungle" Jim Liberman (near lane) and Randy Walls (far lane), enjoyed success in the mid-1960s, running fuel cars, and they both won their share of races at Lions Drag Strip. (Photo by John Ewald/ Courtesy Don Ewald)

American Corvette of Ed Carter. Paula Murphy continued her march into the next round when she easily defeated Bob Bedell's *Wild Thing* Camaro with a 7.68 ET at 193.96 mph to Bedell's 8.10 ET at 184.88 mph.

Jess Tyree, driving the *Bad Bascomb's Ghost* Chevy II Nova, turned a 7.90 ET at 178.92 mph over Jim Adolph's *Vicious Too* Firebird that ran an 8.89 ET at 178.57 mph, as Adolph had problems getting the Goodyears to bite off the line. Larry Fullerton could only sit and watch Marv Eldridge's *Fiberglass Trends* Corvette advance with a 7.65 ET at 187.50 mph pass when Fullerton's *Trojan Horse* Mustang refused to run.

Randy "Mr. Super Nova II" Walls proved to be super when he bested Ernie Nicholson's AA/GS *Flower Power* Barracuda that ran on nitro for this meet. Nicholson's 8.88 ET at 142.18 mph was too little for the Hemi-powered Barracuda to overtake Walls's Rat-powered Chevy's ET of 8.29 at 184.80 mph.

Next up to the line was a pair of Corvettes: Gervase O'Neill's *King Rat* and Mike Snively subbing for Pat Foster in the *Beach City Chevrolet*. O'Neill proved to be king with his 8.24 ET at 176.81 mph win over Snively's 8.69 ET at 191.08 mph. Clyde Morgan's Experimental Javelin dropped a close encounter with the Beebe Brothers's *Dodge Fever* Charger, as Dave Beebe outran Morgan with a 7.46 ET at 192.71 mph to the Chevy-powered Javelin's 7.60 ET at 196.07 mph.

The next run kept the spectators on the edge of their seats, as Steve Bovan ran a 7.61 ET at 192.30 mph to defeat the unpredictable Don Burns's *Durachrome* Bug handled by Warren Gunter. Gunter kept even with Bovan off the line, but as Gunter approached the 600-foot mark, his e-ticket ride began. The Volkswagen proceeded to skate and wander all over the track and forced Gunter to shut off with a 13.49 ET at 69.87 mph.

Closing out the first round of action, "Flash" Gordon Mineo ran a 7.52 ET at 189.87 mph for the win against "Big" Ed Lenarth's *Holy Toledo* yellow Jeepster. Lenarth followed the path of the *Durachrome* Bug as the yellow brick began to fishtail at mid-track and resulted in Lenarth shutting down with a 10.23 ET at 82.56 mph.

Day 1: Round 2

Sixteen cars got underway in the second round with Jess Tyree in *Bad Bascomb's Ghost* against the *Dodge Fever* driven by Dave Beebe. Tyree won with an 8.03 ET at 182.18 mph. Beebe turned a better ET of 8.01 at 195.22 mph but exited off the line out of shape. Marv Eldridge grabbed his second win of the night with a 7.56 ET at

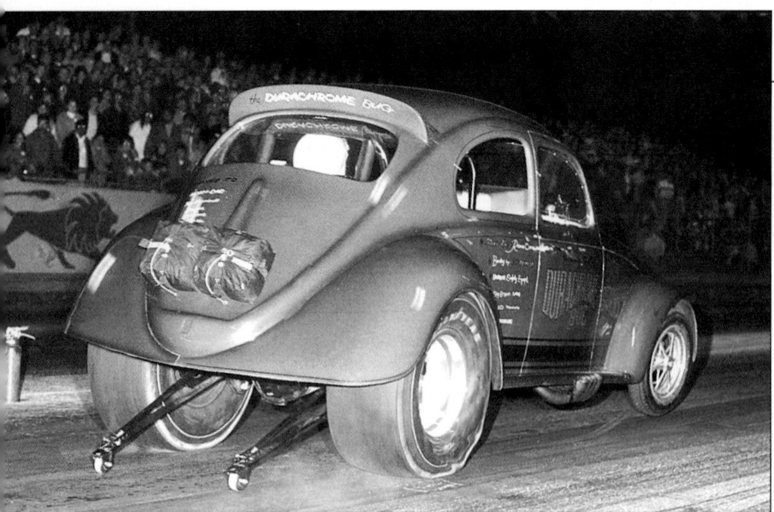

The 427-ci-powered* Durachrome Bug *Volkswagen Beetle of Warren Gunther had its share of handling and performance problems at the Drag News Nationals. Gunther's Volkswagen flopper was a favorite of the spectators, as no one could predict correctly how straight the car would go. (Photo by John Ewald/Courtesy Don Ewald)

189.47 mph over Roger Wilford's 9.02 ET at 98 mph, as the *Mako Shark* lost the engine at mid-track.

Four of the previous round's losers were brought back into the program to make the field complete. Their return was based on the qualifying ETs. One of the returnees, Bob Bedell, made the most of it with a winning 7.65 ET at 189.47 mph over John Lombardo's 8.71 ET at 157.89 mph. Ed Carter returned with a bye run of 7.76 at 170.77 mph when Paula "Miss STP" Murphy broke on the starting line.

Gordon Mineo was slated to face the *King Rat*, but the Sting Ray developed engine troubles in the pits that moved the *Beach City Chevrolet* Corvette back in. Problems with Mineo's Firebird brought Ray Alley up to the line. Snively grabbed the win with a 7.78 ET at 166.97 mph over Alley's 9.33 ET at 172.41 mph. Randy Walls secured a position for Sunday with a winning 7.89 ET at 185.99 mph over Gene Conway, who had a near encounter with the guard rail and shut off early with a 9.39 ET at 95.64 mph.

Clyde Morgan, another low-ET returnee, made it worthwhile when he received a single run when the *Fiberglass Trends* Javelin, driven by Rusty Delling, lost the engine coming off the starting line. Steve Bovan wrapped up the second round and downed Bob Pickett's Javelin with a 7.68 ET at 190.67 mph to Pickett's 7.87 ET at 182.56 mph.

Top speed money of the night went to "Big" John Mazmanian's driver Rich Siroonian with a speed of 198.23 mph in qualifying. The award of low ET went to "Jungle" Jim Liberman for his 7.08, which also put him in the number-one position of the top eight cars.

Day 2: Round 1

The second day of the PDA was greeted by a steady rain shower early Sunday morning. By 1 p.m., the strip was dry, and the Funny Cars were ready and loaded for action. Clyde Morgan started the action with an upset win over the six-seed Dick Bourgeois and the Cook entry. Morgan's ET of 7.55 at 193.92 mph beat the Corvette's 7.58 ET at 188.67 mph.

Chevy powerhouses "Jungle" Jim Liberman and Randy Walls had the makings of a real heads-up race, but at mid-track, Walls's slicks broke loose, and his Nova fishtailed. Liberman wrapped up his 7.56 ET at 191.08 mph over Walls's 8.07 ET at 184.80 mph.

Danny Ongais eliminated Bob Bedell's *Wild Thing* with a 7.25 ET at 198.67 mph to Bedell's 8.57 ET at 118.26 mph. The upset of the race up to this point was that Marv Eldridge's *Fiberglass Trends* Corvette sent favored Richard Siroonian to the trailer. Eldridge's 7.52 ET at 186.35 mph outdistanced the candy red Barracuda of "Big" John Mazmanian that followed closely behind with a 7.56 ET at 189.87 mph. Ed Carter advanced the *Proud American* on a bye run with an ET of 8.63 at 116.78 mph when Fred Goeske suffered transmission woes and shut off.

Tommy Grove pulled a crowd-pleasing wheel-stand on a burnout and went all out for a winning 7.69 ET at 181.81 mph over Mike Snively in the *Beach City Chevrolet* Corvette. Snively, not wanting to be upstaged by Grove, came off the line with an enormous wheel-stand with the back end of the car dragging. After touching back down, Snively made an honest effort to stay in the program, but it was too late. He could only muster a 10.75 ET at 91.27 mph.

Jess Tyree brought the *Bad Bascomb's Ghost* Chevrolet a step closer to another round when the *Hawaiian*, driven by Larry Reyes, had traction problems and went up in smoke. Tyree sailed through the lights with a 7.87 ET at 183.29 mph to Reyes's 15.66 ET at 48.88 mph. For the last pair in round one, Steve Bovan grenaded the rear-end and its contents all over the starting line. Bovan's counterpart, the *Chi-Town Hustler*, sailed through the lights with a 7.36 ET at 195.22 mph.

Day 2: Round 2

Marv Eldridge was the recipient of a bye run, running an 8.05 ET at 127.84 mph when Mickey Thompson's

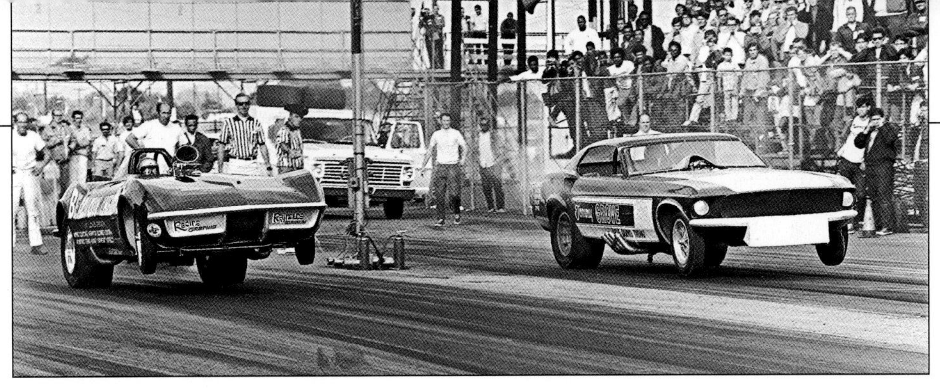

Tommy Grove unleashed a barrage of power in the first round against the **Beach City Chevrolet** *Corvette on Sunday. Grove advanced to the final round to face the* **Chi-Town Hustler** *in a classic East versus West matchup.*

Mach 1 would not fire. Tommy Grove recorded a winning 7.36 ET at 199.11 mph over Jess Tyree when *Bad Bascomb's Ghost* lost control at mid-track and got extremely close to the guardrail. He shut off with a 9.49 ET at 97.71 mph. Pat "Mr. Consistency" Minick, continued his hot streak and took down Clyde Morgan with a 7.25 ET at 200.99 mph to Morgan's 8.96 ET at 99.19 mph. Liberman recorded a 7.50 ET at 193.54 mph on a single when Ed Carter broke off the line.

Day 2: Round 3

Liberman's luck ran out against Tommy Grove in the semifinal round when he flooded the engine and the engine died on the starting line. Grove traveled the distance on a single and turned a 7.32 ET at 198.23 mph.

Next, Marv Eldridge saw his chances diminish when he dropped the hammer too quickly and fouled, handing the win to Minick and the *Chi-Town Hustler*. Even with the automatic win, Minick never let up, lifted the front end several feet off the ground, fishtailed through the top end, and stopped the clocks with a 7.28 ET at 201.34 mph.

Day 2: Final Round

The fourth and final round brought Tom Grove and the "Beast from the East" Pat Minick up to the line. After both cars fired and filled the area with tire smoke after some incredible burnouts, both were locked in and ready to go. Both cars were dead even off the line and saved their best runs of the day for the final. At the finish, it was Minick across the line first with a 7.20 ET at 203.16 mph to Grove's fantastic 7.26 ET at 200.89 mph. The two-day affair drew more than 14,500 spectators and closed out another record year at Lions Drag Strip.

From an interview published in *Drag News*, Ken Coventry, the West Coast tech representative for the AHRA, thanked the crew at Lions Drag Strip regarding the conditions for the two-day Funny Car PDA Nationals. Coventry stated that since the strip was well-organized, his job was easy.

"In my many years being associated with Lions [Drag Strip] and the AHRA, I never had trouble here," Coventry said. "More records are set at Lions than any other AHRA track in the country."

A Stellar Closeout to the Decade

In 1968 and 1969, drag racing was now a full-time business. Attendance numbers rose at record rates at Lions Drag Strip, with the many outstanding promotions offered by the creative staff.

Several local California drag racers successfully made the change from being the weekend hobbyists to full-time professionals. They hired booking agents or took on racing dates on their own across the country and made an upscale living on the road. Another major swing was that Funny Cars were now the popular draw at Lions Drag Strip, dethroning the Top Fuelers.

The proceeds from the drag strip increased, and the Lions Club distributed record amounts of money to local charities. With a new decade on the horizon, the future at Lions Drag Strip was even more promising.

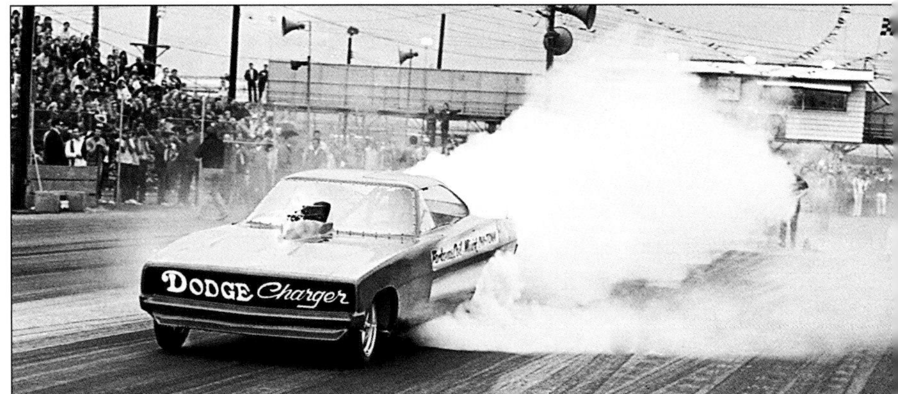

Pat Minick and the **Chi-Town Hustler** *create bellowing smoke clouds. At the Funny Car Professional Dragster Association (PDA) Nationals, the* **Chi-Town Hustler** *beat Tommy Grove in the finals to earn the prize money. Minick recorded the low ET and top speed of the meet with a 7.20 ET at 203.63 mph. (Photo by John Ewald/Courtesy Don Ewald)*

Chapter Six

1970–1971

Lions Drag Strip's Most Spectacular Years Yet

The January 17, 1970, issue of *Drag News* stated, "Weather slows drag racing action nationwide." As for Southern California, there was no end in sight to the erratic downpours. It was one of the rainiest seasons in the history of the South Bay area. Record rainfall and flooding forced the cancellation of the Fuel Funny Car and Top Fuel season opener on January 7. Due to back-to-back-to-back weekends with more rain, dark clouds, fog, and unusually cold temperatures, the action was postponed until January 27.

When Mother Nature finally cooperated, C. J. Hart juggled the schedule and pulled out the "Meet of Meets" with the look of a one-day national event. Multiple fields of injected Funny Cars, Jr. Fuelers, BB/Gassers, and both small- and big-block classes of Jr. Gas dragsters were combined from the two previous

Mike Clancy and Jay Carpenter ran one of the most dominant Junior Fuel dragsters on the West Coast. Clancy powered the Devine-built dragster to ETs in the 7.40s and top speeds of 200-plus mph from the nitro-fueled, 302-ci Chevrolet engine. (Photo by John Ewald/Courtesy Don Ewald)

Fred Kramer lines up in the beams and is ready to compete in the **Gustin & Kramer** *entry at Lions Drag Strip. Jerry Gustin and Fred Kramer hailed from Covina, California, and won class elimination in Saturday's A/FD class at the 1969 NHRA Winternationals. Sunday's Super Eliminator in the first round was a real heartbreaker. The car that pulled the upset of the meet when it beat the* **Adams & Enriquez** *A/FD refused to fire against Carl Heichel's* **Carole's Mink** *A/AA. (Photo by John Ewald/Courtesy Don Ewald)*

Gene Adams and Don Enriquez were considered to be number-one runners in Junior Fuel from the late 1960s through the early 1970s. They set and broke nearly every record in the Junior Fuel class. Adams was one of the original pioneers who ran stockers, gassers, and dragsters. One of his formidable teams was with Leonard Harris and the **Albertson Olds** ***that won 11 consecutive Eliminator titles at Lions Drag Strip before Harris was fatally injured driving another dragster at Lions. (Photo by John Ewald/Courtesy Don Ewald)***

wash-out dates. It was essentially three weekends of racing under a one-day card.

This also included the rained-out City of Garden Grove Challenge from January 10, with four resident Funny Cars that hailed from Orange County: Ray Alley (*Engine Masters* Barracuda), Clyde Morgan (*Experimental* Javelin), Marc "the Kid" Sussman (Chevy II), and the Beebe Brothers (*Dodge Fever* Charger). The standby Funny Car was the *Durachrome* Bug of Warren Gunter out of Don Burns Volkswagen of Garden Grove. To not disappoint both racers and fans, Hart brought in another eight fuel Funny Cars that were all prequalified and paired to race in the first round.

C. J. Hart and the whole Lions Drag Strip crew pulled off near-nonstop rounds of action that started at 9 a.m. and concluded at the 11 p.m. curfew. The action only halted for a dinner break at 6 p.m.

The Grand American Championships

The 1970 AHRA Grand American Championships at Lions Drag Strip featured two full days of jam-packed racing that highlighted three 16-car fields of Top Fuel Funny Cars, Top Fuel Dragsters, and the popular Super Stocks.

Torrential downpours washed out the scheduled $100,000 championships for the weekend of February 28 and March 1, so when the Grand American was rescheduled for the following weekend, the question asked to the racers and fans was, "Where should we go on March 7 and 8?"

With spilt venues for both the Bakersfield Fuel and Gas Championships at Famoso and the rain-delayed AHRA Grand American at Lions Drag Strip, both venues were aware of the precarious situation. They both agreed to go forward to make the best of the situation. With many AHRA competitors chasing elusive series points, they chose to compete at Lions Drag Strip.

Two days of incredible competition at Lions Drag Strip resulted with a dozen new AHRA class records. Richard Tharp, Danny Ongais, and Ed Miller outshined the

By no means did the one-week delay put a damper on the excitement of watching "Big Daddy" Don Garlits smoking it out from the bleach box at Lions Drag Strip. Garlits and George Hutcheson faced each other in the first round, but Hutcheson got off the line sideways, crossed over the centerline, and was disqualified. Garlits went up in a cloud of smoke, broke the rear-end, and coasted through with an 11.32 ET at 65.69 mph. (Photo Courtesy Paul Johnson Collection)

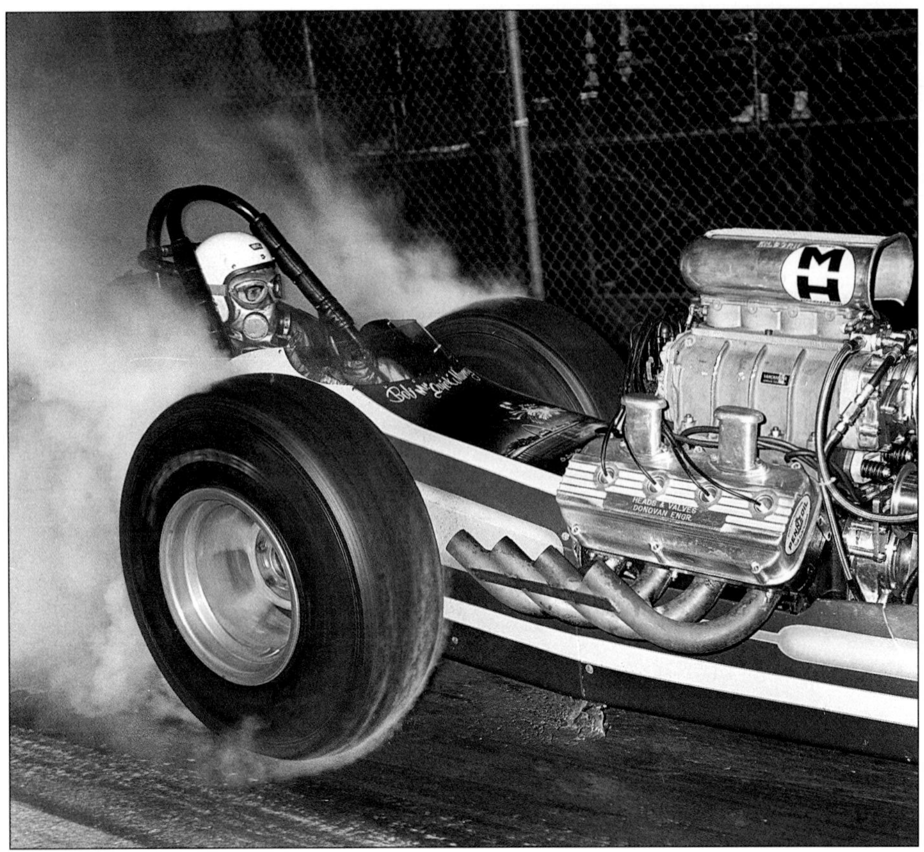

Bob "Mr. Quick" Murray, from St. Louis, Missouri, left the cold Midwest to run in the sun at the AHRA Grand American at Lions Drag Strip. Murray's 7.07 ET at 205.01 mph in the first round couldn't advance him into the second round.

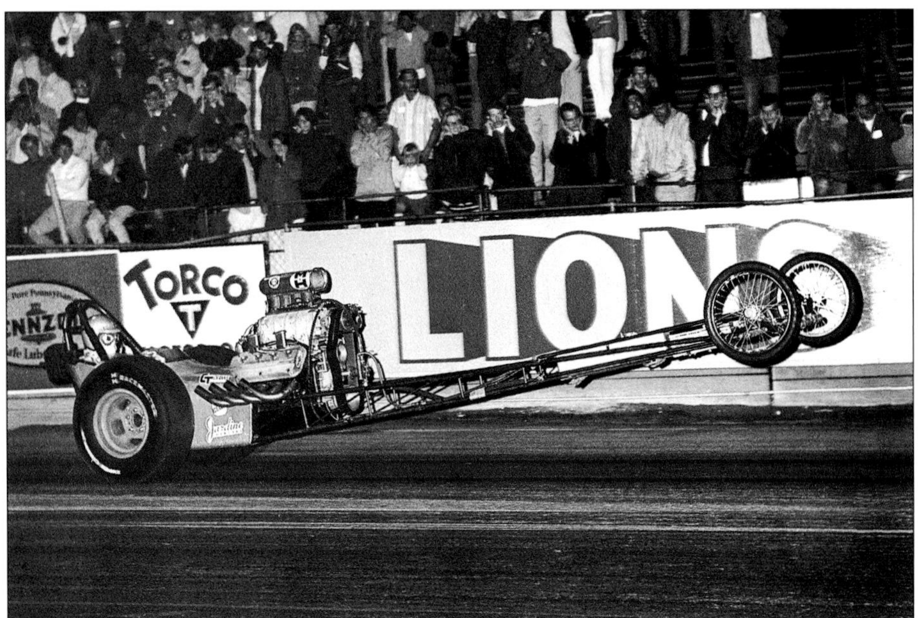

Potter and Glasman fell victim to the bite in the left lane against "King" Richard Tharp in the **Creitz & Donovan** ***fueler. Tharp wasted no time with a 6.62 ET at 221.26 mph to Hippo's slowed 7.88 ET at 178.42 mph.***

competition in their respective classes to take top honors. Even competitors in the lower classes shattered the record book with astonishing performances.

The Bite was Right

Saturday was reserved strictly for qualifying and class and record runs. Many cars discovered and experienced the fantastic bite of the strip. On each run, car after car came off the line and lifted the front wheels high off the strip. Some of the victims that were bitten by the traction were Shirley Shahan, Al Marshall, and Don Grotheer. Records fell when *Ramchargers* driver Leroy Goldstein set both low ET and top speed of the meet on Saturday for Funny Cars (a 7.14 ET at 209.76 mph).

Unpredictable Misfortunes

The one-week delay did not take any of the excitement away for the AHRA Grand American. With all of the accolades received by the winners, the despair of an unfortunate disaster was had by Leroy Goldstein, Chris "The Greek" Karamesines, and "Big Daddy" Don Garlits.

Other victims of track conditions in qualifying included "Flash" Gordon Mineo, who just completed construction of his new Firebird (only hours before), and Clyde Morgan. Each had his hands full in a fishtailing contest and out-dodged each other in the full quarter mile. Both cars made it to the finish line, one behind the other—in the same lane.

Larry Christopherson and the *Bushwacker* each shut off after they headed skyward with giant wheelies toward the guardrail. Leroy Goldstein set both low ET and top speed of the meet on Saturday for Funny Cars (a 7.14 ET at 209.76 mph), but,

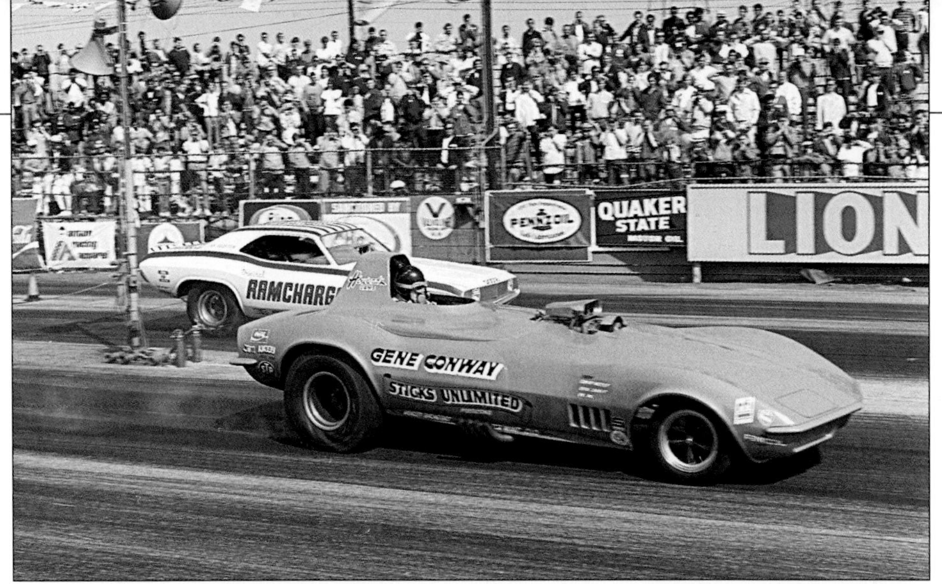

Leroy Goldstein piloted the **Ramchargers** *Dodge Challenger AA/FC to low ET and top-speed honors at the AHRA Grand American with a 7.14 ET at 209.00 mph. Goldstein drew Gene Conway in the first round, where Conway wasted no time on the tree with a holeshot for the win—a 7.54 ET at 182.55 mph to the Dodge's 7.39 ET at 197.80 mph. (Photo Courtesy Paul Johnson Collection)*

unfortunately for Leroy, he couldn't back up the records due to fire damage and minor burns that knocked him from contention.

Don Garlits began his journey of misfortunes in the first round of eliminations against George Hutcheson. Hutcheson got out of shape and crossed over the yellow line for the immediate disqualification. Garlits's *Wynnscharger,* went up in heavy clouds of smoke and broke the rearend in the process. Garlits coasted through the lights with an 11.32 ET at 65.69 mph.

Chris Karamesines was the next casualty during eliminations, as his engine decided to self-implode in the lights against King & Marshall in the second round. Karamesines lost to Jimmy King with a 6.77 ET at 218.44 mph and received multiple facial cuts and burns from hot shrapnel, requiring numerous stitches to his face.

Don Garlits and Don Cook went head to head in the second round, but it was Garlits for the win when he cut a good light and blazed a 6.65 ET at 221.13 mph to Cook's up-in-smoke 7.31 ET at 136.57 mph.

Don Cook blisters the hides in the **Southwind Too** *in his second qualifying attempt at the Grand American. Cook went on to race Bob "Mr. Quick" Murray in the first round. Murray's run went up in smoke, and Cook earned the win.*

John Wiebe was a one-man show with a bye run in the first round when the McCloud & Moore entry broke on the line. Wiebe didn't hold back with a 6.70 ET at 209.70 mph.

Lou Baney's *Folgers Ford Special*, driven by Kelly Brown, put away Jim Nicoll's *Der Wienerschnitzel* fueler in the first round with a 6.63 ET at 223.13 mph to Nicoll's 6.84 ET at 215.31 mph. Unable to make the call for round two, Nicoll replaced the broke Lou Baney but was sent back to the sidelines after he lost to John Wiebe.

Round three saw Don Garlits establish an AHRA and Lions Drag Strip ET record with a winning 6.57 ET at 223.32 mph over John Wiebe, who was right on the heels of Garlits with a 6.63 ET at 223.13 mph. Things looked positive for Garlits going into the final-round against Richard Tharp.

Chris "the Golden Greek" Karamesines boils the hides before his second-round encounter against Jimmy King. King won with a 6.69 ET at 225.00 mph to Karamesines's 6.77 ET at 218.44 mph. As Karamesines crossed the finish line, the supercharger let go and sent fragments of metal into his forehead, which stunned him momentarily. Several stiches were required to close the wound. (Jere Aldereff Photography/ Courtesy Lions Automobilia Foundation Museum)

Jimmy "El Diablo" King singled in the first round when Dan Horan broke on the line and sat helplessly. King ran a 6.68 ET at 224.43 mph.

The multifaceted Gary Southern was up to driving anything during his 30-year career. It is estimated that Southern drove more than 70 cars, including a vast selection of Gassers, Sport Cars, Altereds, Top Fuel and Alcohol front- and rear-engine dragsters, and Funny Cars.

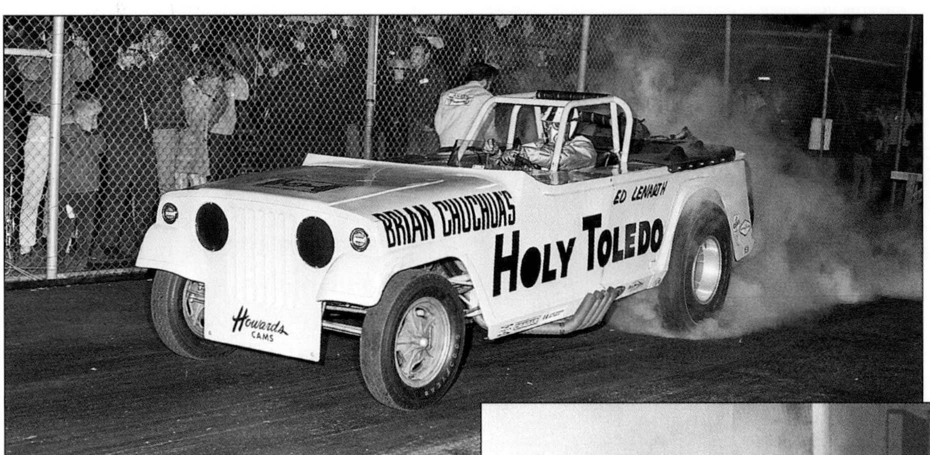

Ed Lenarth's **Holy Toledo** *put up a good fight with a 7.71 ET at 187.89 mph in the first round against Danny Ongais. However, the yellow brick wasn't strong enough to overcome Ognais's 7.42 ET at 197.48 mph. (Photo by John Ewald/Courtesy Don Ewald)*

Jim Nicolls's **Der Wienerschnitzel** *lost in the first round to Kelly Brown when Brown ran a 6.70 ET at 208.81 mph to Nicolls's 6.84 ET at 205.81 mph. In round two, Nicoll was reinstated after Baney & Brown broke, but Nicoll took the rear seat with an 8.97 ET at 205.31 to John Wiebe's 6.69 ET at 202.24 mph. (Jere Aldereff Photography/ Courtesy Lions Automobilia Foundation Museum)*

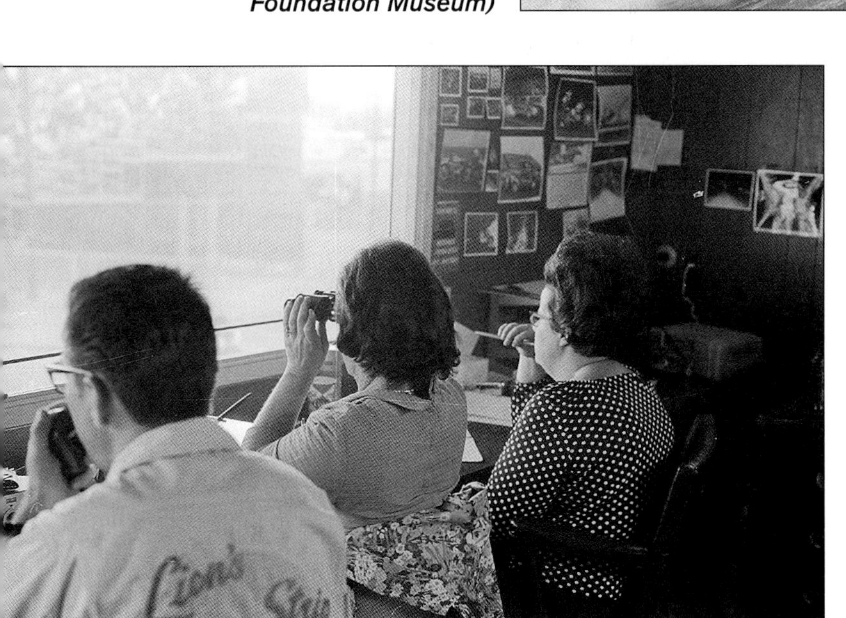

The heroes behind the scenes at the Grand American were announcer Jerry Hart, who called the high-spirited action, while Jerry's wife, Shari, observed the action back down on the strip. Pam Sutton, the Lions Drag Strip statistician, kept the records on all of the hot cars' times and speeds. (Photo by John Ewald/ Courtesy Don Ewald)

Steve Reyes was the dean of drag racing photographers. He attended his first drag race at Fremont Drag Strip in 1963 and brought a Kodak Brownie 620 camera to capture the action. Reyes's success and achievements earned him recognition, as he was inducted into the Don Garlits International Hall of Drag Fame (2002), NHRA California Hot Rod Reunion Honorees (2009), and the East Coast **Drag Times** *Hall of Fame (2011).*

Dick Landy's new Dodge Challenger was in top form but fell a few cars short of making an appearance in the finals. As with his counterparts, Landy found the traction at Lions Drag Strip misleading and sent his Mopar skyward on several runs.

Bill Heisler was one of the most unheralded Chevrolet achievers in the history of the AHRA. Heisler was a drag racing advocate and ran a series of **Mr. Bardahl** *Bill McKay Chevrolet–sponsored race cars that included Corvettes and Camaros. Heisler's acclaimed 1965 Corvette brought him national recognition, where he won nine AHRA titles in a single year.*

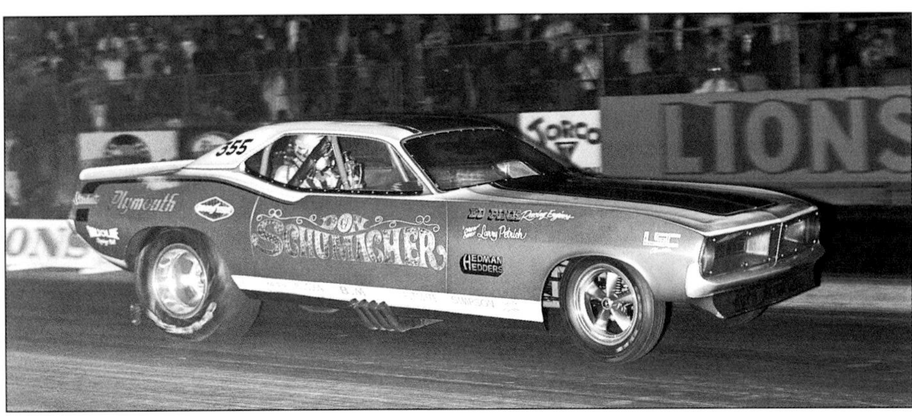

With Don Schumacher competing at the 12th-annual Fuel and Gas Championships in Bakersfield with his **Stardust** *Plymouth Duster, Cliff Zink piloted Schumacher's #2 car at the Grand American. Poor traction and handling kept Zink out of the program.*

The Race That Changed Drag Racing Forever

Don Garlits's *Swamp Rat 13* established the new AHRA and Lions Drag Strip ET record of 6.57 at 223.37 mph in the previous round of eliminations and defeated John Wiebe.

The final round of Top Fuel brought Garlits up to the line to face Texan Richard Tharp, who was driving the *Creitz & Donovan* entry. As the countdown of lights went to green, both drivers dropped the hammer. Tharp shot straight off the line while Garlits moved approximately 10 feet off the line when— *kaboom*! His 2-speed transmission exploded and cut the famous black *Wynnscharger* into two sections.

The front section with the engine skidded to a stop while the rear section with the rear-end and Garlits strapped in the seat stopped just feet away.

It was havoc all around the starting line. Immediately, Mickey Thompson was the first on the scene to aid Garlits, followed by starter Larry Sutton and Garlits's mechanic, T. C. Lemons. They found Don stunned and in a semiconscious state when they noticed the devastating injury to his right leg and foot.

In addition, a large piece of shrapnel from the exploded transmission bounced across the strip surface and took out the powerline to the timing lights before it skipped up into

At exactly 5:25 p.m. on March 8, 1970, the world of drag racing changed in an instant, as national drag racing champion Don Garlits suffered a severe right foot injury when his **Swamp Rat 13** *dragster exploded 10 feet off the starting line against Richard Tharp in the* **Creitz & Donovan** *fueler in the final round of the AHRA Grand American. Garlits's 2-speed transmission exploded and cut the car in half. Garlits was severely injured, as was a young spectator in the grandstands when pieces of shrapnel flew into the crowd. Both were rushed by ambulance to Long Beach Memorial Hospital. The debris seen in the photo narrowly missed Roland Leong and Tom McEwen before it landed in the crowd.*

the stands. A 17-year-old young man was standing in the grandstands watching the race when the debris hit him in the chest and left arm. Blood gushed from his nearly severed arm. Spectators from the rows behind him rushed to the young man and laid him down. Another man in the stands put his thumb into the cut artery in the injured man's arm to stop the bleeding.

Both Garlits and the young man were immediately placed into the ambulance and rushed to Pacific Hospital in Long Beach. Garlits suffered a broken leg and severed toes on his right foot. Unaware of the starting-line catastrophe, Tharp nabbed the Top Fuel honors and ran a 6.65 ET at 200.89 mph. As the car sailed through the lights, the engine let go, which resulted in minor burns to his hands and face.

Funny Car Eliminator

The Funny Cars fared better at the Grand American than in Top Fuel. The first round of 16 Funny Cars got underway when Dick Harrell defeated Gordon Mineo. Roger Wolford got past Tom McEwen when McEwen's *Hot Wheels* Duster's fuel pump broke on the burnout. Danny Ongais in Mickey Thompson's *Mach 1* outran Ed Lenarth's *Holy Toledo* Jeepster. Ray Alley got the easy win over Bob Stuckey, and Gene Conway dropped Leroy Goldstein and the Ramchargers. Larry Reyes and Roland Leong powered Prock & Howell's LSC *Warhorse* Mustang to a win over Marv Eldridge. Gene Snow outpowered Clyde Morgan, and Don Prudhomme advanced into round two of eliminations when Prudhomme drove around Larry Christopher.

In round two, Gene Snow eliminated Larry Reyes. Gene Conway ran into engine trouble and shut off and gave the win to Ray Alley. Prudhomme got the win over "Mr. Chevrolet" Dick Harrell, and Danny Ongais put Pete Everett's *Wild Breed* on the trailer.

In the third round, Prudhomme had the easy path into the finals when Gene Snow's *Rambunctious* could

Wheels Up!

C. J. Hart knew that unusual attractions brought curious-minded folks to Lions Drag Strip, which hosted some of the wildest acts in drag racing.

At the AHRA Grand American, he brought both the *Back-up Pickup* and the *Flying Red Baron* wheel-standers to entertain the crowd between elimination rounds. The Ford Econoline pickup was handled by George Tuers, while famed Fuel Altered pilot Dale Emery built the 1969 *Flying Red Baron* Mustang.

Emery's stint with the *Red Baron* didn't last long, as Dale sold the Mustang that took to the skies in the early 1970s. Emery sold it to Gary "Texas Wheelstand King" Watson, who put Tommy Davis at the controls.

Adding to the excitement of the wheel-standers was the Pennzoil stunt pilot Art Scholl, who performed on Saturday and Sunday with his spectacular maneuvers.

Sponsored by Justice Brother products and Folger Ford, the **Back-Up** *pickup and driver George Tuers brought the crowd to its feet with a shower of sparks as he traveled more than 5,000 feet on the rear wheels. For the encore, Tuers's return trip to the starting line earned cheers and applause from the fans.*

not get into gear. Prudhomme took the single with a 7.74 ET at 153.08 mph, while Ongais earned his way into the final with a winning 7.40 ET at 190.67 mph over Ray Alley's 7.61 ET at 183.08 mph.

The finals in Funny Car followed the finals of Top Fuel, which had been delayed due to the Garlits explosion on the starting line. Since the power lines to both the Christmas tree and timing lights were damaged by debris, both Danny Ongais and Don Prudhomme approved the use of a flag start. A white chalk line marked the starting line, and starter Larry Sutton took his position in front of the cars with both flags.

With both cars locked on the white line, Sutton raised the red flag, dropped the green flag, and both cars were off and running. At mid-track,

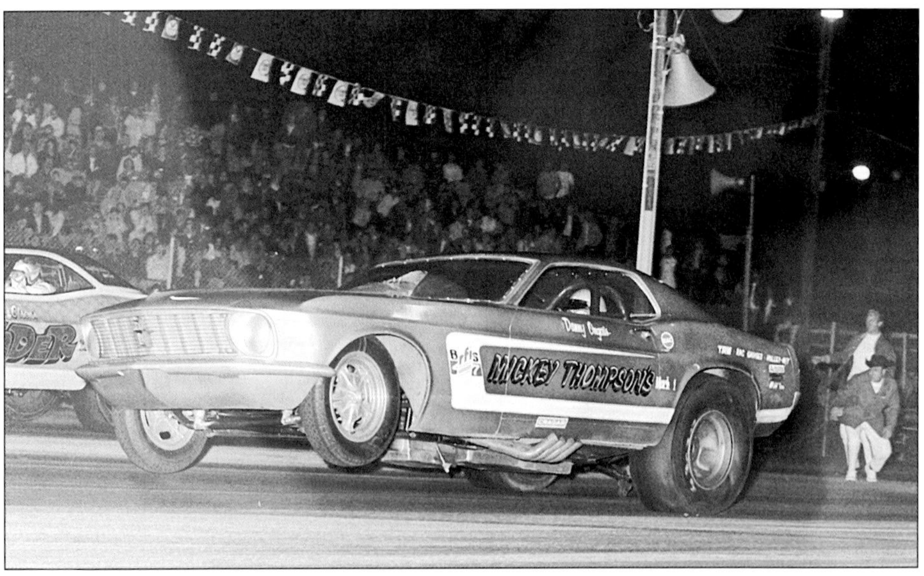

Danny Ongias, in Mickey Thompson's Mach 1, competes against the **Invader** *'Cuda during Saturday's qualifying sessions. Drivers discovered the famous "bite" of the Lions Drag Strip, as cars came off the line with the front wheels high off the strip. Ongais went on to win Funny Car Eliminator on Sunday with a flag-start victory over Don Prudhomme in the finals. Ongais recorded a 7.25 ET at 201.00 mph to hold off Prudhomme's 7.41 ET at 204 mph.*

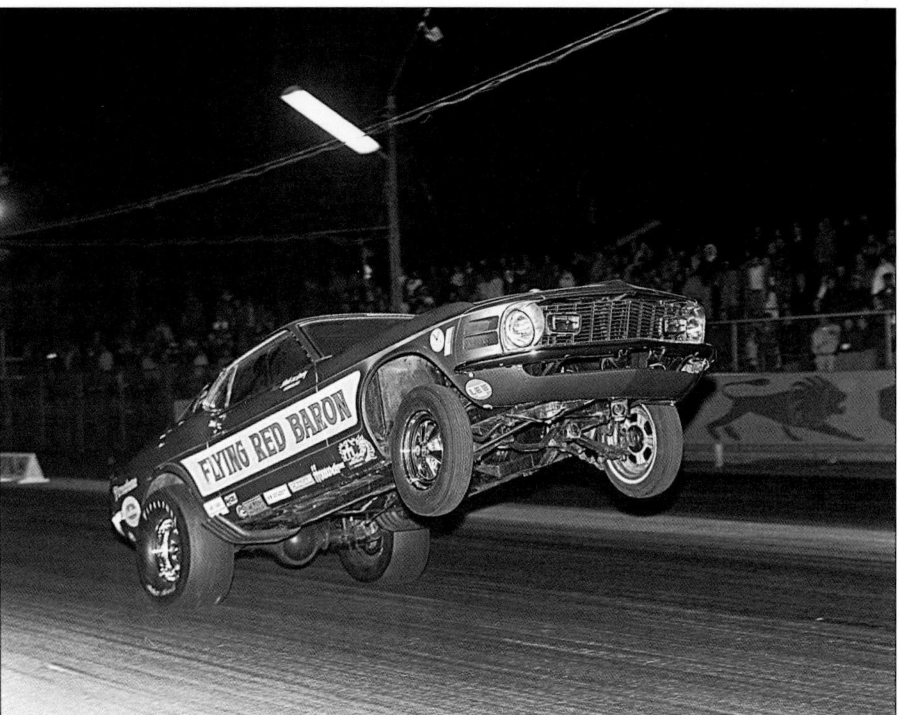

Famed Fuel Altered pilot Dale Emery had a hand in building the 1970 **Flying Red Baron** *Mustang. Emery's ownership stint with the* **Red Baron** *didn't last long, as Dale sold the Mustang to Gary "the Texas Wheel-Stand King" Watson, who put Tommy Davis at the controls.*

Ongais put the move down on Prudhomme and lit up the finish lights first with an estimated 7.25 ET at 201 mph to Prudhomme's 7.41 ET at 205 mph.

Super Stock Competition

The eight-car field was led by "Dyno" Don Nicholson driving his Mr. Gasket–backed Maverick. Nicholson, Bill "Mr. Bardahl" Hielscher, Gary Kimble, and Ed Miller advanced to round two.

A win by Miller over Kimble and a win by Nicholson over the Corvette of Bill Hielscher put a Plymouth and Ford in the final round. Both cars got off the line evenly, but at mid-track, Nicholson was done, as he missed a shift and gave the win to Miller, who reeled off a 10.07 ET at 135.74 mph to the Maverick's 14.13 ET at 67.00 mph.

GT-1 competition was won by Dick Wood driving the Ford-backed Mustang of Ed Terry. The GT-2 winner was Dave Jones in Bill Hielscher's Camaro. Ron Durham, a regular at Lions Drag Strip, powered his 302-ci Camaro to capture GT-3 class. As a side note, Durham kept his undefeated streak intact in GT-3.

"Dyno" Don Nicholson settled for the runner-up position in the Super Stock competition final when Nicholson had trouble shifting into fourth gear against Ed Miller's Plymouth.

Both the Lions Drag Strip and AHRA crews and all the participants were applauded for their efforts toward a well-run Grand American race. Jerry Tice received special recognition for his long hours promoting one of most successful events held at Lions Drag Strip.

Throughout the summer months, Lions Drag Strip remained one of the top spectator attractions on the West Coast with Wednesday night brackets, top drawing cards of fuel Funny Cars, Top Fuel dragsters, Gassers, Fuel Altereds, and the fuel-injected machines of Jr. Fuel and Jr. Gas.

Jet Fuel Cars Rule

Lions Drag Strip hosted a battle of Jet Fuel cars on October 3 that featured Doug Rose's *Green Mamba* and Fred Sibley's *U.S.-1* with the undercard of injected Funny Cars, Jr. Fuelers, and Jr. Gas.

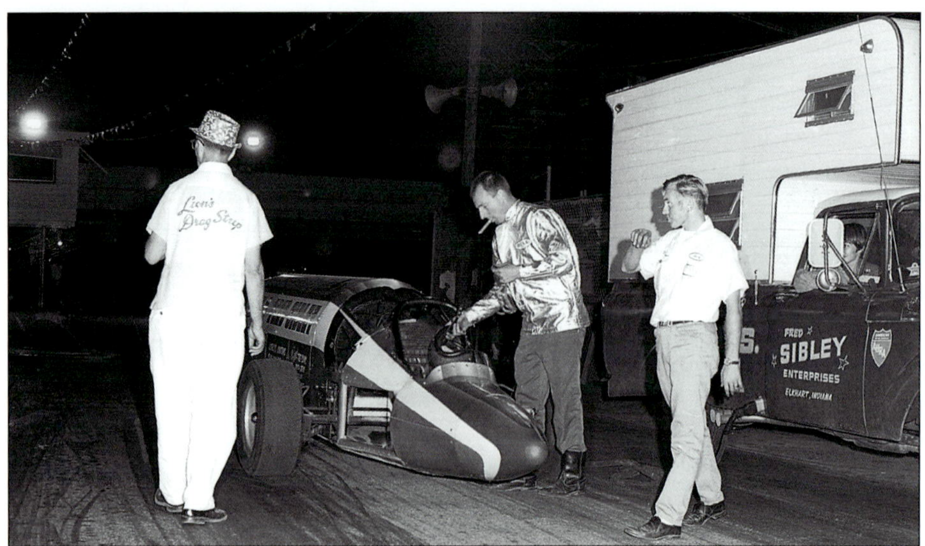

C. J. Hart clears out the lanes behind Fred Sibley's 3,000-pound **U.S. 1** *jet dragster to avoid any damage or injuries from the 30-foot flames produced by the J-37's afterburner. Sibley grabs his helmet while commencing the startup sequence with the auxiliary power unit plugged into the jet engine. (Photo by John Ewald/Courtesy Don Ewald)*

Fred Sibley checks over the pressure and electrical gauges during the startup process of the **U.S. 1** *jet dragster. Sibley had been around racing jet cars since the early 1960s. Sibley's* **U.S. 1** *was built by Bill Frederick. It was originally named* **The Valkyrie** *and was driven for a period of time by Gary Gabelich. The idea was to race the car at Bonneville. However, various problems kept it from running. In 1963, it was taken to the Smokers, Inc. Drags in Bakersfield, California. The* **Valkyrie 1** *was involved with the first side-by-side jet race in drag racing history with* **The Untouchable** *in a best-of-five match race. (Photo by John Ewald/Courtesy Don Ewald)*

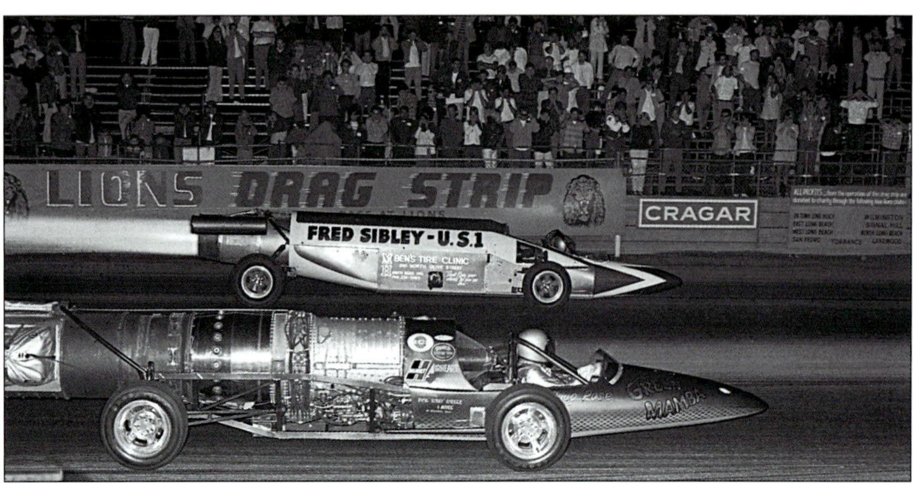

The **Green Mamba** *and the* **U.S.-1** *leave together off the starting line with 25 feet of flame from the high-velocity jet engines. Doug Rose went on to beat Fred Sibley in three straight rounds. (Photo by John Ewald/Courtesy Don Ewald)*

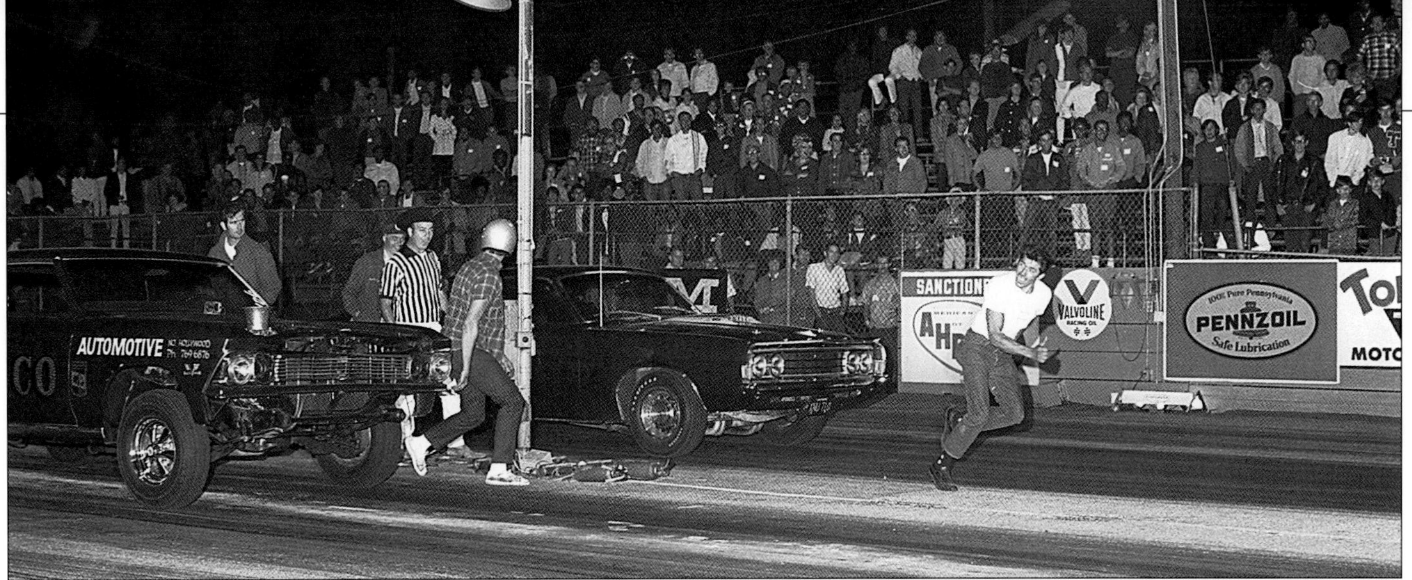

C. J. Hart had a passion for adding something different to the bracket classes, so he came up with the idea of using Le Mans starts. The rules for a Le Mans start were simple: Two contestants pulled up to the starting line, shut off their engines, exited their cars, and placed their keys on the hood. Both drivers stood in the staging area to wait at the green light. Once it was lit, they sprinted to a determined spot, touched it, and returned to their cars. The scheme worked well until participants bent the rules and added a hidden remote starter switch instead of fumbling for their keys. (Photo by John Ewald/Courtesy Don Ewald)

C. J. Hart made the trip to Lions Drag Strip an unforgettable experience for everyone, especially the youngsters in the crowd. Hart chose an unexpected youngster and brought him or her down to the starting line for the opportunity to take part in the winner's circle ceremonies. Whether it was standing with crews or sitting in open-cockpit cars for photos, Hart gave the young fans free passes to Lions Drag Strip. (Photo by John Ewald/Courtesy Don Ewald)

For this match race, Sibley installed a new engine but experienced flame-outs in all three races. Rose secured a win in the first round with a 6.93 ET at 240.00 mph to Sibley's 8.04 ET at 160.35 mph. In the second round, Rose duplicated his first-round ET of 6.93 to Sibley's fizzled-out 9.52 ET. In the third round, Rose posted his best performance of the night with a winning 6.85 ET at 241.78 mph over Sibley's 9.69 ET at 158.17 mph after the afterburner blew out and reignited after he left the line.

Both Rose and Sibley returned to the starting line for post-race interviews, where they announced they would return to Lions Drag Strip by popular demand for another three-round match race.

Sixteenth Anniversary

On Saturday, September 26, Lions Drag Strip celebrated its 16th-anniversary race, which featured an eight-car field of Top Fuelers and eight fuel Funny Cars. Don Moody took top honors in Top Fuel in the *Cerny-Lins-Moody* entry. He let it all hang out when he hammered out a final charge with a 6.63 ET at 221.13 mph. Runner-up honors went to Bill Tidwell in Mike Kuhl's rail with a 6.88 ET at 191.48 mph.

Funny Car honors went to Dave Beebe in the Beebe Brothers *Dodge Fever II* Dodge Challenger over the Corvette of Don Cook driven by Frank Ruppert. Beebe blasted a 7.24 ET at 191.89 mph to Ruppert's 7.42 ET at 199.11 mph.

Memories

Carl Olson

Top Fuel Dragster Driver and Lions Automobilia Foundation Museum Board Member

"In 1968, I got my first ride in a blown Top Fuel Dragster that was owned by Jack Ewell, Tom Bell, and Bill Stecker. Jack Ewell had been the driver for a long time, as I had been around these guys since my early teenage years.

"Shortly after my first race at Lions [Drag Strip], Stecker, who ran a muffler shop in San Pedro, where I was born and raised, recognized me for my passion and interest in those cars. He invited me to start riding with him out to Ewell's house in Torrance (where they kept the car) to help on the car. I did all of the normal menial jobs of polishing the wheels on the car, cleaning oil pans, and taking the parachute down to the local laundromat to foul the washing machines and wash out the oil, grease, and dirt.

"I eventually started going to the races as part of the crew. When I returned to Southern California after my days in the Coast Guard, I immediately hooked up with them again as a crew member. Besides running my Junior Fuel car, I worked as a crewmember on their Top Fuel dragster.

"On one very eventful day at a church parking lot up the street from Ewell's house and garage where they kept the race car, he and I were racing minibikes in this parking lot. In the process of going around one of the turns, Ewell lost his balance, fell over, and broke his leg. Because he could not drive the car until his leg healed, they thought, 'Who in the world are we going to put into this race car until Jack is able to start driving it again?'

"I was over in the corner of the shop, waving my arms and raising my hands, trying to gain as much attention as possible. Finally, they let me move up from my Junior Fuel Car to their Top Fueler, and we got on a roll.

"Ewell decided to formally retire from driving race cars and was happy to remain an owner, partner, and engine builder. I drove front-motor Top Fuel dragsters until the rear engine revolution took over in 1971."

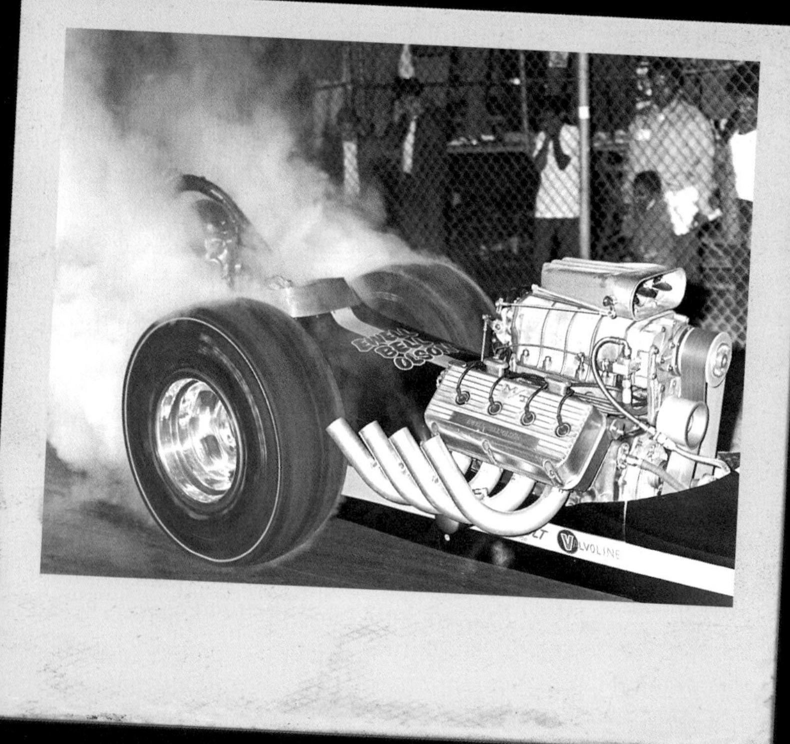

Carl Olson prepares for a successful run in the **Ewell-Bell-Olson** ***AA/FD by heating up the Goodyears and laying rubber onto the surface of Lions Drag Strip. Olson excelled in the Top Fuel ranks as one of the up-and-coming young guns.***

ET brackets and Gassers were on hand for the 16th-anniversary festivities and provided some of the top-notch action. Motorcycles played a huge part in Lions Drag Strip history—going back to opening day in October 1955. Competitors included the *King Rat* of Joe Smith and Lions Drag Strip champion Boris Murray.

Battle of the 6-Second Funny Cars

Midweek racing continued at Lions Drag Strip on November 4 with the nation's eight fastest Funny Cars. The entire eight cars ran three rounds. The field was made up of the East's finest: Candies & Hughes, Don Schumacher,

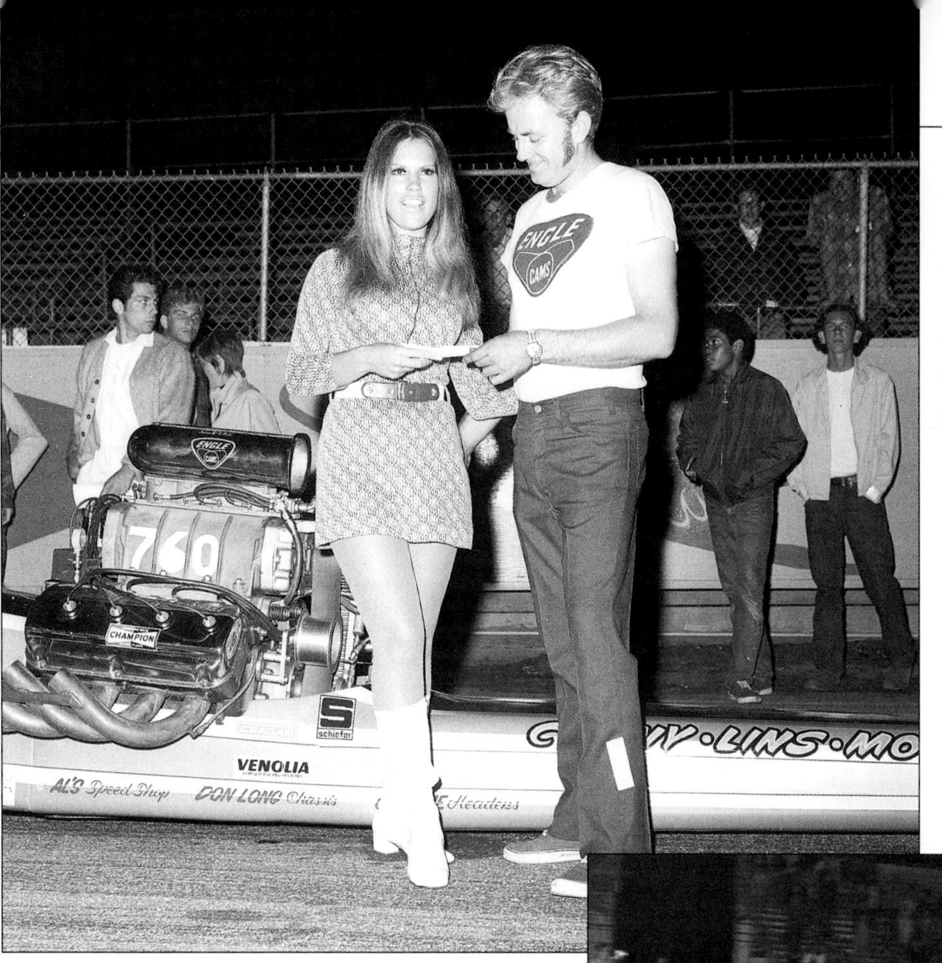

Don Moody accepts a $1,000 check from Lions Race Queen Carolyn Williams after winning Lions Drag Strip's 16th-anniversary meet. Moody defeated Mike Kuhl with "Captain" Billy Tidwell at the helm. Moody ran a 6.63 ET at 221.38 mph in the final.

In the second round of eliminations, Dave Beebe blasted a 7.36 ET at 190.27 mph over John Collins in the **Atlas Oil Tool Special** *that shut down early with a 9.39 ET at 90.18 mph. Beebe set the low ET of the meet with a 7.08 in qualifying and took the win with a 7.24 ET at 191.89 mph over Frank Ruppert in Don Cook's Corvette, who ran a 7.42 ET at 199.11 mph. Collins cranked off the top speed of the meet during qualifications at 209.30 mph.*

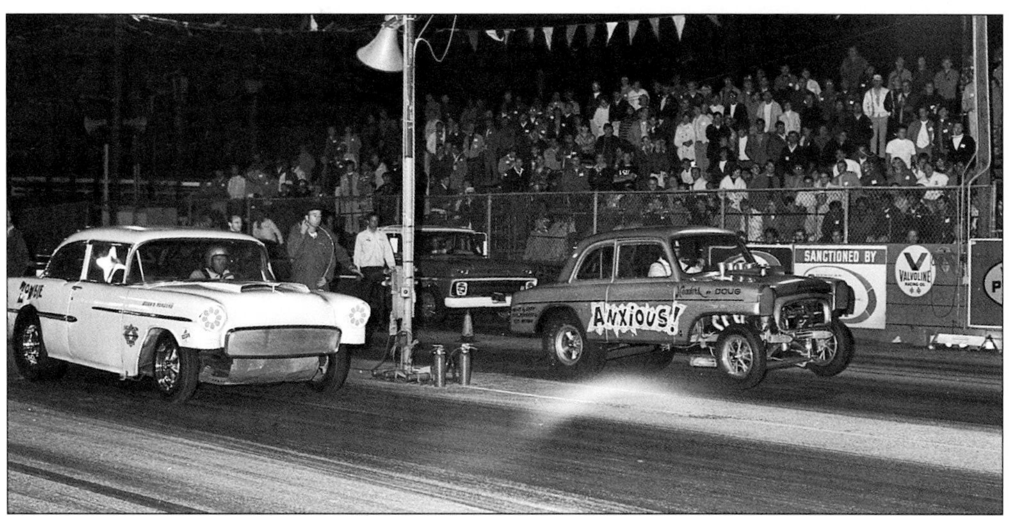

When the drag strip opened in 1955, its main purpose was to get the lawbreaker racers off the streets and into a safe environment, which proved to be very successful. Fast-forward to 1970, and bracket racing was the framework behind the success of Lions Drag Strip. Here's a great example of two competitive cars battling for supremacy at the 16th-annual anniversary meet. (Photo by John Ewald/ Courtesy Don Ewald)

Boris Murray was one of the greatest motorcycle riders in drag racing history. He was a multiple national record holder who campaigned a twin-engine, nitro-burning Triumph that only ran in high gear. Murray was one of the top competitors at Lions Drag Strip's 16th-anniversary meet. He ran at Lions Drag Strip consistently and had a high percentage of wins. On this run, Murray charged off the line at a high rate of torque that shook one of the exhaust header pipes off the twin engine.

Pat Minick annihilates the Goodyears during a 700-foot burnout in the **Chi-Town Hustler***. The undisputed burnout king from Chicago was one of the reasons that spectators came to Lions Drag Strip.*

the *Chi-Town Hustler*, and the *Ramchargers*.

The West roster featured Don Prudhomme, Tom McEwen, Gene Snow, and "Jungle" Jim Liberman. The gates opened at 5 p.m., the first round of competition started at 8 p.m., and admission was $4 with a free pit pass. C. J. "Pappy" Hart pulled off another spectacular show for all of the hardcore Funny Car and drag racing fans.

The Wednesday night affair attracted a record weekday crowd of more than 7,500. Fans witnessed Don Prudhomme take all honors with three consecutive 6-second runs.

Gene Snow captured the low ET and top speed with a 6.76 ET at 218.00 mph. For Prudhomme, this was the one to remember, as it was the swan song for his 1970 *Hot Wheels* 'Cuda. He debuted his new John Buttera–built 1971 *Hot Wheels* 'Cuda

Tom McEwen takes the straight route toward the finish line in his **Hot Wheels** *Duster against Pat Minick and the* **Chi-Town Hustler***. McEwen told the crowd that he was "saving his best for the Chicago boys" and kept his promise with a 7.31 ET at 200.80 mph over Minick's freewheeling 7.43 ET at 192.70 mph.*

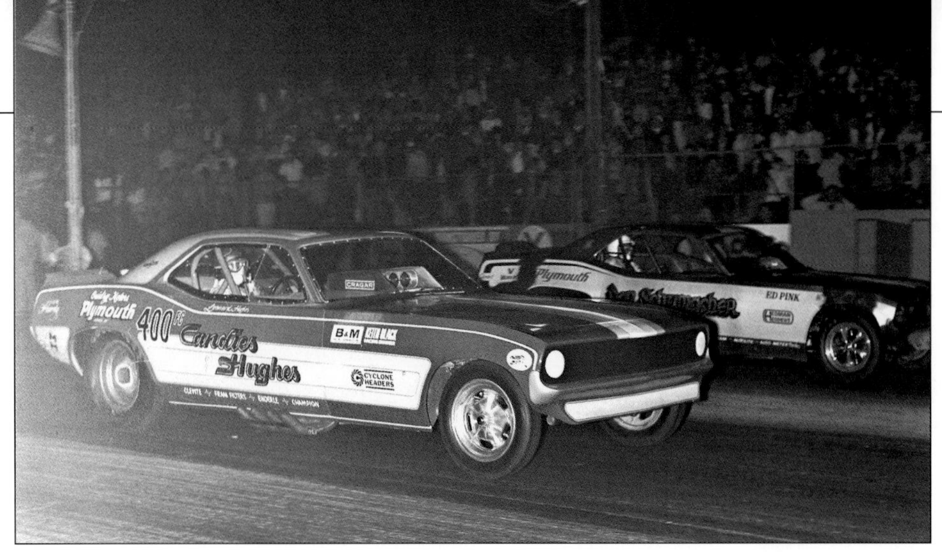

NHRA Gatornationals Funny Car Eliminator winner Leonard Hughes and Chicago's Don Schumacher, who won the Funny Car Eliminator title at the NHRA's 16th-annual U.S. Nationals a few weeks earlier, rekindle the Black-versus-Pink rivalry in this round at Lions Drag Strip.

The battle of the 6-second Funny Cars would not be complete without drag racing's greatest showman: "Jungle" Jim Liberman. His outstanding history at Lions Drag Strip includes many match race and major event wins driving the **Brutus** *GTO and his popular Chevy II machines. Here, Liberman carries on the winning tradition in his 1970 Camaro at Lions Drag Strip.*

Taylor, Michigan, was the home of the famous **Ramchargers** *Dodge Challenger driven by Leroy Goldstein. Goldstein's run at Lions Drag Strip received the approval from the large crowd of more than 7,500 fans.*

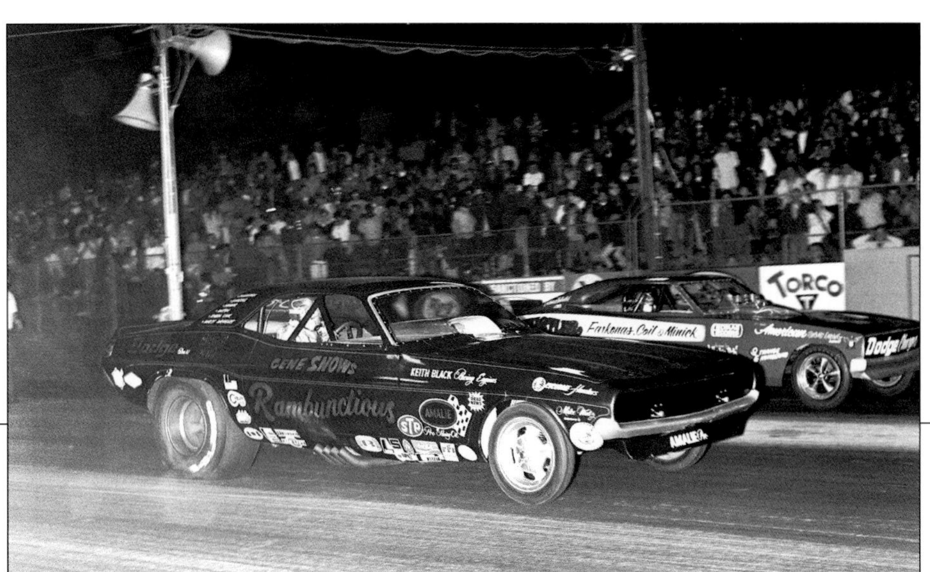

Eight of the nation's fastest and quickest Funny Cars competed during Wednesday night racing at Lions Drag Strip. Each made three full runs for only $4 (including a free pit pass). This setup was the envy of all of the local strips in Southern California. Gene Snow and Pat Minick gave the fans their money's worth with fast times and high speeds.

"Jungle" Jim Liberman and Tom McEwen had been involved in drag racing for years, and both had their own style of racing. Liberman was one of drag racing's original showmen. His charm and antics sold out drag strips all over the country. McEwen's marketing savvy brought Mattel, one of the world's largest toy manufacturers, on board and introduced Hot Wheels to kids and adults who wanted toy collectibles.

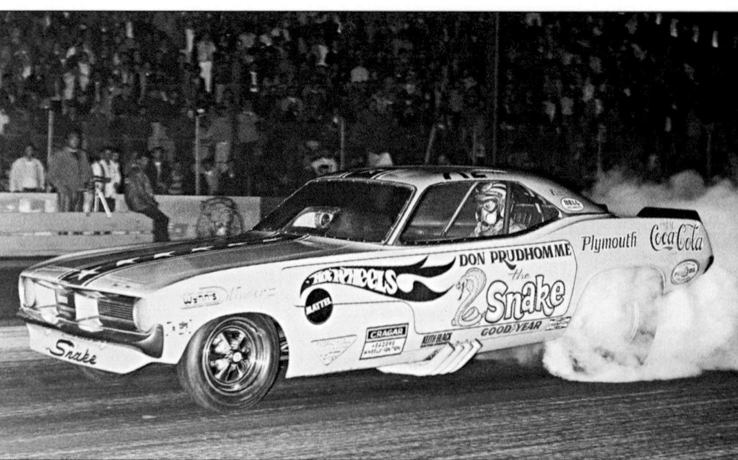

Don Prudhomme made three unbeaten runs in the 6s that earned him the win over Gene Snow's Dodge Challenger in the final round. More than 7,500 fans attended the Wednesday night contest at Lions Drag Strip, which was the swan song for Prudhomme's **Hot Wheels** *Plymouth Barracuda. He debuted his 1971 'Cuda the following week at Orange County International Raceway's Manufacturers Meet.*

Texan Gene Snow (near lane) was one of two unbeatens remaining going into the third round of the battle of 6-second Funny Cars, where he met Don Prudhomme (far lane) for the cash prize and glory. Snow took top honors and set both the low ET (6.76) and top speed of the meet (218.00 mph) but lost to Prudhomme.

the following week at Orange County International Raceway's Manufacturers Meet.

Knievel and Ramsey Share the Spotlight

How do you close out one of the most successful racing seasons at Lions Drag Strip? Track manager and promoter C. J. Hart utilized his circus experience and booked the rare appearance of daredevil and iconic stunt performer, Robert Craig "Evel" Knievel, at Lions Drag Strip on the night of December 12 for the first-ever ramp jump over 13 cars at a dedicated drag strip.

For the estimated 15,000 fans, it was more of a festival-type atmosphere, as they waited to experience Knievel's antics. He had been recovering from injuries he sustained in August from a previous failed jump at the Pocono Raceway in Long Pond, Pennsylvania. Knievel's crash landing at the bottom of the landing ramp resulted in several contusions, cracked vertebras, and a broken shoulder. Unfortunately, his Eagle 750-cc motorcycle was destroyed in the incident.

During the years of making jumps at various tracks, super speedways, a Las Vegas hotel parking lot, and indoor venues, Knievel relied on Norton, Triumph, Honda, and Eagle motorcycles for his jumps.

At Lions Drag Strip, Knievel wheeled out a new pair

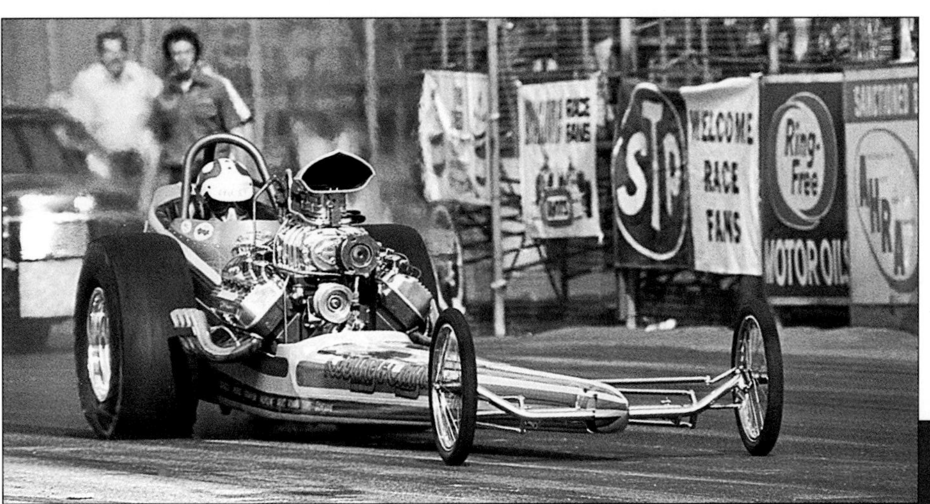

*Rick Ramsey wheeled the **Keeling & Clayton** AA/FD to top honors in the undercard program, as he defeated Gerry Glenn in the final round with a 6.58 ET at 194.80 mph. Ramsey beat Dick Rosberg as well as Tommy Allen for his berth in the finals.*

*Before Evel Knievel's long-awaited jump, C. J. Hart announced the unexpected match race between Dick Rosberg in Mike Kuhl's AA/FD and the AA/FC **Ramchargers** Funny Car of Leroy Goldstein. The reaction from the spectators was the loudest of the night when both cars rolled up to the starting area. Goldstein took the lead, but by mid-track, Rosberg took over the lead and earned the win with a 6.59 ET at 199.65 mph to the candy-striped Challenger's 7.12 ET at 204.54 mph.*

of specially prepared Harley-Davidson XR-750 motorcycles. One was designed especially for the jump, and the second bike was for the trick antics, wheelies, and seat stands.

Along with the featured jump, Hart organized an eight-car invitational Top Fuel field that included the recent inaugural NHRA Supernationals Top Fuel Champion Rick Ramsey to provide entertainment before jump time. Ramsey outdistanced the field when he beat the combination of driver Dick Rosberg and Mike Kuhl in the first round, Tommy Allen in the second round, and recorded a strong 6.58 ET at 194.80 mph to take down a red-lighting Gerry Glenn in the finals.

After the conclusion of the Top Fuel final, the fans reacted favorably

Evel Knievel's tractor and trailer was set up between the drag strip and the fire-up road. Knievel had everything loaded in the rear trailer, including the jump ramps, spare parts, and motorcycles. (Photo Courtesy Steve Brackett)

Evel Knievel's factory Harley Davidson XR-750 motorcycles were used for the first time at Lions Drag Strip. The motorcycles were nearly identical, but one had a modified rear suspension and reinforced handlebars to absorb the impact during landings. The second motorcycle was set up for doing wheelies and show-off riding. Each bike was was geared the same. (Photo Courtesy Steve Brackett)

when the unannounced Leroy Goldstein in the *Ramchargers* Dodge Challenger and the returning Rosberg & Kuhl fueler rolled to the line for a special one-race handicap match race. Both drivers and cars attempted to rewrite the Lions Drag Strip record books, but at the green, the red and white Challenger was off the line first. However, Goldstein relinquished the lead at the eighth-mile marker to Rosberg, who held on to win with a 6.59 ET at 199.55 mph to Goldstein's 7.12 ET at 204.59 mph.

Evel Knievel practices his riding skills and routines on Thursday afternoon before Saturday's show at Lions Drag Strip. Knievel shared the spotlight with an eight-car Top Fuel show that preceded the historic jump. (Photo Courtesy Steve Brackett)

Evel Knievel practices quarter-mile wheelies on an empty strip. On performance days, if any debris or unseen fluids were left on the track, it could be disastrous. (Photo Courtesy Steve Brackett)

Practice time included gauging the distance between the ramps. On jump night, 13 cars and trucks would be sandwiched in the 125 feet between the jump ramps. (Photo Courtesy Steve Brackett)

125 Feet to Glory

The wait was over. The atmosphere was more like a Roman festival, with the arena filled with noise, bright lights, and people who came to see Evel Knievel.

At exactly 9:39 p.m., the entertainer exited his trailer with his helmet and cane in hand. The screaming crowd welcomed the adventurous cyclist when he walked over to his awaiting motorcycle, strapped on his helmet, and climbed onto the bike. Knievel rolled onto the fire-up road in front of a cheering crowd that packed the grandstands. The fences were lined with spectators up to three or four rows deep. Everyone attempted to catch a glimpse of Knievel as they waited to see him perform.

Evel Knievel soars through the air and prepares to touch down on the landing ramp after successfully hurtling over 125 feet of cars and trucks without a scratch. The jump set a record for Knievel at a dedicated drag strip facility. (Jere Aldereff Photography/Courtesy Lions Automobilia Foundation Museum)

With the preparations completed and both ramps and vehicles in place, Knievel made two test runs toward the launch ramp. However, the bike slowly began losing power and was backfiring. In a panic, Knievel signaled franticly over to his mechanic, Steve Brackett. The two looked over the engine before they decided to switch over to his back-up bike and continued with the jump.

His performance was pure insanity.

The elbow-to-elbow crowd thundered their approval when Knievel fired up the new bike and repeated his practice passes alongside the launch ramp before he finally headed down the fire-up road toward the end of the strip.

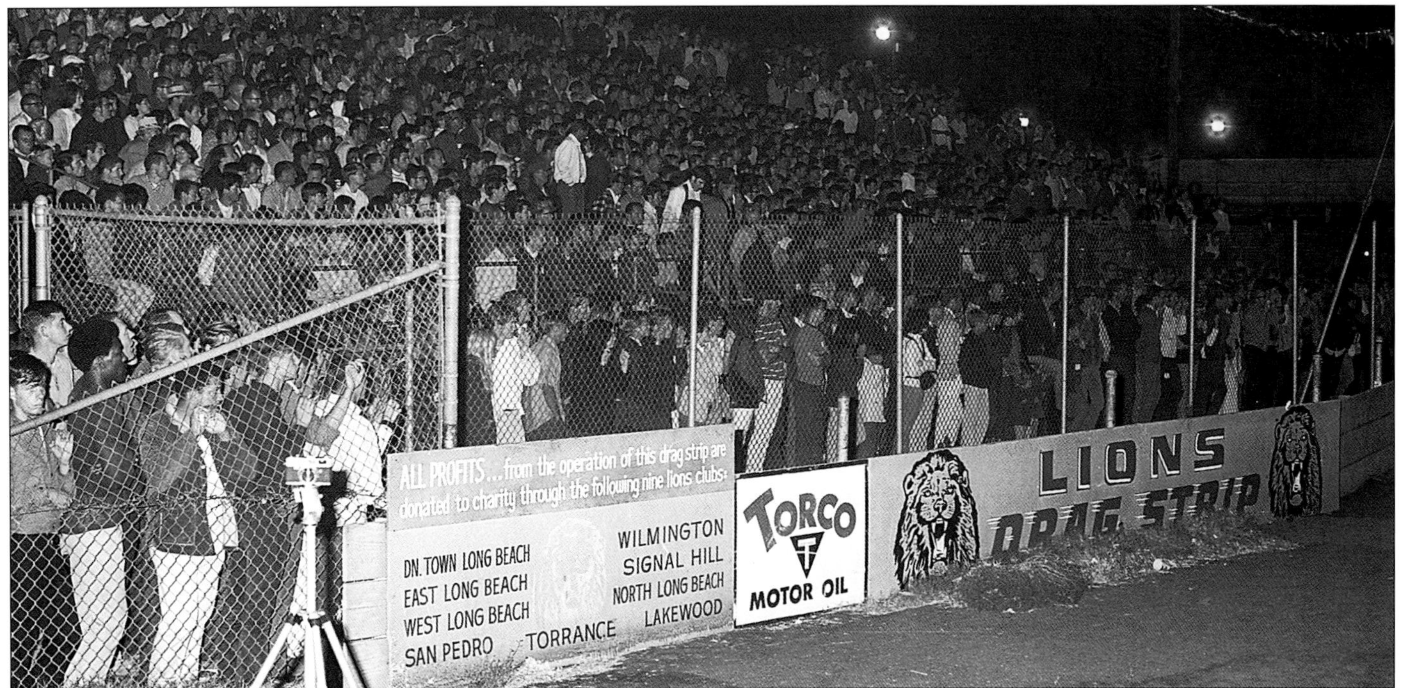

This section of the right-side pit grandstand was the viewing location for some of the 14,000 eager spectators waiting to see if Evel Knievel would succeed or fail. The camera on the tripod is focused on the ramps installed on the fire-up road. (Photo by John Ewald/Courtesy Don Ewald)

Evel Knievel waves to the electrified crowd by raising his helmet after his historic jump. (Jere Aldereff Photography/ Courtesy Lions Automobilia Foundation Museum)

Series of Professional Drag Racing: 1971 AHRA Grand American

The first of 10 races in the 1971 AHRA Professional Drag Racing Series, the Grand American, launched its season opener at Lions Drag Strip on January 9 and 10. The Top Fuel Dragsters and Fuel Funny Cars set the tone that produced some of the quickest (ET) and fastest (top speed) runs ever recorded in both categories.

Don Garlits made his 1971 Lions Drag Strip debut in his new rear-engine Top Fuel Dragster. Throngs of curious onlookers watched his first qualifying attempt. Garlits had the last laugh when he advanced to the money round, where he met Gary Cochran for the title.

The daredevil turned around, and, after a slight pause, he gave the thumbs-up signal. Then, he rode toward the ramps, gaining momentum and speed. As the feverish crowd blocked out any sounds made from his XR-750 motorcycle, Knievel shot up the launch ramp, sailed high into the night sky, and touched down safely on the landing ramp more than 125 feet away.

Knievel circled back, drove up the landing ramp, and stopped at the top of the ramp. The showman dismounted from his bike in front of the exuberant crowd. Calling for his cane, he waved to the crowd with his helmet raised high above his head as he made his way back to his trailer. The flamboyant Knievel was engulfed with legions of his fans who emerged from the stands. Brackett made the right call by switching out bikes, as the magneto failed on the jump bike.

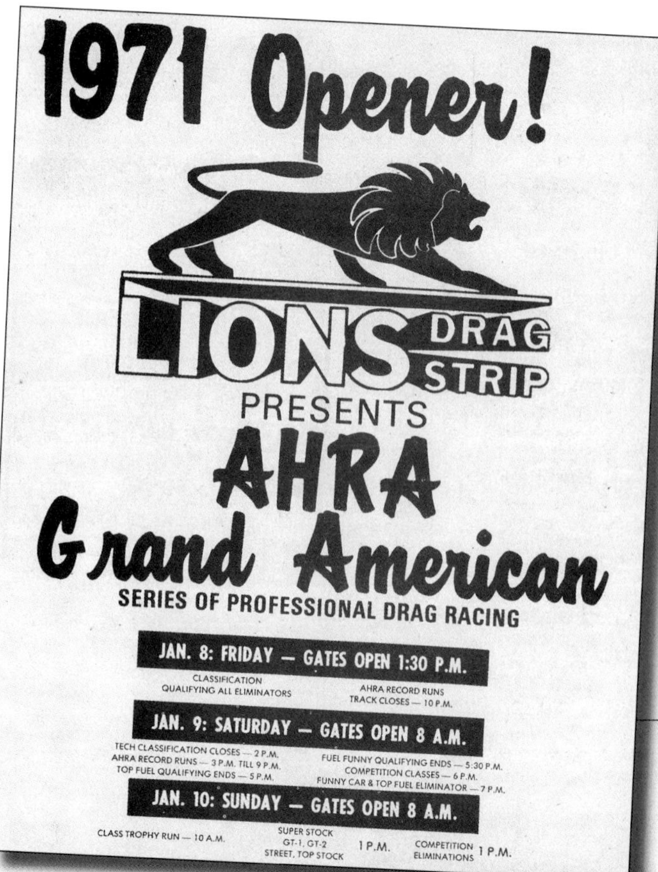

This poster advertised the 1971 opener at Lions Drag Strip. The AHRA Grand American took place over three action-packed days in January.

Memories

Steve Brackett

Maintained the Harley-Davidson XR-750 Motorcycles for Evel Knievel's Record Jump at Lions Drag Strip

"Evel Knievel came to the Long Beach Harley-Davidson shop at 37 Long Beach Blvd. in December 1970. Before making his appearance at Lions Drag Strip, I was personally selected to be his mechanic for the week to assist him in making the jump of 13 cars and set a new drag-strip jump record. This really didn't bother me because I had several years of experience in racing, including dragging motorcycles.

"I took the week off from work, went to Lions Drag Strip daily with Evel, and spent the whole week helping prepare him for the jump and whatever else he needed. He brought two new factory Harley-Davidson XR-750 motorcycles to Lions Drag Strip for me to maintain. The main bike was only for jumping and built with a heavy-duty modified rear suspension and reinforced handlebars to absorb the force on the landing. Bike number two was for doing wheelies and trick riding. Both bikes were completely opposite in riding and handling qualities, but they were both geared the same.

"I helped unload his huge, beautiful red truck and trailer and immediately started to set up the ramps when he arrived at Lions Drag Strip.

"You think Evel would have a crew of 100 to set up the ramps, but it was myself and Harris, his number-one handyman, demanding that we put both ramps close to each other to start with and progressively separate them farther apart throughout the week.

"Along with checking out the ramps every day, feeling the jump, and seeing how everything was in place, Evel practiced riding his bikes doing wheelies, rear-wheel riding, standing-on-the-seat wheelies, and ramp approachment runs. When it came to Saturday, the ramps were the exact length needed to be to clear the jump.

"On Saturday, Evel set the time of 6 o'clock to get to the strip (three hours before the jump) to park the truck and unload the bikes.

"My coworker Len and I headed over to the strip in the shop truck with his cycles strapped in the bed. We created a lot of attention and stares from people checking out his motorcycles while we were on the 405 freeway. We pulled off the exit and drove down the street and into the overflow parking lot. The place was packed. People were everywhere, shoving their way past us, clearing a path to the ticket booth.

"As we slowly inched our way up to the entry gates, the guy in the booth yelled at us saying, 'Sorry, we're full,' and he refused to let us in.

"I told him that if we don't get in, you're not going to have a show. After minutes of going back and forth with track security and the police, they finally let us in. It was pure pandemonium with a sea of people swarming around the truck—everyone trying to catch a closer glance of Knievel's bikes.

Evel Knievel was the definition of exuberant excitement. He entertained crowds wherever he performed. (Photo Courtesy Steve Brackett)

"As soon as the race finished, it was time to finally put the show into motion. While we were making our final inspections of the ramps, we ran into an unexpected problem. The fog began to roll in. The dampness made the ramps wet and slick, which had Evel upset. Using every towel, mop, and rag available to dry the dampness from the ramps, Knievel studied the situation and decided that this would not stop him from jumping, and he went onward with the plan.

"Evel had a trick he used before every jump to get the crowd worked up. He made a few practice runs on the fire-up road before heading back toward the starting-line area. Halfway to the launch ramp, he purposely hit a switch on the handlebar that would short out the ignition and cause backfires. He put the crowd into a frenzy of nervousness and on the edge of their seats, making them think something was wrong with his motorcycle.

"He asked me to get a brightly colored, recognizable hat to wear so I could be easily seen in the crowd, as he wanted to find me for this skit. When the bike started to misfire, he would find me, stop, and have me come over to check out the situation. I wasn't aware of him hitting the button at that time, so I said 'Evel, what I see is the magneto is going out.'

"I suggested that he change bikes and make the jump with the show bike. He didn't want to hear that or make the change to the show bike, as the handlebars were designed for doing wheelies and seat stands only and the suspension was not as rigid on the jump cycle. However, we went forward with the changes and switched over to the show bike. I assured Evel that the backup bike was properly prepared and was ready to go.

"After a few minutes, Evel finally jumped on the show bike and straddled the seat. He started up the bike and gave the throttle a few whacks. He was ready to go and shook his head. I gave him a good shove, and away he went. He brought the bike up to medium speed, going through all the gears to make sure he was ready. On his way toward the end of the strip, he passed by me, winked, nodded, and cracked a smile. Off he went!

"At the end of the night, he successfully made the jump, set the record, and left the thousands of fans ecstatic, including me. It was a lifetime experience that I'll never forget."

Garlits Revolutionizes Drag Racing

Rear-engine vehicles had been in drag racing since the late 1950s. Don Garlits, along with his brother Ed, built an Oldsmobile-powered dragster for Ed to drive. Although the rear-engine technology had little success, Don took the steps to refine it.

Don had actively spent four weeks of construction and logged in the long hours of planning and designing his latest dragster: a revolutionary rear-engine dragster.

On December 27, 1970, at Sunshine Drag Strip in St. Petersburg, Florida, Don made his latest concept of a rear-engine dragster public. Powered by a 1970 Dodge 426 Hemi engine and sporting a 215-inch-wheelbase chassis, the new dragster had a combined weight of 1,250 pounds.

During interviews with the press, Don said, "I decided to build a rear-engine dragster for numerous reasons. Number one, it gives better weight distribution on the rear wheels. It keeps the driver ahead of the engine and away from danger from engine driveline components. In case of an engine explosion, the driver is not subjected to fire, smoke, oil, fuel, and water. The driver would also have a better view of what he's doing."

Don also stated that while the current chassis design had worked successfully and been around for 15 years, he thought that a new design would be a fresh start for AA/FD. The initial quarter-mile test runs resulted in an average ET of 6.81 seconds at 220 mph.

Safety Concerns Addressed

With safety concerns and the uncertainty of Garlits's new dragster, C. J. Hart elected to have Garlits qualify with three single runs. All three qualifying runs brought the curious onlookers and naysayers to the line to see if Garlits's experiment would be a success or failure.

Top Fuel

Garlits started round one of Top Fuel by taking the win with a 6.60 ET at 223.08 mph over Glenn & Shultz. Bob Creitz pulled off a super holeshot with a winning 6.68 ET at 213.77 mph over the *Yankee Packrat* of Jim Paoli, who posted a better 6.59 ET at 217.91 mph. Jimmy King and Don Marshall's *El Diablo* enjoyed the bite and traction of Lions Drag Strip, when King, the pride of New England, defeated Tommy Allen in the *Byron Racing Products* machine with a 6.65 ET at 229.59 mph to a 6.87 ET at 220.58 mph.

"Dapper" Don Moody ran a 6.66 ET at 220.58 mph to defeat Jim Nicoll, who shut off early with a 6.98 ET at 175.09 mph. Chris Karamesines passed Glen Woolsey in the *Cyr & Schofield* entry. John Wiebe set the pace with a 6.61 ET at 193.13 mph over J. D. Hagood's *Spartan* Charger, which was driven by John Nichols.

At the hit, Nichols carried the front end off the line, drifted right, and crossed over into the next lane, where he contacted the guardrail. He coasted through the lights with an 8.42 ET at 116.88 mph. Keeling & Clayton's *California* Charger, piloted by Rick Ramsey, laid down a straight pass of 6.65 at 202.70 mph against an out-of-shape Pete Robinson, who hopscotched to a loss with a 12.96 ET at 63.84 mph. Gary Cochran's 6.74 ET at 196.07 mph was strong enough to get past Don Cook, who posted a 6.83 ET at 211.28 mph to close out round one.

In round two, Ramsey had a single run when Jimmy King lost the engine off the line. Gary Cochran surprised Chris Karamesines with a fantastic holeshot for a 6.79 ET at 208.37 mph to Karamesines's quicker 6.69 ET at 222.22 mph. Don Moody was gifted a single run, as

"Sneaky" Pete Robinson (one of the eight seeded fuelers) ran a 6.50 ET in qualifying at the Grand American. Robinson lost to the **California Charger** *driven by Rick Ramsey in the first round when Ramsey ran a 6.66 ET at 202.70 mph to Robinson's out-of-shape 12.93 ET at 63.00 mph. Two weeks later, Robinson was fatally injured at the 11th-annual NHRA Winternationals, when he entered the lights, lost control when his car came apart, and crashed through the guardrail. (Jere Aldereff Photography/Courtesy Lions Automobilia Foundation Museum)*

The third round of eliminations paired Don Moody in the* Cerny-Lins-Moody *rail with Gary "Mr. C." Cochran for the right to meet "Big Daddy" Don Garlits in the finals. Moody utilized the power of Wes Cerny to post a winning 6.63 ET at 223.32 mph to Cochran's 6.17 ET at 218.97 mph. However, Moody lost the engine at the finish stripe, which eliminated him and resulted in Cochran being reinstated.

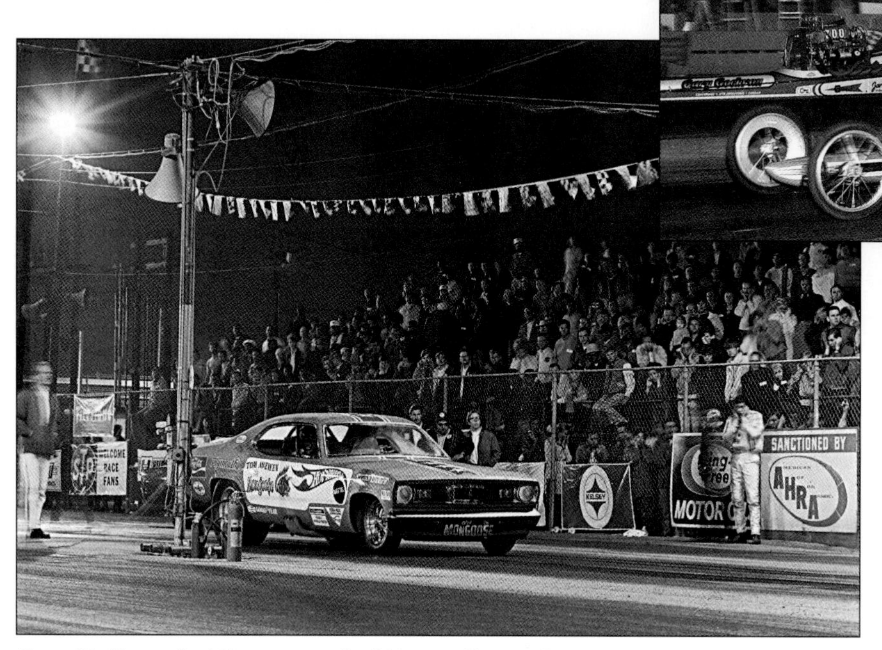

Tom McEwen led the unseeded Funny Cars when he powered his* Hot Wheels *Duster to a jaw-dropping 6.55 ET in the first round of qualifying during Lions Drag Strip's Grand American event. McEwen was unable to back up his earlier 6.55 ET for the new ET record when he lost against Gene Snow. Snow ran a 6.94 ET at 185.18 mph to McEwen's 7.10 ET at 205.94 mph. (Photo Courtesy Paul Johnson Collection)

"Kansas" John Wiebe broke on the starting rollers. Bob Creitz made it easy for Garlits to advance, as he pulled a wheelie off the line and immediately went up in smoke. Garlits secured the win with a 6.65 ET at 225.56 mph.

Ramsey's *California* Charger developed problems after the second round and was forced out of the competition, which brought Karamesines back to face Garlits in the third round. In what looked as if it had the makings of what would've been a highly touted match race at any drag strip, the crowd's excitement quickly dispersed as Karamesines lost fire on the burnout and handed Garlits the easy pass to the finals with an 8.47 ET at 100.11 mph.

Don Moody ran a stellar 6.63 ET at 223.32 mph in the *Cerny-Lins-Moody* rail to take out Gary Cochran's charge with a 6.75 ET at 218.97 mph. Unfortunately for Moody, his all-out assault against Cochran took its toll when the engine self-destructed in the lights and eliminated the team's hopes of meeting Garlits in the final round. This made the way for Cochran to return for the all-important round to pocket the gold and glory.

The final round was a figurative chess match between two champions. Both cars came off the line in a dead heat before Cochran gained the advantage at mid-track and held on for the win with a 6.58 ET

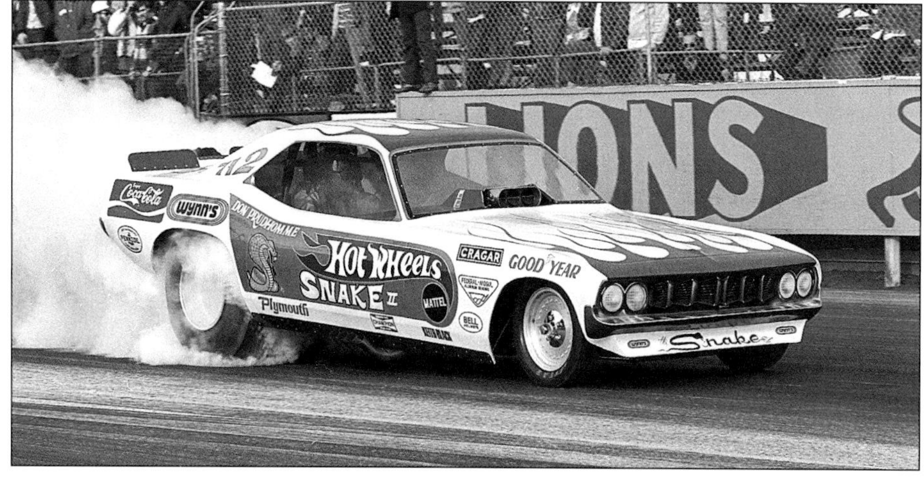

Don Prudhomme sported a new paint on his 1971 Plymouth 'Cuda Funny Car at the Grand American. Prudhomme and Mart Higginbotham met in round one, and Prudhomme set the tone with a 6.88 ET at 212.26 mph to Higginbotham's losing 7.17 ET at 205.74 mph. In round two, Prudhomme faced the candy-striped* Ramchargers *Challenger of Leroy Goldstein. Prudhomme's* Hot Wheels *Plymouth 'Cuda broke coming off the line and sent Goldstein to a winning 7.16 ET at 201.79 mph.

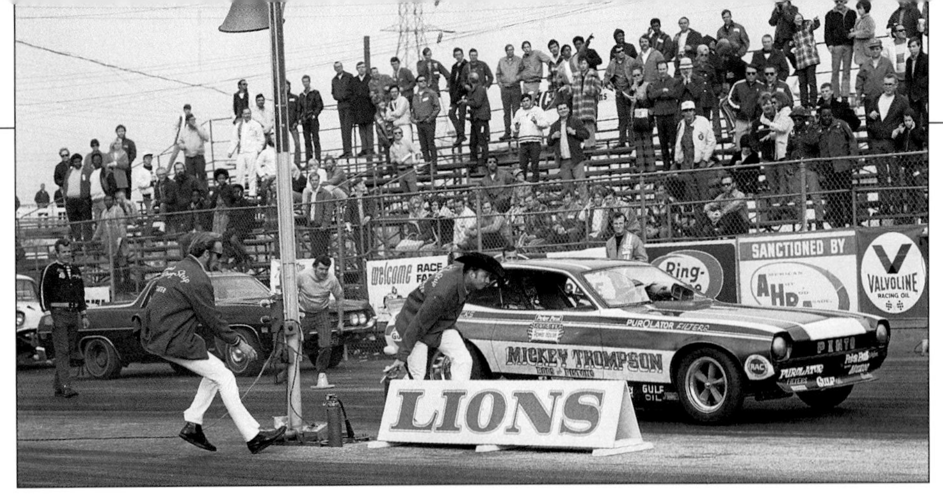

Dale Pulde, one of the eight seeded Funny Cars, experienced a massive blower explosion at the hit in Mickey Thompson's new Pinto. Larry Sutton, Bill Kee, and Mickey Thompson grabbed fire extinguishers and came to the aid of Pulde. (Jere Aldereff Photography/Courtesy Lions Automobilia Foundation Museum)

at 217.91 mph to Garlits's 6.66 ET at 225.00 mph. If anyone had any doubt about the rear-engine dragster, Garlits ended them in a hurry at Lions Drag Strip. Rumors flew around after the race that Karamesines went over to Garlits and ordered a new rear-engine dragster.

One of the season's new Funny Cars that debuted at the 1971 Grand American was the **Custom Body Mini Charger** *driven by Phil Castronovo. Handling and traction issues kept the pink-purplish entry out of the field.*

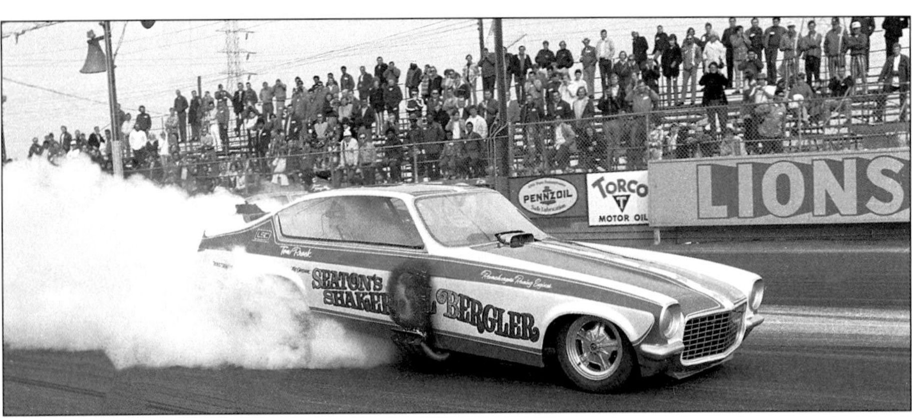

Pete Seaton teamed up with Al Bergler and driver Tom Prock to campaign **The Original Seaton's Shaker & Al Bergler Chevrolet** *Logghe-built Vega. (Jere Aldereff Photography/ Courtesy Lions Automobilia Foundation Museum)*

The 1970 AHRA Top Fuel champion, John Wiebe, launched a winning 6.61 ET at 193.13 mph in the first round over J. D. Hagood's **Spartan** *Charger driven by John Nichols. Nichols carried the front end off the line, drifted sharply over the centerline, smacked against the guardrail, and coasted through the lights with a losing 8.42 ET at 116.08 mph.*

Funny Car

Several new Funny Cars made their debut at the Grand American. This included Mike Burkhart's blue and orange Camaro built by Don Hardy as well as Logghe's latest fleet of new cars (the Dodge Chargers of Phil Castronovo and Roland Leong; the *Ramchargers* Challenger; and the new team of Pete Seaton, Al Bergler, and Tom Prock's *Super Shaker* Vega). In Funny Car, Tom McEwen set the low ET for the unseeded eight Funny Cars with a 6.55 but failed to back it up for the record.

Larry Christopherson and Dick Harrell had a two-car team in 1971 with a Don Hardy–built Chevy Vega. Christopherson qualified well into the program but lost in the first round to Stan Shiroma, the eventual runner-up, who bested the Vega with a 7.71 ET at 189.07 mph to an 8.63 ET at 178.92 mph.

Richard Siroonian annihilates the Goodyears at the start of the second round against Gene Snow. However, Siroonian, in "Big" John Mazmanian's 'Cuda, went sideways, crossed over the centerline within 15 feet of Snow, and drifted to an 8.95 ET at 88.87 mph. Snow played it safe and stayed back from Siroonian to secure the automatic win with a 20.53 ET at 29.73 mph. (Jere Aldereff Photography/Courtesy Lions Automobilia Foundation Museum)

Don Garlits grabbed all of the attention at the Grand American with his new, revolutionary rear-engine dragster. With many scratching their heads, Garlits sliced through the field and downed the **Glenn & Shultz** *entry in the first round. Garlits singled in round two, had a win over Bob Creitz in round three, and received another single in round four before he met Gary Cochran in the finals. In the finals, Garlits fell short with a 6.66 ET at 225.00 mph to Cochran's 6.58 ET at 217.91 mph. (Jere Aldereff Photography/Courtesy Lions Automobilia Foundation Museum)*

Top Fuel Top Eliminator Gary Cochran (middle) poses for a photo with Linda Vaughn (left) and Miss Ruby Davis, queen of the AHRA Grand American. Cochran beat Don Garlits in the final with a 6.58 ET at 217.91 mph. (Photo Courtesy Tim Pearl)

Jim "the Frantic Fireman" Dunn qualified with an ET of 6.75. In the second round of eliminations, he ran a quicker ET of 6.74 at 191.87 mph and set the new Lions Drag Strip Funny Car ET record. Dunn's 1971 'Cuda set the record when he defeated Richard Tharp and the *Blue Max*, who followed with a 6.87 ET at 215.82 mph and ended up in the Lions Drag Strip sandbox.

Super Stock

The Super Stock competition was on Sunday with a 16-car show that featured many of the top doorslammer professionals in the nation. Leading the pack was low-qualifier Bob Lambeck, driving his Hemi-powered Dodge Dart to a 9.71 ET. Right on the heels of Lambeck was "Dyno" Don Nicholson, who drove his Ford Maverick into the number-two spot with a 9.72 ET. Nicholson also set the top speed for the meet at 139.96 mph.

Included in the field were the Mopars of Dick Landy, Butch Leal, and Don Grotheer. Chevy hopefuls in the mix were Bob Anderson, Bill Hielscher, and Tom Jacobson.

For the Super Stock title in the final round, the *Red*

Shirley Shahan experienced tail scrapers in qualifying and eliminations at the AHRA Grand American. The track's bite at Lions Drag Strip was deceiving to many but resulted in good ETs.

On the third day at the Grand American, the doorslammers had their time on the track. Plymouth standout Don Grotheer made strong runs in Super Stock with his new 426 Hemi-powered 'Cuda but fell to the overall winner "Dyno" Don Nicholson.

To offset a relatively slow weekend when all of the hot cars and drivers were up in Bakersfield for the Fuel and Gas Championships, C. J. Hart brought in a non-racing attraction to Lions Drag Strip. "Leaping" Joe Gerlach, a daredevil stuntman and Las Vegas performer, jumped 80 feet from a platform on a hot air balloon basket into an 800-pound sponge on the starting line. Gerlach performed a similar feat when he leaped from the sixth floor of the J. C. Bradford building in downtown Nashville onto an 800-pound sponge in front of a crowd of 200 onlookers.

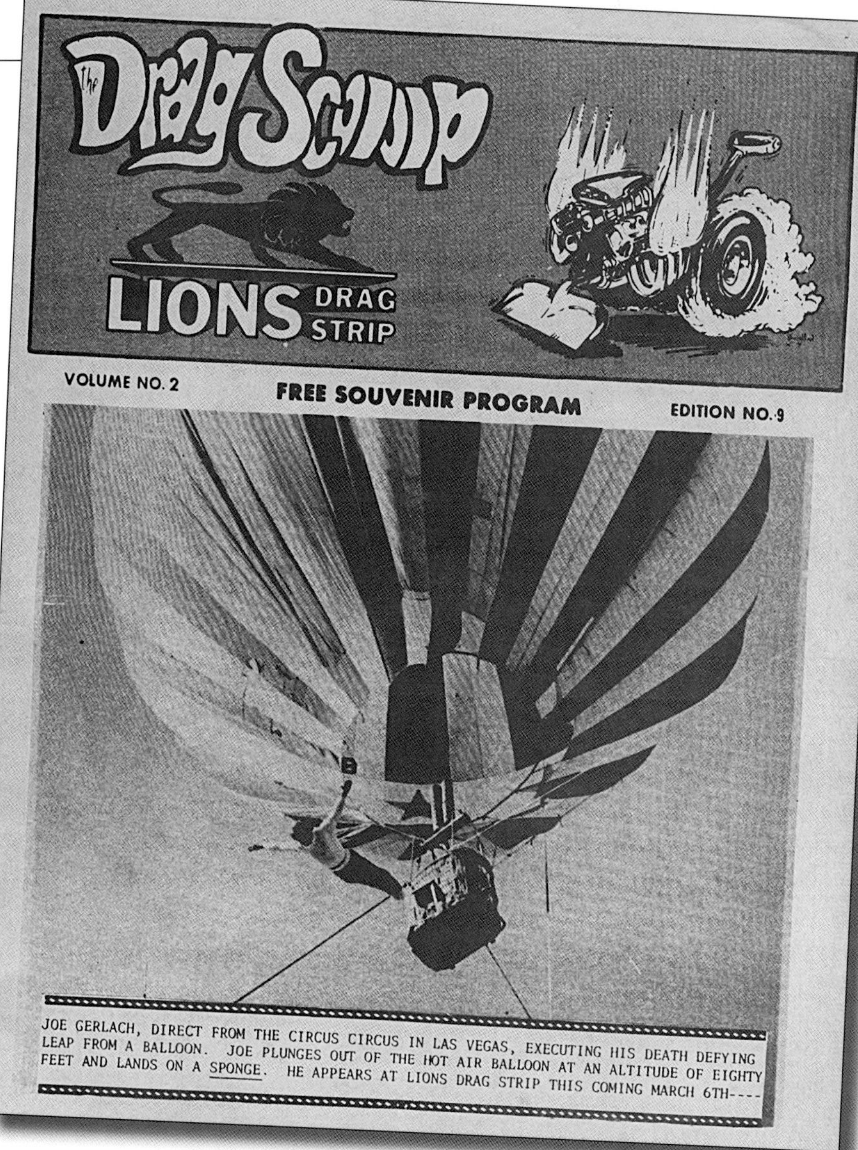

The Drag Scoop
LIONS DRAG STRIP
VOLUME NO. 2
FREE SOUVENIR PROGRAM
EDITION NO. 9
JOE GERLACH, DIRECT FROM THE CIRCUS CIRCUS IN LAS VEGAS, EXECUTING HIS DEATH DEFYING LEAP FROM A BALLOON. JOE PLUNGES OUT OF THE HOT AIR BALLOON AT AN ALTITUDE OF EIGHTY FEET AND LANDS ON A SPONGE. HE APPEARS AT LIONS DRAG STRIP THIS COMING MARCH 6TH----

Light Bandit Dodge Challenger of Bill Bagshaw competed against Nicholson's Ford. Nicholson secured the win with a 9.81 ET at 139.96 mph to Bagshaw's losing (but close) 9.89 ET at 139.31 mph.

"Leaping" Joe Gerlach

With the annual exodus in March of the nitro-fed Fuelers and Funny Cars to Bakersfield for the infamous Fuel & Gas Championships, how would Lions Drag Strip fill the gap with both quality racing and family entertainment? On March 6, C. J. "Pappy" Hart brought in a mixture of colorful and top-performing injected Funny Cars to share the limelight with world-renowned daredevil, Joe Gerlach, who performed his "Sponge Plunge" for the very first performance ever at a drag strip.

With the conclusion of the evening's injected Funny Car show, it was showtime for Gerlack to perform his leap into fame. Gerlach, direct from the Circus-Circus Hotel and Casino in Las Vegas, ascended on a platform that was fixed to the outside of a hot-air ballon. He went approximately 80 feet in the air and was suspended directly over the starting line. Gerlach, a former world championship Olympic diver who defected in 1956 from Hungary, credited two gentlemen who brought his hot air balloon act into existence: expert balloonist George Stokes and Fred F. Barnes, the vice president of operations for Sports Headlines Inc.

Barnes was well-known in the motorsports world and promoted such personalities as Evel Knievel, A. J. Foyt, Mario Andretti, the Unsers, and drag racers Don Prudhomme and Tom McEwen.

Stokes was responsible for keeping the towering balloon steady while Gerlach was perched above the target below: a 6-foot-wide, 12-foot-long, and 3-foot-thick sponge mat.

Gerlach's unique performance captivated everyone in attendance, including the racers who set aside their wrenches to watch this display. The results from his perfect swan dive led to a well-deserved standing ovation. These three men produced this unique one-of-a-kind exhibition that was truly death-defying.

Eighth-Mile Championships

Chilly weather and high winds forced a delay in qualifying for the 16-car Funny Car show on April 24. Track manager C. J. Hart didn't expect the gale-force winds to die down and called a conference with all of the Funny Car drivers. This led to another rare event held at Lions Drag Strip. Hart suggested and then decided (with the approval of the drivers) to have the first-ever 1/8-mile championships.

All of the names were placed into a hat. The first eight names pulled were pooled into the round-robin field, while the remaining eight names were for match races.

Track officials were positioned at the 1/8-mile marker and used flashlights to signal to the tower regarding which car won. No times or speeds were logged for this race, but the ETs were announced to the spectators as the cars drifted through the quarter-mile lights. This 1/8-mile championship event still gave the spectators the opportunity to witness fantastic racing and take all the precautions to keep the drivers safe.

In the first round of the round-robin eight, Bob Pickett secured the win over "Smokey" Joe Lee. Bob Smith, driving Tom Strum's Camaro, won against Gary Densham but lost a head gasket at the finish line. Gary Burgin lost fire on the burnout against Mert Littlefield and watched Littlefield coast to the win. Charlie "the Pie Maker" Wilson and his *Vicious Too* got the chance for the big money when the *Ivory Hunter* Camaro of Mike Halloran broke on the line.

In the second round, the *Mr. Pickett* Javelin got a single when Tom Strum's Camaro dropped a cylinder off the line and called it quits. Wilson got by an ailing Littlefield. The final round win in the round-robin competition went to *Mr. Pickett* over Charlie Wilson on a close race from start to finish.

Over on the match-race side, Randy Walls's *Super Mini-Nova* got the win when Dick Olson tripped the red light. "Mighty" Mike Van Sant, in the new *Stone, Woods, & Cook* Pinto, subbed for the ailing Mickey Thompson Pinto and faced Jim Dunn. Van Sant had a wild, out-of-shape ride to the 1/8 marker and lost to Dunn's 6.86 ET while battling the 50-knot winds.

Dave Beebe and Dick Rosberg were next to brave the winds. Rosberg powered Tim Beebe's *Fighting Irish* Camaro past Tim's brother Dave in Nelson Carter's *Super Chief* that went everywhere except straight and shut off. Dave Condit, driving the *L.A. Hooker*, got the win on a single when Gordon Mineo lost the clutch on the starting line.

The remaining rounds of racing were canceled due to the treacherous winds, as blowing debris and sand left the track with a marble-like surface. Taking in all the considerations and the unusual circumstances that prevailed during the race, all of the drivers and track officials who took part did an outstanding job.

As a side note, controversy unfolded during these unfavorable conditions, as the Lions Drag Strip personnel performed their best to run an unbiased, fair race. Opinions were exchanged in the match race between Jim Dunn and Mike Van Sant, who was driving the *Stone, Woods, Cook, & Keaton* Pinto.

Lions Drag Strip had its two best tech men at the 1/8th-mile marker to determine a race winner. The left lane tech man called Dunn the winner, but the right lane tech called it for Van Sant. An open letter was printed in *Drag News* with numerous comments that favored Van Sant. The outcry for a rematch was made public, but it didn't come about, as Hart ruled that Dunn was the clear winner.

The King of Harts

On Saturday, June 12, 1971, Lions Drag Strip hosted three entertaining fields of eight Top Fuelers, eight Funny Cars, and an eight-car Combination Eliminator. The headline of the evening was the celebration of the retirement of the C. J. "Pappy" Hart, Lions Drag Strip's second general manager/track manager.

To begin the festivities, in the first round of Top Fuel was James Warren, in the *Warren-Colburn-Miller* entry, winning with a 6.83 ET at 202.24 mph over "Giant" Jim Moore's 7.41 ET at 155.70 mph. Jack Martin, in the Northern California *Penner & Beach* entry, wasted no time and set the low ET for the evening with a 6.66 at 218.77 mph over Kuhl & Olson's 6.83 at 215.31 mph.

John Mitchell, in Don Madden's *Howards Cams Special*, picked up the automatic win with a 7.78 ET when Mike Clancy in the *Butters & Gerrard* rail red-lighted as heavy death smoke poured out of the headers at the starting line, indicating engine issues. With the last pair of the first round, John Rodeck's rear-engine machine blasted down the 1320 with a 6.80 ET at 196.93 mph and put away the stand-by *Bright Boys* dual-engine entry with a 7.34 ET at 173.41 mph.

In round two, Martin advanced to the finals with a win over John Mitchell, while James Warren thundered to a winning 6.75 ET at 227.84 mph and set the top speed of evening over John Rodeck's 6.76 ET at 205.01 mph. The finals brought the quickest (ET) and fastest

Northern California's **Penner & Beach** *Top Fuel dragster with driver Jack Martin at the controls returned to Lions Drag Strip after the Grand Premiere debacle. At the Grand Premiere, Martin suffered a disastrous wheel-stand when the throttle stuck open. The new car went straight up and over, crashed down onto the asphalt, and rolled several times before it came to a complete stop. The car was destroyed. In Martin's return to Lions Drag Strip, the results for the team were better, as Martin set the low ET for the evening with a 6.66 ET at 218.77 mph and won the meet.*

(top speed) cars of the evening to see who would collect the cash. After a four-year drought from entering the winner's circle, Jack Martin took the easy win with a 6.69 ET at 213.77 mph over James Warren, who red-lighted and shut off.

As a side note, Carl Olson found a permanent home in the seat of Mike Kuhl's Top Fueler after a short stint in 1970 in Kuhl's fueler when Kuhl's regular driver, Dick Rosberg, was unable to make a few commitments. Early in 1971, Olson built his own dragster but suffered a crash at Fremont that destroyed the car. Olson got a call from Kuhl, and they reunited. Kuhl drove while Olson concentrated on rebuilding his damaged rail. Fortunately for both parties, Olson scrapped the idea of his own dragster, and he and Kuhl formed a new partnership.

In the first round of Funny Car competition, Gene Conway, who was out to make it two wins in a row at Lions Drag Strip, dropped a 6.94 ET at 200 mph to beat "Big" Eddie Lenarth in the Hunter & Chericott's *Malfunction 2* Chevy Nova, which ran a 7.42 ET at 197.36 mph.

The next pair up to the line was Maggio, Stuart, & Thermos's *Sopwith Camel* 'Cuda with driver Ron Rivero and Gordon Swearingen in Carl Griffiths's *L.A. Hooker* Dodge Charger. Rivero made easy work of Swearingen with a 6.95 ET at 207.37 mph to Swearingen's 7.56 ET at 153.04 mph.

Mike Halloran and Tim Grose were next to run. Halloran, driving the *Ivory Hunter* Camaro, was the first to cross over the finish line with a 7.41 ET at 185.56 mph, but he drifted over the centerline at the 600-foot marker and gave Tim Grose the automatic win in Nelson Carter's *Super Chief*. Grose ran an identical 7.41 ET but with a top speed of 149.75 mph.

Memories

Carl Olson

Top Fuel Dragster Driver and Lions Automobilia Foundation Museum Board Member

"My first ride with Mike Kuhl was in 1970, where it was just a one-off race. It was now the *Ewell-Bell-Olson* Top Fuel car, and I replaced Bill Stecker as one of the owners. We were to race over the Fourth of July weekend at two different races. Jack Ewell got sick, and I didn't have a ride for that weekend. Mike got word and asked if I could help drive in those two races—one at Irwindale and the next day at Orange County, where we did very well.

"I went back to our *Ewell-Bell-Olson* car for the balance of the year. In 1971, I built my own race car and crashed and destroyed it at Fremont.

"I went back home to Torrance from the Fremont debacle, the phone rang, and it was Mike Kuhl. He asked if I would be interested in driving his car until I rebuilt mine. I thought it was a good idea, and we went on to win our first race at Orange County. I decided to continue for the foreseeable future to see where that relationship went, and it lasted for the next 50 years."

Mike Kuhl and Carl Olson formed one of Southern California's most popular and successful Top Fuel dragster teams. Kuhl mastered the Chrysler 392 to the tune of setting record ETs and top speeds. Olson spent time behind the wheel of the **Ewell-Bell-Steckler** *fueler in 1969 before he connected with Kuhl in early 1971. Kuhl & Olson won their first NHRA Top Fuel Eliminator title at the 1972 Winternationals.*

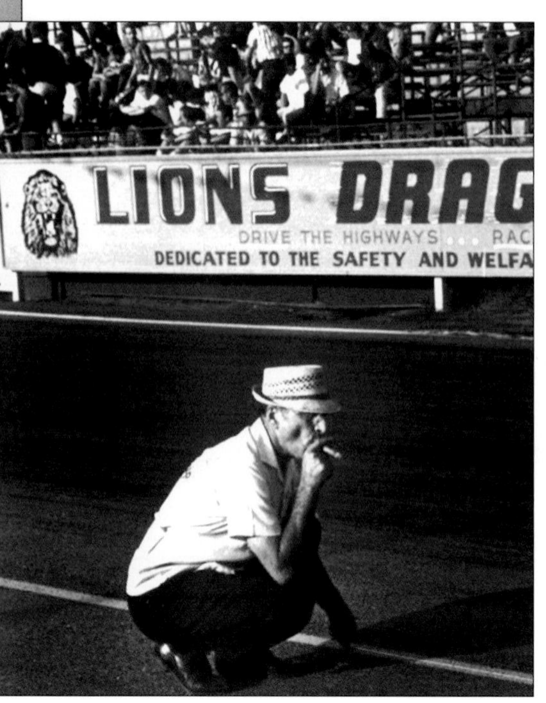

When C. J. Hart stepped away from Lions Drag Strip, he left a void at the strip and in the world of drag racing. He had brought some of the most entertaining racing personalities to the venue. In the June 19, 1971, issue of **Drag News**, *C. J. and his wife, Peggy, printed a statement of gratitude: "Thanks to so many . . . the racers, the spectators, and the many strip employees for making these past 21 years the greatest. [It's the] people who made the tremendous sport of drag racing what it is, and those same people made our past 21 years so great."*

Farewell to Hart

When Lions Drag Strip was constructed on a narrow, mile-long finger of land in 1955, it provided a safe and legal venue for car and motorcycle enthusiasts to drag race. Due to the track's popularity and prosperity, funds were generously given back to community charities.

When then-manager Mickey Thompson, who worked tirelessly through the strip's early developmental years, left Lions Drag Strip to pursue his own business interests, his replacement, C. J. Hart, took over and served as drag racing's popularity significantly grew. Hart took the extra steps throughout the community and used his diplomatic ways to keep the peace. He provided the surrounding neighborhood and the Navy families that were housed nearby with free lunches and free passes to Lions Drag Strip for all to experience the sights and sounds of the sport. These gestures were directly from Hart, who believed that positive community relations were a necessity.

With the rumors swirling about the changes coming to the facility, Hart decided that he had enough and resigned. He cited his displeasure with the Lions Club's board of director's decision to install a closed-course motorcycle track over a simulated rough-terrain surface to offer the top and local professional riders to ride every Thursday night.

On Saturday, June 19, another chapter in the history of Lions Drag Strip came to an end, as C. J. Hart's six-year reign as general manager ended. The active, hands-on leader was a colorful, strong-willed person and the greatest manager that the drag racing world knew. Hart was given the respect and praise from all the employees, racers, media, and spectators that he rightly deserved.

Chopper Drags

Lions Drag Strip had seen more motorcycle action than any other drag strip in the nation, and all types of motorcycles were welcomed. One of the most interesting competitions of the two- and three-wheel kind was on Sunday, July 18, 1971. More than 125 motorcycles from 16 different clubs got together for a day of Chopper Drags.

Every year, Lions Drag Strip hosted these hard-running, high-performance machines, which represented groups, including the Chosen Few, Road Runners, Choppers of Los Angeles, the Palo Alto Soul Brothers, Oakland Vagabonds, Magnificent 7, and the East Bay Dragons of Northern California. The high number of Harley-Davidson

All makes and types of motorcycles competed at Lions Drag Strip, as is shown by owner and driver Ed Stor from Long Beach, California. Store rides his custom Harley-Davidson 883 Sportster chopper at the Nationals. (Photo Courtesy Steve Brackett)

Sidecar racing was a huge attraction at the Chopper Nationals. This husband-and-wife team out of the Harley-Davidson of Ventura camp show how low to the surface this racing sidecar passenger (also known as the "monkey") was positioned in the sidecar. It was only inches from off the ground, and without safety restraints, one sudden mishap could lead to serious injury or death. (Photo Courtesy Steve Brackett)

Sportsters, Hondas, and Full Dresser clubs gave the enthusiast much to watch.

No cars were allowed to run, so the bike riders were able to use all of the track facilities. Track attendants, along with members from the various clubs, kept the meet moving smoothly and organized without incident.

Competition was fierce in all of the classes, as the final win light told the outcome in these classes. Ed McDonald (Top Gas) and Joe Smith (Fuel) led the big-inch Harley-Davidson contingency, as both made runs through the traps with ETs in the 10.60s at 130 mph, while Borris Murray led the Triumph faithful in the competitive fields in both the Fuel and Top Gas classes.

Bikes of every color, size, and description, along with all the beautiful women, made the meet an enormous success. Pat Miller's triple-engine B/Gas drag bike ran three Yamaha 350-cc, two-stroke engines, and each one was 60 hp. Miller was one of the first to use a slipper clutch for a motorcycle and an oversized trail-bike sprocket to transfer power to the 4-inch rear slick. It didn't always work the way that it was designed—to smoke the tire for the entire quarter mile. However, when it did, the cycle was

The New Voice at Lions Drag Strip: Track Manager Steve Evans (1970–1972)

Replacing C. J. Hart with a new manager at Lions Drag Strip was no easy task. The Lions Club board of directors focused on the personable Steve Evans whom they nominated and elected to the position. On June 26, 1971, Evans began his work as general manager and track manager at Lions Drag Strip.

Evans had served as track manager at Fremont Speedway and Champion Raceway. He brought 20 years of racing experience to Lions Drag Strip, where he was well-known for being one of the best and most knowledgeable announcers and promoters in motorsports.

Evans was heard over the radio waves in his entertaining and outrageous radio advertisements promoting the Big Match Race between highly competitive foes.

The top priorities for Evans as the new manager included bringing Lions Drag Strip back to NHRA sanctioning, which had been absent for six years, and the immediate construction of the new motocross facility.

On July 3, Lions Drag Strip was officially sanctioned as an NHRA track. As for the future, Evans announced that the venue needed a major facelift to keep pace with the professionalism of drag racing.

"Lions Drag Strip already has the sport's quickest asphalt, the finest metropolitan location, and one of the finest teams of officials that a manager could ask for," Evans said.

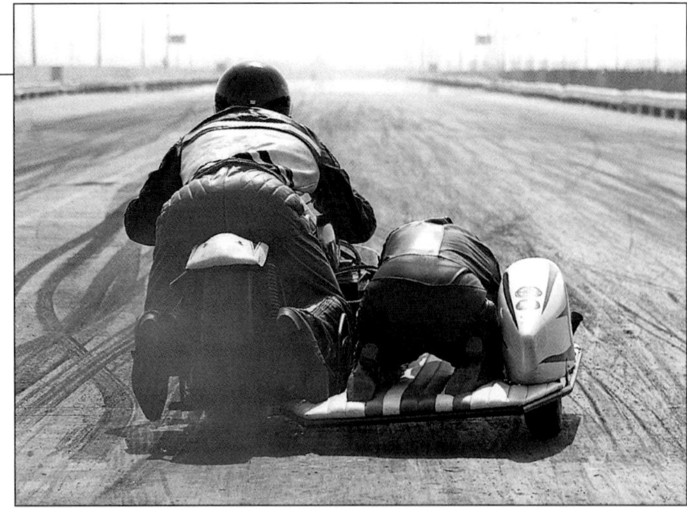

This is a rear angle view of the exact moment that the rider goes full throttle, and it demonstrates the dangers on how low to the surface the "monkey" was positioned in the sidecar. (Photo Courtesy Steve Brackett)

Pat Miller's B/Gas Cycle ran triple Yamaha TR2 350-cc factory road-racing engines that each produced an estimated 60 hp. Miller's cycle was one of the first to incorporate a slipper clutch. He was able to run in the low 10s with speeds averaging 145 mph. (Photo Courtesy Steve Brackett)

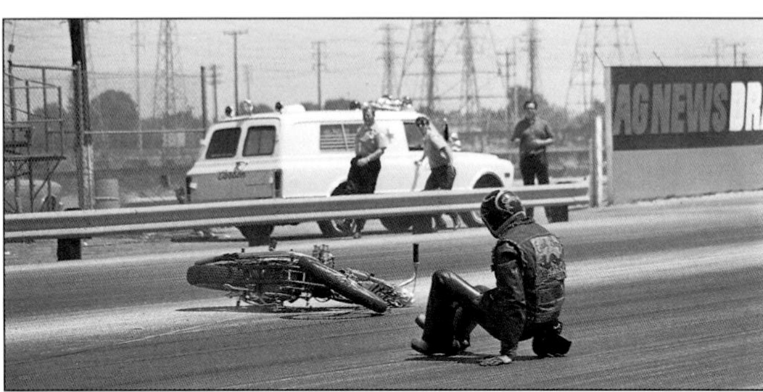

Accidents of any type were uncommon at the Chopper Nationals. The most serious misfortune of the meet was when this rider from the northern California East Bay Dragons lost control off the line and dumped his bike. The rider quickly got up and walked off without a scratch. Anyone who thought that choppers were not powerful machines was proven wrong. This bike featured Weber carburetion. (Photo Courtesy Steve Brackett)

Joe Smith and his son Gene accept the accolades of winning the Top Fuel Chopper Nationals Eliminator and top speed trophies from race queen and Playboy Playmate, Molly Blue. Smith, also known as the "West Coast king of Harley Drag Racing," rewrote the record books numerous times when he mastered the power of the big-inch Shovelhead-based engine. Smith's **King Rat** *Harley-Davidson was the first motorcycle in NHRA competition to break the 8s with an 8.97 ET at 166.05 mph at the 1971 Bakersfield March meet. (Photo Courtesy Steve Brackett)*

Another Sportster cyclist prepares to speed down the strip on this custom-built chopper, which peaked at about 95 mph in the quarter mile. The Chopper Nationals gave riders and owners the opportunity to see their machines perform in a safe, controlled setting—instead of on public highways. (Photo Courtesy Steve Brackett)

When Steve Evans was hired as the new general manager at Lions Drag Strip, his first task was to return it to NHRA sanctioning. The second task was to build a new, permanent motocross track to generate revenue. The track originally only operated on Friday nights, but Evans expanded the schedule to three nights a week. It drew the riders but the decision soured quickly around the neighborhood. (Photo Courtesy Don Gillespie)

exceptionally quick, and ETs were in the low-10-second range with speeds of more than 140 mph.

More than 400 choppers were entered, and the popular Honda fours were seen throughout the pits among chopper builders. Many of the Hondas featured modified front ends, fenders, seats, and fuel tanks.

CMC Motocross

Stu Peters, the president of CMC Motocross, and Steve Evans oversaw the design and construction of a new and challenging 5/8-mile motocross course in the parking lot behind the scoring tower.

The course was erected from tons of dirt and had multiple obstacles. The layout of the track included all of the basic sections: numerous rollers (rounded bumps in the dirt), rhythm sections (areas where riders continuously gain rhythm to complete double or triple jumps on the track), whoops (smaller continuous bumps), and booters (medium jumps that occur before the finish line).

Stu Peters, a Continental Motosports Club president and motocross promoter, and Steve Evans designed and built a permanent dirt track at Lions Drag Strip. It was complete with lights, bleachers, jumps, and berms. This added extra traffic and noise pollution to the neighborhood. (Photo Courtesy Don Gillespie)

Professional Quartz lighting, new grandstands, and permanent restrooms and snack bars highlighted the advertised "finest night-lighted motocross course in the United States." It opened in the fall of 1971.

MAD at Lions Drag Strip

Despite a temperature of 92°F, 10,000-plus fans and jobbers turned up at Lions Drag Strip for the first-annual Manufacturers Appreciation Day (MAD) on July 31 that featured 17 manufacturers exhibiting their products and answering questions about their wares.

A sample of the groups that participated included Hurst Performance, RFI, TRW, Hedman, Edelbrock, Holley, Savage, Keystone, American, Autolite-Ford, and Autosentials.

While the wholesalers had their time during the day, the afternoon and evening were devoted to racing. The spectators were treated to a program that featured three eight-car fields of action: Funny Cars, AA/Fuel Altereds, and the intriguing battle of front-engined versus rear-engined dragsters.

The finals in the Top Fuel challenge were the front-engine rails of Don Moody and Jerry Glenn. Moody emerged as the winner and clocked a 6.53 ET. Glenn was a very close second with a 6.55 ET.

Explosion in Motion

In what had to be one of the wildest shows at Lions Drag Strip, the AA/Fuel Altereds kept true with their unpredictable travels down the 1320.

Dennis Geisler's *Instant T* was the first to take a win over "Dangerous" Danny Collins in Don Green's *Rat Trap*. Geisler stopped the clocks with an 8.74 ET to Collins's 9.86, as Collins pulled a wheelie 100 feet off the line, landed hard, and shut off.

Gary Hazen was next up in the *Panic* and turned in a 7.28 ET win over Tim Perry and the *Yellow Submarine*. Dave Hough and Stan Lucas made things interesting when Hough in the *Nanook* had everyone hold their breath as he uncontrollably bounced around on three wheels and eventually gained control with a 7.76 ET. Lucas also two-stepped his way to the win with a 10.12 ET. The last pair up to the line was the *Stone T* of Graf & Yoshioka and Tocco, Harper, & Garten. Mikio Yoshioka picked up the win with a 9.44 ET, as Roger Garten crossed over the centerline.

The second round of the raging band of Altereds turned out to be the final round. Dennis Geisler and Gary Hazen led off the round, and Hazen took the win with a 7.19 ET at 201.77 mph, which was the low ET of the night. For unknown reasons, Hazen tried for the longest run ever attempted at Lions Drag Strip and plowed deep into the giant sandbox at the end of the track, which fouled him out. Geisler was also disqualified for crossing over the centerline. Mikio Yoshioka also fouled when he crossed the centerline, which awarded the win to Stan Lucas with an 8.40 ET.

Gary Hazen qualified the **Panic!** *with a 7.24 ET and turned in a winning 7.28 ET at 186.34 mph over the* **Yellow Submarine** *of Tim Perry, who shut off with an 11.84 ET at 73.11 mph. Hazen let it all out for round two to grab the win and take low ET of the meet with a 7.19 ET at 201.77 mph. For Hazen, he made a trip deep in the giant sandbox that damaged the* **Panic!** *beyond returning. (Jere Aldereff Photography/Courtesy Lions Automobilia Foundation Museum)*

It seems like that only happens with the Fuel Altereds. The confusion that took place couldn't be put down on paper to figure out, so the final decision was made by track manager Steve Evans.

Dave Hough's **Nanook** *(near lane) and Stan Lucas's* **Scrounger** *(far lane) made things interesting in the first round when Hough red-lit and gave the automatic win to Lucas. The excitement continued when the* **Nanook** *did some bouncing around on three wheels when Hough eventually settled down with a 7.76 ET at 162.33 mph. Lucas took the win with a 10.12 ET at 124.33 mph. (Jere Aldereff Photography/Courtesy Lions Automobilia Foundation Museum)*

In the first round, the **Stone T** *of Graf & Yoshioka faced the* **Tocco-Harper-Garten** *entry. The* **Stone T** *moved on to round two, as "Rapid" Roger Garten blew the tires and crossed into the other lane (losing by disqualification). (Jere Aldereff Photography/Courtesy Lions Automobilia Foundation Museum)*

Evans decided that Dennis Geisler, Stan Lucas, and Mikio Yoshioka would share the final-round money. Evans awarded Hazen the low ET money along with all the sand that was stuck to the *Panic* after it was pulled out of the sand traps.

Shiroma's 6.63 ET Record

Stan Shiroma recorded the third-quickest Funny Car ET in quarter-mile history with a 6.63 ET in the *Midnight Skulker* Plymouth 'Cuda. Only Gene Snow (6.59) and Don Prudhomme (6.62) ran quicker than the bespeckled Shiroma.

Shiroma began his march toward the Lions Drag Strip ET record with a 6.73 ET at 208.33 mph to beat the Dodge Charger of Glenn, Glenn, and Schultz (Jerry Glenn, Jim Glenn, and Bill Schultz), which ran a 7.16 ET at 200.89 mph. In the second round, Pat Foster laid down a long, smoky burnout. When the smoke cleared, the *Damn Yankee* was nowhere to be seen. The failed brake system was to blame, so Foster had no choice but to idle slowly down to the end of the strip and stop. Shiroma took a step closer to the record as he singled his way to the win with a 6.69 ET at 210.12 mph.

Shiroma's final-round opponent was Gary Burgin, who needed to cut a quick light to outdistance Shiroma. All was for naught for Burgin, as he left the line a little too fast and fouled. Shiroma thundered off the line, took home the win, and set the new Lions Drag Strip ET record of 6.63 at 215.31 mph.

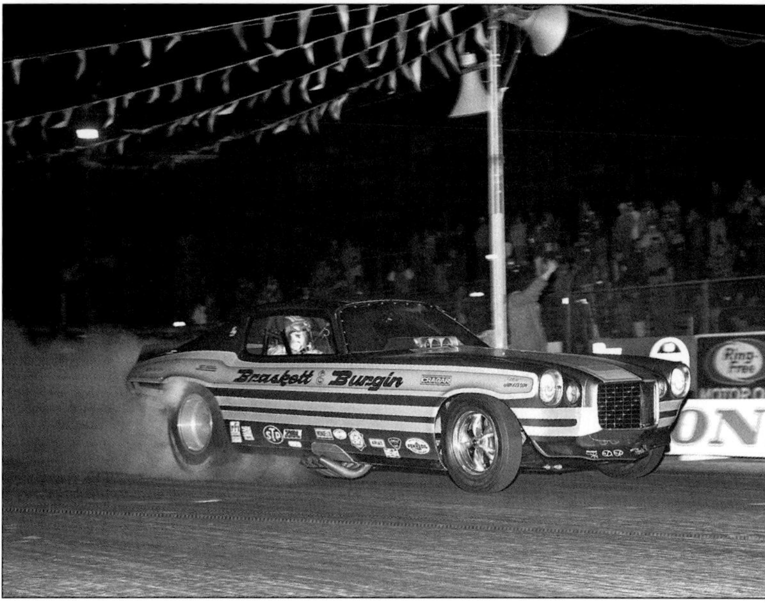

Gary Burgin knew he needed to cut a perfect light to have a chance to put away Stan Shiroma, but he got a little too quick on the countdown and red-lit. This gave the automatic win to the **Midnight Skulker** *gang, who set the Lions ET record with a 6.63 ET at 215.331 mph.*

The first round of Funny Car racing saw Gene Conway, an old-time favorite of Lions Drag strip, go down in defeat. He ran a 7.24 ET at 172.41 mph as Stan Shiroma and the **Midnight Skulker** *took the path toward the ET record and won with a 6.73 ET at 206.33 mph.*

The triumphant crew of the **Midnight Skulker** *celebrates in the winner's circle after setting the new Lions ET record (6.63) and winning Top Eliminator. In the top row (left to right) are crewman John Leonard, manager Steve Evans, crew chief Ray Zeller, and Zeller's girlfriend Samantha. In the bottom row (left to right) are driver Stan Shiroma and crew members Terry Ludwig and Doug Finley. (Jere Aldereff Photography/Courtesy Lions Automobilia Foundation Museum)*

Memories

Stan Shiroma

Midnight Skulker *Funny Car Driver*

"Keith Black was there that day when we set the [Lions Drag Strip] ET track record. Acting as a consultant, Keith and Ray Zeller had the engine running better than ever. It was the quickest we ever ran, and with him being there, it was just pure magic. Keith always did the right things to make the car quick and fast.

"My thoughts about Lions? We always ran well there, and the weather was great for making horsepower. Although it wasn't the best-looking drag strip and the odors from the nearby refineries were unpleasant at times, the conditions were always favorable for racing."

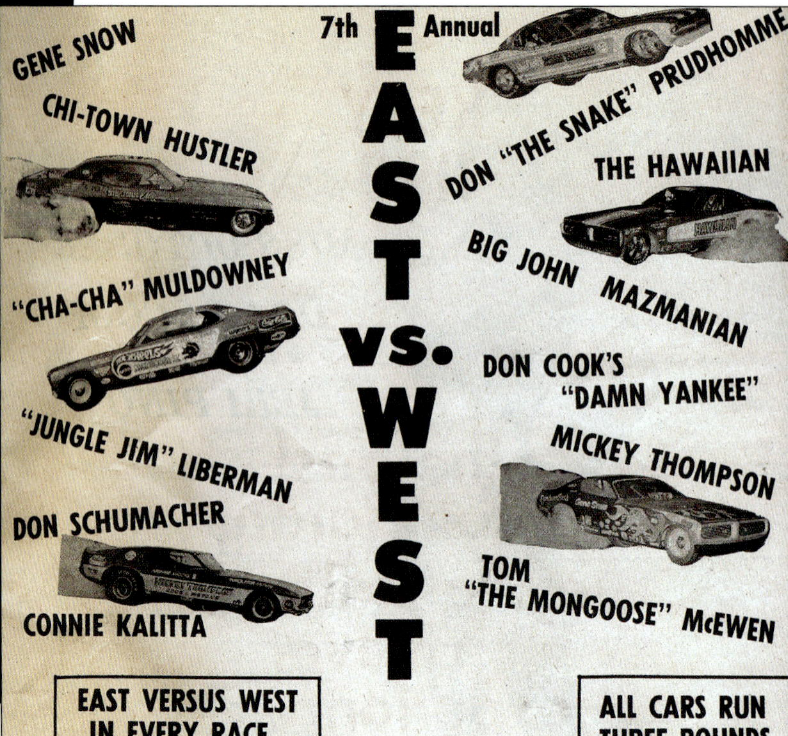

7th Annual
EAST vs. WEST
GENE SNOW
CHI-TOWN HUSTLER
"CHA-CHA" MULDOWNEY
"JUNGLE JIM" LIBERMAN
DON SCHUMACHER
CONNIE KALITTA
DON "THE SNAKE" PRUDHOMME
THE HAWAIIAN
BIG JOHN MAZMANIAN
DON COOK'S "DAMN YANKEE"
MICKEY THOMPSON
TOM "THE MONGOOSE" McEWEN
EAST VERSUS WEST IN EVERY RACE
ALL CARS RUN THREE ROUNDS
SATURDAY, OCTOBER 16
GATES OPEN 1:30 - ELIMS at 7
ADMISSION $5.00
PIT PASSES $1.00
CHILDREN 8-12 $1.00
UNDER 8 FREE

This poster was used to advertise Lions Drag Strip's seventh-annual East-West racing event. The poster was displayed mostly in the Wilmington area.

East versus West versus Mother Nature

The seventh-annual East versus West Spectacular was Saturday, October 16, at Lions Drag Strip. The crowd of 12,000 spectators contemplated a question: which region (the East or the West) has the fastest Funny Cars? Well, the question remained unanswered, as Mother Nature disrupted racing with on-and-off showers that put an end to racing during the third round that day.

Representing the East team was Connie Kalitta, "Jungle" Jim Liberman, Shirley "Cha-Cha" Muldowney, the *Chi-Town Hustler*, Don Schumacher, and team captain Gene Snow.

Don "the Snake" Prudhomme anchored the West team with Tom "the Mongoose" McEwen, "Big" John Mazmanian, Roland Leong's *Hawaiian*, Mike Snively in Mazmanian's candy red machine, Dale Pulde in Mickey Thompson's Pinto, and Ron O'Donnell in Don Cook's *Damn Yankee* 'Cuda.

Pre-race driver introductions around the starting line included (from left to right) Tom McEwen, Shirley Muldowney, **Hawaiian** *owner Roland Leong, and Lions Drag Strip starter Larry Sutton. (Photo Courtesy Steve Brackett)*

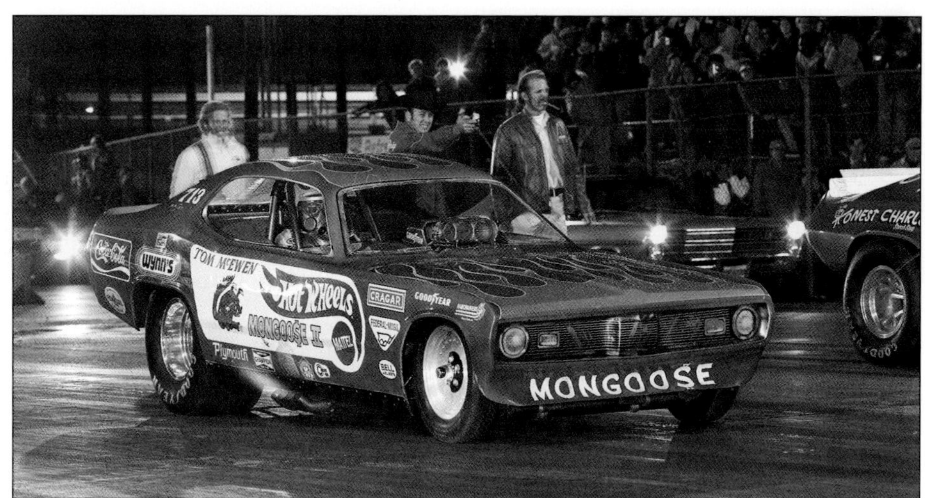

With traces of rain surrounding the area, round one opened with Tom McEwen facing "Jungle" Jim Liberman. Liberman got the East team off to a winning start and earned the first point when he outran McEwen.

As the opening ceremonies concluded, the call went out for the first pair of Funny Cars to get to the line. Representing the East team was Liberman, and McEwen represented the West. They brought the crowd to its feet. Liberman scored the East's first point when he defeated the Mongoose with a 6.72 ET over McEwen's out-of-shape 7.23 ET.

Next, Ron O'Donnell evened the score for the West when he disposed of Connie Kalitta with a 6.74 ET at 168.67 mph to the *Bounty Hunter*'s 6.90 ET at 184.42 mph.

Don "the Chicago Kid" Schumacher, focuses on the tree against Mike Snively, who is driving the **Plymouth Dealers Association** *'Cuda of "Big" John Mazmanian. Snively won with a holeshot.*

Muldowney earned a point for the East when she posted a win over Pulde in the Mickey Thompson Pinto, as Pulde carried the front wheels from off the line and broke the rear-end in the process.

Snow received a single run when the *Hawaiian*, driven by Bobby Rowe, broke the blower belt on the line. Snively, in Mazmanian's 'Cuda, dropped a holeshot and turned it into a win (a 6.84 ET at 217.39 mph) over Don Schumacher, who recorded a quick 6.77 ET at 213.77 mph.

The final pair to run in the first round was the *Chi-Town Hustler*, which had Clare Sanders in the seat against Prudhomme, who was piloting his *Hot Wheels II* Plymouth 'Cuda. Prudhomme knotted up the score 4-4 with the win (a 6.81 ET at 201.34 mph) to Sanders's 7.02 ET at 209.30 mph.

Pulde got round two off and running with a winning 6.86 ET at 210.77 mph over an out-of-shape Don Schumacher, who crossed over the line around the 600-foot mark when the front of the car went airborne. Schumacher recovered, brought his car back into his lane, and avoided running into Pulde.

Sanders tied up the score when he drove the *Chi-Town Hustler* to the finish line with a 7.05 ET at 210.28 mph after McEwen, in his no-go Duster, broke the driveline off the starting line. Prudhomme was up next against Kalitta but received a single run when Kalitta took the first exit off the strip when he lost fire on the burnout. Prudhomme's

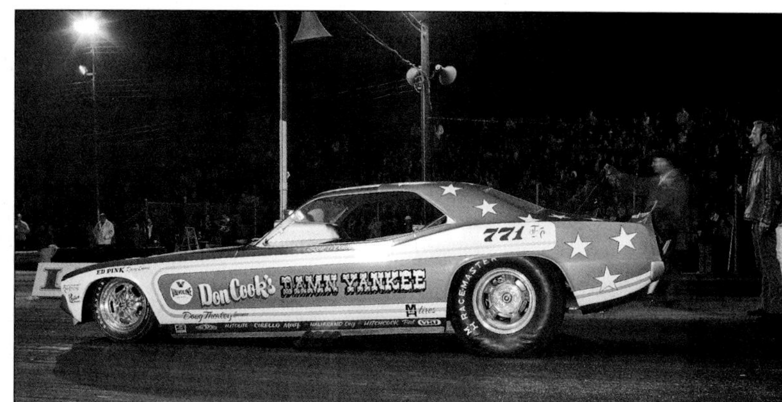

Ron O'Donnell in the Don Cook **Damn Yankee** *scored a point for the West team with a win over the* **Bounty Hunter** *Mustang of Connie Kalitta.*

Clare Sanders, who was from Chicago, drove the **Chi-Town Hustler** *Dodge Challenger of John Farkonas. Austin Coil and Pat Minnick met Don Prudhomme in the first round and lost to the Snake when Sanders apparently used up all of the power on the 1/8-mile burnout.*

7.05 ET at 210.28 mph gave the West a 1-point lead.

Snively kept the win streak going for the West with the win and the point when he put away Liberman in a heads-up race. Both cars were on a rail toward the finish line when Liberman suddenly got out of shape midway down the strip. Snively was first to the finish line with a 6.90 ET at 187.89 mph, but Liberman never let up on the pedal and ran right on Snively's bumper, where he ran an identical ET of 6.90 with a top speed of 203.61 mph.

Muldowney gave the East hope with a win and a point over Rowe, as both cars were in a dead heat toward the top end. Muldowney crossed the finish line first and

Bobby Rowe (in Roland Leong's **Hawaiian***) failed to earn a point in either round of competition. In round one, Rowe lost a blower belt right at the starting line against Gene Snow. In round two, Rowe lost to Shirley Muldowney in what was one of the closest races of the night, as Muldowney ran a 7.07 ET at 206.89 mph to the* **Hawaiian's** *7.07 ET at 200 mph.*

In the second round, alternate Tom Hoover replaced Ron O'Donnell's **Damn Yankee** *when the 'Cuda suffered from engine woes. Hoover went on to run the wildest ride of the night, as his Charger got completely out of shape and came close to the guardrail. Hoover recovered but lost to the East captain, Gene Snow, who set the low ET of the meet with a 6.71.*

Shirley "Cha-Cha" Muldowney's first visit to Lions Drag Strip was a successful one, as she collected two points for the East team with wins over Dale Pulde in Mickey Thompson's Pinto and the **Hawaiian.**

Don Prudhomme pulls on the gloves for his second-round encounter against the Mustang of Connie Kalitta. Prudhomme co-anchored the West team with Mike Snively, as both earned two points. Prudhomme took a single-run win against Kalitta when Kalitta took the first exit from the strip after his burnout. (Photo Courtesy Steve Brackett)

The East team's "Jungle" Jim Liberman had one win and loss on the evening. Liberman won his point against Tom McEwen in the first round, but in the second round, he lost a nail-biter against Mike Snively. Liberman got crossed up mid-track and stayed in it to the delight of the fans, as he nearly pulled out the win. Each car ran identical 7.07 ETs.

won by the margin of a bumper with a 7.07 ET at 206.89 mph to the *Hawaiian's* 7.07 ET at 200 mph.

Tom Hoover's *White Bear* Dodge replaced the ailing *Damn Yankee* against Snow. At the hit, Hoover got completely out of shape, lifted, and nearly met with the guardrail. Hoover still netted an ET of 8.76, but Snow went on to win and set the low ET of the meet with a 6.71.

Lightning Forces 6-6 Tie

Each team entered the third and deciding round with the score tied 6-6. Up to this point, Snow, the East captain, held the meet's low ET of 6.71, while Snively claimed the top-speed mark of 217.39 mph. As the first two cars prepared for the third round, a bolt of lightning hit a transformer near the starting area and knocked out the public address system, the staging and timing lights, and a light bank around the starting line.

After a brief delay, starter Larry Sutton let the show go on and prepared the first two cars for a flag start. The remaining races were to be run under those conditions, but as

A huge wheel-stand in the first round damaged the rear-end, but Dale Pulde won in round two against Don Schumacher. Schumacher got out of shape past mid-track and crossed over the centerline. He recovered quickly and moved back into his lane before he came up on the rear of Pulde's Pinto.

Mechanical problems plagued Connie Kalitta's **Bounty Hunter** *Mustang the entire evening in his return to Lions Drag Strip. Kalitta lost to Ron O'Donnell in the first round, as O'Donnell ran a 6.74 ET at 168.67 mph to Kalitta's 6.90 ET at 184.42 mph.*

Captain Gene Snow of the East team won his two rounds against the West and set the low ET of the meet with a 6.71 in the first round. The third round had all the makings of a slugfest, but the overall top eliminator of the night was the weather, as heavy showers washed out the meet, which ended in a 6-6 tie.

Mike Snively and Don Prudhomme carried the weight for the West team with two points apiece before going into the third round. Mike Snively had "Big" John Mazmanian's 'Cuda running strong when Snively laid claim and set the top speed of the meet at 217.39 mph.

soon as the next pair of cars fired up, the skies opened to a steady downpour, and the race ended abruptly. Because the time curfew was near and the conditions of the strip were poor, the meet was halted. Due to the power failure and rain, the track officials determined that only the first two rounds counted in the team scoring.

17th Anniversary Race Championships

Seventeen years ago, 6-second ETs seemed unattainable. However, on October 30, Lions Drag Strip celebrated its anniversary by making it a reality for fuel Funny Cars to net a 6.92 or better and for Top Fuelers to net a a 6.5 or better to find a spot in the eight-car field.

Twenty-seven Funny Cars and 34 Top Fuelers were on hand at Lions Drag Strip's 17th anniversary championship meet. All tried to cut a set number for a spot in the eight-car fields. The top of the leader board in Funny Car was Ron O'Donnell, who cut a supreme 6.61 ET at 218.82 mph driving Don Cook's *Damn Yankee* Plymouth 'Cuda.

"Kansas" John Wiebe sent many of the 34 entries back to the drawing board when he led the pack of eight Top Fuel dragsters with an astounding 6.46 ET at 226.23 mph. The newcomer in Top Fuel was 17-year-old sensation Jeb Allen. He rounded out the eighth slot in the field with an impressive 6.59 ET at 218.44 mph.

Wiebe Dominates

In the first round, Wiebe's 6.56 ET at 221.13 mph easily disposed of Frank Bradley's 6.84 ET at 225 mph. For the start in round two, Wiebe ran past James Warren with a 6.54 ET at 223.32 mph to Warren's respectable 6.60 ET at 222.77 mph. In the final round, Wiebe faced Larry Dixon. At the first sight of the green, both cars left evenly, but Wiebe was given a clear path to the winner's circle when he posted a 6.75 ET at 226.13 mph, as Larry and Pat Dixon's *Astrolo Special* developed engine troubles and allowed Dixon to coast his way through the lights with a 10.99 ET.

Fires in the First Round

In the Funny Car lineup, Bobby Rowe and the *Hawaiian* Charger chalked up a round-one victory with a 6.64 ET at 194.38 mph over Gene Conway, as Conway shut off early with an 8.42 ET at 100 mph. Unfortunately for Leong's *Hawaiian*, the Keith Black Elephant dropped a rod at the finish line that resulted in a fire that was quickly extinguished.

After the lengthy cleanup, Stan Shiroma disposed of Dunn & Reath, and Bill Leavitt upset number-one-qualifier Ron O'Donnell with a holeshot win (a 6.81 ET at 208 mph) to O'Donnell's 6.72 ET at 217.39 mph.

Jake Johnston ran a stellar 6.61 ET at 217.39 mph over Tom McEwen, as the *Hot Wheels* Plymouth Duster went up in a ball of flames just before the finish line and burned off the chute from the car. McEwen had to ride it out using just the brakes. He experienced the worst fire of his driving career and escaped without serious injuries or burns to himself. The same couldn't be said for his car.

Johnston Outlasts the Field

In round two, Ron O'Donnell and the *Damn Yankee* was called back to replace the broken *Hawaiian* against Bill Leavitt. This time, O'Donnell reversed the tables from round one with a winning 6.69 ET at 211.76 mph, as Leavitt broke mid-track, shut off early, and stopped the lights with an 8.48 ET at 106.00 mph.

Next up to the line were Shiroma's *Midnight Skulker* and the popular Jake Johnston. The *Rambunctious II* got out of shape mid-track, but it wasn't enough to slow the Dodge Charger. Johnston won with a 6.81 ET at 205.47 mph to Shiroma's 7.07 ET at 189.47 mph. With Keith Black lending aid to the *Rambunctious II* team, Johnston prevailed in the final round with a winning 6.62

When you arguably have the best engine builder, tuner, and teacher in drag racing in your pit, it's good to learn from him. Jake Johnston confers with Keith Black on tuning techniques at the 17th-annual Anniversary race at Lions Drag Strip. Whatever Black suggested, it made a difference, as Johnston made it to the winner's circle.

Memories

Jake Johnston

Rambunctious *Dodge Charger Funny Car Driver and Tuner*

"I always enjoyed racing at Lions Drag Strip, and I had considerable success there too. It had so much history, and it was such a popular place to go to when we toured out on the West Coast in the fall and winter months. The proximity to the ocean with the ideal temperatures, air density, and traction made racing perfect.

"So many historical memories and performances made Lions Drag Strip one of the magical strips to race. I always had a great time there at that distinguished track."

In the battle of the elephants, Jake Johnston powered the **Rambunctious II** *Dodge Charger past Ron O'Donnell in the final round with a 6.62 ET at 218.97 mph over the Ed Pink–powered* **Damn Yankee** *'Cuda of Don Cook. O'Donnell's 6.82 ET at 196.07 mph fell short due to engine issues before it went through the finish lights.*

ET at 218.97 mph over O'Donnell's 6.82 ET at 196.07 mph. O'Donnell experienced engine woes before going through the finish lights.

Leavitt Sets All-Time Funny Car Record

Bill Leavitt from Chula Vista, California, made his first-ever run in his new *Quickie Too* Mustang fuel Funny Car in May 1971. Just seven months later, Leavitt drove his *Quickie Too* Mustang to the upper echelons of the Funny Car world and became the quickest Funny Car in the world.

On December 4, at Lions Drag Strip's Grand Finale Funny Car meet, Leavitt made his assault toward the world record when he qualified number one in the 16-car field with the low ET of 6.53. For Leavitt, this was just the beginning for the self-established racer.

Described as a low-buck racer, Leavitt's history-making evening got underway in round one with a winning 6.65 ET at 211.76 mph over Omar Carrothers's off-pace 6.97 ET at 212.76 mph. Next, in round one was the entry of Pat Foster and Barry Setzer against Mike Snively driving John Mazmanian's 'Cuda. It was Snively from the get-go with a 6.80 ET at 214.28 mph, as Foster slowed through the lights with a 10.50 ET and a broken rear-end.

In round two, Leavitt set the record with a 6.51 ET at 209.71 mph, as he streaked past Gary Burgin, who lifted after getting crossed up and drove over the centerline. Leavitt was in jeopardy of watching the record go to Pat Foster, who returned from a broken rear-end. Foster singled in the Ed Pink–prepped Barry Setzer Vega with a 6.49 ET at 222.04 mph.

Leavitt made an easy pass with a 7.99 ET at 110.29 mph in round three, as Ron O'Donnell in Don Cook's *Damn Yankee* was forced to remain in the pits when the transmission locked in reverse. Foster returned for another single attempt and needed a 6.62 ET or quicker to set the record but fell short with a 6.67 ET at 220.04 mph.

The final round brought Leavitt and Johnston to the line. At the green, Johnston jumped out to the lead and pulled away at mid-track with Leavitt in hot pursuit. Suddenly, the *Rambunctious* Charger struck the tires, which caused Johnston to back-pedal and shut off with a 6.97 ET at 177.10 mph. Leavitt and the *Quickie Too* went the distance for the win and the title for being the quickest Funny Car in drag racing history with a fantastic 6.48 ET.

This closed the curtain on another incredible season.

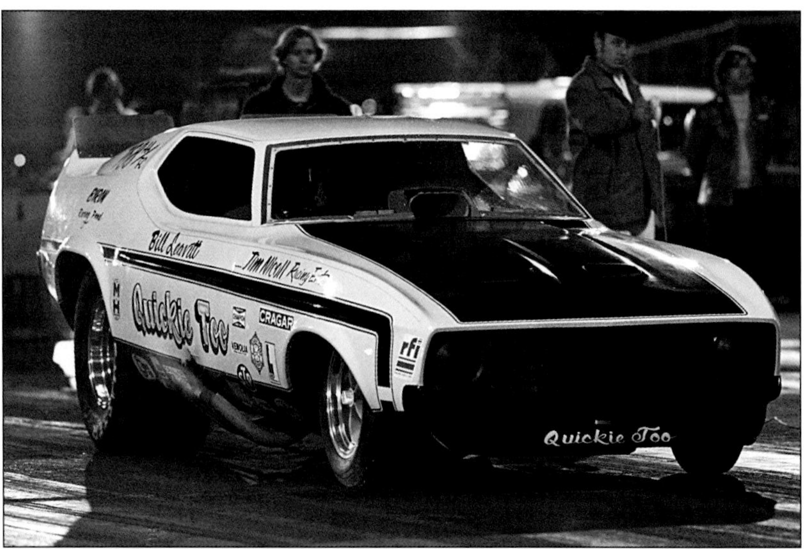

Bill Leavitt astounded the drag racing world on December 4 at Lions Drag Strip when he recorded the quickest ET ever for a Funny Car with a 6.48 at 213 mph. Leavitt backed up his time when he ran a 6.53 ET during eliminations. The new record pumped new life into 392 Chrysler Hemi users.

Chapter Seven

1972

A Dark End in Hot Rodding History

The entrance to Lions Drag Strip was a short distance from Interstate 405, and 223rd Street led straight to the parking lot and pit area. The Grand Premiere opened the 1972 season and set the expectations for another record year. Look closely at the proximity of homes in the neighborhood that later became a major factor of the fate of the drag strip. (Jere Alderef Photography/Courtesy Lions Automobilia Foundation Museum)

The first official NHRA season opener at Lions Drag Strip was the first-annual Grand Premiere. It was brought to the attention of many that the untouchable 5-second barrier would not withstand the onslaught of the fuel dragsters much longer.

Another item entered the drag racing record books when Don Prudhomme and John Wiebe turned in the world's quickest Top Fuel race.

Record performances and top times were not just limited to the nitro group. Every class brought out the best with its own super performers at Lions Drag Strip.

This poster (featuring teenage sensation Jeb Allen) announced the first-annual Grand Premiere at Lions Drag Strip. The event opened the 1972 drag racing season. (Image Courtesy Tim Pearl)

The staging lanes begin to fill up for the first-annual Grand Premiere at Lions Drag Strip. Before spectators went to get a spot on the bleachers, it was common to go to the concession stand. Since opening day in October 1955, the Taylor family had been the sole concessions proprietor. It was fitting that the family debuted a new item at the Grand Premiere to complement the regular menu of hot dogs, chili, tamales, fries, candy, soda, and popcorn. Butch Taylor put together a double stack of various cold cuts on an extra-long submarine-style roll that was loaded with all of the fixings. Butch's wife suggested "the 1/4-mile sandwich" as the name for the sandwich. (Jere Aldereff Photography/Courtesy Lions Automobilia Foundation Museum)

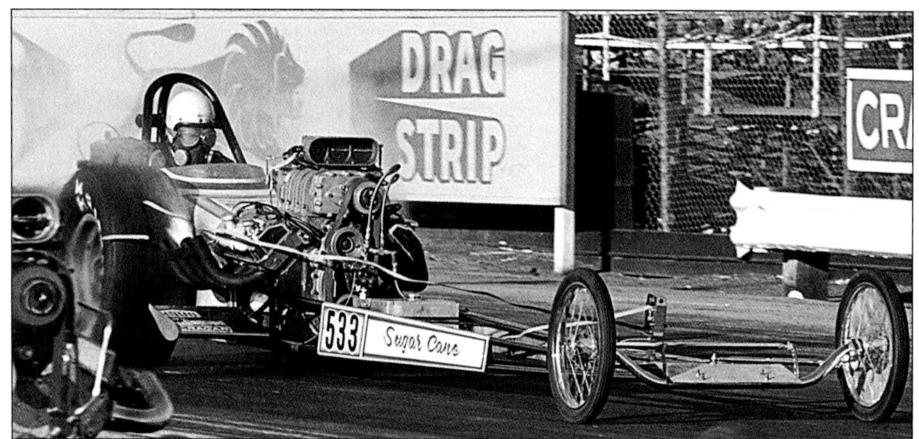

Howard Ditzel of Boulder, Colorado, attempts to put the **Sugar Cane** *Top Fueler of owner Otis Campbell into the program during the Grand Premiere at Lions Drag Strip. Unfortunately, Ditzel was unable to make the show, and the* **Sugar Cane** *shook so violently coming off the line that it forced the movie camera to open, exposed the film, and unrolled the entire reel.*

The Schley Brothers' chopped-top H/G Volkswagen made the quickest run ever for a Volkswagen-powered race car (an unbelievable 11.28 ET). The team of Dave Brasket and Gary Burgin ran back-to-back 6.72 and 6.75 ETs to set the national Funny Car ET record at 6.72. "Dyno" Don Nicholson set the new national Pro Stock ET mark with a 9.58, Ken Veney set the record of 8.33 in an injected Funny Car, and Tony Nancy set the NHRA national top-speed record of 233.16 mph and backed it up with a 236.22-mph run.

Lions Drag Strip was the premiere track in the country if you wanted to go fast.

The Beach Bite

The super Long Beach bite (traction at the starting line) resulted in record performances in all brackets. Some machines ran 0.3 seconds under their national marks, but a few experienced the ferocious aggressiveness of the strip.

During Saturday's last qualifying session, in the new *Penner & Beach* Top Fuel entry, driver Jack Martin found that the fabled beach bite was more than he could manage. Martin backed off the throttle, but the throttle linkage jammed and caused the injectors to go wide open.

During Saturday's qualifying session, this sequence of four photos captured a surprised John Martin in the new and unpainted **Penner & Beach** *Top Fuel dragster that fell victim to the fabled "beach bite." At the hit, Martin headed skyward when the throttle stuck wide open, providing the momentum for a giant wheel-stand. The engine bogged on the way down, and a series of rollovers ensued. Martin was shaken but walked away from the mangled mass of steel with minor injuries. Notice the tire distortion of the left wheel in the last photo that indicates the engine's freewheeling momentum.*

Pre-race festivities at the Grand Premiere began with driver and car introductions. The parade of racing dignitaries included Miss Hurst Golden Shifter Linda Vaughn, and Bill Balance, the popular Southern California talk show host of the Feminine Forum radio program on KGBS. (Jere Aldereff Photography/Courtesy Lions Automobilia Foundation Museum)

This view looking toward the starting line shows the jam-packed grandstands during the first round of Top Fuel at the Grand Premiere with Jim Brissette and Don Moody. (Jere Aldereff Photography/Courtesy Lions Automobilia Foundation Museum)

The car went into a gigantic wheelstand that resulted in a blow-over, and it flipped and tumbled several times down the track. The new car was destroyed, but Martin walked away unscathed.

Top Fuel History Made

With the conclusion of the pre-race introductions and the playing of the national anthem, the first round of Top Fuel was underway. John Wiebe shut off before the lights with the win and a 6.54 ET at 179.64 mph, and Jim Nicoll lost the blower at the finish line with a

The first round in Top Fuel had "Kansas" John Wiebe shut off early with a winning 6.54 ET at 179.64 mph over a troubled Jim Nicoll, who lost a blower at the finish line but managed to run a 6.60 ET at 196.07 mph. (Jere Aldereff Photography/Courtesy Lions Automobilia Foundation Museum)

The major upset at the Grand Premiere unfolded in the third race of the first round of Top Fuel when Bob Noice in the new **Brissette & Noice** *Top Fueler streaked past number-one contender Don Moody in the* **Cerny & Moody** *machine. Noice, the unexpected winner, surprised Moody with a near-perfect light off the line and ran a 6.47 ET at 225.00 mph to Moody's 6.48 ET at 222.22 mph. (Jere Aldereff Photography/Courtesy Lions Automobilia Foundation Museum)*

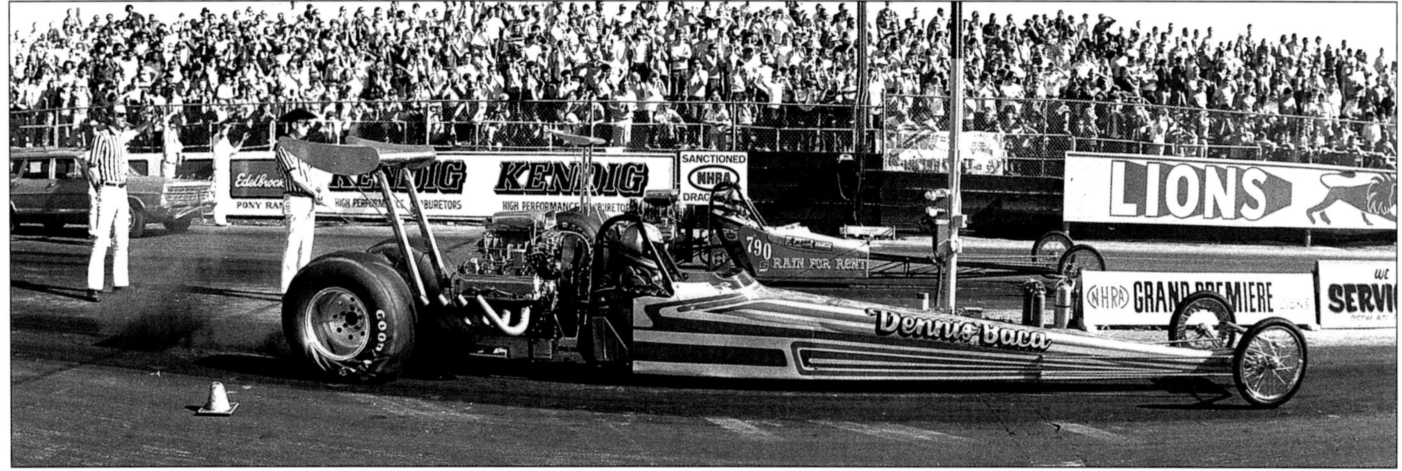

James Warren (far lane) and Dennis Baca (near lane) put on one heck of a race in the opening frame at Lions Drag Strip. Both drivers cut near-perfect reaction times and raced side by side through the traps, and Warren earned the win. He laid down a 6.44 ET at 231.36 mph to defeat Baca, who ran a 6.47 ET at 229.59 mph. (Jere Aldereff Photography/ Courtesy Lions Automobilia Foundation Museum)

High schooler Jeb Allen continued to improve his driving abilities and impress the seasoned veterans in Top Fuel. However, he was stopped by John Wiebe, who repeated his Supernationals semifinal-round defeat. Wiebe jumped out to an early lead and beat the youngster with a 6.41 ET at 232.55 mph to Allen's 6.44 ET at 229.59 mph.

6.60 ET at 196.07 mph.

Don Prudhomme began his march toward the finals when the normally consistent Carl Olson left too early and drew a red light in the *Kuhl & Olson* machine.

The unexpected drubbing of the meet occurred in the first round of Top Fuel when underdog Bob Noice, driving the *Brissette & Noice* entry, cut a perfect light over the favored *Cerny & Moody* entry to seal the upset win. Noice's lightning-like reflexes were better than Don Moody's, as Noice jumped out first, never backed off, and crossed the finish line with a 6.47 ET at 225.00 mph to Moody's 6.48 ET at 222.22 mph.

Prudhomme singled when the *Berry Brothers & Hughes* fueler failed to make the call to the lanes due to three broken motor mounts. In round three, Prudhomme found his groove and ran a 6.39 ET at 207.37 mph to put away Bob Noice, who ran a 6.52 ET at 200.85 mph.

Wiebe, driving his Donovan 417-powered, front-motored dragster, took a similar path to that of Prudhomme on his way to the finals. In the first round, Wiebe shut off early during a winning run with a 6.54 ET at 179.64 mph over Jim Nicoll, who launched the blower at half-track. In the second round, Wiebe received a free pass to the next round when Randy Allison red-lit and proceeded to obliterate the lights at the finish line. The third round brought "Kansas" John Wiebe up to the line against Jeb Allen, the 17-year-old sensation. Allen was late off the line and found himself playing catch-up. He lost to Wiebe's 6.41 ET at 232.55 mph with a 6.44 ET at 229.59 mph.

Don Prudhomme showcased the first appearance of his new* Yellow Feather *Top Fuel dragster at the Grand Premiere event. He contracted Kent Fuller to build it with an ultralight frame and a Keith Black cast-iron engine that was secured between the chromoly tubing. (Jere Alderef Photography/Courtesy Lions Automobilia Foundation Museum)

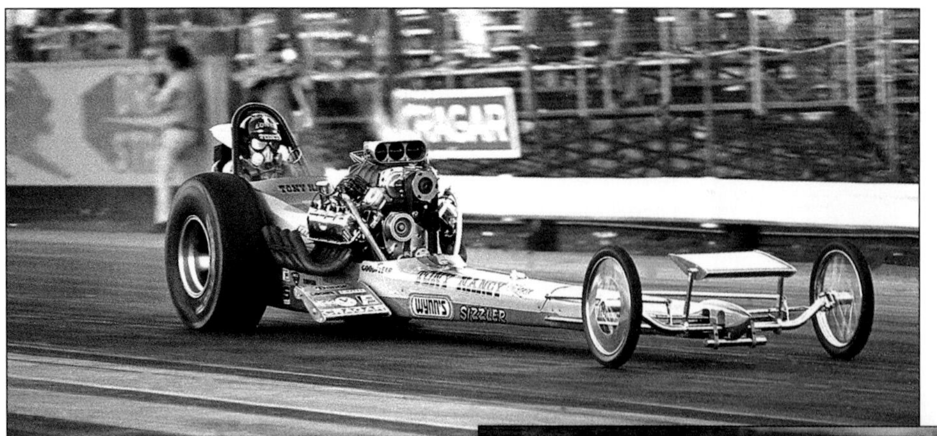

Tony Nancy astonished the crowd when he drove his ***Wynn's Sizzler*** *to a new NHRA national top-speed record of 233.16 mph for Top Fuel during Saturday's qualifying session. Considering that the feat was performed by a conventional front-end dragster, both John Wiebe and Nancy dropped the big numbers over the newer-generation dragsters.*

The final in Top Fuel Eliminator at the Grand Premiere went down as the quickest side-by-side run in drag racing history. With an unbelievable 6.174 ET at 235.60 mph, Don Prudhomme won a nail-biter over John Wiebe.

Quickest Side-by-Side Final in Drag Racing History: 6.174 to 6.175

The final round brought the two dominant cars to the line for the highly anticipated start. Both cars left evenly at the hit, but the results finished the same for Wiebe, as he finished second best.

Prudhomme won with an unbelievable 6.174 ET at 235.60 mph to Wiebe's nearly identical 6.175 ET at 236.22 mph, which went down into the record books as the quickest Top Fuel final ever. Although, Don Garlits held the official NHRA national ET record of 6.24. Prior to that, the quickest ET was officially a 6.21, which was also set by Garlits.

For Wiebe, it was deuces wild. He finished number two in the finals, owned the second-quickest Top Fuel dragster (a 6.175 ET), and had the second fastest Top Fueler, tying Tony Nancy for top speed of the meet (236.22 mph).

Funny Cars Debut

Never in the history of Lions Drag Strip had the field in Funny Car Competition been sprinkled with so many new cars.

Rich Guasco made the jump from Fuel Altered to Funny Car with a new Don Long Dodge Demon that still carried the *Pure Hell* branding with Elwyn "Honker" Carlson in the seat. "Super" Sidney Foster was another owner/driver who debuted a new

Memories

Don "the Snake" Prudhomme

Hall of Fame Drag Racer:
International Motorsports Hall of Fame and Motorsports Hall of Fame of America Member

"In 1971, I had the 'wedge' car that John Buttera built for me, and Nye Frank built the body. It was a great looking car, but it was just too damn heavy compared to [Don] Garlits's car that weighed almost nothing compared to the wedge.

"I had Kent Fuller build me a new car that was really light. It was so light that it weighed 1,250 pounds, and I named it the *Yellow Feather*. Keith Black and I put a cast-iron block in it. We put it in a mill that shaved any excess material on it and drilled a few holes in it to lighten it. We debuted the car at the Grand Premiere and ran John Wiebe in the finals, who had a conventional front-engine car. This was the quickest side-by-side final in drag racing history. We both ran identical 6.17s, which was pretty cool."

machine for 1972 at the Grand Premiere.

Among the new unveilings were Mart Higginbotham's Ramchargers-powered Vega, two Mickey Thompson entries, a Ford Pinto driven by Dale Pulde, Henry Harrison's new Chevrolet Vega, and fireman Jim Dunn's radical rear-engine 'Cuda.

During Funny Car qualifying on Friday, Kelly Brown surprised all qualifiers by taking the number-one position with a 6.64 ET at 213 mph in the *Mr. Ed* Dodge Charger.

Crash-a-Palooza

Funny Cars proved to be as exciting as Top Fuel with the added flair that unfolded in the first round of eliminations.

Right out of the gate, Dale Pulde (in Mickey Thompson's Ford Pinto) got crossed up and went out of shape. He recovered in time to take the win with a 6.79 ET at 215.82 mph over Bill Leavitt in his *Quickie Too* Mustang, which ran a 7.11 ET at 169.17 mph.

Memories

Stan Shiroma

Midnight Skulker *Funny Car Driver*

"At the 1972 Grand Premiere, I was racing Tom McEwen in the first round of eliminations and was well ahead of him at the finish line when the top half of my car instantly ripped off from the body, turning it into a convertible.

"There weren't any problems with the engine. It was fine and running perfectly. When I got out of the car, McEwen came up to me to see if I was alright and jokingly said, 'Stanley, I guess you would do anything to beat me!'

"I won the round, but I was out of the race."

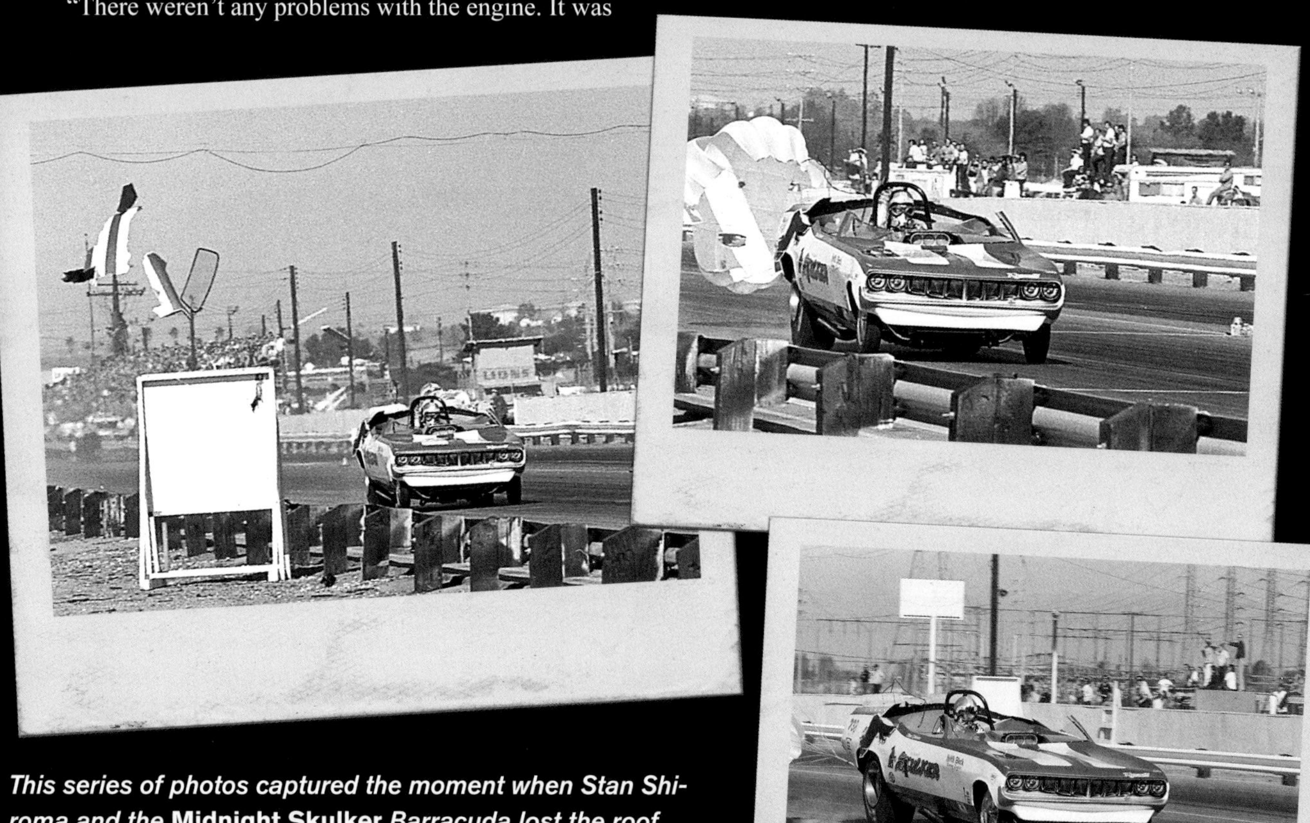

This series of photos captured the moment when Stan Shiroma and the **Midnight Skulker** *Barracuda lost the roof of the car before it entered the finish lights. Shiroma took advantage of Tom McEwen's slow start off the line and won with a 6.94 ET at 190.27 mph to McEwen's quicker 6.85 ET at 217.39 mph. The cause of the roof failure was the stress of severe body flexing. In the lights, the stunned Shiroma appeared to reach out for the missing roof.*

Kelly Brown in the **Mr. Ed** *Charger was the number-one qualifier in Funny Car Eliminator with a 6.64 ET at 213 mph, but he lost in round three against the* **Hawaiian** *driven by Bobby Rowe. Brown took an early lead, but the* **Hawaiian** *blasted to a 6.57 ET at 222.77 mph to beat Brown, who ran a 6.76 ET at 214.79 mph. (Jere Aldereff Photography/Courtesy Lions Automobilia Foundation Museum)*

Mickey Thompson unveiled his "one-two punch" at the Grand Premiere. The pair of floppers were both sponsored by the Peter Paul Candy Manufacturing Company. Thompson used bodies from two different automotive manufacturers. Henry Harrison piloted Mickey's Chevy Vega, while Dale Pulde handled the controls of the Ford Pinto. By the crowd's reaction, both cars were a huge hit at the Premiere, especially when candy samples were tossed into the crowd. (Jere Aldereff Photography/Courtesy Lions Automobilia Foundation Museum)

With luck on his side, Stan Shiroma in the *Midnight Skulker* Plymouth 'Cuda caught a napping Tom McEwen off the starting line and had enough power to out-distance the *Hot Wheels* Plymouth Duster with a 6.94 ET at 190.27 mph to the McEwen's quicker 6.85 ET at 217.39 mph. For Shiroma, his good fortune quickly vanished when he approached the finish line. The body flexed significantly, which resulted in the roof being ripped off the car and removed the *Skulker* from contention for the rest of the day.

Pat Foster secured the win in Barry Setzer's Ed Pink–powered Chevrolet Vega, and the excitement continued with "Mighty" Mike Van Sant, driving the *Stone-Woods-Cooke* Mustang, when he crossed over the centerline and got up on Foster's rear bumper and chased him through the finish lights.

The carnage continued with the next pair of Joe Winter and Gary Burgin, who set the new NHRA national ET record during qualifying on Saturday with a 6.72 ET. Burgin saw his chances to advance evaporate when the *Braskett & Burgin* Vega (Dave Braskett and Gary Burgin) experienced an uncontrollable wheel-stand, veered sharply into

Rich Gausco made his mark in drag racing and campaigned **Pure Hell**, *which was one of the most dominating and feared AA/Fuel Altereds in the history of the sport. For 1972, Gausco dropped the bantam-bodied altered, switched to the Funny Car class with his new Don Long–built Dodge Demon, and continued to carry the original name. Gausco had Elwyn "Honker" Carlson as his driver. (Jere Aldereff Photography/Courtesy Lions Automobilia Foundation)*

the opposite lane, and collided with Winter. Burgin's car received extensive damage when it spun around completely, slammed into the guardrail, rolled over, and came to a stop upside down on its roof. Winter received the automatic win but was unable to continue due to the considerable fiberglass damage to the Mustang's body and front end.

Sidney Foster was one of the early drag racing pioneers and began racing in the 1950s. He ran several brands of cars in the early days, including the famed **Black Trash** *Chevy, throughout the Southeast. Foster formed an alliance with Ford and drove everything from factory-backed Thunderbolts to SOHC nitro Funny Cars. Foster's Ed Pink–powered* **Foster's King Cobra** *Mustang was one of a few Funny Cars to make its debut at the Grand Premiere. (Jere Aldereff Photography/Courtesy Lions Automobilia Foundation Museum)*

Henry Harrison is at the controls of Mickey Thompson's Chevy Vega. Harrison qualified deep into the program but was on the receiving end of a Frank Rupert holeshot in the first round. The **Bays & Rupert** *Vega shut off early for the win with a 6.93 ET at 166.66 mph to Harrison's losing 6.99 ET at 210.82 mph.*

La Mirada, California, fireman Jim Dunn debuted his new revolutionary rear-engine Plymouth-bodied Barracuda Funny Car at the Grand Premiere. Lions Drag Strip's bite once again proved be too much to handle and prevented Dunn from extracting a full run all weekend.

The NHRA record keepers were busy on Saturday at the Grand Premiere, as relative newcomers Dave Braskett and Gary Burgin put together back-to-back ETs of 6.72 and 6.75 to set the national Funny Car ET record. (Photo Courtesy Tim Pearl Collection)

After setting the new NHRA national record in Saturday's qualifying round, the immaculate **Braskett & Burgin** *Vega was the favorite to win it all in eliminations. However, a wheel-stand in the first round veered Gary Burgin into the right lane in front of Joe Winter. Winter ran into the rear of the Vega, and spun Burgin's car around on its roof and along the top of the guardrail.*

Joe Winter won the round when Gary Burgin was disqualified after crossing the centerline into Winter's lane and causing a collision. Winter continued down the strip with excessive body damage, which ended his day.

Super Bowl Viewing on the Starting Line and Back to the Action

Due to the continuous downtime from all of the mishaps in the first round, photographer Jim Kelly went to his car and brought his portable TV to the starting line to catch the action between the Dallas Cowboys and the Miami Dolphins in Super Bowl VI. Guessing by the score of the game (Dallas won 24-3), the action on the strip was more exciting.

Gene Snow's 6.69 ET at 218.12 mph soundly defeated Gene Conway's 7.12 ET at 165.13 mph. Kelly Brown and the *Mr. Ed* Dodge Charger (the number-one qualifier with a 6.642 ET) ran a 6.71 ET at 213.77 mph to beat Leroy Goldstein's 6.89 ET at 210.28 mph in the *Candies & Hughes* 'Cuda.

The first round continued with the biggest upset of the race. The Richard Bays & Frank Ruppert underdog *Black Plague* Vega slipped past Henry Harrison in Mickey Thompson's new Chevy Vega and shut off. Ruppert's holeshot, which led to a 6.93 ET at 166.66 mph, was enough to outlast Harrison's 6.99 ET at 215.82 mph.

The last pair in the first round pitted Bobby Rowe in Roland Leong's *Hawaiian* Dodge Charger against Omar "the Tentmaker" Carrothers, who was from Joplin, Missouri. Rowe muscled past Carrothers and never relinquished the lead. He ran a 6.71 ET at 216 mph to Carrothers's on-fire 6.90 ET at 184.42 mph. Despite the fire, Carrothers was unscathed.

In round two, Frank Ruppert nearly duplicated his performance from round one when he met Dale Pulde, who was driving Mickey Thompson's new Pinto. Dale Pulde won the round when he overcame Frank Ruppert's holeshot and came from behind with a 6.79 ET at 211.26 mph over Ruppert's 6.92 ET at 182.75 mph.

Gene Snow and Bobby Rowe received easy singles when Joe Winter was unable to repair damage from the first round and Stan Shiroma's instant-convertible incident kept him on the sidelines. The upsets continued, as Kelly Brown, who showed tremendous starting-line form, hung a holeshot on Pat Foster in the *Barry Setzer* Vega and held on for the win. Brown's *Mr. Ed* Charger recorded a 6.58 ET at 223.88 mph to Foster's quicker 6.54 ET at 233.32 mph. For Brown, it was a sweet victory to beat his former ride.

In round three, Snow was once again on the receiving end of a single run when Dale Pulde couldn't make the call to the line due to breakage.

Bobby Rowe and Kelly Brown closed out the round. Rowe overcame a holeshot by Brown to win with a 6.57 ET at 222.77 mph to Brown's 6.76 ET at 214.79 mph.

Bob McFarland had the worst luck at the Grand Premiere when the engine of his new Dodge Demon flopper exploded at mid-track during qualifying, and the car turned into a rolling inferno. Blinded by flames and the massive clouds of black, toxic smoke, McFarland crashed against the guardrail in the shut-down area at more than 100 mph before coming to a complete stop in the sandbox. Unable to exit the burning car, Mickey Thompson was first on the scene with one fire extinguisher. He freed McFarland from the carnage. McFarland suffered from smoke inhalation and burns to his hands and feet. His Funny Car was a total loss. (Photo Courtesy Dick Bain)

Snow Storms to Victory

The final round was the closest race of the day from start to finish. Both Dodge Chargers got off the line together, and by mid-track, both cars were dead even. By the top end, it was Snow with the necessary distance to win with a 6.54 ET at 222.79 mph to Rowe's 6.55 ET at 226.13 mph.

"Dandy" Dick Landy had been a fan favorite at Lions Drag Strip since his early days of running factory-backed Dodge Stockers and A/FXers. The popular Southern California Pro Stock driver debuted his latest Pro Stock Dodge Challenger at the Grand Premiere with a new paint scheme that resembled a popular soft drink. Landy was beaten in the second round by eventual winner "Dyno" Don Nicholson.

Gene Snow swept top honors in Funny Car Eliminator at the Grand Premiere. Snow kept his Keith Black–powered car on track with a winning 6.54 ET 222.77 mph over Bobby Rowe, who was driving Roland Leong's Keith Black–powered **Hawaiian** *and ran a 6.55 ET at 226.13 mph. (Jere Alderef Photography/Courtesy Lions Automobilia Foundation Museum)*

Bob Lambeck picks up the front wheels during a burnout during his first-round encounter against NHRA Division 6 champion Ken Van Cleve. Lambeck, the driver of one of the six Chrysler products in the field of eight, was eliminated when he went up in smoke.

"Rapid" Roger Garten concentrates on the tree in the **Tocco-Harper-Garten** *AA/FA during his qualifying attempt in Competition Eliminator. Garten was one of a few Fuel Altered drivers to qualify in the field of 16 with a 7.19 ET. However, his chances for the eliminator title went up in smoke when he lost traction off the line and smoked his tires.*

Don Nicholson proved that consistency was the direct route to the winner's circle, and he did just that when he ran ETs of 9.61, 9.68, and 9.58 to shut down the Pro Stock competition during Lions Drag Strip's Grand Premiere. Nicholson's 9.58 ET in the final round set the NHRA's new national Pro Stock ET record.

Pro Stock

Out of the eight-car Pro Stock field, six of the cars that qualified were Chrysler products, one was a Chevrolet, and one was a Ford. The Ford was the Maverick of "Dyno" Don Nicholson, who steamrolled through the field like a hot knife cutting through butter. In the third and final round of Pro Stock Eliminator, Nicholson's holeshot led to a win over Butch Leal and the *California Flash* Plymouth Duster with a 9.59 ET to a 9.57 ET.

The unpredictable AA/Fuel Altereds were fan favorites at the Grand Premiere. This included the **Winged Express,** *which was driven by one-handed "Wild" Willie Borsch. The Marcellus & Borsch entry was the low qualifier for Competition Eliminator with a 7.06 ET. Borsch, who never ceased to amaze the crowds with his unique driving habits, red-lit in the second round against Gene Brasel.*

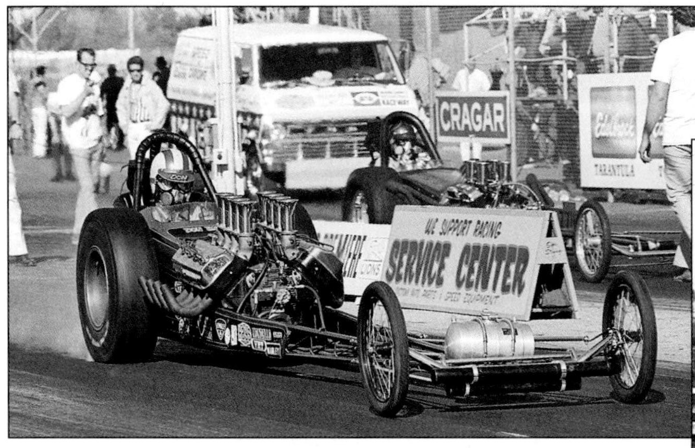

Before race cars utilized computers to optimize performance, Jr. Fuel had its own computerized team of tuner and driver Gene Adams and Don Enriquez. Adams and Enriquez were in sterling form at the Grand Premiere, with Adams reeling off consecutive 7-second passes before running a 6.93 ET at 200.00 mph for a solo run in the Competition Eliminator finals.

The first test of the new combination of Stock and Super Stock cars in one class proved to be a great success, as one of each met in the finals at the Grand Premiere. Jim Clark, driving the **DeFrank & Cohen** *SS/DA Dodge Dart, held off the '55 Chevy of 1971 Supernationals Stock Champion Paul Dilcher. Clark ran near-record numbers in the final with a 10.40 ET at 132.15 mph to Dilcher's 13.94 ET at 96.46 mph.*

Competition and Modified Eliminators

"Wild" Willie Borsch held down the number-one position with a 7.06 ET in the famed Marcellus & Borsch *Winged Express* AA/FA but red-lit in the second round to Gene Brasel. Brasel reported as being broken before appearing in the final round against the injected dragster of Gene Adams & Don Enriquez. After bombarding the Competition Eliminator class with low-7-second blasts, Enriquez soloed in the final with a 6.93 ET.

The Modified Eliminator title was won by Darrell Vittone and the I/G EMPI *Inch Pincher* Volkswagen Beetle with an 11.89 ET at 112.35 mph over the Kallas, Rinaudo, & Berry A/SR's 9.39 ET at 141.73 mph.

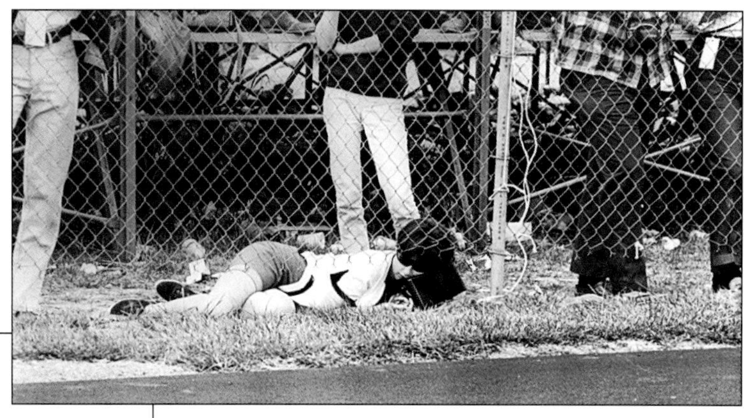

The excitement of all of the record-breaking performances and unfortunate mishaps at Lions Drag Strip's Grand Premiere took its toll on this young lady. (Jere Aldereff Photography/Courtesy Lions Automobilia Foundation Museum)

The Volkswagens were a major force in Modified Eliminator. Darrell Vittone set the tone with the **EMPI Inch-Pincher Too!** *Vittone's final-round victory over the A/SR of Kallas & Rinauro earned the mighty Beetle the prize money and glory.*

With the only Ford in the field of Pro Stock, "Dyno" Don Nicholson accepts the accolades of winning another Pro Stock title and set a new national ET record of 9.58. From the left are mechanics Bob Mandel and Dave McGrane, Miss Drag Scoop, Nicholson, unknown, and the NHRA's Bernie Partridge. (Jere Aldereff Photography/Courtesy Lions Automobilia Foundation Museum)

Super Stock and Stock Eliminators

Super Stock honors went to the SS/AA Dodge Dart of DeFrank and Cohen driven by Jim Clark with a winning 10.40 ET at 132.15 mph over Paul Dilcher, who ran a 13.94 ET at 96.46 mph.

Stock Eliminator came down to a pair of Buicks. Chuck Capsel and the Dead End Kids team's A/SA Buick secured the win with a 12.90 ET at 107.14 mph over the red-lighting C/SA Buick of Dave Benisek, who posted a 13.88 ET at 100.44 mph.

NHRA World Championship Series: July 1972

Records in any sport are made to be broken. One or two in a single game or a season is a feat in and of itself. So, setting 2 Top Fuel, 1 Funny Car, and 11 Sportsmen national records in one meet was a significant accomplishment that would be nearly impossible to repeat.

On the third leg of the NHRA's Western Conference Division VII World Championship Series at Lions Drag Strip, many records were broken.

Clayton Harris, driving Jack McKay's *New Dimension* Top Fueler, established the new low ET national record with a 6.15 on his second tune-up pass and eclipsed his first pass of 6.17 in the early Friday afternoon session. Harris's performance spring-boarded him onto the national scene, when he became the first to record four consecutive 6.20 ETs and set the low ET at the 1972 NHRA U.S. Nationals in Indy. Not to be upstaged, "Captain" Billy Tidwell took charge and guided the *Rossi & Lisa's* ironing-board Fueler to an incredible 239.36 mph to surpass his earlier run of 237.46 mph.

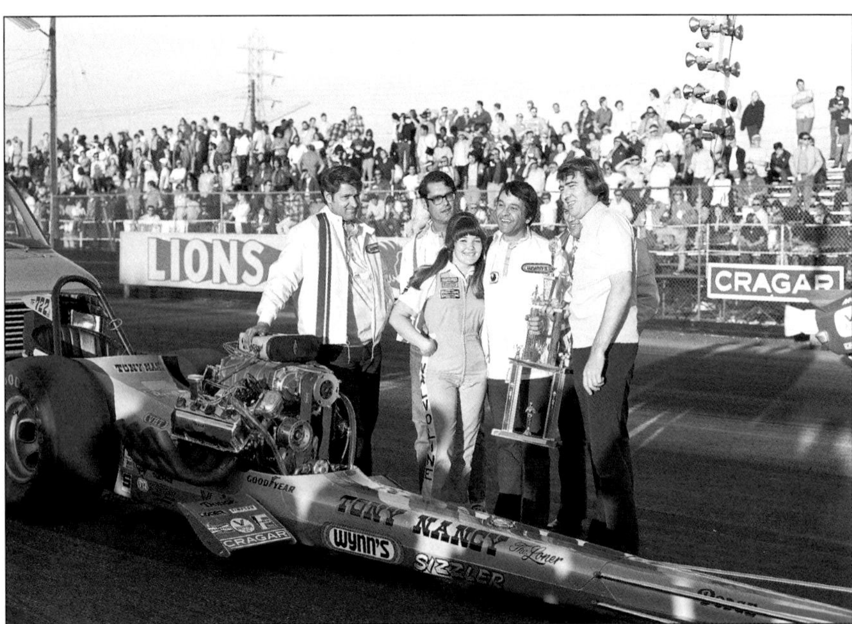

Tony Nancy and his **Wynn's Sizzler** Top Fueler set the new NHRA's top speed record at 233.16 mph on Saturday and backed it up with an even faster 236.22-mph run. He received the prestigious honor for the Best Appearing Car award at the first-annual Lions Grand Premiere. Celebrating (from left to right) are John Peters (crew chief), unkown, Jeanie Allen, Nancy, and Steve Evans (Lions Drag Strip's general manager). (Jere Aldereff Photography/Courtesy Lions Automobilia Foundation Museum)

The team of Joe Pisano and Sush Matsubara gave notice to the fuel Funny Car field by setting a new national ET record (6.49) and backing it up with a phenomenal run of 237.52 mph.

What seems to be par for the course in drag racing, the record setters invariably exit before they make it to the finals—and this event was no exception.

The newly crowned NHRA record holders in Top Fuel met in the first round of eliminations. After a drawn-out staging standoff, Billy Tidwell jumped off the line at the green

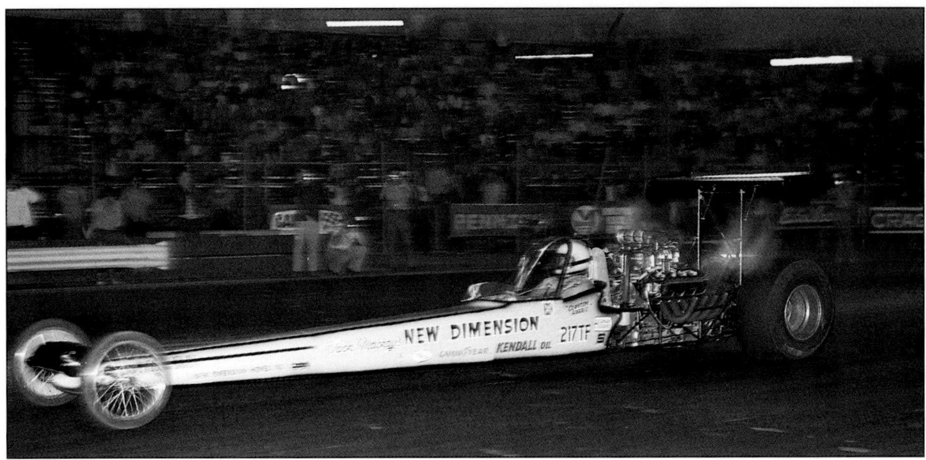

Clayton Harris made the trek from Mississippi to compete at the NHRA Division VII World Championships at Lions Drag Strip, and he found the conditions of the track to his liking. Harris set the national ET record with a 6.15 and backed it up with a 6.17 run in Jack McKay's **New Dimension** *T/F dragster.*

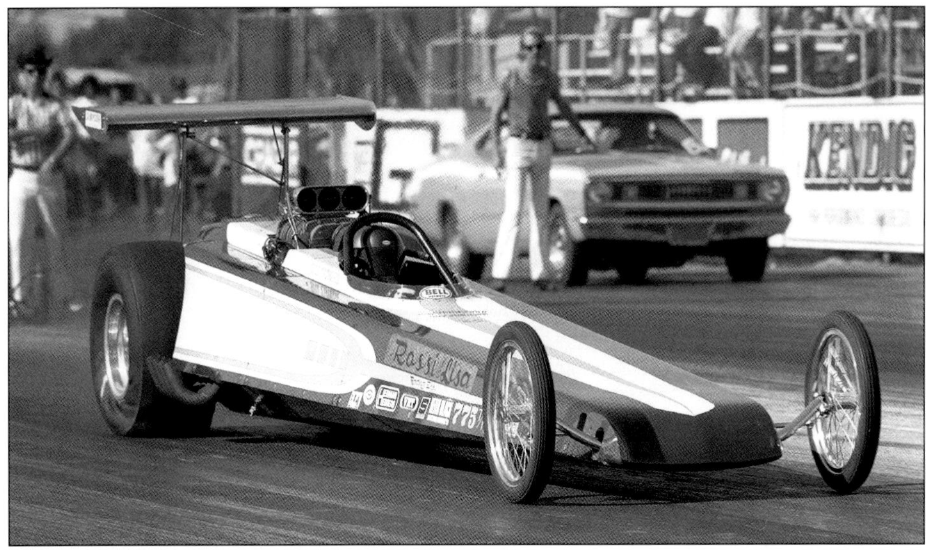

The two newly crowned NHRA national record holders in Top Fuel met by coincidence in the first round of eliminations. The national low ET holder Clayton Harris (6.15) and "Captain" Billy Tidwell, the national top speed holder (239.64 mph), held a somewhat prolonged staging contest before making tracks to the finish line. Tidwell hung on for the win with a 6.36 ET at 238.72 mph to Harris's quicker-but-losing 6.25 ET at 231.95 mph.

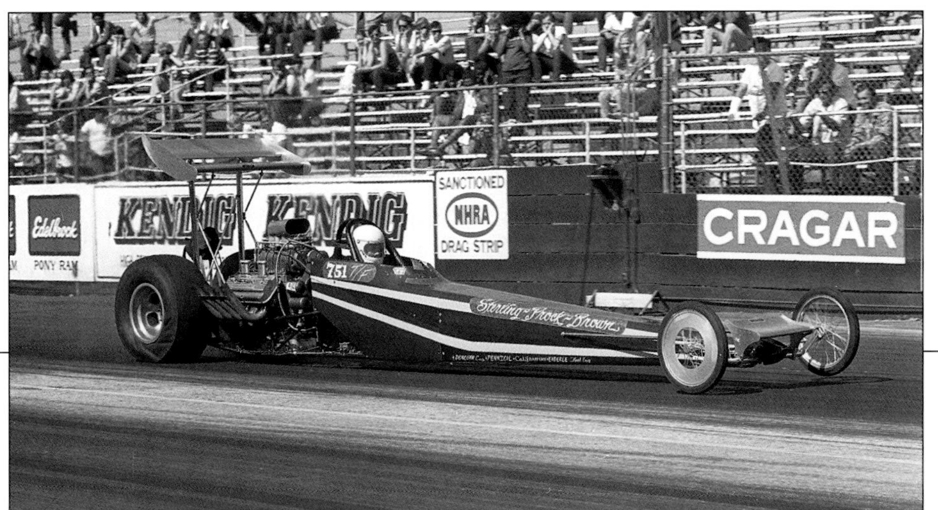

and opened a sizeable lead over Clayton Harris. Tidwell hung on for the win with a 6.36 ET at 238.72 mph to Harris's quicker but losing 6.25 ET at 231.95 mph.

In other pairings in the first round of 16, Wayne King tripped the red light and shut off on the starting line to give James Warren the automatic win. In his first competition appearance in Top Fuel, Bob Bommarito made his best pass of the weekend with a 6.79 ET at 205.01 mph, but it was not enough to hold back veteran Larry Bowers, who ran a 6.46 ET at 226.71 mph.

Next, Herm Petersen made a statement when he ran the quickest pass of the round (a 6.16 ET at 226.70 mph) to beat the Norm Wilcox and Simpson *California Skyjacker*, which ran a 6.41 ET at 217.39 mph). Roger Gates went up in smoke and shut off against Randy Allison. World champion Gerry Glenn scored a win with a 6.88 ET at 161 mph when Walt Rhoades, driving the *Safeway Sandblasting* car, lost the engine mid-track and got out of shape while making a desperate attempt to stop Glenn. The team of Sterling-Prock-Brown advanced with a 6.52 ET at 181.08 mph to soundly dispose of Dunlop-Fuller-Walsh, which ran a 6.61 ET at 214.28 mph.

To close out the first round, Dennis Baca, who was the number-two qualifier with a 6.26 ET, went up in smoke at the hit against Bob Noice, who sailed through lights with the win and a 6.43 ET at 195.65 mph.

The **Sterling-Prock-Brown** *car got off to a good start with a 6.52 ET at 181.08 mph for a first-round win over the* **Dunlap-Fuller-Walsh** *machine, which ran a 6.61 ET at 214.28 mph. Frank Prock's chances for advancement ended with a red-light start in the second round against James Warren.*

Bob "Underdog" Noice, the Division VII points leader, went all-out against Dennis Baca, who was the number-two qualifier with a 6.26 ET. Baca was hopeful for a 5-second run but went up in smoke to give the win to Noice, who ran a 6.43 ET at 196.65 mph. Brissette & Noice's **The Avengers** *car lost in the third round against "Big" Herm Peterson.*

Herm Petersen of Poulsbo, Washington, and his Donovan 417 engine was known to have the horsepower edge. In the finals, he met James Warren, who had only one strong competition run under his belt. As the lights went down, Warren came off the line, hooked up for a great start, and took the win with a 6.24 ET at 230.76 mph over the **Northwest Terror***'s quicker 6.20 ET at 222.22 mph.*

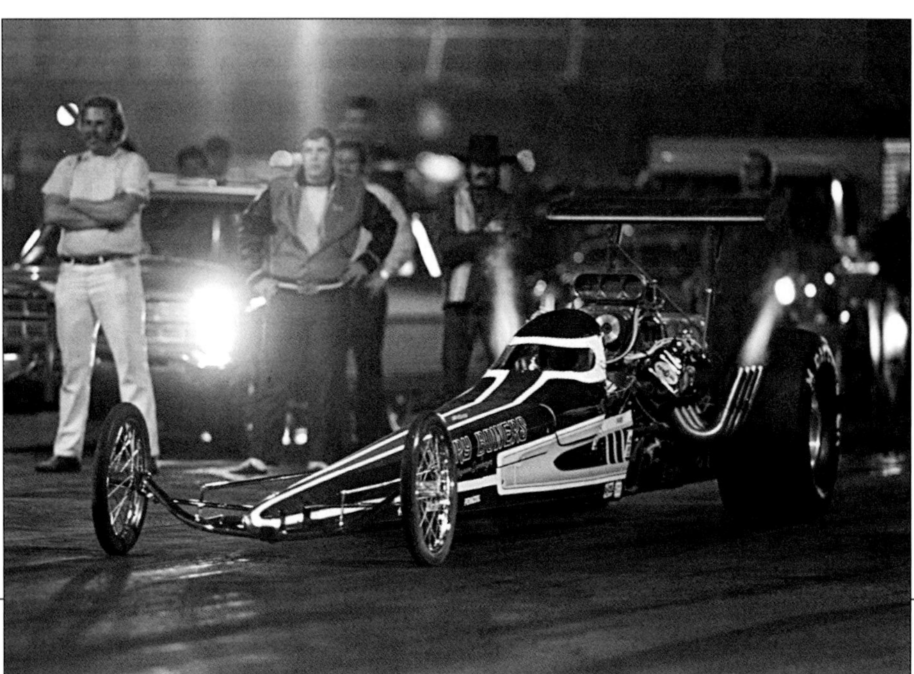

It can be difficult to get out of the funk from bad luck, but Larry Bowers persevered. Around this time, Bowers encountered violent clutch and engine explosions, as clutch discs and engines shot out of the car and had spectators and track personnel running for cover. Bowers qualified seventh at the World Championships and defeated newcomer Bob Bommarito in the first round. In the second round, Bowers met Randy Allison and lost with a 6.52 ET at 233.16 mph to Allison's 6.35 ET at 222.32 mph. It appeared that the unlucky streak had snapped.

One of the most respected teams in all of drag racing hailed from the city of Bakersfield, California. James Warren and Roger Coburn were known as the Ridge Route Terrors. As crowd favorites, Warren met Herm Petersen in the finals and ran a winning 6.24 ET at 230.76 mph. Peterson nearly pulled out the upset win in the lights and recorded a better-but-losing 6.20 ET at 222.22 mph.

In round two, James Warren singled when Bill Tidwell experienced a small fire at the line. Bob Noice had an easy win when Prock drew the red light, and Petersen singled when Gerry Glenn was a no-show. Randy Allison had to work for his next adversary, Larry Bowers, as the cars left the line side by side and were nearly even at the lights. Allison crossed the stripes first with a 6.35 ET at 222.32 mph to Bowers's 6.52 ET at 233.16 mph.

Round three brought together the battle of the Waterman "elephants," with Warren & Colburn and Randy Allison. Warren's 6.24 ET at 218.44 mph was enough to outlast Allison's 6.35 ET at 193.54 mph. In the other semifinal round, the all-Donovan 417 matchup between Noice & Brissette and Herm Petersen went to Petersen, who recorded a 6.21 ET at 211.7 mph over Noice's 6.53 ET at 203.61 mph.

The fourth and final round for the points and cash pitted the Bakersfield duo of James Warren and Roger Colburn running a Sid Waterman–prepared engine and Herm Petersen running his Ed Donovan 417 engine. Petersen had the horsepower advantage, and Warren came into the finals after only one strong run. Warren, who was out first and hooked up like on a rail got the win with a 6.24 ET at 230.22 mph to the *Northwest Terror*'s quicker 6.20 ET at 222.22 mph.

Funny Car Records Fall

The Funny Car field of 16 proved to be the favorite of the standing-room-only crowd of 12,000-plus when the first pair of fuel Funny Cars roared to life.

Low qualifier and new NHRA national ET record holder Sush Matsubara continued his charge of low-6-second runs and put away Danny Ongais in "Big" John Mazmanian's 'Cuda with 6.53 ET at 221.13 mph to Ongais's 6.67 ET at 220.58 mph.

Bob Pickett, driving *Pete's Lil' Demon*, received a free pass when the subbing "Lil' John" Lombardo failed to show. Lombardo replaced Pat Foster in Barry Setzer's Vega, as Foster developed engine woes on a run before eliminations for the Funny Car ET record that Foster established on his first run on Friday at 6.52. Gary Hazen's *Panic* Vega squeaked out a win over Gary Burgin in the *Braskett & Burgin* Vega as Hazen posted a 6.86 ET at 209.79 mph to

Joe Pisano and Sush Matsubara gave the fuel Funny Car field something to aspire toward. They set a national record with a 6.49 ET that stood with the backup charge of 6.52. Matsubara continued the charge in the first round with another mid-6-second run (a 6.53 ET at 221.13 mph) in a win over Danny Ongais and a 6.67 ET at 220.58 mph win over "Big" John Mazmanian's 'Cuda.

The Dodge Charger of "Smokey" Joe Lee from San Diego posted a 6.68 ET at 215.82 mph, but it wasn't strong enough to overtake Dave Beebe's 6.61 ET at 222.22 mph in the **Whipple & Mr. Ed** *Plymouth.*

HELP SAVE LION'S DRAG STRIP & MOTOCROSS TRACK!

To Whom It May Concern:

Lion's Drag Strip in Wilmington, California, has provided a place for hot rodders and motorcycle riders to race in competition and complete safety. Racers from all over, every week use this facility and thousands of spectators pay to watch. Where are we the people going to go if Lion's Drag Strip is closed?

Keep Drag Racing on the strip, and off the streets.

Save Lion's Drag Strip Committee

Dave Brewer
Don Dieckman
Paul Doty
Gary Lane
Larry Lane

For information please contact us: 423-6426

After 5:00 p.m. leave phone number with answering service, or voice your opinion directly to:

Bernard J. Caughlin
P.O. Box 151
San Pedro, Calif.
90733
(213) 775-3231

Several "Help Save Lion's Drag Strip & Motocross Track!" committee members circulated this letter of concern throughout the South Bay area to petition and keep Lions Drag Strip open. The project was spearheaded by Bernard Caughlin, who composed the idea of the letter. It drew a great amount of interest, but the effort fell short of stopping the closure of the track. It was too little, too late. (Image Courtesy Brian Pain)

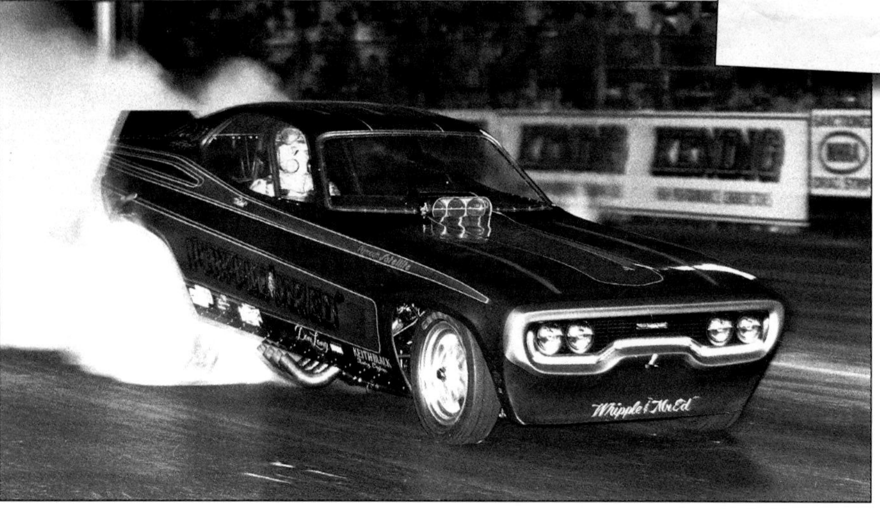

Dave Beebe, the driver of the new team of Art Whipple and Mr. Ed Willits, compiled ETs of 6.51 ,6.53, and 6.48 to win honors in the Funny Car field at the World Championship. Beebe defeated Bob Pickett in Pete Everett's **Pete's Lil' Demon** *in the final. Pickett lost an engine in the final but still clocked a 6.71 ET at 222.17 mph for the runner-up spot.*

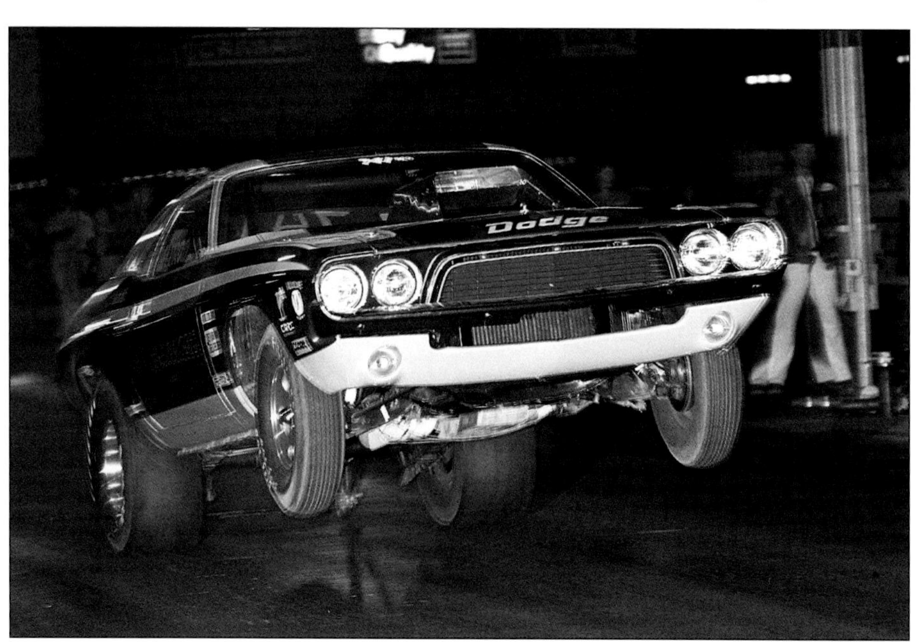

Bill Bagshaw entertained the crowd with the wheel-standing escapades of the **Red Light Bandit** *Pro Stock Dodge Challenger. Bagshaw's 9.66 ET at 141.28 mph produced a win in the final round of the World Championship Series.*

Posters that advocated to save Lions Drag Strip flooded the areas around the Wilmington, Long Beach, Lakewood, and South Bay area in California. Although all was for naught, it was a valiant effort by the committee.

The cover of the Last Drag Race program at Lions Drag Strip shows the date of December 2, 1972, which is exactly 16 years to the date when the first drag race at Lions Drag Strip took place under the lights.

The Last Drag Race poster was highly sought-after as a collectible. It was rapidly removed from telephone poles, buildings, and windows by people who wanted to grab a piece of Lions Drag Strip history.

Burgin's close 6.88 ET at 213.27 mph. Dave Beebe posted a 6.51 ET at 222.22 mph for a win over "Smokey" Joe Lee, who ran a 6.68 ET at 215.82 mph.

The second round brought Dave Beebe and the newly crowned national record ET holder, Sush Matsubara, up to the line. Beebe came out the winner of this unbelievable race with a 6.53 ET at 223.32 mph over Matsubara's near-perfect blast (a 6.49 ET at 225.69 mph), which held up as the top speed of the meet.

With Dave Beebe's best run of the meet (a 6.48 ET at 223.88 mph), he won Funny Car honors against Bob Pickett, who made a late charge but lost with a 6.71 ET at 222.77 mph.

Think Pink

When it came to the record-breaking performances, Pink power prevailed at the NHRA World Championship series at Lions Drag Strip. In Top Fuel, Clayton Harris regained his national record status with a 6.15 ET and backed it up with a 6.17 ET, while the nearly identical Vega twins of Pisano & Matsubara and Barry Setzer were the only two Pink-powered Funny Cars at Lions Drag Strip. Matsubara set the national ET record at 6.49 and backed it up with a 6.52.

The Red Light Bandit *Dominates*

Bill Bagshaw captivated the crowd with his flair, performing spectacular wheel-stands during burnouts and runs. He also dominated the Pro Stock field in performance and showmanship.

Bagshaw started his strong performance with a 9.68 ET at 140.89 mph in the first round to single for a win over the Baker & Smith *Chevy West* Camaro that broke coming off the line. In the second round, Bagshaw scored the win with a 9.72 ET at 141.50 mph over Tom Jacobson's Chevrolet, which ran a 9.91 ET at 138.47 mph.

The final round paired the Mopars of Bill Bagshaw and Butch Leal. In true style, Bagshaw raised the front wheels high in the air and settled back down for a win with a 9.66 ET at 141.28 mph over Leal's Plymouth Duster, which tripped the red light.

Sportsman Competition

The 16-member Competition Eliminator field was captured by Jimmy Scott driving the *Weiss & Scott* BB/GD, as he defeated the perennial favorite Adams & Enriquez B/Dragster with a 7.30 ET at 194.80 mph to Enriquez's 7.93 ET at 171.42 mph.

Modified Eliminator was picked up by the A/SR roadster of Fred Badberg, who ran away from Ed Sigmon's B/A Opel with a 9.26 ET at 143.76 mph to Sigmon's 9.04 ET at 153.52 mph.

Super Stock and Stock honors were won by the Zoelle Bros. and the Crader SS/T '55 Chevy, respectively. The Crader SS/T '55 Chevy won with a 13.27 ET at 101.23 mph over Vaughn Currie's SS/DA Dodge, which ran an 11.12 ET at 124.13 mph.

Dave Benisek continued his supremacy in Stock Eliminator in his C/SA 1972 Buick with a winning 13.16 ET at 90.54 mph. Benisek came from behind to catch Matt Espinosa's L/Stock Ford Pinto in the final. Espinosa held off the Buick with a 16.63 ET at 79.92 mph.

Nuisance in the Neighborhood

Heading into the fall months, manager Steve Evans came up with an idea to increase business and revenue at Lions Drag Strip. Evans extended track operations to five days a week. Grudge racing was on Wednesdays, motocross was increased to three nights during the week (Tuesdays, Thursdays, and Fridays), professional drag racing was on Saturdays, and bracket racing was on Sundays. Evans also made the strip available for private test sessions, which usually took place all day on Friday.

As the vehicles became more powerful and louder, more complaints went to strip management and were ignored. The main complaint by the neighborhood was due to the noise, and the loudest complaints came from a nearby senior citizens housing development. Other complaints were due to the excessive dust from the motocross track, the pollution, the traffic congestion, and the lack of parking. The pressure from nearby homeowners was accompanied by threats to file a $1,000,000 class-action lawsuit against the City of Wilmington, all nine area Lions Clubs, and the Los Angeles Harbor Department (the owner of the land occupied by the drag strip).

Lions Club International and the Los Angeles Harbor Commission felt that the envelope had been pushed too far and decided that they had enough.

Save Lions Drag Strip

For 17 years, Lions Drag Strip had been a home and sanctuary for young and old hot rodders, racers, and gearheads who were driven by power and speed.

Recognized as one of drag racing's leading facilities in the country, Lions Drag Strip officials issued a statement that the Los Angeles Harbor Department held the title to the land and wanted it back. As the rumors ran rampant about the racing venue closing, the Committee to Save Lions Drag Strip was formed and co-chaired by members Dave Brewer, Don Dieckman, and Paul Doty. The committee members took matters into their own hands and composed and circulated a letter of concern titled "Help Save Lions Drag Strip & Motocross Track."

This meaningful message mentioned the

consequences that would occur if the drag strip closed. Brothers Gary and Larry Lane formed a 24-hour information hotline and hoped for a tremendous public outcry to save the drag strip. There was always a chance to save it before the bulldozers and graders showed up in December.

Notice to Vacate

The entire staff of Lions Drag Strip (Michael Nestor, president; George Keens, vice president; O. Rugg Barnard, secretary/treasurer; Steve Evans, general manager; Jane Hickey, office manager; and Harold Wallace, maintenance chief; as well as Stu Peters, [CMC Motocross president]) were served with written notices to cease operations and vacate the premises from Fred B. Crawford, the assistant general manager of the Los Angeles Harbor Department.

Crawford also notified the nine area Lions Clubs that their permit to use the land at 233rd and Alameda had been revoked. In addition, he gave a notice to vacate the 200-acre property and to return it back to the Los Angeles Harbor Department in its original state on or before December 31, 1972.

A final appeal of the decision on October 10 was rejected by the landowners, so Lions Drag Strip was forced to close its gates.

Date Set for the Last Drag Race

On October 13, the officials of Lions Drag Strip announced that the final event at the legendary facility would be on the Friday and Saturday nights of December 1 and 2. For the "Last Drag Race" event, Lions Drag Strip and the NHRA worked together to produce a complete NHRA-style national event that featured all classes of competition. A schedule of events was made available to all competitors on November 1.

The Last Drag Race attracted virtually every big-name drag racer in the country. The final event on the world's most tractive strip would hopefully produce the sport's first 5-second ET.

Racer Appreciation Week

The final weeks at Lions Drag Strip featured a full slate of racing loaded with larger purse incentives.

The final weeks began Friday night, November 24, with the last motocross event. It drew more than 300 of the top riders from across the South and Northwest regions, and the competitors went all out for the advertised big-money triple purse.

The following night, on Saturday, November 25, the last bracket race took place with double payouts awarded in all brackets, including the last "King of the Hill" run-offs. On Wednesday night, November 29, the last grudge race and fuel testing was from 5 to 10 p.m. for $2 per person.

These last events led up to the grand finale: the Last Drag Race. A shared purse of $26,000 was up for the taking in the Top Fuel, Funny Car, Injected Funny Car, Pro Stock, Competition, Modified, Super Stock, and Stock categories, and bonuses were awarded for setting new national records in all of the pro classes.

Going out with a Bang

The inevitable became a reality. The most famous drag strip in the history of drag racing was turning off the lights permanently, but it didn't go out quietly. It was a spectacular 18-year run. The feeling was surreal to racers and fans. Within hours, Lions Drag Strip would become a memory. With the strip no longer available, would hot rodders and the dangers of racing return to the streets? The Los Angeles Harbor Department was in need of land for development, and rising property values were reasons behind the closure of the strip. If this was happening to Lions Drag Strip, how much time remained for the other nearby facilities with complaints? Only time would tell.

Moody-Foster-Leal Lead Pro Divisions

On Friday, December 1, the gates at Lions Drag Strip opened at 3 p.m. Qualifying and professional national record runs were underway at 4 p.m. and concluded at 10 p.m. The Super Nationals champion, "Dapper" Don Moody, grabbed the number-one position in Top Fuel in the *Walton-Cerny-Moody* entry. Carl Olson was next with Kuhl & Olson's *Da Fast Guys* entry. Olson posted an unreal 6.092 ET at 221.67 mph, which stood as the best ET until Moody's 6.04 on Saturday afternoon.

Following Olson, the field consisted of the new machine of Keeling & Clayton driven by Rick Ramsey with a 6.11 ET at 225.00 mph, Jerry Ruth (a 6.16 ET), Dennis Baca (a 6.17 ET at 224.43 mph), James Warren (a 6.19 ET), the 392-ci Chrysler entry of John Blanchard piloted by Denver Schutz (a 6.23 ET at 238.72 mph that

The name "Mooneyham" is mythical in the history of drag racing. At Lions Drag Strip, it dates back to the 1950s and 1960s when Gene Mooneyham campaigned his trademark **554** *blown coupe and the* **Jungle 4** *Top Fuel dragster to numerous wins. Carrying on the Mooneyham legacy, Gene's son Fred piloted the family Top Fuel dragster,* **California Cajan**, *here at the Last Drag Race. Fred failed to qualify.*

stood for the top speed of the meet), and Mike "Mr. 5.97" Snively, who powered "Diamond" Jim Annin's beauty to a 6.23 ET at 225.56 mph.

Others entered in the field of 16 included nationals champion Gary Beck, Walt Rhoades, Herm Petersen, Bob Noice, Larry Bowers, Flip Schofield, and the lone front-motored car of the Berry Brothers & Hughes, which took the 16th position with a 6.41 ET. The lone alternate was "Kansas" John Wiebe.

Don Moody, who powered the *Walton-Cerny-Moody* entry to an unreal 6.02 ET, followed that run with a 6.04 for the new NHRA national record. The top speed of the meet went to the

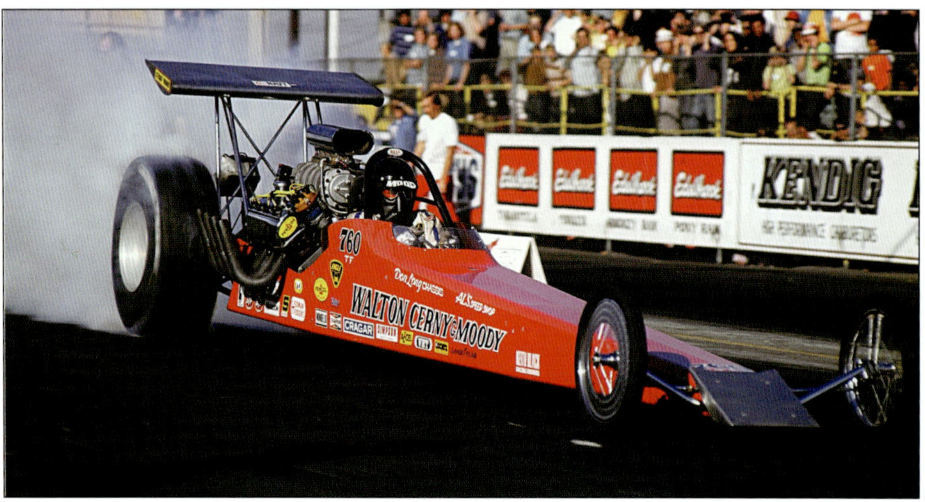

Off of his recent win at the NHRA Supernationals at Ontario, Don Moody was the number-one qualifier in Top Fuel at the Last Drag Race in the Walton-Cerny-Moody car. He ran a 6.04 ET at 225.00 mph, and the backup pass of an earlier run was 6.13 for the national ET record. (Photo Courtesy Don Prieto)

Veteran driver Gary Southern makes his second attempt in the Top Fueler of the little-known team of Nick Cirino and Andy Lopiccolla of West Covina, California. Cirino and Lopiccolla were both former blown-fuel boat racers who were involved in a heated controversy at the NHRA Supernationals. Running a boneyard-bought 392-ci Chrysler with a 1/2-inch stroker kit, Southern recorded the quickest run in drag racing history, a 6.036 ET at 210.28 mph during qualifying at the super speedway. NHRA officials questioned the inconsistency with other ETs (6.175 for the second qualifier) and disallowed Southern's time.

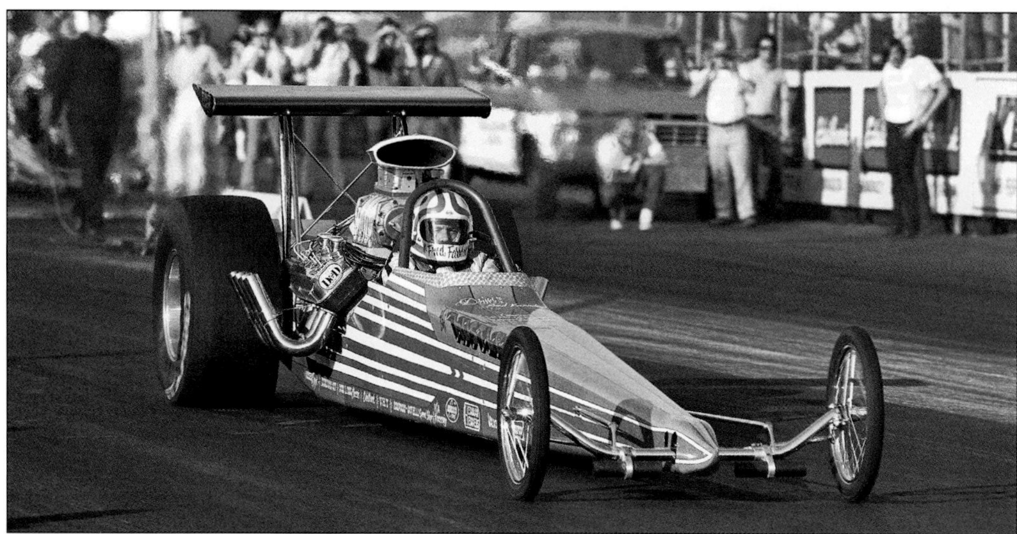

Fred Farndon powers his **Hustler** *dragster toward the top end and attempts to crack the stellar field in Top Fuel. Farndon began his drag racing career in 1958 at age 18 and competed regularly over the years at Lions Drag Strip.*

Memories

Don Ewald

Top Fuel Dragster Owner and Driver

"We pulled into the pits early Saturday morning knowing that qualifying was going to be hectic, as we had only two shots of getting into the 16-car field.

"Late in the afternoon, I made my last attempt and unfortunately missed the cut. We pushed the car to a saved spot on the return road and went to the pits for our trailer. We mated the two and watched Eliminations from 'loser's row.'

"It sucked not being in the show, but the racing was great and so was the Coors we had brought by the case.

"The crowd got crazier as the night went on. When it got closer to the finals, people were already coming out of the stands and over the fences with wrenches and pliers to remove pieces of the guardrail or anything that could be unbolted and carried off. My thoughts were, 'This is absolutely insane!'

"We went along with the whole party atmosphere until [Larry] Sutton got pulled down the track in an outhouse. Then, just like that, it was over."

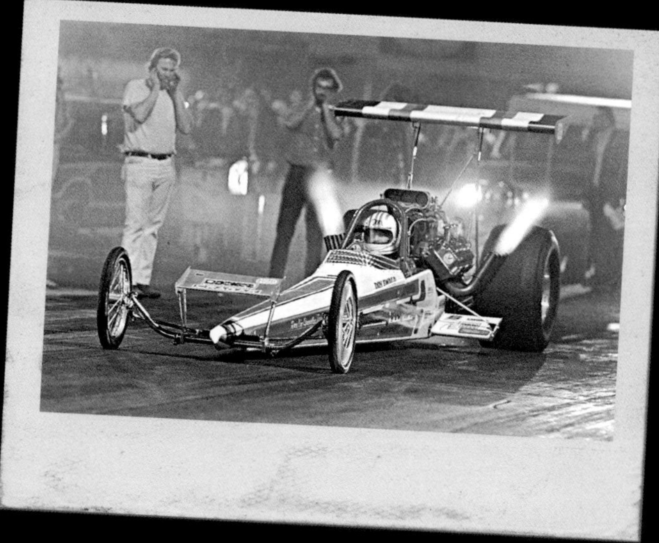

Many local racers in the Top Fuel ranks made Lions Drag Strip their home, including Don Ewald, who competed with front-motor and rear-engine dragsters. Ewald carefully stages his **Community Property** *machine for his all-out attempt to crack into the field of 16. Unfortunately, his performance fell short of making the show, and he finished second behind alternate John Wiebe.*

The wild Fuel Altereds were present at the Last Drag Race and competed in Competition Eliminator. Starter Bill Kee looks over the **Nanook** *of Dave and Linda Hough. The AA/Fuel Altereds lost their class and were regulated to the new Pro Competition Eliminator bracket for the upcoming 1973 season.*

Gary Beck made his way down from Edmonton, Alberta, Canada, after he competed at Ontario Motor Speedway for the NHRA Supernationals. He had never raced at Lions Drag Strip, and he hung around the entire week to close out the racing venue's final chapter. The Nationals champ found the strip's surface to his liking, as he turned in a stout 6.24 ET in qualifying.

Howard Haight occupied the seat of Harry and Maxine Lehman's futuristic **American Way** *streamliner Top Fuel dragster at the Last Drag Race. Byron Blair fabricated the chassis, Tom Hanna crafted the stealth-like body, and Kenny Youngblood applied the patriotic-themed colors. The heart of the* **American Way** *was a reliable, cast-iron 392 Hemi that featured a 6-71 GMC supercharger and Enderle fuel injection. (Jere Aldereff Photography/Courtesy Lions Automobilia Foundation Museum)*

Gary "Mr. C" Cochran was a regular competitor at Lions Drag Strip throughout the years. He raced in C/Altered, Top Gas, and Top Fuel and won his share of races. One of Cochran's most unforgettable wins at Lions Drag Strip took place at the 1970 AHRA Grand American, when he drove his conventional front-end dragster to a win over Don Garlits and his new rear-engine dragster. At the Last Drag Race, Cochran attempts to add his latest entry into the field of 16.

The only front-motored car to qualify in Top Fuel for the Last Drag Race was the **Berry Bros. & Hughes** *dragster. Driver Dwight Hughes ended up in the bump spot (16th) with a 6.416 ET at 221.56 mph.*

unheralded Denver Schutz, who drove John Blanchard's 392 Chrysler-powered entry and hit 238.72 mph.

Funny Car Eliminator

Joe Pisano and Sush Matsubara held the number-one spot with a 6.38 ET at 225.00 mph on Friday night that held until the last qualifying session on Saturday.

With everyone expecting it, veteran Pat Foster once again proved that the sleek *Barry Setzer* Vega was simply the best in drag racing, as he grabbed the number-one spot with a thundering 6.36 ET at 229.59 mph. Not only did Foster rock the Lions Drag Strip crowd but it also proved to be costly for him, as both parachutes completely ripped off the car and he plowed into the sandbox at more than 100 mph. The damage was too extensive to repair in time for the first round of eliminations.

Danny Ongais and "Big" John Mazmanian followed closely behind with a 6.38 ET at 225.00 mph. Pisano & Matsubara held onto the third slot. Don Prudhomme's latest Hot Wheels edition, the *Black Snake III* 'Cuda, nailed down the fourth position with a 6.521 ET at 215.82 mph.

Tom McEwen followed suit with another 6.524 ET at 223.88 mph in his *Hot Wheels* Duster. Teenager Billy Meyer (6.58 ET), Supernationals champion Jim Dunn (6.59), and Dave Condit (driving the *L.A. Hooker*) rounded out the top eight in the field.

Sitting in the unlucky ninth spot was Canada's Gordie Bonin with a 6.64 ET at 210.28 mph. Dale Pulde debuted Mickey Thompson's new Pontiac Grand Am with a fine 6.68 ET at 203.49 mph. Closing out the remainder of the field was Missouri's Omar "the Tentmaker" Carrothers, who made it into the program as a replacement for Pat Foster; Mert Littlefield; Kelly Brown's Vega panel *WonderWagon*; John Lombardo's Vega; Bill Leavitt's *Quickie Too* Mustang, Gordon Swearingen's *Sopwith Camel* 'Cuda; and, on the bump bubble, Bob Pickett driving Pete Everett's *Pete's Lil' Demon*.

For Pat Foster, the good and bad frequently go hand in hand. For the good, Foster grabbed the number-one qualifying spot with an unbelievable 6.365 ET at 229.59 mph. For the bad, after the run, both parachutes ripped off the car in the lights and sent Foster and the **Barry Setzer** *Vega into the sandbox. The extensive damage to the car was unrepairable and prevented Foster from coming back for the first round of eliminations.*

Pro Stock

Although they were absent from the California Pro Stock scene for quite some time, the Mopars were back and stronger than before. Butch "the California Flash" Leal led all the qualifiers in his Duster with a quick 9.44 ET at 145.63 mph. Behind Leal was Larry Breaux, who turned a 9.48 ET at 144.69 mph in his Dodge Demon, while the *Red Light Bandit* Dodge Challenger of Bill Bagshaw earned a close third-place finish with a 9.50 ET at 144.92 mph.

Danny Ongais and "Big" John Mazmanian secured the second spot in the field of 16 with a 6.38 ET at 225.00 mph. They hoped for a better outcome at the Last Drag Race, but Ongais idled Mazmanian's 'Cuda off the strip with brake problems and allowed Bill Leavitt to advance his Mustang into round two.

After Don Prudhomme qualified fourth overall in his new **Snake III** *1973 'Cuda, teammate Tom McEwen followed suit and nailed down the fifth spot with a 6.52 ET at 223.88 mph during Friday's night session.*

Starter Larry Sutton assists one of the Top Fuelers to back into its tracks after its burnout during a late Friday afternoon qualifying session. (Photo by Jim Kelly/Courtesy Lions Automobilia Foundation)

Other notable entrants were Chevy hopeful Sonny Bryant and Bob Lambeck in his Plymouth Duster. The remaining field continued down the ladder to the 16th qualifier, Ken Dondero, in his new Ford Pinto. Unfortunately for Dondero, his car broke on the last qualifying run.

Final Sunrise over Lions Drag Strip

When dawn broke early on Saturday, December 2, hundreds of people had been waiting in line for hours for the spectator gates to open for the last time. When they finally opened at 8 a.m., the line was several miles long. Word traveled that the area supermarkets and liquor stores had been cleaned out of alcohol, beer, ice, sodas, and snacks.

Qualifying for the Sportsman classes began at 9 a.m. and concluded at noon. Qualifying and record runs for only the Pro classes commenced at 12:30 p.m. and ended at 5 p.m.

Track manager Steve Evans and his staff didn't know what to expect, as they watched the size of the crowd increase minute by minute. As the crowd poured in all day long, management realized that its prediction of a crowd of around 10,000 people was underestimated. By 6 p.m., the crowd was roughly at 20,000, and more were coming in.

The local sheriff's department forced track officials to close and secure the gates due to the size of the gathering. The thousands who were denied entry hung around outside the gates and waited hours for the outcome. A party of some sort was going on in every area of the parking lot.

Red Carpet Welcome

By 3 p.m., every drag racer who was not racing held a party. Mostly of them were camped out on the return road. Racers who retired a decade ago came out to see it all happen.

With all of the liquid refreshments consumed, one would think that the good times were plentiful, but this wasn't the case. Under the mask of gaiety was a mood of finality. Everyone knew that this day would be irrevocable. The last race at the famous racing facility made all the smiles seem empty and hopeless.

Racers reminiscing of better and happier times couldn't overcome the mood of melancholy and sadness. Frank Pedregon (whose earlier performances at Lions Drag Strip earned him the name of "Flamin' Frank" due

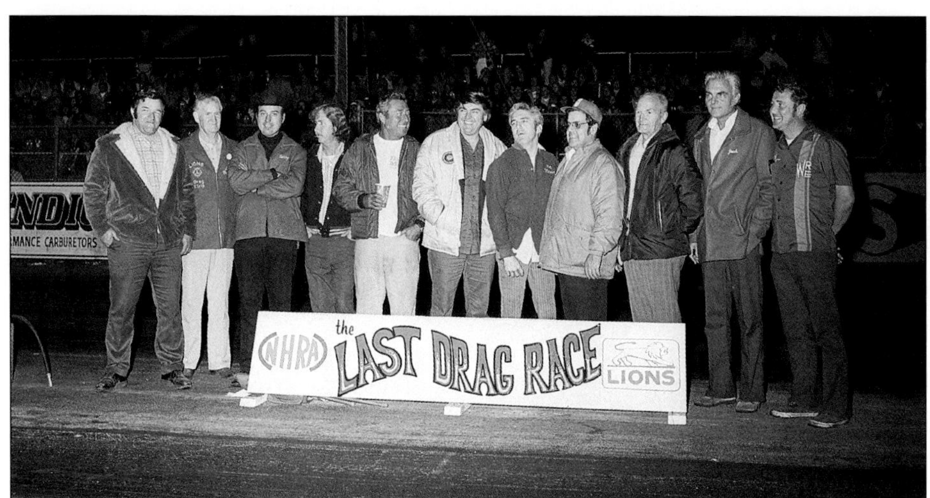

Those who were on hand on opening day (October 9, 1955) posed for a photo during the Last Drag Race to bid farewell to the strip. From left to right are Lonnie Botts, Dr. Roy M. Stokes (president of the Harbor Area Lions Club and Lions Drag Strip), Larry Sutton, Don Hampton, unknown, Mickey Thompson, Don Ratican, Lou Baney, Red Leggitt, Jack Ewell, and Sid Waterman. (Jere Aldereff Photography/Courtesy Lions Automobilia Foundation Museum)

to the many times he ran down the strip on fire) brought a semitruck full of people, parked it on the return road, and set up shop with a selection of sprits. This included everything from cognac to bourbon, rye, and Añejo tequila for all of his family and friends to celebrate (not mourn) Lions Drag Strip.

A partial list of celebrities on the red carpet of Lions Drag Strip with Flamin' Frank included "Big" John Bateman; Leland Kolb; Freeman & Sons; Frank Fedak; Fred and Shirley Crow; Bob Muravez; John Mitchell; Tommy "Watchdog" Allen; the Purple Gang of Rapp, Rossi, and Maldonado; and John and Beverly Peters of *Freight Train* fame, who stopped by after the wedding of Linda Vaughn and Bill Tidwell to bid adieu to Lions Drag Strip.

Pomp and Circumstance

The Long Beach Junior Concert band, the Music Man, was selected to perform the national anthem for the final time at the Last Drag Race. Marvin Marker, the director of the marching band, led the group of young musicians from down the track and up to the starting line. After the playing of the national anthem, the first two cars rolled off the roller starters, and the Last Drag Race was ready to begin.

Top Fuel Eliminations

Jeb Allen and Denver Schutz brought the standing-room-only crowd to near silence as they rolled to the starting line. Allen, the teenage veteran, wasted no time in getting the show going with a solid 6.40 ET at 222.77 mph and won easily over Schutz, who got out of shape and shut off the potent 392 Chrysler of John Blanchard.

The second race of the night led to an upset, as Canada's finest, Gary Beck, got an early advantage and held on

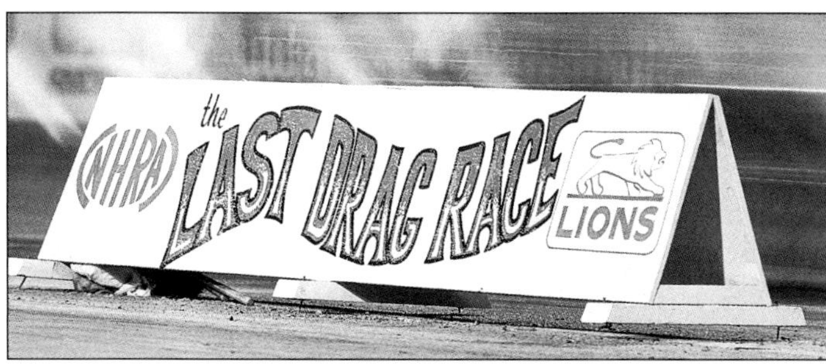

The Last Drag Race starting line A-board became the number-one targeted memento of the 20,000 attendees at the event. Any souvenirs that weren't anchored down quickly disappeared. (Jere Aldereff Photography/Courtesy Lions Automobilia Foundation Museum)

The Music Man (the Long Beach Junior Concert Band) marched from mid-track to the starting line for the presentation of the National Anthem. The distinguished band was selected from a group of award-winning bands in Southern California to perform at the Last Drag Race. (Photo by John Ewald/Courtesy Don Ewald)

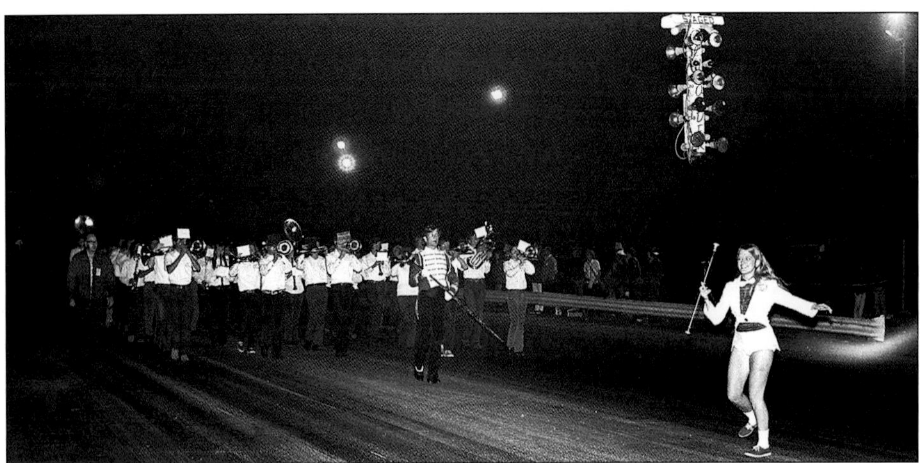

Marvin Marker, the founder, director, and head of the Music Man, keeps pace with the band. Marker organized the group in 1952, and it was selected by the Lions Club officers to perform at the Last Drag Race. (Photo by John Ewald/ Courtesy Don Ewald)

for the win with a 6.31 ET at 206.89 mph over the *Walton-Cerny-Moody* entry's up-in-smoke 6.46 ET at 227.84 mph. Bob Noice was forced to shut off and took the short exit off the track, giving the win to Dennis Baca, who ran a quick 6.14 ET at 231.95 mph. Carl Olson's 6.33 ET at 206.89 mph was enough to advance to round two with a win over Walt Rhoades, who ran a subpar 6.73 ET at 198.67 mph.

James Warren muscled a 6.48 ET at 215.31 mph on alternate John Wiebe, who replaced Flip Schofield, who broke before the start of the first round. Larry Bowers was forced to shut down against Jerry "the King" Ruth, who won with a 6.32 ET at 223.32 mph. With a 6.28 ET at 222.22 mph, Mike Snively outdistanced the lone front-engine dragster in the field that belonged to the Berry Brothers & Hughes, who ran a 6.52 ET at 208.33 mph.

The first round concluded with Herm Petersen coming from behind to nip Rick Ramsey right at the lights after Ramsey's holeshot 6.44 ET at 211.76 mph fell short against Petersen's quicker 6.22 ET at 210.77 mph.

In the second round of eliminations, Supernationals champ Don Moody was back in the program due to Gary Beck suffering extensive damage when the clutch let go in the previous round. Dennis Baca was the unlucky party to face the dangerous Moody, as Moody ripped off a winning 6.15 ET at 215.31 mph to Baca's 6.39 ET.

Jeb Allen advanced to the next round with a 6.45 ET at 213.31 mph over "Big" Herm Petersen when the 2-speed transmission decided that it had enough. James Warren suffered from driveline problems and had to watch Carl Olson make a single run of a great 6.19 ET at 212.26 mph for the win.

Lions Drag Strip starters Bill Kee and Larry Sutton smoke cigars to celebrate the camaraderie and connections they made throughout the years. This took place as Sutton makes the call for the first round of Top Fuel eliminations. (Photo by John Ewald/Courtesy Don Ewald)

Jeb Allen and Denver Schutz kicked off the first round of eliminations in style, as Allen took care of business with a winning 6.40 ET at 222.77 mph over Schutz, who got out of shape and turned off his engine.

Next up for a solo run was Mike Snively in "Diamond" Jim Annin's fueler, as Jerry Ruth broke the engine mounts in the previous round and elected not to run. In the week before, at the NHRA Supernationals at Ontario Motor Speedway, Snively made drag racing history when he became the first driver to crack the 5-second barrier with a 5.97 ET at 235.69 mph. Snively laid down a superb 6.15 ET at 209.79 mph in a "let it all out" attempt to run the first 5-second run at Lions Drag Strip.

The semifinals shaped up to be one of historic proportions in all of drag racing. Three of the four cars in the round had won a 1972 NHRA national event, while the

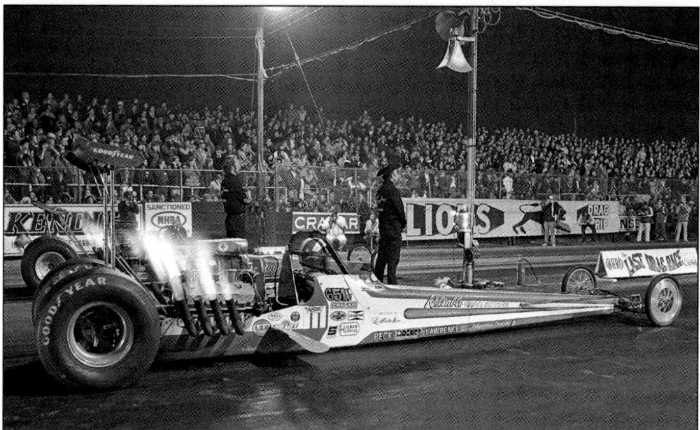

Gary Beck, who won the U.S. Nationals at Indy in September, pulled the upset in the second race when he got out first on Don Moody and parlayed the advantage into a victory with a clutch-destroying 6.31 ET at 206.89 mph to the **Walton-Cerny-Moody**'s *tire-smoking 6.46 ET at 227.84 mph. Beck's first appearance at Lions Drag Strip was unforgettable at the Last Drag Race, but his win damaged the car beyond the point of repair, which allowed Moody back into the program.*

The new **Keeling & Clayton** *machine, with Rick Ramsey behind the wheel, qualified third overall with a 6.11 ET at 225.00 mph. Ramsey was on a mission with a holeshot on Herm Petersen, but Peterson reeled in Ramsey like he was standing still and won the race. (Jere Aldereff Photography/Courtesy Lions Automobilia Foundation Museum)*

"Kansas" John Wiebe began the year at the historic Grand Premiere and finished as the runner-up to Don Prudhomme. They ran the quickest-ever side-by-side run in the final round (a 6.17 ET at 235 mph to a 6.17 ET at 236 mph). Eleven months later, Wiebe returned to Lions Drag Strip but had to settle for the first alternate spot. Flip Schofield, who qualified late Saturday, was unable to compete due to unrepairable damage. The call went out for Wiebe to fill in for Schofield, but it was all for naught, as James Warren ran a 6.48 ET at 215.31 mph to Wiebe's losing 6.66 ET at 189.87 mph.

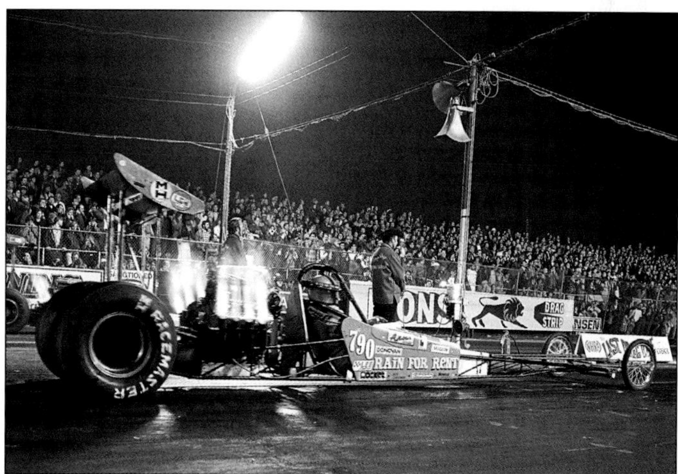

With James Warren's best-ever 6.19 ET, he qualified behind Carl Olson's 6.09 ET, but Warren's excitement didn't last, as he encountered driveline problems a few hundred feet off the line. He watched as Olson streaked past him for the win. Olson ran a 6.19 ET at 212.26 mph and advanced to the next round to face Mike Snively.

Dennis Baca advanced to round two, but he was the unfortunate one who had to face the reinstated Don Moody, who got back into the program after Gary Beck destroyed his clutch in the first round against Moody. Baca fell victim to Moody's 6.15 ET at 215.31 mph, despite a valiant 6.39 ET.

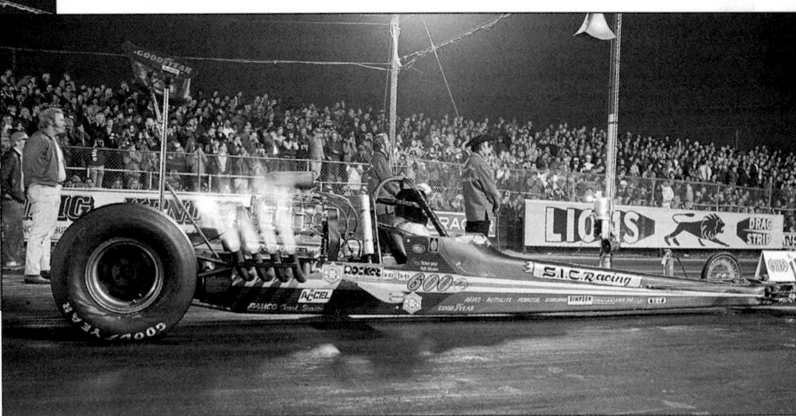

"Big" Herm Petersen ran the race of the meet when he came from behind to put Rick Ramsey on the trailer. Ramsey's holeshot 6.22 ET at 211.76 mph lost to Petersen's slower 6.44 ET at 210.77 mph.

Carl Olson's 6.33 ET at 206.89 mph was enough to advance to round two with a win over Walt Rhoades, who recorded an up-in-smoke 6.73 ET at 198.67 mph. Standing behind Olson are Don "Fats" Mackay, Mike Kuhl, Daryl Woods, and Bob Stroup, who helped that day in the truck. (Jere Aldereff Photography/Courtesy Lions Automobilia Foundation Museum)

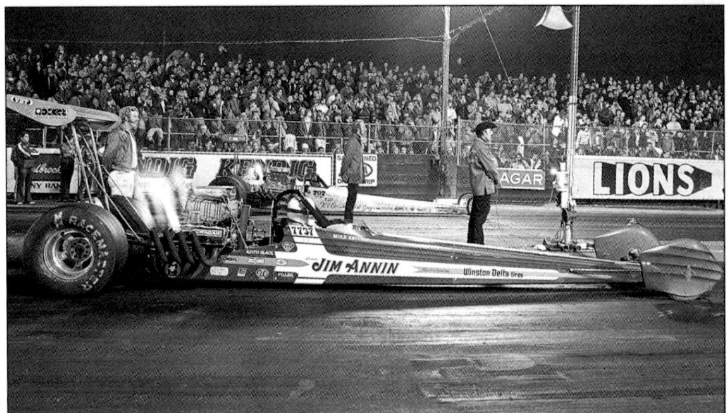

Round three of Top Fuel Eliminations paired "Mr. 5-Second" Mike Snively in "Diamond" Jim Annin's machine against Carl Olson. Snively seemed to have more power than needed, as he smoked the tires to a disappointing loss while Olson advanced to the final round with a solid 6.21 ET at 222.77 mph.

other was the first in the 5.90s.

With Moody given the reprieve to return in the second round, he found the right combination of power and ran the low ET of the meet (6.02) at 232.55 mph to defeat Jeb Allen's off-pace 6.50 ET at 214.79 mph. Olson advanced to the important final round with a 6.21 ET at 222.77 mph when Snively overpowered the track and smoked the tires nearly all the way to the finish line.

The unruly and disruptive crowd put more stress on the racers and crews who tried to return to the pits for the finals, as beer bottles and loud boos were directly aimed at the Walton, Cerny & Moody team. The team decided to pull out of the race and leave the facility before attempting a 5-second run. This allowed Jeb Allen to be in the final against Carl Olson.

Funny Car Eliminations

Launching off the Funny Cars was the *Lil' Demon* of Pete Everett against the Beaver Brothers & Dave Condit driving the *L.A. Hooker* Mustang, who prevailed with a 6.65 ET at 213.27 mph to Bob Pickett's trailing 6.79 ET at 192.71 mph.

The new *Wonder Wagon* Vega panel driven by Kelly Brown broke something in the driveline and watched hopelessly as Texas teenager Billy Meyer streaked past for the win with a 6.69 ET at 211.26 mph. Omar Carrothers got into the program as the replacement for Pat

Omar Carrothers and Gordie Bonin made it interesting, as they posted identical ETs (7.10 to 7.10) in their first-round duel. Bonin shut off before the lights and lost to Carrothers in the* Tentmaker *Mustang.

Sponsored by the Continental Baking Company, Kelly Brown's new* Wonderwagon *Vega panel wagon broke something in the driveline at the hit against Billy Meyer, who streaked to a winning 6.69 ET at 211.26 mph in his Texas-based Mustang.

Foster and beat Gordie Bonin's Vega in a wild 7.10 to 7.10 back-and-forth duel. Tom McEwen soloed for a win with a 6.92 ET at 161.00 mph when Mert Littlefield shut off his Vega on the starting line. Jim Dunn's rear-engine Barracuda took a win over "Lil' John" Lombardo when Lombardo broke after the burnout.

Dale Pulde took the first turn-off road when something went sour in Mickey Thompson's new Grand Am while Prudhomme went on for the win with a 6.51 ET at 203.61 mph. Gordon Swearingen encountered driveline trouble and shut off with an 18.71 ET, while Sush Matsubara posted the quickest ET of the round with a 6.42 at 210.77 mph. Closing out the first round, Danny Ongais drove off the end of the strip in John Mazmanian's 'Cuda and into the sandbox with chute failure.

Round by Round

The closest race in round two was between Tom McEwen and Omar "the Tentmaker" Carrothers. It was a nearly even start with both racing side by side until McEwen crossed the line first with a 6.60 ET at 219.51 mph that just nipped Carrother's 6.62 ET at 216.86 mph. Supernationals winner Jim Dunn kept his quest going when he hit his second 6.54 ET in eliminations at 217.39 mph over Pisano & Matsubara as Matsubara lost traction and lifted with a 6.74 ET at 209.30 mph. The Texas kid, Billy Meyer, disposed of former Lions Drag Strip record holder Bill Leavitt with a 6.81 ET to a losing 6.87 ET. Don Prudhomme advanced to round three with a 6.66 ET at 204.54 mph to beat the *L.A. Hooker*'s 6.83 ET at 200.89 mph.

In the semifinal round, Tom McEwen made his all-time quickest trip down a quarter mile in his Funny Car with a 6.40 ET at 225.67 mph to end Jim Dunn's bid for back-to-back wins at a major NHRA event. Dunn's solid 6.63 ET at 183.67 mph proved that the performance of his rear-engine Funny Car was the real deal.

Confusion unfolded with the last pair in the semifinals, as Billy Meyer was late getting to the lanes, which put Omar Carrothers back

The rear-engine 'Cuda of the recent NHRA Supernationals Funny Car Eliminator champion Jim Dunn took the win over John Lombardo's Chevy Vega. After Lombardo qualified with a 6.76 ET, the Vega shut off with a subpar 7.47 ET at 157.97 mph when the motor broke at mid-track. (Jere Aldereff Photography/Courtesy Lions Automobilia Foundation Museum)

Dave Condit and the Beaver Brothers' sleek **L.A. Hooker** settled for the eighth position in Funny Car Eliminator. In the second round, Condit stepped up to battle Don Prudhomme's new **Snake III** Barracuda. Prudhomme prevailed with a 6.66 ET at 204.54 mph to the Mustang's 6.83 ET at 200.80 mph.

A young Billy Meyer qualified sixth with a 6.58 ET at 219.66 mph. He advanced past Kelly Brown in the first round when Brown broke after his burnout and disposed of Bill Leavitt's **Quickie Too** Mustang in round two with a 6.81 ET. Confusion unfolded in the third round when Meyer was late getting up to the line, which led to Omar Carrothers facing Don Prudhomme. Eventually, Meyer fired up and tried to squeeze into the race against Prudhomme, but starter Larry Sutton quickly shut him down.

In the first round of Funny Car Eliminations, Dave Condit prevailed with a 6.65 ET at 213.27 mph over Bob Pickett in Pete Everett's **Pete's Lil' Demon**. Pickett, who qualified last in the field of 16, trailed with a 6.49 ET at 192.71 mph.

Sush Matsubara was considered to be the favorite to take home the Last Drag Race Eliminator title after he set the low ET early on Friday with a 6.38 at 225.00 mph for the Ed Pink–powered Vega. He recorded the best ET in round one with a winning 6.40 ET at 218.33 mph over Gordon Swearingen in the broken **Sopwith Camel** Barracuda.

Billy Meyer was late getting to the staging lanes in round three of eliminations, which allowed Omar Carrothers back in to face Prudhomme's dew-covered **Snake III** 'Cuda. Prudhomme made it an all–Hot Wheels/Wildlife Enterprises finale when he ran a winning 6.67 ET at 193.64 mph to Carrothers's 6.74 ET at 214.28 mph.

into the show. Both cars cut identical lights, but the Snake struck first with a 6.67 ET at 193.64 mph to Carrothers's 6.74 ET at 214.28 mph.

Pro Stock Eliminations

Things were not looking up for Leal to advance out of the first round, as his transmission launched before the lights. He lost with a 10.10 ET to the winning 9.99 ET of the new Colorado-based Chevy Vega of Lynn Harrison.

Bob Lambeck kept the Mopar hopes alive with a winning 9.48 ET at 144.00 mph over Gary Dodd, who could only muster a 10.03 ET at 131.38 mph. Larry Johnson's Camaro took care of Bob Mazzolini, and Bill Bagshaw ran an easy 9.86 ET at 144.23 mph, as Jim Baker's Camaro broke and slowed to an ET of 12.07. Larry Breaux ran a 9.55 ET at 143.54 mph to beat Roger Adsit, who could only net an off-pace 11.87 ET. With a 9.75 ET at 141.72 mph, Larry Huff's Mopar dropped the Duster of Jim Warren, which ran a 10.42 ET at 128.88 mph. Dean Tait scored an easy single with a 14.70 ET when Dondero was a no-show. In the first round, Tom Jacobson, with a 10.13 ET, upset Sonny Bryant when Bryant missed a shift and posted a 10.23 ET.

The second round opened with the Chevrolet Vega of Lynn Harrison suffering from new-car bugs against Lambeck's Duster, as Lambeck reeled off a winning 9.46 ET at 144.46 mph to Harrison's 9.86 ET at 138 mph.

Winners Crowned

Dave Benisek and Bill Trevor won the Stock Eliminator class at the Last Drag Race. The team also kept its unbeaten streak intact at Lions Drag Strip, as Benisek drove the national-record-holding C/Stock Automatic Buick Grand Sport past the L/Stock Ford Pinto of Matt Espinosa with a 13.16 ET at 90.54 mph. Benisek's Buick GS was sponsored by Bill Trevor, and they had been partners for years.

Ron Zoelle won Super Stock when he powered his SS/QA '56 Chevy wagon past Andy Cohen's SS/AA Dodge Dart for the prize money and the honor of winning the Last Drag Race. Zoelle reset the Lions Drag Strip record book in the SS/QA class with a 12.78 ET at 106.00 mph.

Modified Eliminator featured the toughest field of 32 competitors that assembled for the event. Ed Sigmon's Opel GT, Fred Bamberg's A/Street Roadster, the European contingent of Paul and Mark Schley, Darrell Vittone, Rick Anderson, Jim Kuykendahl, Rich Herrera (driving Van Prothero's Camaro), and J. R. Barona aimed to write

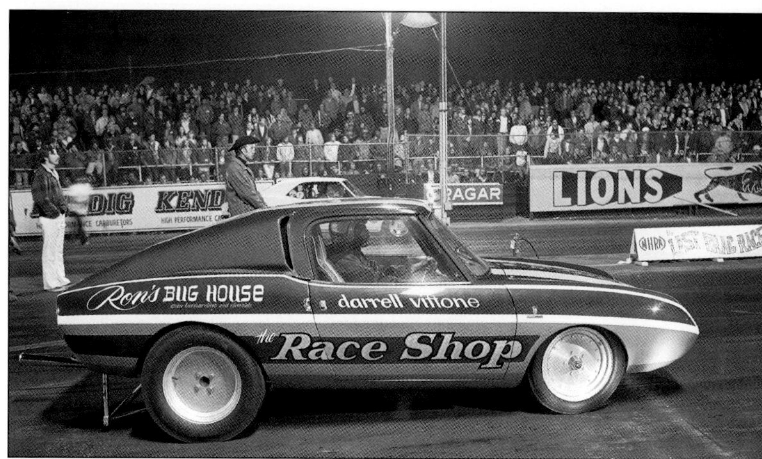

The European contingent dominated the Modified class, which included the Opel GT of Ed Sigmon and the Volkswagen Beetles of Jim Kuykendahl, Paul and Mark Schley, and the Anderson Brothers. In the third round of eliminations, Darrell Vittone's* The Race Shop *H/Gas Fiat met Van Prothero's E/Gas Camaro (driven by Rich Herrera) and tried to gain a spot in the semifinals. Herrera's 11.64 ET outdistanced Vittone's H/Gasser's 12.81 ET.

their names in drag racing's history book. In the end, the Modified Eliminator title went to veteran competitor Ed Sigmon, who beat the I/Gas Volkswagen of Rick Anderson. Sigmon's Opel GT uncorked a final-round 9.06 ET at 165.10 mph to Anderson's losing 11.84 ET at 112.21 mph.

Competition Elimination featured one of the wildest fields of qualifiers who had won at least one NHRA Competition Eliminator title. The top-seeded cars that went into the elimination rounds were Don Enriquez, Steve Woods, Jimmy Ige, Lou Gasperilli, Dale Armstrong, Jimmy Scott, John Evans, and Kay Sissell.

Jimmy Scott and Kay Sissel were the last survivors to race for the coveted Last Drag Race title. Despite watching Sissell gain the advantage off the starting line (due to the large handicap head start), Scott calmly waited as the light went green and shot off the line. At mid-track, he motored his BB/Dragster past the 6-cylinder D/Dragster and sailed past the finish line first for the victory with a record ET of 7.40 at 184.04 mph to Sissell's 9.12 ET at 131.38 mph.

The king of the California injected Funny Cars, Ken Veney, shredded everything in sight throughout the elimination rounds. Staying true to form, Veney led the 16-car field with an unreal 8.09 ET at 165.74 mph and never looked back. In the final round, Veney stormed his

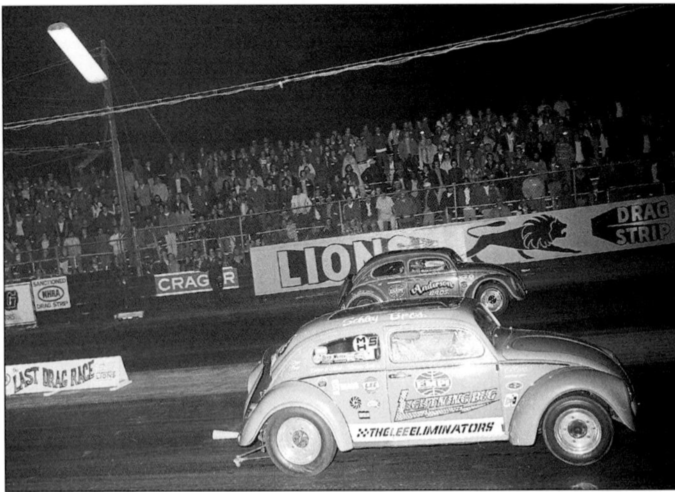

The two quickest Volkswagen Beetles were the Schley Brothers' **Lightning Bug** *and the* **Anderson Brothers** *car. They faced each other in round eliminations for the Modified Eliminator class at the Last Drag Race. Rick Anderson came from behind to nip Paul Schley's H/Gasser with a 11.78 ET at 113.36 mph to Schley's 12.81 ET at 113.92 mph. (Photo by Jim Kelly/Courtesy Lions Automobilia Foundation Museum)*

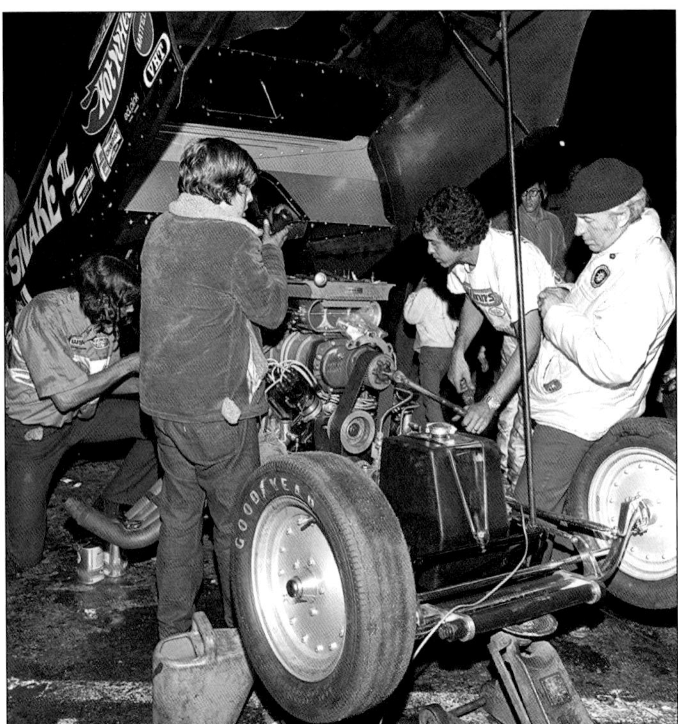

Don Prudhomme, Ed Pink, and the crew prep the car for the all-important Funny Car final against longtime adversary Tom McEwen. Prudhomme and McEwen both employed Pink-powered "Elephants." (Photo by Jim Kelly/Courtesy Lions Automobilia Foundation Museum)

way to a win over "Wild" Wilford Boutilier with an 8.12 ET at 165.74 mph to Boutilier's losing 8.63 ET at 154.90 mph.

Disarray and Confusion

As the clock ticked during the final hours of the event, officials had planned for the onslaught of people trying to grab historical or noteworthy keepsakes. With crews on hand in preparation for the hysteria, even manager Steve Evans didn't expect what was about to happen.

"We figured all the billboards and track signage would be the first souvenirs taken by the hunters, but we didn't expect anything to happen like the other incident," he said.

The incident to which Evans referred happened before the final rounds of eliminations. A few groups of fans exited from the stands with tools in hand and began to dismantle sections of the Armco railing that was approximately 800 feet down the track. When the security guards finally subdued the unruly fans, they were bombarded with debris that was thrown by the people in the stands.

With the event scheduled to end at midnight, it was clear that it would continue into the early morning hours of Sunday, December 3. Interruption after interruption delayed the Pro Stock, Funny Car, and Top Fuel finals. The thousands of people who remained outside the track stormed the facility from other locations, knocked down additional sections of the 8-foot cyclone fencing, rushed in, and marched their way through the pits. Security guards escorted the event personnel and their families up to the tower for their safety, as there were unconfirmed reports of gunshots. People funneled their way around and onto the starting line, causing more delays.

The Pro finalists making their way up through the lanes were forced to maneuver around the masses of people who were blocking the road to the rollers. The starting line and safety officials, along with some of the remaining racers and crews, ushered the Pro Stock, Funny Car, and Top Fuel cars to the starting area and rounded up the surrounding crowd and distanced them behind the rollers and starting line. Finally, the stage was set. The time was now.

Bagshaw Bags Breaux

It was an all-Mopar final in Pro Stock as Bill Bagshaw and Larry Breaux left the line evenly, but Bagshaw held a slight performance edge over Breaux that was enough to put the *Red Light Bandit* into the winner's circle. Bagshaw's final run, a 9.43 ET at 145.16 mph, got him past Breaux's 9.49 ET at 144.23 mph.

Snake and Mongoose Conclude Rivalry at Lions Drag Strip

The storyline in Funny Car was fitting for a Hollywood ending and starred two of the longest running arch-rivals in the history of Lions Drag Strip.

Facing each other for the final time in the track's history, Tom "the Mongoose" McEwen and his longtime friend (and nemesis), Don "the Snake" Prudhomme, would finally settle the score. They traded friendly barbs, insults, jabs, and all of the hype that carried on for years. Any way you looked at it, it was the good guy versus the villain. Both mighty warriors flexed their Ed Pink muscle in one last joust at Lions Drag Strip.

Bill Bagshaw (left) celebrates with Miss Lions Lynn Reck and Larry Sutton after winning Pro Stock at the Last Drag Race. Bagshaw's* Red Light Bandit *defeated Larry Breaux in the final. (Photo by Jim Kelly/Courtesy Lions Automobilia Foundation Museum)

The cars came to life simultaneously, and both bodies were lowered and locked securely. With burnouts completed, each car rolled into the pre-stage and staging beams. With anxiety at its highest level, the outcome would be over in 6 seconds. At the green, it was the perfect start for both drivers. Neither veteran let anyone down, and the outcome went to the crafty Mongoose, who crossed the finish line first. He posted a career-best Funny Car run at Lions Drag Strip with a 6.39 ET at 225 mph.

This was the pinnacle for McEwen, especially since Lions Drag Strip is where he gained much of his fame and glory. For the runner-up Prudhomme, his 6.97 ET at 163.04 mph was the best overall showing for his new car.

Top Fuel Finale

The *Da Fast Guys* Top Fueler of owner Mike Kuhl and driver Carl Olson exited the rollers for the final time along with Jeb Allen in the Allen family's *Praying Mantis*.

After both drivers completed their burnouts, they brought their cars up to the staging beams for the last

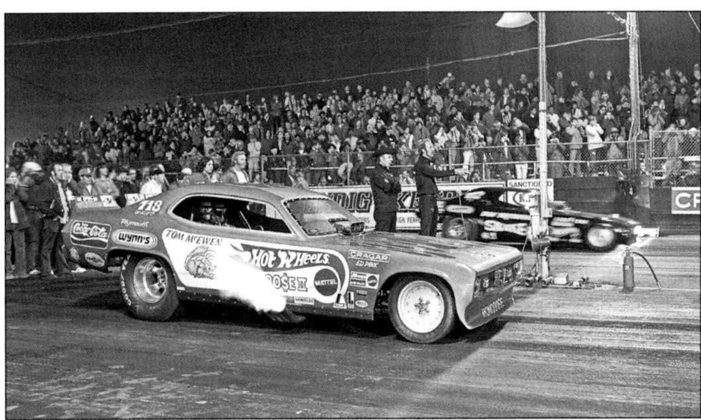

In the early hours on Sunday morning, December 3, 1972, starter Bill Kee activates the countdown on the tree for the Funny Car final at the Last Drag Race. The traditional battle between Don Prudhomme and Tom McEwen was a fitting final, as neither veteran let down the fans. McEwen couldn't have been any happier with the outcome, as he ran his career best with a winning 6.39 ET at 225.00 mph. Prudhomme's runner-up finish, a 6.97 ET at 163.04 mph, was the best showing yet for his new car.

Memories

Don "the Snake" Prudhomme

Hall of Fame Drag Racer: International Motorsports Hall of Fame and Motorsports Hall of Fame of America Member

"My last drag at Lions was in a Funny Car," said Don Prudhomme. "I raced Tom [McEwen] in the finals, and he flat-out beat me. I was so pissed off that I got beat. Being that it was the Last Drag Race, it was certainly the end of an era for us. Both of us were there pretty much from the early beginnings of the track until they closed it down. It was a cool place to race that made a lot of memories for us."

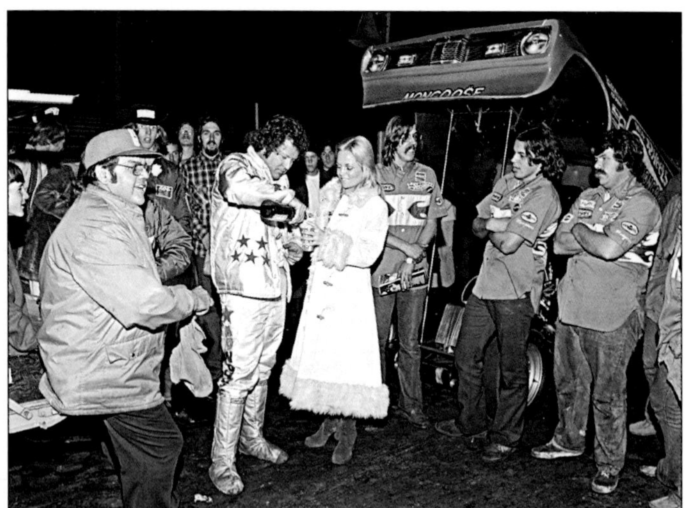

Tom McEwen pours the celebratory champagne for the crew while Miss Lions Lynn Reck holds the cups for the crew and Lou Baney cracks open another bottle of champagne. (Photo by Jim Kelly/Courtesy Lions Automobilia Foundation Museum)

When the Walton-Cerny-Moody team could not make the final round and the hopes of the first 5-second run at Lions Drag Strip were dashed, Jeb Allen was brought back to clash against "Da Fast Guys" Mike Kuhl and Carl Olson. The "final go" honor went to the celebratory cigar-toter Larry Sutton, who started the finale as both cars raced side by side for the final time. Olson's 6.20 ET at 223.76 mph prevailed over Allen's runner-up 6.45 ET at 227.34 mph.

Fans, friends, and family of the formidable "Da Fast Guys" team of Carl Olson and Mike Kuhl relish the moment and enjoy the accolades of winning Top Fuel Eliminator at the Last Drag Race. (Photo by Jim Kelly/Courtesy Lions Automobilia Foundation Museum)

time. This was it. Seventeen years of history would end in a matter of 6 seconds.

The chaotic final began with many fans sitting on the guardrails, and others were still piling through and jumping over the fences when Olson and Allen launched off into the darkness. Just like that, the thundering sounds of horsepower were silenced forever.

Lions Drag Strip's prestigious history ended as Olson crossed the finish line first with a 6.20 ET at 233.76 mph. Olson won the Lions Top Fuel Eliminator title, but for Allen, the 18-year-old teenager's determined charge netted a respectable 6.45 ET at 277 mph.

The Last Drag Race, one of the largest events ever witnessed in drag racing, was now history.

Scavenger Hunters Converge

Chaos erupted throughout the establishment like a riot on the Sunset Strip. With most of the 21,000-plus (estimated) crowd still in attendance, souvenir hunters were like piranhas. They took any momentous relics or memorabilia to prove that they were at the Last Drag Race.

The grandstand fences were torn down, and spectators swarmed from the stands like aggressive ants, brandishing wrenches, cutters, screwdrivers, hammers, and chisels that they had concealed from the security. It was the moment everyone was waiting for, as anything that was unbolted or unsecured was gone. Chunks of starting line asphalt were chiseled out of the strip. Signs, such as those for Hooker Headers and Cragar, were quickly taken. One treasure hunter climbed up the front of the

Carl Olson

Top Fuel Dragster Driver and Lions Automobilia Foundation Museum Board Member

"Anticipation of the Last Drag Race at Lions was very bittersweet. On one hand, we knew it was going to be an excellent event with many of the premiere cars and teams around the country committed to be there for all the right reasons. Part of it was to demonstrate everyone's respect for Lions [Drag Strip] and what it had meant to us in our lives, but at the same time, it was going to be a funeral of sorts. Saying goodbye to Lions was going to be like saying goodbye to your best friend. It was a very bittersweet feeling.

"On Friday, our feelings were normal for qualifying. We made two runs and were very fortunate with both being good runs, as we wound up qualifying second out of all of the entries. Nothing about that evening stands out in my memory.

"Saturday was an entirely different situation. On Friday night, after qualifying, we took the car back to our shop to service and prepare for Saturday's eliminations. When we got back to the track early on Saturday morning, we were shocked to see the enormous line of cars, miles long, leading into the facility and moving at a very slow pace. Because we were towing a trailer with a race car, we were fortunately waved around by a lot of people waiting to get into the spectator parking lot. We were finally able to get into the pit area to secure our pit spot and prepare for final eliminations.

"As we were busy preparing the race car, we couldn't help but notice the huge numbers of people who continued to show up. Well, this was beyond any of our expectations, and it was turning out to be a very unusual event.

"When we neared the time for the final eliminations to start, the place was filled. From our vantage point in the pit area, we saw that the sheriff's department was attempting to close the gates because the facility, in their opinion, had reached the maximum acceptable number of attendees.

"The sheriff ordered general manager Steve Evans to secure the gates and not allow anyone else in, which made sense from our perspective, as there were people everywhere. The grandstands were full, and people were lining up on the return road—all the way to the end of the shut-off area. It was just crazy. I remember when they closed the gates, cars continued parking in the adjacent bean field next to the return road, with people on the east side of the facility pushing up against an 8-foot-tall chain-link fence. They soon knocked it over to the ground. People poured in like endless streams of ants, and they were coming in from everywhere!

"Interruptions took place for hours leading up to the first rounds of eliminations, as people were still flocking in from the bean field. It became very difficult to get around the facility because there were so many people jammed in there.

"The delays dragged on further into the night, as nobody was leaving. I don't remember seeing many people getting too unruly at that time, but the thing I do remember was seeing most of the security staff leave when they looked around and decided that it was too much of a hopeless cause. Them being there was likely to do more harm than good. I can only describe it as it looked like total anarchy.

"I heard others say that people were sitting on the guardrails with their feet dangling over and onto the racetrack surface. I heard some others deny that, but as we reached the head of the staging lanes for the first round of eliminations, we could see that it was true. Parties were going on adjacent to the return road. There were bonfires popping up, and beer cans and beer bottles were piling up everywhere. To be perfectly honest, there were heavy clouds of the unmistakable odor of marijuana as we worked our way down the return road and past the grandstands at a time when that was seriously illegal in California.

"On the one hand, it seemed like the world's biggest party, while on the other, it was surreal that this was all happening. I thought that as it got later into the night, the pandemonium should start winding down, but it did not. It kept escalating and getting crazier.

"By the time we were going into the final round of eliminations against Jeb Allen, we slowly progressed our way through the staging lanes, went under the infamous walkover bridge and the timing tower for the last time, and finally made it to the roller starters. It was well past 2 a.m. on Sunday morning when I glanced around and saw that there was total chaos. By now, the crowd had become decidedly unruly. Fires were still burning everywhere. Some people were trying to unbolt sections of the guardrails, and others were standing by with pickaxes, ready to break up pieces of the track surfaces for souvenirs.

"Just before we ran, my partner Mike Kuhl and I got together with Jeb Allen and his family. We decided that after we made Lions' final run, we would stop on the racetrack in the shut-off area and wait until the two crews came down behind us and it was safe to get back up to the starting line for the post-race ceremonies. We waited for more than a half-hour for the chaos to subside, and when it was safe enough, we returned to the starting line to get our bottle of celebratory Cold Duck [sparkling wine] from Steve Evans and have a few photos taken for posterity."

For all the winners of the Last Drag Race, it was a time that undoubtedly will be remembered in the years to come. For those who didn't win or just attended the festival, they can say they were a part of the Lions Drag Strip finale. Their names were to be etched into Lions immortality.

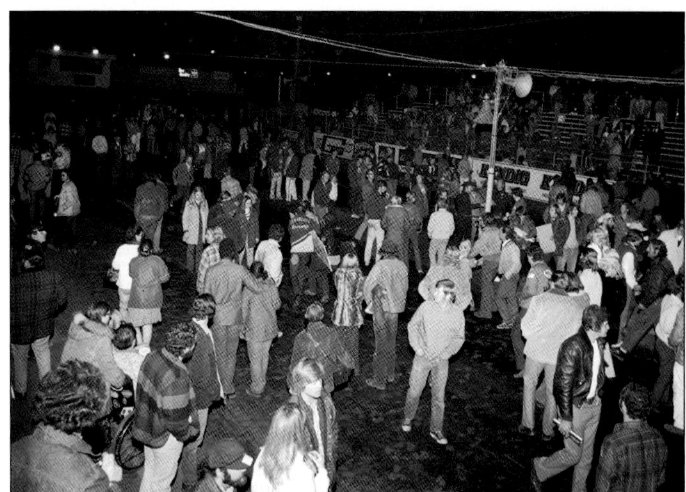

Pandemonium and chaos broke out around the starting line after Carl Olson and Jeb Allen crossed the finish line for the last quarter-mile run at Lions Drag Strip. (Photo by Jim Kelly/Courtesy Lions Automobilia Foundation Museum)

Nothing was left untouched by the packs of souvenir hunters and scoundrels. All advertisement signs and banners were the first to go. Chunks of asphalt were broken away from the starting line, and Lions Drag Strip signs were stripped clean from the fences. (Photo by Jim Kelly/Courtesy Lions Automobilia Foundation Museum)

timing tower for a sign, removed it, and yelled, "Look out below." He dropped it 15 feet into the waiting hands of his friends.

One official described the tag-team effort of a pair of young scavengers who attempted to take a speaker down from one of the starting-line poles. One of the scroungers stood on the shoulders of his friend, who appeared to weigh 30 pounds or more than he did. Unfortunately for the scavengers, it was a losing battle for the prized memento, as the man on the bottom failed to keep his friend aloft, thus ending their quest.

During what seemed like an eternity, the hunt for souvenirs was over in the short span of 15 minutes from when it started. The track had been picked clean of any signage of any type of automotive or Lions commercialism.

If you were one of the lucky ones who were there on that final night at the Last Drag Race, you will always remember that spectacular finish and the brilliant history of one of the greatest facilities in the sport of drag racing: Lions Drag Strip.

That's a Wrap

Lions Drag Strip was more than just a drag strip. It was a second home to many and will be remembered as helping to foster lifelong friendships, relationships, and partnerships. It was the countless hours and efforts by its volunteers and the civil-minded citizens that helped make it all come true.

Lions Drag Strip will mostly be remembered because it gave back to those who were disadvantaged in the local communities and that it supported the Lions Club charities. No other drag strip in the country can make that admirable statement.

Farewell to the "Giant of the West." You'll be long remembered.

Honoring the Brave Men Who Lost Their Lives at Lions Drag Strip	
Name	**Date**
Dave Gendian	January 15, 1956
Joe Koper	July 15, 1958
Mickey Brown	September 12, 1959
Leonard Harris	October 22, 1960
Boyd Pennington	September 5, 1964
Clyde "Pete" Petre	April 17, 1965
Joe Jackson	February 5, 1966
Herrell Amyx	May 21, 1966
Johnny Hoffman	March 30, 1968
Tom Polkinghorne	November 23, 1968
Tim Lampley	April 16, 1969
Ken Kotalac	October 12, 1969

In the following days, everything was removed, taken down, and boarded up. The fencing and grandstands were dismantled and torn down. Once hailed as the greatest drag strip in America, the land was returned to the Los Angeles Harbor Department to make space for overseas shipping cargo containers, which is what it is used for to this day at 223rd Street and Alameda Street in Wilmington, California. (Photo Courtesy Don Gillespie)

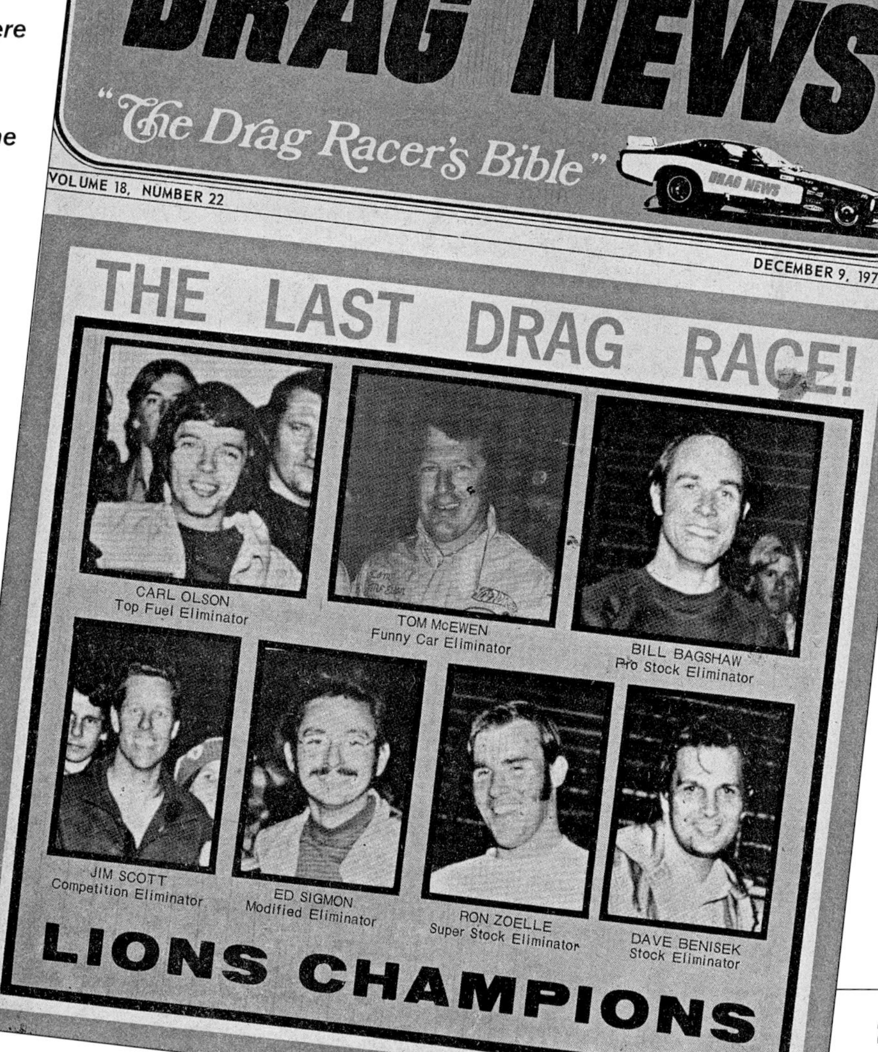

DRAG NEWS

"The Drag Racer's Bible"

VOLUME 18, NUMBER 22

DECEMBER 9, 1972 35¢

THE LAST DRAG RACE!

CARL OLSON
Top Fuel Eliminator

TOM McEWEN
Funny Car Eliminator

BILL BAGSHAW
Pro Stock Eliminator

JIM SCOTT
Competition Eliminator

ED SIGMON
Modified Eliminator

RON ZOELLE
Super Stock Eliminator

DAVE BENISEK
Stock Eliminator

LIONS CHAMPIONS

The December 9, 1972, issue of **Drag News** *(Volume 18, Number 22) includes a tribute to all the class winners at the Last Drag Race at Lions Drag Strip for a final goodbye to the legendary drag strip.*

Preserving the Legacy of Lions Drag Strip

Rick Lorenzen, the founder of the Lions Automobilia Foundation and Museum in Rancho Dominguez, California, brought his vision to reality in 2019.

Lorenzen celebrated the grand opening of the non-profit foundation museum, which embraces the automotive past to maintain and protect Southern California's distinctive car culture and its motorsports history.

It was many years in the making, and Lorenzen's perceptiveness was the driving force behind the creation of the foundation and museum, which were created to honor the spirit of Lions Drag Strip.

Lorenzen never raced at Lions Drag Strip, but he enjoys telling stories about watching the races at the venue as a young man with his friends. He met the many legends who traveled down Lions Drag Strip's quarter mile when they have visited this treasured museum. Lorenzen stopped by on a daily schedule to visit the museum and start up his favorite car, a 1941 Willys coupe named *Periwinkle*.

Lorenzen enjoys seeing all of the smiles that go along with the "oohs" and "aahs" of great satisfaction by the museum's many visitors and friends.

Museum guests enter through a 1950s speed shop and take a journey back into a simpler time (the 1950s through the 1970s) in Southern California. The museum showcases an impressive collection of vintage cars, including classic muscle cars, hot rods, race cars, racing boats, commercial vehicles, and many rare, low-production cars.

The museum features beautiful hand-painted murals in each room of the 110,000-square-foot facility. There are interactive exhibits that allow visitors to learn about the mechanical and creative designs of these vehicles along with the legends who actively competed in the motorsport in Southern California.

Honoring the great history of Lions Drag Strip, the Lions Drag Strip Foundation Museum recreated the famous bridge and tower that expanded over the staging lanes and starting line. It shows the infamous gasser wars with the* Swindler 1 *1941 Willys of Stone, Woods, & Cook and a "Big" John Mazmanian Willys that once blazed down the quarter mile at Lions Drag Strip.

Rick Lorenzen, the founder of the Lions Automobilia Foundation Museum, sits behind the wheel of his beloved 1941 Willys coupe* Periwinkle. *Lorenzen's love for Willys cars dates back to 1960, when he purchased his first 1941 Willys Americar Coupe for $65. He spent his time hot rodding the Willys in hopes of racing it at Lions Drag Strip. Today, the Lions Automobilia Foundation Museum has more than 60 different models of Willys Overland cars in the collection, including Rick's first coupe.

The Hot Rodders of Tomorrow Engine Challenge

The Lions Automobilia Foundation is a proud supporter of the Hot Rodders of Tomorrow, which is a nationwide high-school engine-building competition. As a host of the Hot Rodders West Coast competition, which includes timed engine teardowns and rebuilds, several teams have earned national recognition and have competed at national challenges at the Specialty Equipment Manufacturers Association (SEMA) and Performance Racing Industry (PRI) trade shows.

The mission of the Lions Automobilia Foundation is to honor and preserve the legacy of motorsports and car culture in Southern California for future generations. The Lions Foundation Youth Engagement and Career Path Programs were designed to create community awareness by revealing the safety and performance innovations that were developed in motorsports. These innovations have helped students discover many career paths in the motor, automotive, and transportation industries.

George Hurst made an astute observation when he said, "Young men and women with a wrench in their hands are one of America's natural resources. We've got to do anything and everything we can to keep them interested in their car and carry out the solutions of the industry."

The Hot Rodders of Tomorrow team takes time to interact with the legendary Ed "Isky" Iskenderian (also known as the "Cam Father"), for a job well done in the team engine competition. Frequently seen at the Lions Automobilia Foundation Museum, the 103-year-old Iskenderian takes the time to talk and answer questions about the history of hot rodding.

The future is in the hands of the youth, as they test their skills at the Lions Automobilia Foundation's Spark Plug Challenge. It's a timed activity that is a fun competition between two future hot rodders. Brothers Ethan and Tyler Yax experience the challenge as their father, Mathew Yax, and Lions Youth Engagement Volunteer Russ Bacarella supervise.

A tradition that was established in 2022 is the annual class of the Lions Automobilia Foundation Hall of Fame Inductees Awards Dinner and Fundraiser, which honors individuals who made a major impact in California motorsports. The 2023 hall of fame honorees included Tom "the Mongoose" McEwen, Keith Black, Ed Pink, Linda Vaughn, Bones Balogh, Doug "Cookie" Cook, Gary Gabelich, and Jim Dunn. The ceremony included (left to right) Mike Cook Jr. (accepting for Doug Cook), Rick Lorenzen, Linda Vaughn, Ken Black (accepting for Keith Black), Robert "Bones" Balogh, Rae Gabelich (accepting for Gary Gabelich), Ed Pink, Jim Dunn and granddaughter Johnna Dunn, and Kathleen Sarna (Tom McEwen's daughter).

Additional books that may interest you...

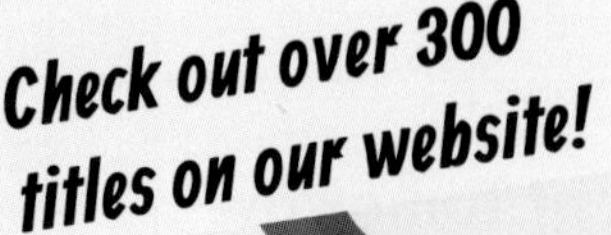

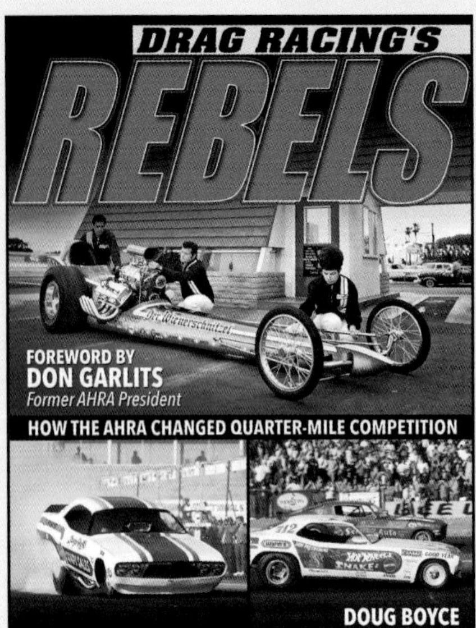

DRAG RACING'S REBELS: How the AHRA Changed Quarter-Mile Competition *by Doug Boyce*
In this first book ever published on the AHRA, get previously unrevealed stories about how the drivers, tracks, and sanctioning bodies operated in the golden era (and, as some argue, the most interesting era) of drag racing. 8.5 x 11", 160 pgs, 450 b/w & color photos, Sftbd. ISBN 9781613257661 Part # CT691

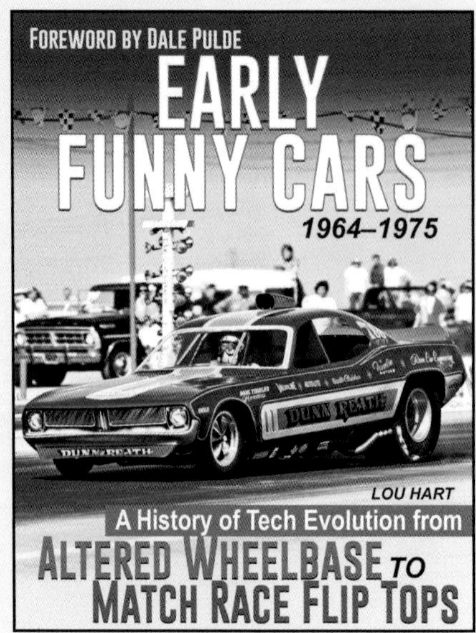

EARLY FUNNY CARS: A History of Tech Evolution from Altered Wheelbase to Match Race Flip Tops 1964–1975 *by Lou Hart*
Blast through the evolving early years of Funny Car drag racing when doorslammers morphed into flip-top rail monsters. The era features historic mounts from Arnie "the Farmer" Beswick, Al "the Flying Dutchman" Vanderwoude, Don "the Snake" Prudhomme, and many more! 8.5 x 11", 192 pgs, 452 photos, Sftbd. ISBN 97816132569858 Part # CT683

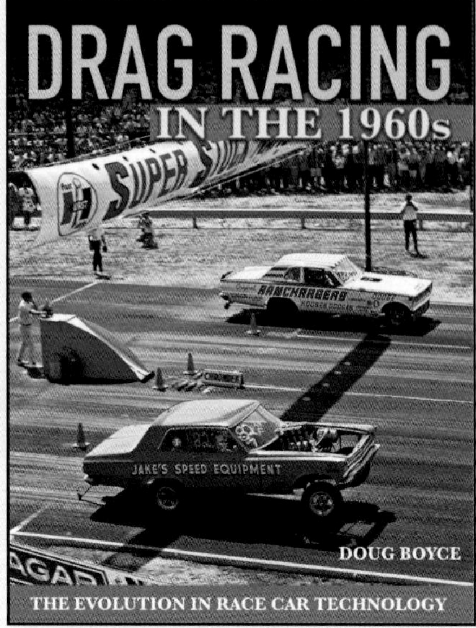

DRAG RACING IN THE 1960s: The Evolution in Race Car Technology *by Doug Boyce*
In this book, veteran author Doug Boyce takes you on a ride through the entire decade from a technological point of view rather than a results-based one. 8.5 x 11", 176 pgs, 350 photos, Sftbd. ISBN 9781613255827 Part # CT674

Check out our website:

CarTechBooks.com

✓ Find our newest books before anyone else

✓ Get weekly tech tips from our experts

✓ Featuring a new deal each week!

Exclusive Promotions and Giveaways at www.CarTechBooks.com!

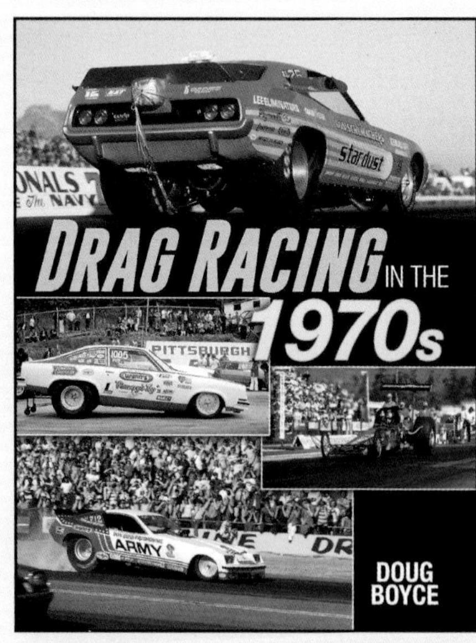

DRAG RACING IN THE 1970s *by Doug Boyce*
Veteran racing author Doug Boyce takes you chronologically through the entire exciting decade, covering the cars, the classes, and the future hall of fame drivers that piloted them. 8.5 x 11", 192 pgs, 433 photos, Sftbd. ISBN 9781613258422 Part # CT699

www.cartechbooks.com or 1-800-551-4754

LIONS
TONY NANCY
VHT
DODGE
GOODYEAR
SIMPSON
CRAGAR
CHAMPION
VALVOLINE
TONY
WYNN'S
722